S0-BYX-311

BCMSN: BUILDING CISCO® MULTILAYER SWITCHING NETWORKS

BCMSN: Building Cisco® Multilayer Switching Networks

Thomas M. Thomas II
John C. Bass
James E. Robinson III

McGraw-Hill
New York   San Francisco   Washington, D.C.
Auckland   Bogotá   Caracas   Lisbon   London
Madrid   Mexico City   Milan   Montreal   New Delhi
San Juan   Singapore   Sydney   Tokyo   Toronto

McGraw-Hill

*A Division of The **McGraw·Hill** Companies*

Copyright © 2000 by The McGraw-Hill Companies, Inc. All rights reserved. Printed in the United States of America. Except as permitted under the United States Copyright Act of 1976, no part of this publication may be reproduced or distributed in any form or by any means, or stored in a data base or retrieval system, without the prior written permission of the publisher.

2 3 4 5 6 7 8 9 0   DOC/DOC   0 5 4 3 2 1 0 9 0

P/N 0-07-212472-5
PART OF ISBN 0-07-212474-1

The sponsoring editor for this book was Steven Elliot and the production supervisor was Clare Stanley. It was set in Century Schoolbook by D&G Limited, LLC.

Printed and bound by R. R. Donnelley & Sons.

 This book is printed on recycled, acid-free paper containing a minimum of 50 percent recycled de-inked fiber.

I would like to dedicate this book to my family and friends. These people who know me and understand me. They know that I value them and our relationship. It is only through their understanding and support that I have been able to achieve my goals. I can only pray that I have made a positive impact in your life. Thank you.

Thomas M. Thomas II

This book is dedicated to my wife Carole and son Connor. I would like to thank them for sticking it out with me for the many late evenings, spoiled weekends, and my overall nasty disposition while working on this book. Her support of my work and overlooking my insufferable behavior is amazing. There is no doubt that I couldn't have married a more wonderful woman.

John C. Bass

This book is dedicated to my wife, Stacy. Thanks for your loving support and hard work which allowed me the time to work on the manuscript. This is an accomplishment for both of us. I Love You.

James E. Robinson III

CONTENTS

Contents

Contents

Contents

PREFACE

It's no secret that the networking industry is lucrative for manufacturers, service providers, investors, and employees. All the elements are in place to make a job market that will last for a long time to come. Unfortunately, the personal benefits do not come for free. The price we must pay is keeping up with the technology.

In the old economy, seniority and experience were the main components that defined an employee's position. In today's economy, knowledge is the key—not just any knowledge, but knowledge of current technology. Experience is valuable, but the best advantage is the willingness to put the past behind and forge on toward the future.

Those that choose to live in the past and not learn new technology will find themselves wondering why the younger crowd is making more money and is afforded more opportunity. It has little to do with age and much to do with staying current. If you are new to the field of networking, use your newfound enthusiasm to your advantage. Read everything networking related you can get your hands on. If you have been in the computer, communications and networking industry for a while, use your experience to your advantage. You have an advantage that few have in this industry. Regardless of your current position, there is no substitute for diligent study.

So what now? You understand your position and that you need to learn lots of new things, but you aren't sure where to start. That's where industry certification comes in to play. Industry certification is a great guide for your development in the fast changing network field. Cisco Systems has developed an excellent roadmap guide you through the broad field of networking.

This book offers you a great view of one certification test for the *Cisco Certified Network Professional* (CCNP) certification. This book covers topics from network design and configuring virtual LANs to implementing IP multicast and security policies. Careful study of these topics will prepare you for success in passing the exam and allow you the opportunity to stay current in data communications—the key to success in your career.

ACKNOWLEDGMENTS

Without the help, support, advice, guidance and feedback of many folks, this manuscript would be only simple text. Creating a book that is a valuable tool, reads well, is technically correct and visually appealing is the result of hard work of a large team. We would like to thank the following people for being a part of that team.

First, we would like to thank the Lord, our God, for this wonderful opportunity.

Thanks to Tom Thomas, series editor, for asking us to participate in this series of books. Opportunities are precious, we will be forever grateful for his generosity.

Thanks to Carole Bass and Stacy Robinson for their support and assistance with diagram creation.

Thanks to Richard M. Benoit and John P. Streck for their thorough and valuable input in the technical review process.

Taking several documents and diagrams and turning them into a book is no trivial task. Thanks to Beth Brown and the staff of D&G Limited, LLC for their hard work. We really appreciate Beth working closely with us and saving us many, many hours of work.

Last, but hardly least, coordinating the team takes an enormous effort; the McGraw-Hill staff tackles these challenges every day. It has been a real pleasure to work with the quality people at McGraw-Hill. Thanks to: Regina Brooks, Steven Elliot, Franny Kelly, Jennifer Perillo and Maria Tahim. There are many more folks behind the scenes . . . Thank you for making a difficult job enjoyable.

Many thanks to my good friend James Robinson. He is a pleasure to work with, but more than that he has a character of gold. James is a great example that still waters run deep.

JOHN C. BASS

Thanks to John Bass for being a good friend and a joy to work with. John is a man of integrity, honesty and values; I count it a privilege and blessing to work with him.

JAMES E. ROBINSON III

When I first met John and James I knew that they had the ability to make an extensive contribution to the Networking Industry. Since that time we have become good friends and I have worked hard to earn their respect. I am glad to have been able to help them achieve both a personal and professional goal, this is what friendship is all about! I echo their sentiments above and the wonderful folks that they have acknowledged, however in the end they are the ones that I would like to acknowledge, well done my friends.

THOMAS M. THOMAS II

ABOUT THE AUTHORS

Thomas M. Thomas II is the series editor and founder of NetCerts (www.netcerts.com), a leading training and education site for Cisco certification. He was previously a Course Developer for Cisco Systems and has worked on the Advanced Systems Solutions Engineering Team for MCI's Managed Network Services. He is currently an Instructor/Consultant for Chesapeake Network Solutions (www.ccci.com).

John C. Bass has worked in the networking industry for more than 10 years as an engineer, consultant, and author of numerous trade magazine articles. He is currently the technical director of Centennial Networking Lab at North Carolina State University (www.cnl.ncsu.edu). John develops test tools and system tests for networking and server equipment.

James E. Robinson III has worked for more than seven years as a software programmer and network engineer. He is currently the lead test engineer for Centennial Networking Lab at North Carolina State University (www.cnl.ncsu.edu). James develops network software applications and test tools for benchmarking and troubleshooting networking and server equipment.

ABOUT THE REVIEWERS

As the leading publisher of technical books for more than 100 years, McGraw-Hill prides itself on bringing you the most authoritative and up-to-date information available. To ensure that our books meet the highest standards of accuracy, we have asked a number of top professionals and technical experts to review the accuracy of the material you are about to read.

We take great pleasure in thanking the following technical reviewers for their insights:

Richard Benoit, CCDA, CCNA, MCNS, MCSE, serves as the Technology Manager for an international entertainment conglomerate headquartered in Orlando, Florida. Currently, his work focus is on enterprise network design, management, and security issues. Formerly, as a consultant, he has worked with many customers in the design, implementation, and support of large-scale network solutions. He holds a BS in Management Systems from the Milwaukee School of Engineering.

John Streck is Associate Director for Advanced Technology Development at NC State's Information Techology group as well as a member of the Senior Technical Staff for NC State's Centennial Networking Labs. Mr. Streck has degrees from Rensselaer Polytechnic Institute at Troy, New York, BS in Electrical Engineering in 1972 and an MS in Electrical Engineering in 1974. He was granted his P.E. license in 1977.

Introduction

Building Cisco Multilayer Switching Networks is designed to give the reader a ground up view of creating multilayer switched networks by using Cisco equipment. Design concepts, networking concepts, real-world configuration examples, and case studies are provided throughout the book so that you can build a strong understanding of the book's objectives. The practical nature of the book makes it applicable to networking professionals who need to understand Cisco multilayer switched networks and networking professionals who are working toward Cisco certification.

This book is composed of 11 chapters; this first chapter is the introduction. The rest of the chapters are as follows:

- Chapter 2, "Multilayer Switching Network Design Basics"
- Chapter 3, "Identifying Cisco Products for Multilayer Switching Networks"
- Chapter 4, "Connecting the Campus Network"
- Chapter 5, "Layer 2 Configuration"
- Chapter 6, "Unicast Layer 3 Configuration"
- Chapter 7, "IP Multicast Configuration"
- Chapter 8, "IP Multicast Routing Configuration"
- Chapter 9, "Access Control"
- Chapter 10, "Classful IP Routing Protocols"
- Chapter 11, "Classless IP Routing Protocols"

Chapters 2 and 3 cover the design principles in creating a campus network and choosing the appropriate equipment. Chapters 4–9 cover the concepts necessary for configuring Cisco equipment to implement your network objectives. Chapters 10 and 11 provide information on configuring IP routing architectures in your network. Each of these chapters is outlined in greater detail later in this introductory chapter.

Who Should Read This Book

CCNP Candidates

Cisco Certified Network Professional (CCNP) candidates will receive valuable information in working toward CCNP certification. This book covers the concepts you will be tested on in the *Building Cisco Multilayer Switched Networks* (BCMSN) exam. The next section covers the type of material that appears on the BCMSN exam.

This book covers the material you need to know to build multilayer campus networks using Cisco equipment. We will strive to show the most pertinent information that you will be tested on in the exam.

We break the information down into sets of concepts that are covered in great detail. These concepts then are reinforced with real-world examples of how to implement the concepts. This approach will help you to better understand the concepts and the Cisco syntax necessary for configuring your network. The best approach to taking the BCMSN exam is to fully understand the concepts and then drill down to the details of the implementation.

CCIE Candidates

Those working toward CCIE certification will get a valuable distillation of the issues surrounding the design and implementation of multilayer switched networks. The practical hands-on approach of this book will prove invaluable in understanding many of the concepts you will be grilled on in the CCIE exam.

The CCIE exams are long, grueling, full of detail, and cover a broad range of concepts. This book refreshes your knowledge of the concepts and configuration of an IP-based campus network that must support IP routing and IP multicast and provide adequate security.

Networking Professionals Supporting Multilayer Switching Networks

If you are in the position of designing, maintaining, or supporting multilayer switching campus networks, this book is for you. You will receive a comprehensive and practical view of the elements of design and the implementation of multilayer switched networks.

Campus networks are being deployed worldwide. All major corporations have campus networks to support their operations and information delivery. It's no longer a question of whether a campus network can increase company productivity. It's now a question of corporate survival. A company with a poorly designed and maintained campus network puts itself at great danger of losing ground to its competitors. The ability to properly design and maintain a campus network creates a great opportunity for networking professionals to directly contribute to the success of their companies. The ability to design, build, and maintain efficient and feature-rich campus networks is in high demand. This book can provide you with the technical foundation that will place you in high demand in today's job market.

The BCMSN Exam

The BCMSN CCNP exam covers a wide range of material. You will be given three hours to complete the exam. Fortunately, the material is focused on a few subjects. The following subsections list the scope of the BCMSN exam.

Expected Material on the BCMSN Exam

The BCMSN exam focuses on the following areas:

- Campus Area Networks *(CANs)* The exam focuses on the principles and concepts that apply to campus area networking. Although some of the principles may apply to *Metropolitan Area Networks* (MANs) and *Wide Area Networks* (WANs), no direct coverage of WANs and MANs is on the test. This entire book is focused on campus area networking.
- *OSI Model* The OSI Model is the basis for all networking principles covered on the test. This model helps organize how the principles relate to each other. Chapter 2 covers the OSI model.
- *Ethernet* Ethernet is the physical layer network protocol of choice for the BCMSN exam. Ethernet is the most widely used physical layer protocol in campus networks today. Chapter 4 covers the topic of Ethernet.
- Virtual Local Area Networks *(VLANs)* VLANs solve a number of problems in today's campus networks. The BCMSN exam includes many questions on this topic. Chapter 5 covers the concepts and protocols associated with VLANs.

- Internet Protocol *(IP)*   The Internet Protocol is the standard network layer protocol used in the majority of campus networks, not to mention the whole Internet. The BCMSN exam focuses on IP in terms of a network layer protocol. Chapter 6 covers IP.

- Multilayer Switching *(MLS)*   Cisco provides a mechanism to allow for cut-through switching of IP packets. This mechanism is covered in great detail later in the book. The BCMSN exam also covers this topic in great detail. Chapter 6 covers MLS.

- Spanning Tree Protocol *(STP)*   The STP gives Layer 2 networks the capability to scale by removing the possibility for bridge loops. The BCMSN exam covers this topic in detail. We also give STP lots of coverage in this book, particularly in Chapter 5.

- *Link Aggregation*   Fast EtherChannel is Cisco's method for combining multiple Ethernet links into one logical link. This combination provides bandwidth scalability and fault tolerance between network devices. The BCMSN exam covers this topic in detail. Chapter 5 covers link aggregation.

- *IP Multicast Principles*   The BCMSN exam covers a sampling of IP multicast principles. This book gives a complete look at IP multicasting and the protocols that make it work to prepare you for multicast questions. Chapters 7 and 8 cover IP multicasting fundamentals, group management protocols, and IP multicast routing protocols.

- *Access Control*   Security and traffic control are important requirements of a campus network. The BCMSN exam reflects this by having several questions on access control. This book covers these topics in detail in Chapter 9.

Material Not on the BCMSN Exam

The following material is not on the BCMSN exam. Use this information to make optimum use of your study time.

- Asynchronous Transfer Mode *(ATM)*   ATM is not covered by the BCMSN exam. Instead, the BCMSN exam focuses on Ethernet.

- Fiber Distributed Data Interface *(FDDI)*   The FDDI physical layer networking protocol is not covered by the BCMSN exam. Instead, the BCMSN exam focuses on Ethernet.

- *WAN* WAN principles and concepts are not covered; the BCMSN exam is focused on campus area networking.

- *IP Routing Architectures and Configuration* Chapters 10 and 11 in this book cover many of the principles and protocols associated with designing and implementing IP routing architectures in a campus network. However, the BCMSN exam does *not* cover this material. Chapters 10 and 11 were included to give the reader a full view of creating a campus network using Cisco multilayer switching equipment.

- *IPX* Novell's network layer protocol, IPX, is not covered by the BCMSN exam in great detail. Instead, IP is the focus of the BCMSN exam in terms of a Layer 3 protocol.

- *Appletalk* Apple Computer's Appletalk is not covered on the BCMSN exam. Instead, the exam focuses on Ethernet in terms of the physical layer.

- *DECNet* DECNet will not be covered on the BCMSN exam.

The following section describes the content of each of the subsequent chapters in this book. Any material in Chapters 2–9 should be fair game on the BCMSN exam, but it is highly recommended that you concentrate on the main topics to optimize your time. Do not expect the material in Chapters 10 and 11 (IP routing protocols) to be on the BCMSN exam. This material was incorporated into the book to give readers a full view and understanding of building campus networks.

Overview of Chapters

Chapter 2, "Multilayer Switching Network Design Basics"

The second chapter introduces the basic design concepts that define the building blocks for multilayer switched network design.

This chapter begins with a network overview including the definition of a campus network, a description of the multilayer data communications model and functionality, and basic traffic flow models. The following is a list of the layers from lowest to highest in the multilayer networking model.

- Layer 1—Physical Layer
- Layer 2—Data Link Layer
- Layer 3—Network Layer
- Layer 4—Transport Layer
- Layer 5—Session Layer
- Layer 6—Presentation Layer
- Layer 7—Application Layer

This list more or less defines the flow of the book. After we cover details of Cisco equipment in Chapter 3; we cover the physical layer in Chapter 4; we cover the data link layer in Chapter 5; we cover the network layer in Chapters 6, 7, and 8; and we cover the transport layer in Chapter 9. In Chapters 10 and 11, we cover more details of Layer 3 forwarding. We placed these two chapters at the end because the material is not covered on the BCMSN exam.

Next, a detailed list of network design criteria is covered, including current and emerging network design issues and switching technologies. Chapter 2 ends with a discussion of the concept of a *switch block* and *core block*.

Often the hardest part of undertaking the design of a complex system is determining where to start. The first task at hand is to define the problem. "Defining the problem" means defining the requirements of the campus network. This chapter covers this subject in great detail, giving you a solid view of the core objectives in building campus networks.

The objectives of a campus network are as follows:

- *Fast Convergence*   The network must learn about available paths between sources and destinations in a minimal amount of time.
- *Deterministic Paths*   The path or paths that a packet can take through the network should be somewhat static. If path choices constantly change in a network, the user has little chance of a consistent experience while using applications and services throughout the network.
- *Deterministic Failover*   When links or devices fail, a known failover backup should exist. This aids in the troubleshooting of the problem

and, more importantly, creates a stable environment in the presence of a network failure.

- *Scalable in Size and Throughput*   As the need for the services and information on networks grow, networks get bigger and require more capacity. The network should have an adequate design to allow for growth in the number of devices on the network and growth of the capacity of the links connecting the devices.

- *Centralized Storage*   Campus networks must be able to support a common location for file and application storage. This offers an environment where these services can be supported at a much lower cost.

- *The 20/80 Rule*   As you will discover in Chapter 2, modern networks have distinct traffic patterns that are quite different from the traffic patterns of earlier networks. Today, networks must be designed with the assumption that 20 percent of the traffic on a local network will stay on that local network and that the remaining 80 percent is destined for hosts outside the local network.

- *Multiprotocol Support*   Campus networks must have the capability to carry many different types of networking protocols such as the IP, Novell's IPX, and Apple's Appletalk. Even though networks are becoming predominantly IP networks, some legacy applications and hosts require other types of network protocols. Even in IP-only networks, the upper layer protocols must be supported by the network. This book is focused on explaining the concepts and configuration behind IP-only networks.

- *Multicast Support*   Today's networks must have support for multicast traffic streams. *Multicasting* is the mechanism by which users can transmit and receive network video in an efficient manner.

Building an effective and efficient campus network that can meet these objectives is difficult. At first glance, it seems virtually impossible to put all the functionality necessary to meet the requirements into one network. The final topic in this chapter will help you organize the functions of the network in an easy-to-visualize hierarchical model. Each of the components of this model can be modified to meet the specific needs of the network you are designing. Now, the problem can be broken down into many smaller pieces that are easier to design.

The chapter closes with two case studies of the initial network design. The first case study is a simple network with a few services to improve office efficiency in a small business. The second case study is a large network design project to implement a campus network with urgent business demands and pressure to get the job done.

This chapter leaves you with the requirements of campus networks and how to define the building blocks for an initial design. Two case studies top off the information with a practical view of how to apply the concepts introduced in this chapter.

Chapter 3, "Identifying Cisco Products for Multilayer Switching Networks"

In Chapter 2, we cover the basic requirements of campus networks and the logical organization to meet these requirements in a systematic way. Chapter 3 builds on this knowledge and covers how Cisco products should be used in a campus network.

Each member of the Cisco switching product line is described in terms of its hardware and software capabilities. After discussing these product line families, we cover how they should be used in the hierarchical structure described in Chapter 2.

The Cisco multilayer switching product families are as follows:

- Cisco 1900 series
- Cisco 2926 series
- Cisco 2900 series
- Cisco 3500 series
- Cisco 5000 series
- Cisco 6000 series
- Cisco 8500 series

After reading this chapter, you will have a good understanding of how to choose and place Cisco equipment into your multilayer switched network design.

The case study at the end of this chapter gives you a practical example of how Cisco switches would be chosen and placed in a campus network by building on the case study of Chapter 2.

Chapter 4, "Connecting the Campus Network"

In the previous two chapters, we cover the methodology for logically building the campus network and how to choose Cisco equipment to be placed in the network. In this chapter, we begin filling in the details about how these devices are connected and how to configure the devices.

In this chapter the concepts and principles of Ethernet operation are covered. Along with the theoretical concepts of Ethernet, we cover the different types of Ethernet interfaces and the types of cabling used with these interfaces. We cover the following types of Ethernet interfaces:

- 10Base2
- 10Base5
- 10BaseT
- 100BaseT
- 100BaseFX
- 1000BaseSX
- 1000BaseLX

Because these interface types are used to interconnect the campus network devices, the types of cabling and pinouts for these Ethernet interface types are covered. This discussion gives you a good foundation in building Ethernet networks, which are the core interconnect method in building campus networks.

In addition to Ethernet connectivity, the following concepts are covered:

- Password configuration
- Hostname and system name configuration
- Setting up an IP address for the device
- Naming the Ethernet ports
- Configuring the speed and duplex mode for the Ethernet ports
- Testing your initial setup

Knowledge of each of these topics is crucial in setting up the individual network devices on the campus network. In addition the packet formats of Ethernet, IP, TCP, and UDP are covered. The packet formats are illustrated through diagrams to show how information from each of these protocols is transmitted. This information is used extensively throughout the remainder of the book to show how protocols necessary for meeting the needs of a campus network relate to each other.

To reinforce these configuration and cabling concepts, a case study is provided at the end of the chapter to illustrate a real-world example of putting together the first steps in building a campus network

Chapter 5, "Layer 2 Configuration"

Now that a lot of the preliminary information about campus networks and Cisco equipment is out of the way, we get into the details of the protocols that run over switched networks. In this chapter, we take a progressive look at how Layer 2 switching works. Here, we cover VLANs, STP, and link aggregation.

VLANs are a way to distribute Layer 2 networks throughout the campus network. Before VLANs, Layer 2 networks were restricted to a localized geographical area. With VLANs, they can span large networks to make distant hosts appear to be on the same local area network. Open standards and Cisco proprietary standards provide the mechanisms for this to work. Here, we cover the advantages and disadvantages of each mechanism and how they can help you make decisions on how to implement VLANs in your network.

The STP is used to eliminate bridging loops in the network. We cover what bridging loops are, why they are detrimental to your network, and how STP eliminates these loops. We also look at how Spanning Tree is implemented over VLANs. Another topic we cover in dealing with Spanning Tree is how to make it run faster to reduce the convergence time.

Link aggregation is the last topic in this chapter. Link aggregation is the ability to bundle links together between switches to create one virtual link. Here, we describe how link aggregation works and how to configure it in your network. We cover the advantages of link aggregation such as increased bandwidth between switches and increased fault tolerance if a link goes down.

A case study is included to give a real-world example of how to implement VLANs, STP, and link aggregation in your campus network.

This chapter prepares you to design and implement Layer 2 networks throughout your campus network. The next step is to learn how to connect the Layer 2 networks together. This is where the information presented in Chapter 6 applies.

Chapter 6, "Unicast Layer 3 Configuration"

In the previous chapters, we cover what a campus network is, what a campus network's requirements are, how to pick Cisco multilayer switch equipment to build a campus network, and how to implement Layer 2 networks throughout the campus network. At this point in the book you are equipped with the knowledge to build a campus network with several disconnected Layer 2 networks.

In this chapter, we tackle the mechanisms necessary to connect together disconnected Layer 2 networks. Forwarding at Layer 3 is needed to provide communication between Layer 2 networks. The tried and true Layer 3 protocol of choice is the IP. Not only in this chapter, but throughout the whole book, we focus on IP.

The following IP concepts are covered in detail.

- *IP Address Classes* The organization of IP addresses are covered here.
- *Subnet Masks* With subnet masks, a network designer can divide up a campus network's IP address space to logically group devices.
- *IP Router Functions* The function of a device that forwards packets based on Layer 3 information is discussed here. This chapter provides information on what happens to a packet when a router processes it.
- *IP Routes* This chapter provides the foundation for understanding IP routing. We cover the principles and methodology for manually configuring routing information in a router so that multiple routers can exist in the campus network.

With a strong understanding of IP addressing and the functions of a router, we move on to the topic of InterVLAN routing. This mechanism enables IP routing functionality in Cisco multilayer switched networks. The hardware and software requirements are listed and described to aid you in choosing the proper Cisco equipment for implementing InterVLAN routing.

To optimize the performance of IP routing using Cisco multilayer switching equipment, Cisco has devised *Multilayer Switching* (MLS) to provide cut-through switching of IP sessions (flows) between two hosts. This mechanism stores information in the switch about IP flows so that the switch knows where to send the packets without having to make a routing decision. This functionality greatly speeds up the processing time it takes to route a packet. The tradeoff is a more complex switch configuration. Here, we cover these issues to provide you with the necessary information needed to implement MLS in your network.

The last topic in this chapter is fault-tolerant routing with the *Hot Standby Routing Protocol* (HSRP). HSRP provides a mechanism by which several routers can have the appearance of one router. That way, if one of the routers were to fail, another router in the HSRP router pool would take over the routing function. The result is a more reliable and fault-tolerant routing architecture.

This chapter ends with a case study that shows the implementation of the principles covered in this chapter in a real-world network. Here, you can see some of the decisions that need to be made to properly implement these IP routing functions.

After completing this chapter, you have a strong foundation in how to design and build multilayer switching networks using Cisco equipment to provide optimal Layer 2 and Layer 3 forwarding capabilities. Up to this point, however, we have discussed only unicast packet forwarding. A unicast packet is a packet that is directed to only one destination host. In the next two chapters, we cover the concepts of multicasting in which packets are directed to more than one destination but not necessarily to all destination hosts.

Chapter 7, "IP Multicast Configuration"

As we mention in the previous section, only unicast transmission has been covered up to this point. This chapter looks into the concept of IP multicasting. Multicasting is a transmission model by which sources transmit packets to groups of destination hosts. In a unicast transmission model, a source transmits to only one destination host. This chapter begins by exploring the differences and benefits of unicasting, multicasting, and broadcasting.

One of the chief benefits of multicasting is the capability to efficiently transmit packets to a group of destination hosts. The same result can be achieved by using unicasting, but with unicasting separate streams have to be set up for each of the destination hosts. This results in a large number of the same packets on the network with different destination addresses.

Multicasting enables the network to decide where the multicast stream should go. This is a complicated concept, and it requires a number of protocols to make it happen. Before delving into the details of the protocols involved in IP multicasting, the IP multicast addressing scheme is explored. The following concepts are covered in this section of Chapter 7:

- IP multicast addresses
- IP multicast to Ethernet address mapping

An entire class of IP addresses is dedicated to IP multicasting, but there must be a way to translate these addresses into Ethernet addresses; otherwise an address resolution protocol for multicast has to be devised. Because multicast groups can span the entire campus network, a multicast address resolution request packet would have to be flooded to the entire campus network. Lots of these requests could bring a campus network to its knees. To avoid this situation, IP multicast addresses are mapped to special Ethernet addresses that each host in the multicast destination group assumes. It sounds simple, but there is a catch—a one-to-one mapping of IP multicast addresses to Ethernet addresses does not exist. This is discussed in Chapter 7.

Now we are down to the crux of the matter with IP multicasting. How does a host join a multicast group? This concept is the focus of Chapter 7, and Chapter 8 considers the responsibilities of forwarding multicast traffic through multiple routers.

Three protocols are available to provide a host with the ability to join a multicast group. The ability for a host to join or leave a group is known as group management. The protocols covered in this chapter that are used for IP multicast group management are as follows:

- *Internet Group Management Protocol Version 1* (IGMPv1)
- *Internet Group Management Protocol Version 2* (IGMPv2)
- *Cisco Group Management Protocol* (CGMP)

In all three cases, the hosts communicate with a multicast-enabled router. The router is able to use the information gathered from the hosts to know which multicast groups to forward through the router.

IGMPv1 is a simple group management protocol that enables a host to join a group. When the host wants to leave a group, it stops refreshing the join request. IGMPv2 is an improvement over IGMPv1 in which the host can explicitly leave a group. IGMPv2 has other improvements as well. Both IGMPv1 and IGMPv2 are open standards.

CGMP is a Cisco proprietary group management protocol. It works in concert with IGMP. IGMP talks with multicast-enabled routers, and the routers then communicate with the switches to let the switches know where to forward multicast traffic. With IGMP only, the multicast traffic is forwarded to the entire Layer 2 network, on which resides the multicast host.

This floods the entire network with multicast traffic. With IGMP and CGMP, the multicast traffic can be sent directly to the hosts that need it, therefore reducing the overall amount of bandwidth consumed in the Layer 2 network.

This chapter closes with a real-world case study that shows how to implement group management in a campus network.

After completing Chapter 7, you will have a strong grasp of the configuration concepts involved with implementing multicast group management in your campus network. With this knowledge in mind, you are ready to tackle the forwarding of multicast traffic between routers in your campus network. This information is covered in Chapter 8.

Chapter 8, "IP Multicast Routing Configuration"

Chapter 7 covers the concepts and configuration syntax for implementing group management through your campus network. Chapter 8 takes this knowledge one step further and covers the multicast routing concepts necessary for understanding how routers forward IP multicast traffic streams between each other to create a campus network mechanism that can efficiently carry IP multicast traffic.

Before delving into the concepts of multicast routing, this chapter focuses on the differences between unicast routing and multicast routing. The notion of a multicast distribution tree is covered also. The distribution tree is a structure that the routers in the network define to determine the path that packets take from the multicast source to the destination hosts of a multicast group. Two types of distribution trees exist:

- Source-Based Trees
- Shared Trees

Source-based trees set up a multicast tree for each source in a multicast group. A shared tree multicast network sets up one tree for the whole group. IP multicast routing protocols can be divided up into either source-based tree multicast routing protocols or shared tree multicast routing protocols.

Multicast routing protocols can be further divided into sparse-mode and dense-mode IP multicast routing protocols. Sparse-mode protocols assume that bandwidth should be conserved at all costs and that the density of the multicast destination hosts are very low. Dense-mode protocols assume that bandwidth is cheap and that the network is filled with multicast destination hosts.

The following IP multicast routing protocols are covered in Chapter 8:

- *Distance Vector Multicast Routing Protocol* (DVMRP)
- *Multicast Open Shortest Path First* (MOSPF)
- *Protocol Independent Multicast–Dense Mode* (PIM–DM)
- *Core Based Trees* (CBT)
- *Protocol Independent Multicast–Sparse Mode* (PIM–SM)

DVMRP is a source-based tree, dense-mode multicast routing protocol. It is prevalent in the MBone—a multicast overlay network on the Internet. It has a built-in routing protocol to build a special multicast routing table that is based on the *Routing Information Protocol* (RIP).

MOSPF is a dense-mode multicast routing protocol that uses a source-based tree. It uses an OSPF-like routing protocol to build a special multicast routing table. However, MOSPF is rarely used.

PIM–DM is a widely accepted multicast routing protocol that is a shared tree dense-mode (as the name implies) routing protocol. It is protocol independent in that it has no built-in routing protocol that is based on any particular unicast routing protocol. Instead, it uses the existing routing table to determine multicast routes.

CBT is a rarely used multicast routing protocol that is a shared distribution tree-based protocol.

PIM–SM is a widely accepted multicast routing protocol that is a shared-tree sparse-mode (as the name implies) routing protocol. Like PIM–DM, it is not dependent on a built-in routing protocol to build a special multicast routing table. Instead, it uses the existing routing table to determine multicast routes. PIM–SM is especially well suited for carrying multicast traffic over WAN links because it is frugal with bandwidth.

For each routing protocol that is implemented in Cisco multilayer switching equipment, the configuration syntax is discussed. To complete the chapter, a real-world case study is described to show the decision-making processes and configuration examples for implementing multicast routing in your campus network using Cisco multilayer switching equipment.

This chapter completes the exploration of the unicast and multicast networking material covered on the BCMSN test. The next chapter covers the security and access control issues covered on the exam.

Chapter 9, "Access Control"

The previous chapters give a strong and deep foundation for understanding how to implement the networking concepts necessary to deploy Cisco multilayer switching networks. Chapter 9 explores the mechanisms and concepts necessary for maintaining security and controlling access in your campus network.

The following concepts, which pertain to access of the management console of the multilayer switching equipment, are covered in Chapter 9:

- Physical Security
- Passwords
- Privilege Levels
- Banner Messages
- Virtual Terminal Access
- Controlling HTTP Access

These topics basically cover the protection of the management interface to secure the integrity of the network. This discussion ranges from making sure that the equipment and wiring is locked away in an environment that protects the equipment to setting passwords and restricting connections to the management interfaces of the equipment.

Next, the concept of restricting access into the periphery of the network is covered. This is achieved by restricting the Layer 2 addresses that can be forwarded through switches that connect directly to hosts.

After the hosts that can access the network are known and the management interfaces have been secured, the traffic inside the network can be controlled by setting up access lists. An access list is a mechanism by which a Cisco device can filter certain types of packets that enter the device. Because this book is focused on IP, we cover IP access lists, but be aware that Cisco devices can filter on many other types of packets. Two types of IP access lists exist—standard IP access lists and IP extended access lists.

Standard IP access lists can filter on the source IP address of a packet. This list is the simplest and the easiest for the device to support. Many restrictions can be implemented by using this type of access list. The matching criteria in the access list can be either permitted or denied.

IP extended access lists enable the administrator to set up restrictions based on many criteria within the IP packet. Some of these criteria can be source and destination IP address, source and destination port addresses, and protocol type. Because this type of access list can filter based on the port number and address, we can say that the device can operate at Layer

4. Layer 4 restrictions give the device more control over the applications that flow over the network.

These methods of filtering packets through a Cisco switch enable the administrator to set routing policies based on destination route and routing protocol type. This gives another level of control over the routing architecture of the network.

Chapter 9 closes by giving a real-world example of implementing security and filtering in a campus network. After completing this chapter, you are well on your way to implementing security policies, usage policies, and routing policies in your network to allow your network to perform in a way that conforms to your company's business practices and policies.

By the end of Chapter 9, you will have covered all the material that you will be tested on in the BCMSN exam. The following chapters give an introduction to Layer 3 routing protocols and how they are implemented in real-world networks. This material along with Chapters 2–9 will give you a well-rounded, practical foundation in designing, implementing, configuring, and maintaining your campus network using Cisco multilayer switching equipment.

Chapter 10, "Classful IP Routing Protocols"

The material in this chapter is not covered on the exam but will help give you an introduction to the operation, use, and configuration syntax of a certain category of IP routing protocols. This material is crucial to grasping a full understanding of how campus networks are built.

Chapter 10 begins by describing the different categories of routing protocols. These categories are as follows:

- Interior and exterior routing protocols
- Distance vector and link state routing protocols
- Classful and classless routing protocols

Because this book is focused on building campus networks, our discussion of routing protocols is limited to interior routing protocols. Interior routing protocols are used for routing IP packets within a campus network. Exterior routing protocols are for routing IP packets between campus networks. This chapter is focused on classful IP routing protocols. The following classful routing protocols are covered.

- *Routing Information Protocol Version 1* (RIPv1)
- *Interior Gateway Routing Protocol* (IGRP)

RIP was the first IP routing protocol to be developed. It is a distance vector interior routing protocol. Its operation is relatively simple and is covered in great detail in Chapter 10. This protocol has limitations, however. These limitations are covered in great detail as well.

IGRP is another interior classful distance vector routing protocol. It was developed by Cisco and is a proprietary standard. Because it is a proprietary standard, details of its implementation are not open to the public. Its method of operation has been documented by Cisco and is covered in Chapter 10. IGRP solved some of the limitations that RIP has, but IGRP does not solve all of RIP's problems.

Chapter 10 describes the configuration syntax of RIP and IGRP and closes with a real-world discussion of a routing architecture design and implementation in a campus network. This example gives you a good idea of how RIP and IGRP can be used in a campus network.

Now that you understand the operation, configuration, and limitations of a couple of the original routing protocols developed by the Internet and Cisco, you can move on to Chapter 11 where details of classless routing protocols are discussed. Many of the limitations of RIP and IGRP are solved by using these IP routing protocols.

Chapter 11, "Classless IP Routing Protocols"

Chapter 11 begins by recapping the difference between classless and classful, distance vector and link state, and interior and exterior routing protocols. In this chapter we cover classless routing protocols. These routing protocols solve many of the limitations of RIP and IGRP also covered in Chapter 10.

We cover the following routing protocols in Chapter 11:

- *Routing Information Protocol Version 2* (RIPv2)
- *Enhanced Interior Gateway Routing Protocol* (EIGRP)
- *Open Shortest Path First* (OSPF)

RIPv2 is basically RIPv1 with a few enhancements. It solves many of the limitations of RIPv1. It is a distance vector interior classless IP routing protocol. The operation of RIPv2 is very similar to RIPv1. A few differences exist in how the routing table is maintained as well as the type of information that is carried by the protocol. The details of the operation and configuration of RIPv2 are covered in great detail in Chapter 11.

EIGRP is an enhanced version of IGRP as the name implies. The differences between EIGRP and IGRP are much greater than the differences between RIPv2 and RIPv1. EIGRP is basically a completely different protocol than IGRP. EIGRP, like IGRP, is a proprietary IP routing protocol developed by Cisco. EIGRP is a distance vector interior classless IP routing protocol. It is technically a distance vector routing protocol, but it has many of the features of a link state protocol as you will see in the Chapter 11. It is oftentimes called a hybrid routing protocol due to it similarities to both distance vector and link state routing protocols.

OSPF is the last routing protocol covered in Chapter 11. It is a link state routing protocol as opposed to a distance vector routing protocol. This gives this protocol a number of performance advantages in a large network. The downside to OSPF is that it is complex and requires a lot of resources on the routing device to implement. OSPF, unlike IGRP and EIGRP as its name implies, is an open standard. Therefore, all vendors' equipment that correctly implements OSPF should interoperate. This chapter covers the details of OSPF and how it is configured on Cisco routing equipment.

This chapter concludes with a case study that gives a real-world example of how to implement these routing protocols in your campus network.

After completing Chapters 10 and 11, you will have a broader base of knowledge by which you can build more elegant and sophisticated campus networks using the powerful IP routing protocols covered here.

This information, along with the topics covered in Chapters 2–9 will give you a wealth of understanding and will be a great reference for studying for the BCMSN exam and for building and maintaining networks in your career.

These are exciting times in networking. The industry is young and growing fast—work hard and enjoy the benefits of contributing to your company and community!

Now, on to the details of *Building Cisco Multilayer Switching Networks*. Good luck!

2

Multilayer Switching Network Design Basics

It's old news that networks are growing at an explosive rate. Not only has the size of networks changed, but the perception of networks has changed from being a nifty gadget with questionable returns to becoming a mission-critical business tool. These realities of today's campus network have driven networking equipment manufacturing companies, namely Cisco, to provide network devices that can keep up with the fast pace of changing perception and the demand for networking features.

To be better equipped to build networks that meet heavy demands of its users, you need to understand basic design principles. Strong knowledge of the fundamental components, definition of the requirements, and an understanding of the building blocks of the campus network are all ingredients you need to build a reliable and responsive mission-critical network.

Objectives Covered in the Chapter

This chapter lays the foundation you need to understand the basics of multilayer switched networks. The following topics are covered:

- Campus network definition and description
- Multilayer network model and function definition
- Network design requirements
- Multilayer switching technologies
- Hierarchical design concepts

Campus networks are complex systems that must meet a rigorous set of requirements. This chapter defines a campus network and its requirements. After defining the campus network design problem, a discussion of emerging switching technologies follows. At this point, solving the problem of a complete network design may seem daunting considering the design problem and the many ways of coming up with a solution.

Building a network to meet expected requirements is an enormous job, but developing a systematic approach to placing network devices in a campus network makes the problem manageable. This chapter closes by describing a system for designing a campus network using network building blocks formed by multilayer switches.

This chapter equips the network professional with tools to understand campus networks and to determine their functional design requirements. In addition, it covers how to build campus networks using a systematic approach to network design.

Network Overview

Campus Network Definition

When speaking of networks, you will hear colleagues use the acronyms LAN, CAN, MAN, or WAN. These acronyms are used to convey the notion of the size of a network. Understanding the scope of a network is critical from a design perspective. Let's look at each of these acronyms and their definition, which will help you understand the design concepts that follow.

A *Local Area Network* (LAN) refers to networks ranging in size from a single room to a building (see Figure 2-1). A LAN is owned and administered by a single organization.

The *Campus Area Network* (CAN) is a collection of LANs (see Figure 2-2). A CAN consists of a building or multiple buildings located in a fixed geographical area. It is also owned and administered by a single organization or may be a portion of an organization at a single location.

Figure 2-1
Local Area Network
(LAN)

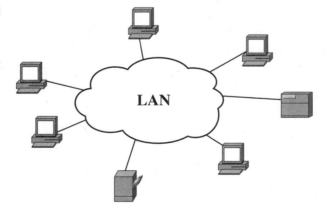

Figure 2-2
Campus Area
Network (CAN)

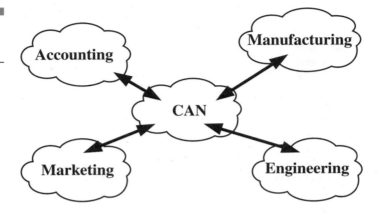

Figure 2-3
Metropolitan Area
Network (MAN)

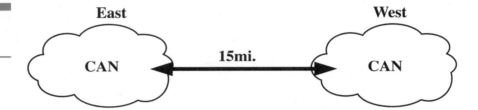

The *Metropolitan Area Network* (MAN) is a sparse collection of campuses (see Figure 2-3). A MAN may be owned and administered by multiple organizations.

The *Wide Area Network* (WAN) is a conglomeration of LANs, CANs, and MANs connected over large distances (see Figure 2-4). A WAN is likely owned and administered by several organizations.

The concepts covered in this text are focused on the CAN; however, references to the WAN are made as appropriate. If you learn how to design and build a CAN, you will have the knowledge to apply to LANs and MANs.

What's in the CAN?   The company that owns the network usually owns the physical wiring. For the remainder of this text, we'll assume that Ethernet technology is deployed over that infrastructure. Because the CAN is a collection of LANs, to fully understand the CAN, you must first understand the concepts associated with a LAN. First, we'll look at the network communications architecture. Next, you will be introduced to traditional network traffic models and management.

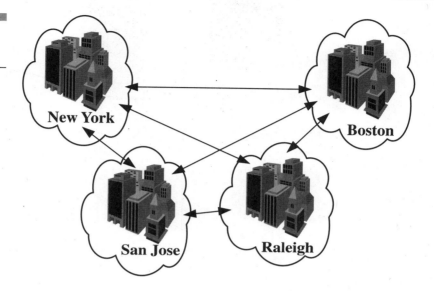

Figure 2-4
Wide Area Network
(WAN)

Multilayer Model

Palindrome Architectures   No matter what the size of the network, the *Open Systems Interconnect* (OSI) architecture was designed to facilitate the characterization of many types of communication. In addition, OSI architecture laid the groundwork, as a reference model, for defining standard protocols. These standards enable heterogeneous systems to communicate with each other. The OSI model is modular, which greatly aids in the troubleshooting of networks implemented using the model.

The *International Standards Organization* (ISO) created the OSI model to describe the theoretical layers (that often map to reality, although difficult at times) that all networks have in common. The layers serve as a frame of reference for standards-making bodies when describing how protocols interact with each other. Each layer is described in detail in this chapter.

The OSI Model   The seven OSI layers are shown in Figure 2-5 and are as follows:

- Physical
- Data Link
- Network

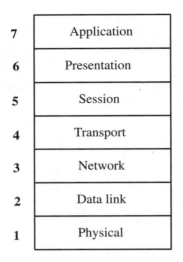

Figure 2-5
OSI 7-layer network
model

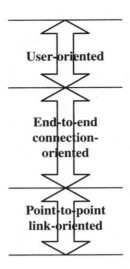

- Transport
- Session
- Presentation
- Application

The physical layer refers to the transmission media used for communication. Common media include electricity, light, and radio waves. The physical layer manages sending the data, in a serial fashion, over the medium. The physical layer understands only that the datum is raw bits.

The data link layer describes how the communication takes place over the physical layer. The various physical layers will, of course, require that different methods be defined for transmitting data over the media. The data must also be *framed* (packaged) for transmission. The data link layer is made up of two sublayers—the lower sublayer is the *Media Access Control* (MAC) sublayer, and the upper sublayer is the *Logical Link Control* (LLC) sublayer. The data link layer must try to provide for reliable transmission over the selected media, which means retransmission in the event of an error. Layer 2 switching takes place at the data link layer.

The network layer provides a layer of abstraction for the remaining layers from the transmission media. This layer provides for managing connections, either at end points, or pass-through nodes. The network layer also handles converting logical addresses into physical, or MAC, addresses. The

Internet Protocol (IP) resides at this layer. Layer 3 switching takes place at the network layer.

The transport layer is responsible for providing reliable, transparent communication to the session layer. This communication includes such features as flow control and end-to-end error recovery. The *Transmission Control Protocol* (TCP) and *User Datagram Protocol* (UDP) reside at the transport layer.

The session layer provides the structure for managing connection-oriented service between applications. This layer handles creating node-to-node channels for communications, as applications require them.

The presentation layer acts as a translator for the application to send data over the network. This layer shields the application from potential differences in data representation by ensuring that the format is correct for the application layer.

The application layer is the interface between the user application and the rest of the OSI layers. Typically, this software interface is available to applications.

As Figure 2-6 shows, each layer is responsible for communicating with its peer layer. As data travels down the stack, each layer adds the necessary information it needs to function properly. On the receiving end, each layer uses the information to perform its task, and passes the remaining data up to the next layer for processing.

In an ideal world, each layer would be independent and have a common interface that would make it possible to substitute protocols at each layer

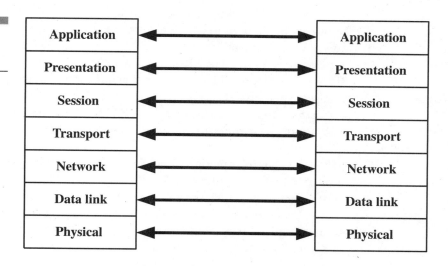

Figure 2-6
Network layer communication

and still have communication ability. Although the latter is not likely, the architecture is still applicable in modern networks. For more information on the OSI Model, see Appendix E.

Putting It To Work   The layers we will concentrate on are Layers 2–4: data link, network, and transport. Layer 2 switching takes place at the data link layer. Layer 3 switching takes place at the network layer. Access control can take place at Layer 2, 3, or 4. These functions can be implemented in software or hardware. Typically, the functions are developed in software and evolve to hardware. Hardware implementations of these functions are typically much faster than software implementations. That's where multilayer switches come into play. These devices typically implement the Layer 2–4 switching functions in hardware.

Traffic Model

As we look at the campus area network, and Layers 2–4, we must understand how we expect traffic to traverse the network. Traffic patterns significantly affect network design; however, before charging into design, we need to understand some historical theories on traffic models.

LANs were created to enable users to share local resources. These LANs usually were Ethernet networks.

Ethernet   The Ethernet specification allows for 1024 devices within a single collision domain, with a maximum of 100 taps, or devices, per segment. When connecting multiple devices to a shared media, you create contention for the medium. If more than one device attempts to transmit at the same time, a collision occurs. For more information on Ethernet theory, see Appendix D.

As the number of users increases, a repeater, or hub, must be used to connect multiple segments to prevent exceeding the 100-tap limit. Repeaters enable you to exceed the 100-tap limit; however, you are extending only the collision domain. As traffic load increases with use, you must reduce the size of the collision domain. A collision domain that is too big results in a large amount of collisions, which increases overall network delay.

A collision domain can be split up with a bridge. A bridge enables you to connect multiple segments, each having their own collision domain.

As we look at the concept of the collision domain, you need to understand the history of the physical layer as it relates to contention. As shown

Figure 2-7
Ethernet bus
structure

Bus Architecture

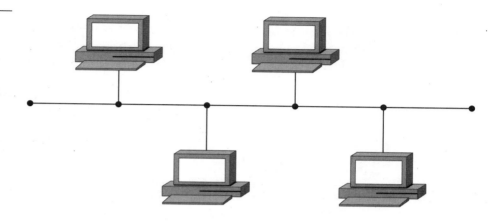

Figure 2-8
Modern Ethernet
structure

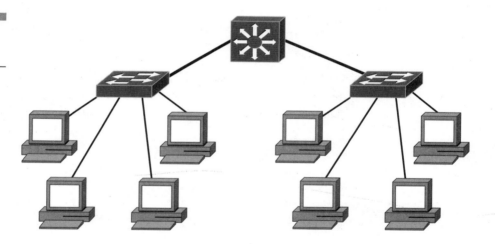

Today, the bus has been replaced with point-to-point physical links (see Figure 2-8). This includes twisted pair and fiber optic cable. Each end of a point-to-point connection has a transmit line and a receive line. Initially, the point-to-point connections were half-duplex (one end could transmit at a time); later full duplex was implemented. With both ends capable of transmitting and receiving at the same time, the effective throughput is doubled!

The point-to-point architecture has made the concept of the collision domain almost obsolete. The following section describes the operation of bridges.

Bridging A bridge works by learning which network devices are connected to each port. A bridge looks at the packets that are transmitted by devices on that port and creates a forwarding table. When the bridge sees a message, it looks at the destination MAC address in the packet and looks up that address in the forwarding table. If the address exists, the bridge forwards the message on that port as long as the destination is not the same port on which the packet was received.

Figure 2-9 shows Host A, connected to Port 1 of a bridge, and Host B connected to Port 2. When Host B needs to communicate with Host A, Host B sends a broadcast packet to find the physical address of Host A based on the logical name. First, the switch learns which port Host B is connected to by examining the broadcast packet and the source address. Second, a switch forwards all broadcast packets; it retransmits the broadcast packet out all other ports of the bridge. Because all hosts listen for broadcast packets, Host A receives the packet and examines it to find out that someone wants to communicate with it. Host A replies to Host B to inform Host B of its physical address.

As this reply crosses the bridge, the bridge adds Host A to its forwarding table based on the source address. The bridge then examines the destination address and looks it up in the forwarding table to see whether it exists.

Figure 2-9
Bridging

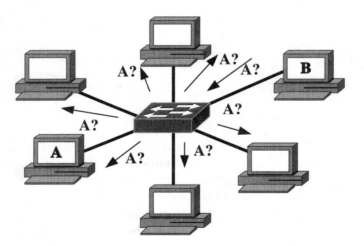

Because Host B exists, the bridge forwards the packet out the port associated with Host B.

The term *switch* usually refers to a Layer 2 switch. A Layer 2 switch performs the same tasks as a bridge, only faster.

Broadcast Domains   Bridges enable you to reduce the size of the collision domain; however, the size of the broadcast domain only increases. As devices communicate, they must use broadcast packets to determine physical addresses. For example, a host sends a broadcast packet to find the MAC address associated with IP address `10.0.2.1`. The host with IP address `10.0.2.1` responds with a packet directed back to the host that sent the original request.

With more and more devices communicating, broadcast traffic increases. Because *every* machine must examine the broadcast to determine whether it requires a response and because broadcast packets must contend for the shared medium as with any other messages, we have another problem that needs solving—broadcast storms. *Broadcast storms* are the result of many devices on a broadcast domain. A significant amount of available network resources are used for broadcast traffic in this situation.

As noted earlier, even though we have moved away from the shared bus model, point-to-point connections are still considered shared media when they terminate into a repeater. Only one device on the repeater may be transmitting at a time. A good rule of thumb is a maximum of 250 devices per broadcast domain (see Figure 2-10). We use bridges to segment the collision domain; we have to use another device to segment broadcast domains. Layer 3 switches or routers are used to segment broadcast domains.

Routing   Bridges operate at Layer 2, looking at only physical MAC addresses. To segment broadcast domains, you must add another layer of abstraction. Multiple LANs are connected with routers to form a campus area network.

Because bridges operate at Layer 2, it follows that routers operate at Layer 3, the network layer. As multiple networks are connected together, the router handles routing data between each network.

Figure 2-11 shows how multiple LANs are connected via a router. The router has several jobs. First, as devices attempt to communicate with devices on another LAN, broadcast packets are used to determine the physical address based on the logical address. The router examines these broadcast packets and determines whether it knows how to get to the logical

Figure 2-10
Broadcast domains

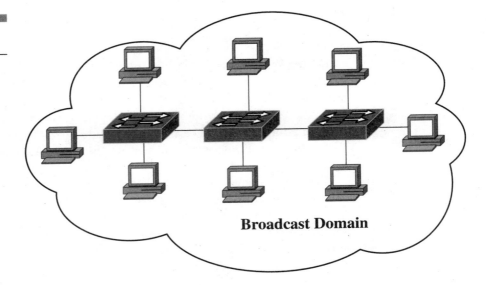

Broadcast Domain

Figure 2-11
Routing

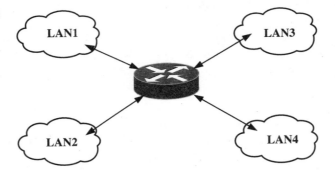

address. If the logical address is connected on another router port, the router must respond to the broadcast to let the device know where, physically, to address the packet. The router gives the device the physical address of itself. When the router receives the packet, addressed to itself from the device, it must further examine the packet to look for the actual logical destination of the packet.

The router must be configured to know what Layer 3 IP addresses are connected to it. If the IP address is connected, the router then looks in its own tables to see whether it knows the MAC address that corresponds with the IP address. If the MAC address is not listed in its own tables, it sends a broadcast packet only to the port where the IP address should exist and waits for a reply from the destination device. If it already has the MAC address in memory, it simply forwards the packet to the device, addressing it appropriately.

Routers have a lot to do—receiving packets, examining packets, making decisions and forwarding packets. This technology gives you the ability to scale networks from small to very large.

The 80/20 Rule   The 80/20 rule says that you should expect 80 percent of the traffic to remain local, which implies that 20 percent of the traffic is destined for, or coming from, remote locations (see Figure 2-12).

The assumption is that most of the traffic is communicating with local file servers or application/database servers. The 80/20 rule is the classic notion of LAN traffic patterns. The 80/20 rule may not apply due to network services that are moving off individual LANs to a centralized location in the campus network. In the case of Internet resources, some network services can move off the campus network.

Network Design Considerations

Requirements

Now that you have a basic understanding of what a campus network is, the next order of business is to understand what features a campus network

Figure 2-12
80/20 rule

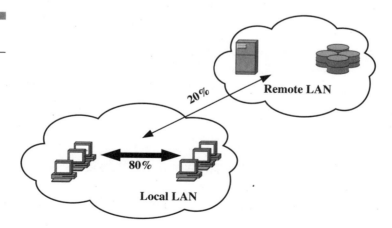

should have. Modern campus networks have several common requirements. These requirements must be considered when designing any campus network:

- Fast convergence
- Deterministic paths
- Deterministic failover
- Scalable in size and throughput
- Centralized storage
- 20/80 rule
- Multiprotocol support
- Multicast support

These requirements guide the decisions you make when designing networks. Let's look at each of the requirements individually.

Fast Convergence   Convergence is the act of Layer 2 switches and Layer 3 switches adapting to network changes by using mechanisms in the protocols at Layer 2 and Layer 3. A change in the network could be a broken link, a failed router, a failed bridge, or a new router, link, or bridge. As networks grow, the number of links, hosts, and routes grows, making more probable the occurrence of a random change in the network.

Regardless, if the network change happens intentionally or unexpectedly, the network must have intrinsic capabilities to adapt to the change quickly. This capability gives a network scalability as well as minimal downtime during disruptions.

Deterministic Paths   Consistency in a network is a virtue. Whether in traffic patterns, response times, jitter, or uptime, both users and network administrators demand consistency. The largest component of guaranteeing consistency is a logical topology that forces traffic to flow over a set of links in a predictable way. This predictability makes the path choice deterministic.

If two hosts can communicate with each other over multiple paths and the choice of paths can be random, the response times between the two paths could be radically different. Think of the poor network administrator that has to troubleshoot this network when one of the randomly chosen paths has a failure. The symptoms would not quickly lead the administrator to the problem resulting in unnecessary downtime, user frustration, and network administrator stress.

Deterministic paths result in consistent network performance and help to minimize troubleshooting efforts.

Scalable Size and Throughput   Networks often simultaneously grow in the number of users and individual user demand. This means that your network design must handle an increased number of connections as well as handle more bandwidth over the network's internal links.

If a network is designed without this in mind, you could reach an unexpected point where the network can no longer handle the addition of new links without a fundamental design change. This type of change could cost not only large amounts of time but also large amounts of money.

Centralized Storage   We've come full circle. In the beginning of multiuser computing, the mainframe was the core device that housed the majority of storage and processing power. After the invention and accelerated development of the PC, the storage and processor power migrated to the desktop. The problem encountered with the fully distributed model of computing with a PC on every desktop is the inconsistency in information system uniformity and administration.

The new requirement is much like that of the mainframe in terms of application management. Instead of a user accessing a mainframe from a remote terminal, a user now accesses a server or a cluster of servers from his desktop. This centralized approach to file and application management requires that all users have adequate access to this resource (see Figure 2-13).

20/80 Rule   In the past, it was a fair assumption that 80 percent of traffic originating on a network remained on the network. This meant that bandwidth within a network or workgroup LAN was large and that the bandwidth to connect with other networks or workgroups could be small.

With the flexibility of modern campus networks and centralized storage, this rule has completely reversed. Now it's a fair assumption that 20 percent of the traffic originating on a network remains on a network, and the rest of the traffic is destined for another network (see Figure 2-14). This means that the connections between networks must be large and allow for scalability.

Multiprotocol Support   Even with the current popularity of the IP, other legacy protocols must be supported, including Novell's IPX and Apple

Figure 2-13
Centralized storage

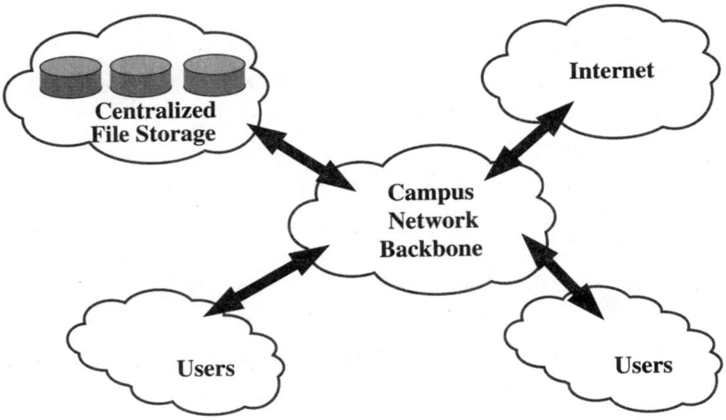

Figure 2-14
20/80 rule

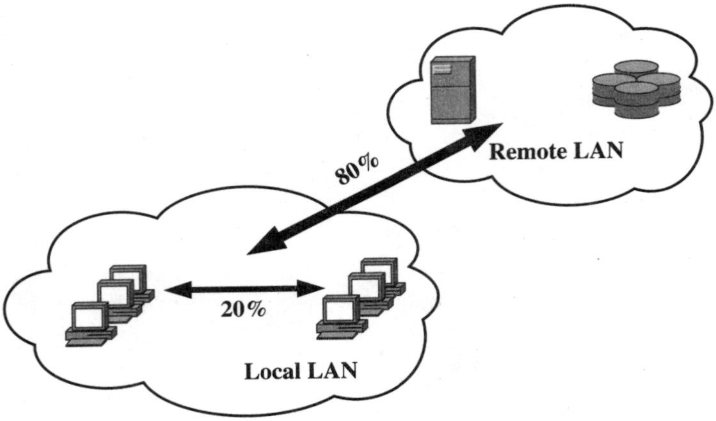

Computer's Appletalk. These protocols are waning because most new networking products are IP-centric.

Even considering an IP-only network, many new protocols that ride on top of IP are emerging. These protocols include multimedia protocols, multicast protocols, and routing protocols. To maximize the life of your network design, these protocols must be supported.

Multicast Support   With new applications like teleconferencing, video on demand, and new networking protocols, multicast support is a must. The legacy view of traffic flow was one-to-one (unicast) as in Figure 2-15 or one-

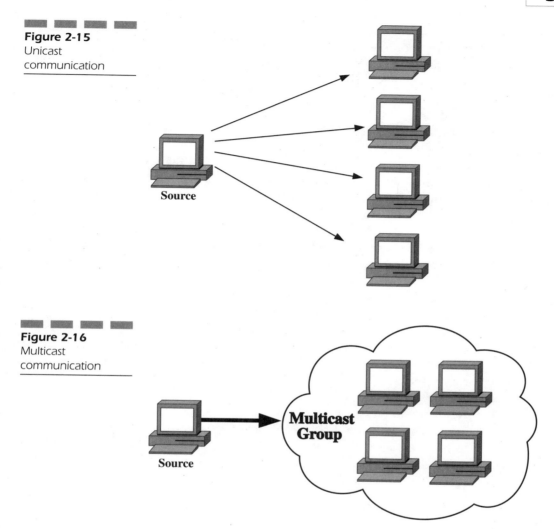

Figure 2-15
Unicast
communication

Source

Figure 2-16
Multicast
communication

Multicast Group

Source

to-all (broadcast). Multicasting is a mechanism by which a source sends traffic destined for a group of hosts (see Figure 2-16). This concept of one-to-some is providing a means to greatly reduce the occurrence of unnecessary traffic on the network and to increase the reliability and response of new multimedia teleconferencing applications.

A new network design that doesn't take multicast into consideration has the potential of being inefficient and needing costly upgrades in the future.

The list of requirements discussed here is constantly changing due to new expectations of campus networks, new application functionality, and new network functionality. This list is sure to grow, but for now, these requirements will be your basic objectives in designing a campus network.

Campus Structure

The network design requirements discussed in the preceding section show a definite shift from the classical way traffic patterns were viewed throughout the network. Instead of a campus network linking several geographically grouped workgroup LANs, now a campus network is made up of services linked together in a way that affords efficient traffic flow. The network services are grouped into three types: local services, remote services, and enterprise services.

Local Services Local services are network services accessible from within the same local workgroup (see Figure 2-17). For example, network print services could be considered local services. Traffic for these services typically remains in the same broadcast domain (i.e., is switched at Layer 2) and does not appear on the backbone of the campus network (i.e., is not routed at Layer 3).

Remote Services Remote services are services that users access outside their own workgroup LAN (see Figure 2-18). For example, applications such as file services could be considered a remote service. Traffic corresponding

Figure 2-17
Local services

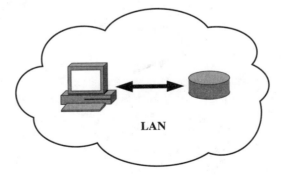

LAN

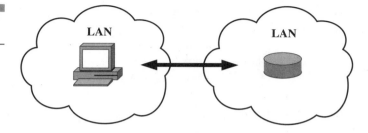

Figure 2-18
Remote services

to these services crosses broadcast domains and is forwarded across routers at Layer 3.

Enterprise Services   Enterprise services are accessible to all users throughout the campus network (see Figure 2-19). For example, applications such as email and intranet services would be considered enterprise services. These services are typically placed near the logical center of the network to allow equal access by all users. Depending on the scale of the enterprise services, these services may or may not be grouped in the same broadcast domain.

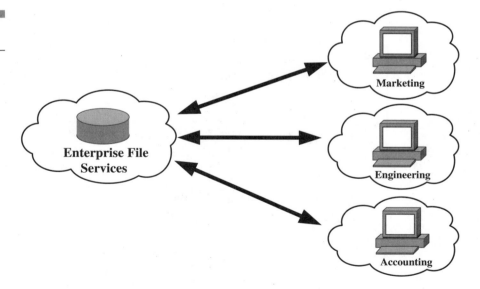

Figure 2-19
Enterprise services

Accommodating all three types of services efficiently in the campus network is a must.

Switching Technologies

Earlier in this chapter, we discussed the multilayer network model. This book focuses on the first four layers of that model. Each of these layers is encoded inside each frame that traverses a physical network. Each layer has its own definition of how its protocol data unit is formed. Here is an example of how the various layers' PDUs are organized with respect to each other.

Let's start with Layer 2 using Ethernet for this example. The Ethernet PDU, called a *frame*, consists of a header, payload, and trailer. The header includes source and destination MAC or hardware addresses. These addresses correspond to physical Ethernet devices on that local Ethernet segment. The Ethernet trailer is a checksum code for verifying the correctness of the frame.

Inside this Ethernet payload is an IP PDU or packet. A unit of transmission at Layer 3 is typically called a *packet* (see Figure 2-20). A unit of transmission at Layer 2 is typically called a frame. Sometimes the terms packet and frame are used interchangeably. This IP packet includes a header and payload. The header, among other things, includes the source and destination IP addresses for this packet.

Inside this Ethernet packet is a fragment of a TCP PDU or message. This TCP message fragment has a header that includes a source and destination TCP port number. The destination port numbers are used by the destination hosts to determine which application gets the TCP message.

Figure 2-20
Exploded view
of a packet

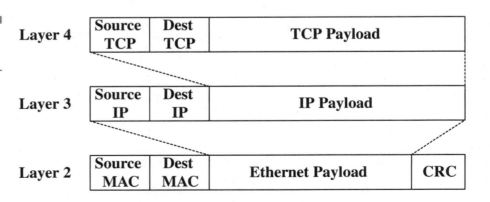

Layer 4	Source TCP	Dest TCP	TCP Payload	

Layer 3	Source IP	Dest IP	IP Payload	

Layer 2	Source MAC	Dest MAC	Ethernet Payload	CRC

In this example Ethernet MAC addresses correspond to Layer 2 addresses; IP addresses correspond to Layer 3 addresses; and TCP ports correspond to Layer 4 addresses. Note that each higher layer address is farther inside the Ethernet frame. In addition, the higher layer address locations are often dependent on the header information found in the lower layer PDUs.

Forwarding at Layer 2 and Layer 3 is typically called *bridging* and *routing*, respectively.

An important implication can be drawn from the preceding example. It is more difficult (i.e., more steps are involved) to forward at Layer 3 than at Layer 2 because the information used to determine the Layer 3 destination address is farther inside the Ethernet frame than the Layer 2 MAC address. The time it takes to forward at Layer 3 is greater that at Layer 2. Another result of the relative difficulties of forwarding at Layer 3 is more of the forwarding device's resources are consumed for each Layer 3 PDU to be forwarded through it. Each function that the router must perform consumes memory and processor power. The more functions the multilayer switch has to do, more memory and processor power is used. At worst, the switch becomes unable to perform its functions as it runs out of memory or if the processor becomes saturated. At the least, the switch causes increased forwarding latencies, which affect network performance. This limitation of switches must be considered when implementing functions in networks.

These implications are true in a software-based router, which is typical of older network devices. However, advancements have been made that allow these forwarding decisions to be made in hardware. Because hardware operations are much faster than software operations, the differences in forwarding Layer 2 and Layer 3 PDUs are negligible. If a Layer 2 or Layer 3 forwarding device performs its functions in hardware, it is called a Layer 2 or Layer 3 switch. Layer 3 switches can forward packets at Layer 3 much faster than software-based routers. The time it takes a switch to do Layer 2 or Layer 3 forwarding is nearly equal. However, Layer 3 switching still takes 50–100 percent more time than Layer 2 switching.

Layer 2 Switching Operation Layer 2 switching is fairly simple. The switch keeps a table that associates a MAC address to a port. If a packet arrives that has an unknown destination MAC address, it forwards it to all ports. If a packet arrives with a broadcast address for the destination address, it is forwarded to all ports. Layer 2 switching is complicated by media translation and loop protection.

If a Layer 2 switch has ports of different media types, such as FDDI and Fast Ethernet, the switch has to reformat the Layer 1 (physical layer) PDU into the destination media type. In some cases, the switch may have to fragment the packet if the maximum PDU length of the destination media type is smaller than the packet destined for it.

Loop protection is absolutely necessary for any bridged network. Imagine three switches connected with three links. A broadcast packet would never stop being forwarded through all the switches. Assuming that the switches can forward at wire speed, the ultimate result is that all three links will be completely saturated with this single broadcast packet causing a bridging loop (see Figure 2-21).

To avoid this scenario, Layer 2 switches use the *Spanning Tree Protocol* (STP) (see Figure 2-22). This protocol finds all other bridges in the broadcast domain and places each of the switches in a tree structure so that there is only one path between any two switches. If redundant links exist, their corresponding ports are set to blocking mode and will not forward packets. This function removes the chance of a bridge loop situation.

Layer 2 Scalability   As the number of hosts that are connected with Layer 2 switches increases, the number of broadcast packets that traverse

Figure 2-21
Bridging loop

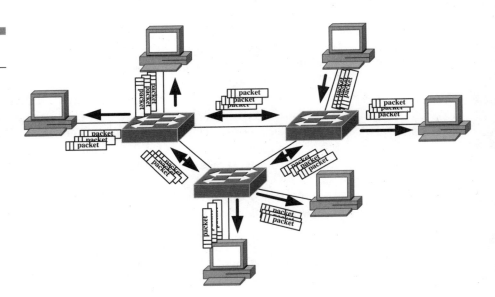

Figure 2-22
Bridging loop
with STP

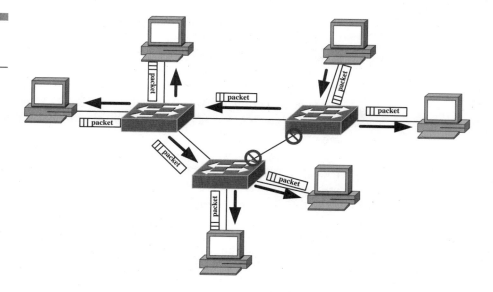

the Layer 2 network increases. The broadcast packets begin to have an adverse effect on the network when the bandwidth used by these packets begins to take up a significant portion of the available network bandwidth. This situation is called a *broadcast storm*. Therefore, Layer 2 networks do not scale infinitely. Broadcast storms can be contained within broadcast domains. The only way to connect broadcast domains is through routing (i.e., Layer 3 switching).

Layer 3 Switching Operation   Routers have been around for years, but it wasn't until recently that routing could be done virtually at the same speed as Layer 2 switching. Regardless of the method of performance, the operation is the same.

When a packet arrives on the port of an IP router, the router looks toward the destination IP address and determines the port to forward the packet on, based on its routing table. The IP checksum is verified; the packet's *time to live* (TTL) field is decremented; and the destination MAC address is updated before forwarding.

The routers routing table is built by keeping up with the Layer 3 networks directly connected to the router and by receiving routing updates from other routers if a routing protocol is used. These routing updates include information about routes elsewhere on the network.

Layer 3 switching is highly scalable. In fact, the entire Internet is built from Layer 3 forwarding devices. However, no control over application-specific traffic exists once the path between hosts is determined.

Layer 4 Switching Layer 4 switching enables forwarding decisions to be made on Layer 4 port addresses. Note that Layer 4 port addressing is a way to create multiple logical connections over one path defined by Layer 3. The most common Layer 4 protocols are TCP and UDP. Many applications have well-known TCP and UDP ports. That way, an application knows to listen to a particular port address for communication to and from a particular application.

The Layer 3 source and destination addresses along with Layer 4 source and destination port pairs define a session also known as a *flow*. Because the paths that the flows travel over are already defined, the Layer 4 switch can determine whether a session should be allowed or denied, creating a firewall device. The Layer 4 switch can also define at what priority these flows pass through the switch. This is defining a *quality of service* (QoS) for the flow.

Determining what application a flow is associated with is not always easy because some applications are *stateful* in that a control flow sets up a data flow on a negotiated port number. This topic is beyond the scope of this book, but keep in mind that the situation exists.

Multilayer Switching A multilayer switch can bridge at Layer 2, route at Layer 3, and provide firewalling and QoS capabilities at Layer 4—all in hardware. This book is devoted to describing how to design campus networks that use these switches.

Multilayer switching is a recent innovation and provides a wealth of new opportunities for network designers who must solve the multidimensional problem of meeting all the campus network design requirements.

Hierarchical Design

Access, Distribution, and Core Layers

The first approach to tackling any system design is to identify the main components of the system. In keeping with our design requirement for a campus network, pockets of services and user connectivity need to be connected together in a way that optimizes bandwidth, stability, and fairness for all users. These main components are the *Core Layer*, *Distribution Layer*, and *Access Layer* (see Figure 2-23). We'll describe each component starting with the user and working toward the center of the network.

Access Layer   The Access Layer component handles user access to the network (see Figure 2-24). Typically, the Access Layer is made up of Layer 2 switches, although hubs can be used instead of switches to share the bandwidth of an Ethernet segment.

Switched Access Layer networks provide more bandwidth to the user than shared networks. However, switched networks are more costly than shared networks even though the per-port cost of Layer 2 switching is quickly decreasing. The decision between using switched versus shared Layer 2 networks at the Access Layer is based on user requirements and cost.

Virtual LANs (VLANs) can be configured to group users into functional groups instead of by geography. VLANs are covered in depth in a later chapter.

In a nutshell, the Access Layer provides high port density and low cost access between users and the campus network.

Figure 2-23

Hierarchical network design layers

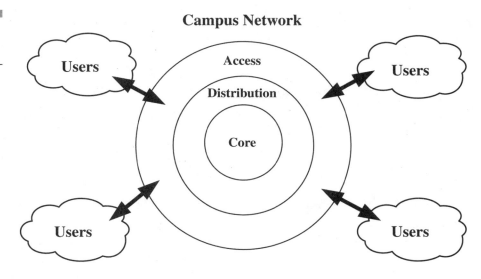

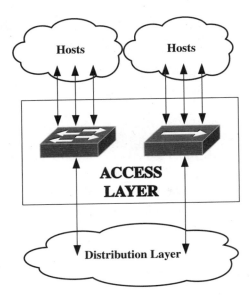

Figure 2-24
Access Layer

Distribution Layer   The Distribution Layer is the boundary between the Core and the Access Layers of the network (see Figure 2-25). From a logical perspective, the Distribution Layer is used to aggregate users together into workgroups.

Functionally, the Distribution Layer provides connections between broadcast domains, routing between VLANs, multicast optimization, and security. This layer typically handles the Layer 3 routing function of the campus network.

Core Layer   The Core Layer ties together the Distribution Layers (see Figure 2-26). Typically, no routing occurs in this layer. Because few Distribution Layer devices typically exist, Layer 2 switching is used because it is fast and simple.

The big design requirement with the Core Layer is speed and reliability.

Network Building Blocks

Now that we've broken down the campus network into three topological layers—Access, Distribution, and Core—we will further dissect the network

Figure 2-25
Distribution Layer

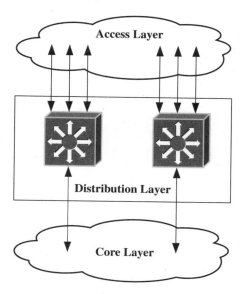

Figure 2-26
Core Layer

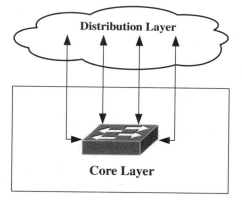

into network building blocks. Types of network building blocks that exist:
the *switch block* and the *core block*.

The Switch Block   A switch block is a group of switches with Layer 2
(bridging) and Layer 3 (routing) functionality and can span the Access and
Distribution Layers (see Figure 2-27). A switch block contains broadcast
storms because the routing function acts as a boundary between broadcast

Figure 2-27
Switch Block

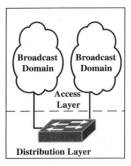

domains. Typically, a switch block is a set of distribution devices that connect access devices together.

The switch block performs the following functions:

- Defines a broadcast domain
- Defines a boundary for STP
- Terminates a subnet or VLAN
- Provides redundancy at the Access Layer

The containment of broadcast domains gives the capability for switch blocks to be interconnected in a scalable fashion. If a broadcast domain spans the entire campus network, the amount of traffic devoted to broadcasts could have a significant effect on network performance. To compound matters, the behavior of the network with large broadcast storms could be sporadic, creating frustrated users.

Another feature of the switch block that promotes scalability is spanning tree termination. The STP is a necessary function of a production network that provides protection against bridging loops. Operating a network without spanning tree turned on could consume a switch in unnecessary traffic if redundant links are inadvertently created by a simple cabling mistake. The problem with STP is that it is not scalable. Forming the spanning tree graph structure within the switch consumes memory and network bandwidth. Terminating the spanning tree network at the boundary of a switch block helps bound the scope of the spanning tree network and conserve network device resources.

Subnets and VLANs are typically terminated on the boundary of a switch block to provide a logical boundary to a subnet or VLAN. Because routing takes place between subnets and VLANs, this neatly defines where routing should take place in the Distribution Layer of the network within the switch block. Remember that the Core Layer typically does not provide routing functionality.

Redundancy is an important feature in a production network. Redundant paths provide a backup path in the case of a link failure. Because STP spans the switch block, redundant paths can be safely implemented to provide redundant connections between the Access and Distribution Layers. If a redundant path exists in the switch block, one of the paths is disabled by the STP by setting the appropriate ports to blocked mode, which disables packet forwarding. If one of the redundant paths fails, STP activates the disabled path to regain connectivity.

Switch Block Limitations   The conventional rule of thumb is to limit the number of users per switch block to 2000. This limits the number of hardware addresses in the bridging tables of Layer 2 switches. Overrunning a Layer 2 switch's bridging table can create unnecessary traffic that is flooded to all ports of the switch because an increased probability exists that a particular destination hardware address could be missing from the bridging table. This situation can create random behavior that makes troubleshooting the problem much more difficult.

Aside from the number of users, a switch block size should be limited so that the routing capacity of the Distribution Layer switches is not overrun. As the number of routes in the switch block increases, the amount of resources consumed within the switch increases. The processor of the switch may also be stressed to the point that network performance is affected.

Broadcast domains within the switch block may also begin to create a problem if the switch block grows too large. The amount of traffic used for broadcasting may cause an adverse effect on network performance. The size of the broadcast domain is related to the scope of the STP, which consumes memory in the switch.

No hard and fast rules for sizing a switch block exist. After the network is designed, you must monitor it to keep a close eye on situations that can degrade performance. Fortunately, these problems are limited to the individual switch block instead of the entire network. The solution to an oversized switch block is to split it up or devote more resources to the problem area.

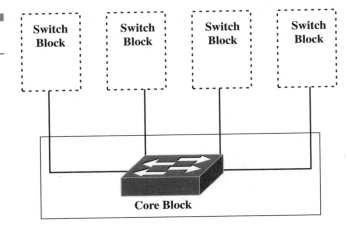

Figure 2-28
Core block

The Core Block   The core block connects multiple switch blocks (see Figure 2-28). Because the majority of traffic processing takes place in the Distribution Layer, the focus of the Core Layer is maximizing speed and minimizing delay. Typically, Core Layer devices only do bridging to minimize the time it takes to forward traffic; therefore, routing is left to the Distribution Layer.

Because the core is the aggregation point of the entire network, this layer must have the capacity to handle a large amount of traffic. This requires that the Core Layer must have adequate processing power and bandwidth to handle all the backbone traffic on the campus network.

Two basic forms of core block topologies exist: *collapsed core* and *dual core*. The collapsed core merges the Distribution and Core Layers. The dual core provides redundant links in a separate set of switches. In both forms, redundancy is key. The core block must have redundant links to protect the most critical links in the campus network.

The collapsed core topology merges the distribution and the core functionality in the same device (see Figure 2-29). The links connecting the switch blocks are situated such that more than one path exists between switch blocks. A separate spanning tree domain from the Distribution Layer protects the core block from bridging loops.

The second core block topology form is the dual core (see Figure 2-30). The dual core provides the Core Layer functionality in a separate set of switches, which enables each switch block to be connected to redundant core block switches to provide redundancy. If a core link or a network device

Figure 2-29
Collapsed core
topology

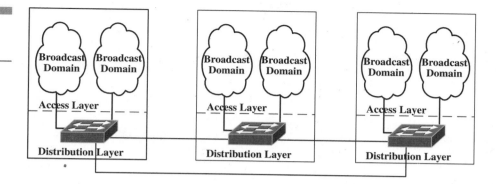

Figure 2-30
Dual core topology

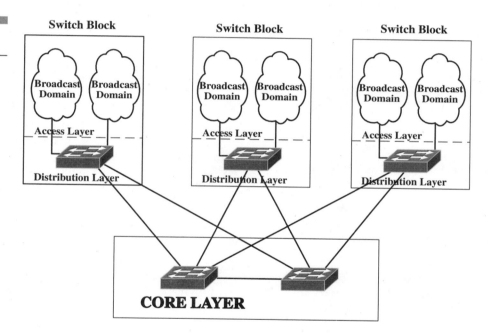

in the core block fails, the Core Layer still remains operational. This architecture requires more core devices and, therefore, costs more money. A tradeoff often exists between redundancy and economy.

The core block typically does not run the STP to minimize the amount of extra traffic in the core and to maximize performance. To implement redundant links in this case, redundant paths are used between the routing domains in the Distribution Layer. The routing protocols allow redundant links and can even load balance between the links. This takes the burden of handling loops away from the core block.

Core Block Limitations   The core block is limited by the amount of aggregate traffic that must traverse the core as well as functional limitations of routing protocols in the Distribution Layer and the number of switches in the Distribution Layer.

The Core Layer switches must be able to handle the amount of aggregate traffic between switch blocks. It is good to oversize this capacity to allow for future growth. The switch capacity is found by solving the following equation:

$$BW_{switch} = N \times BW_{link}$$

where BW is bandwidth and N is the number of links to the Distribution Layer.

Note that this equation assumes that all links to the Distribution Layer are the same type. If the links from the distribution are different media types, adjust the equation accordingly. This simple calculation, with the addition of a safety margin, will ensure the capacity of the core switches.

Even though the core block is not responsible for routing, the core block connects switch blocks that are responsible for routing. Therefore, the core must pass routing protocol traffic between the switch blocks so that all switches that are responsible for routing are aware of all the routes within its routing domain. Limitations to the number of peer routers that a routing protocol supports do exist. Routing protocols are discussed in much greater detail later. For now, simply accept that OSPF and EIGRP can support only 50 peers, and RIP can support only 30 peers. The number of peers are multiplied by the number of redundant links between the switch blocks. For typical redundancy, two paths exist between each switch block. Therefore, OSPF and EIGRP can support 25 switch blocks, and RIP can support 15 switch blocks.

To limit the amount of peering between switch blocks, routing can be implemented in the core block to create a hierarchical routing structure. Several things must be considered before attempting to deploy routing in the core. First, the complexity of the network is increased tremendously with the implementation of hierarchy in the routing architecture. Secondly, routing in the core creates performance degradation for the most critical links and devices in the network. Therefore, you should limit the implementation of hierarchical routing architectures within the core block to campus networks in which the amount of peering is a limiting factor.

Keeping these core block limitations in mind will increase the scalability of your campus network.

Chapter Summary

As you can see from this chapter, designing or even defining a campus network is far from trivial. The campus network is a complex system that is divided up into the following layers:

- Physical
- Data link
- Network
- Transport
- Session
- Presentation
- Application

The campus network must satisfy the following requirements:

- Fast convergence
- Deterministic paths
- Deterministic failover
- Scalable in size and throughput
- Centralized storage
- 20/80 rule
- Multiprotocol support
- Multicast support

The campus network services can be classified into local, remote, and enterprise services based on the traffic patterns of the services.

Multilayer switches can perform bridging at Layer 2, routing at Layer 3, and flow-based prioritization and firewalling at Layer 4.

The campus network can be divided topologically into the Access, Distribution, and Core Layers. The Access Layer connects the user to the network and typically is responsible for only Layer 2 switching. The Distribution

Layer connects groups of users to each other and typically handles all the routing functionality of the network along with some bridging functionality. The Core Layer provides the high-bandwidth switching between the distribution devices and switch blocks.

To implement the three-layer topological model in a scalable fashion, broadcast domains must be limited to switch blocks. The switch blocks handle the routing between each other. The core block handles the connectivity between the switch blocks. The core block is typically limited to bridging, but on rare occasions, as in the case of large networks, the core block may conduct routing.

Frequently Asked Questions (FAQ)

Question: What is a CAN?

Answer: A campus area network collection of LANs, in a fixed geographic region, owned and operated by a single organization

Question: What are the 3 layers used in multilayer switching?

Answer: Layer 2, data link. Layer 3, network. Layer 4, transport

Question: What function does a bridge perform?

Answer: A bridge isolates collision domains. It also performs Layer 2 forwarding, in that the bridge learns Layer 2 MAC addresses based on source addresses and forwards to ports based on destination MAC address.

Question: What is the difference between Access and Distribution Layers?

Answer: Access provides connectivity to users, while the Distribution Layer is responsible for grouping users into workgroups, managing multicast, and routing traffic through the core.

Question: What is the difference between the switch block and the core block?

Answer: The switch block represents connections at the Access and Distribution Layers. The switch block performs Layer 2 and Layer 3 forwarding. The core block maps directly to the Core Layer. The core block usually performs Layer 2 forwarding only; however, in very large networks, the core block may perform Layer 3 also.

Case Study

Beansprout Bargain Basement Network Design

Objective: Your task is to identify the networking technology to implement a small network for *Beansprout Bargain Basement* (BBB).

Scenario: BBB owns a single building with five offices and a small warehouse. They want to network the five offices and the warehouse to achieve basic file and print sharing. Only one machine will be connected in the warehouse.

Approach: Identify the number of devices that will be connected. Always be sure the solution allows for some growth. For BBB, it looks as though they will have six connections initially. Later, they may wish to add a central file server, or perhaps a networked printer. You should also consider the expected usage. BBB says they will periodically share files and do some printing.

Results: Wiring BBB with twisted-pair and deploying a single repeater that all users connect to has created a small network that fits their needs. With only a few devices, collisions and broadcast traffic are non-issues. BBB is an example of an Access Layer problem only. Users only need access to local services. In the future, BBB may invest in a local file server to provide a central file repository and backup. To provide more bandwidth and reduce the collision domain, replacing the repeater with a switch would be an easy and inexpensive upgrade as the BBB network grows. See Figure 2-31.

Cubby Products International Network Design

Objective: Your task is to identify the networking technology to implement a large campus area network for the headquarters of *Cubby Products International* (CPI). CPI is a multinational furniture manufacturer and ice cream producer. Your deliverable will be a high-level diagram detailing the network components necessary to create the CAN.

Scenario: CPI's headquarters consists of 10 buildings across 128 acres (see Figure 2-32). Currently, a smattering of LANs are across the campus to handle interdepartmental communications services. File sharing is virtu-

Figure 2-31
BBB network design

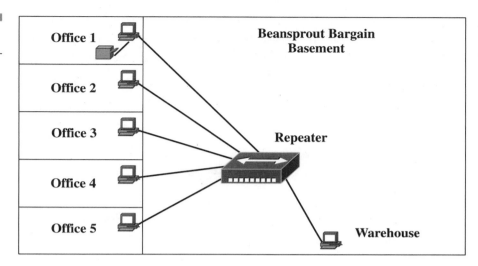

Figure 2-32
CPI campus layout

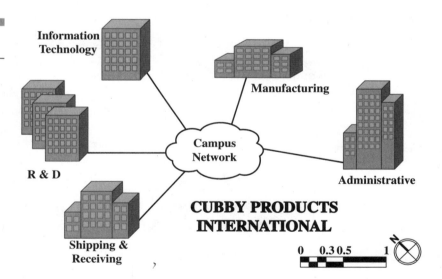

ally impossible between departments because there is no network between them. Workers must use transfer disks and tapes to share files between departments. Printers are everywhere. There is no policy or means for providing print services across the campus.

Meanwhile, at a friendly business golf game, Burt Baskins, CPI's VP of Operations, learns how his friend (a competitor's VP of Operations) installed a campus network six months ago and efficiency tripled resulting in increased profits, a fattening stock portfolio, and a huge bonus at Christmas. Burt quickly convinced CPI's CEO and board that a campus network is not only a way to increase profits, but a necessity to stay in business.

CPI requires high speed and high availability communications between all their departments and buildings at the headquarters campus. Your job is to make Burt happy.

Approach: You need to gather more information regarding the location of the departments, the expected network usage of the departments (perhaps specific applications), and the number of devices that will be plugged into the network in each building. With that information in hand, you can begin planning your Access, Distribution and Core Layers and subsequently placing your switch blocks and core blocks at the respective layers.

Results: After the necessary information gathering, you can construct a diagram that displays the desired location of the network components (see Figure 2-33).

The number of users that are already using some form of network is staggering. For the Access Layer, you use high port density workgroup switches to handle the large number of users and to maximize speed, provide low latency, and eliminate the concern for collisions. You design the Distribution

Figure 2-33
CPI network architecture

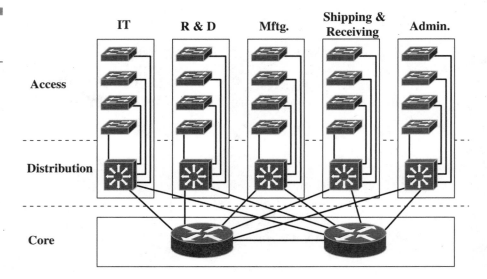

Layer to have routing, multicast support, and support for redundant path routing in a dual core design. The dual core design was chosen to maximize the reliability of the overall network. You feel that redundant paths inside the Distribution Layer are unnecessary at this point, but it is an option if the reliability of the current architecture proves to be inadequate.

Questions

1. What is Layer 2 in the OSI model called?

   a. presentation

   b. transport

   c. data link

   d. data transport

2. What is Layer 3 in the OSI model?

   a. physical

   b. network

   c. session

   d. application

3. What is Layer 4 in the OSI model?

   a. web

   b. session

   c. network

   d. transport

4. What device(s) operate strictly at Layer 2?

   a. router

   b. repeater

   c. hub

   d. bridge

5. What device(s) operate at Layer 3?

   a. router

   b. repeater

   c. hub

   d. bridge

6. What device isolates broadcast packets?

   a. router

   b. repeater

   c. bridge

   d. switch

7. What are some of the network requirements of a modern campus network?

    a. deterministic paths
    b. deterministic failover
    c. web access
    d. multiprotocol support

8. The new 20/80 rule states that 20 percent of traffic is remote and 80 percent of the traffic is local.

    a. True
    b. False

9. Emerging applications such as video on demand and teleconferencing need _____ enabled networks to be efficient.

    a. unicast
    b. pointcast
    c. multicast
    d. flycast

10. Centralized storage refers to _____ or _____.

    a. filing cabinets
    b. mainframes
    c. file servers
    d. warehouse

11. Remote services refers to:

    a. dialup services
    b. services outside the local workgroup
    c. services in another country
    d. ISP services

12. The Ethernet header includes:

    a. payload
    b. source hardware address
    c. destination hardware address
    d. checksum

13. The Layer 3 address within a packet is:

   a. MAC address
   b. hardware address
   c. source and destination IP address
   d. street address

14. It takes more time to forward at Layer 3 than at Layer 2.

   a. True
   b. False

15. When forwarding, a packet may be fragmented if:

   a. it is a malformed packet.
   b. media conversion is necessary, and the packet is too large for the new media.
   c. the fragment bit is set.
   d. the device has high utilization.

16. If a loop occurs in your bridged network, the following will happen:

   a. Users will be mad.
   b. All bandwidth on the connected networks will be taken by a single packet.
   c. The network will crash.
   d. You might be offered early retirement.

17. The basic network architecture includes:

   a. access
   b. distribution
   c. transport
   d. core

18. The basic network building blocks are:

   a. distribution block
   b. core block
   c. switch block
   d. access block

19. The switch block includes devices capable of switching:
    a. Layer 2
    b. Layer 3
    c. Layer 4
    d. Layer 5

20. The core block includes only Layer 2 functionality.
    a. True
    b. False

Answers

1. **Answer:** c

   Layer 2 in the OSI model is the data link layer.

2. **Answer:** b

   Layer 3 in the OSI model is the network layer.

3. **Answer:** d

   Layer 4 in the OSI model is the transport layer.

4. **Answer:** b, c, and d

   Hub is an alias for a repeater. Both repeaters and bridges operate at Layer 2.

5. **Answer:** a

   Routers handle routing/forwarding at Layer 3.

6. **Answer:** a

   Broadcast refers to Layer 2, or hardware broadcast. Because routers operate at Layer 3, they may listen to and process broadcast packets but do not forward.

7. **Answer:** a, b, and d

8. **Answer:** b

   The new 80/20 rule states that 80 percent of the traffic is Internet, and 20 percent is local.

9. **Answer:** c

   Multicast enables new technologies to deliver data from multipoint to multipoint connected devices while using network bandwidth effectively.

10. **Answer:** b and c

    Mainframes were centralized storage of the past; today file servers provide centralized storage.

11. **Answer:** b

    Services accessed outside the LAN are referred to as remote services.

12. **Answer:** b and c

    The source and destination hardware addresses are included in the Ethernet header.

13. **Answer:** c

    The Layer 3 address is the IP address.

14. **Answer:** a

    Layer 3 requires more processing to look farther into the packet, although hardware has made this process faster.

15. **Answer:** b

    Each media has a maximum PDU size that it can accommodate. If the outgoing media is smaller than the incoming media, packets over the maximum PDU size of the outgoing media must be fragmented.

16. **Answer:** a, b, c, and d

    The most important thing to realize is B, a single packet will be forwarded continually, as fast as the devices can transmit the packet. This will consume all network resources, rendering communication impossible.

17. **Answer:** a, b, and d

    The Access, Distribution and Core Layers are fundamental to designing today's campus area networks.

18. **Answer:** b and c

    The core and switch blocks will be our network building blocks.

19. **Answer:** a and b

    The switch block performs routing and switching (bridging).

20. **Answer:** b

    The core block may perform routing in very large campus network deployments.

Identifying Cisco Products for Multilayer Switching Networks

With a solid understanding of the basic building blocks required to build a campus area network, you must also be able to map the network architecture into a set of physical devices. Furthermore, it is imperative that you choose the hardware that will provide the best solution to the design problem.

Hardware selection is important. Correct selection includes hardware with the correct number of interfaces. These interfaces must be of the correct type and software to offer the features necessary to make the hardware perform optimally.

This chapter introduces the various multilayer-switching products produced by Cisco Systems. By the end of the chapter, you will have an understanding of the architectures, interfaces, and features of each product line. Furthermore, you'll be able to identify which hardware series can be used in the switch block and core block.

Objectives Covered in the Chapter

This chapter will aid you in making the right hardware selection when deploying a network. The following topics will be covered:

- User interface differences
- Cisco product descriptions
- Description of available interfaces
- Software selection
- Installing the hardware
- Adding hardware

You will be introduced to the user interfaces present in the different hardware series. This includes the different *command line interfaces* (CLIs), Web interfaces, and a menu-driven interface.

As each product series is introduced, you will learn about the architecture. Each series included is based on a back-plane that includes a switch fabric. The switch fabric is the mechanism used by the device to move data between ports. As you will see, each product line has a different switching capacity. Two common parameters are the total switching capacity of the back-plane in *bits-per-second* (bps) and the number of *packets-per-second* (pps) the switch can process. In either case, the higher the capacity, the better the hardware will be.

Each series has different network interfaces available. Interface availability is based on the switch capacity. Putting high-speed interfaces on a device that could not switch high-speed traffic would not make sense.

The *Cisco Internetworking Operating System* (IOS) is the brains behind the multilayer switching hardware. It has been honed over the course of many years and has a variety of options available.

We'll touch on hardware installation and additions briefly. We'll also discuss mounting options and examine possible upgrade options for existing equipment.

In addition to gaining an understanding of the architectures, interfaces, and features of each product line, you'll be able to identify which hardware series can be used in the switch block and core block. First, let's look at each product line in detail.

Cisco Switching Products

As each product line is introduced, we'll look at the internal architecture (capacity of the switch fabric), types of chassis, and cards available. Furthermore, we will examine the physical aspects of the hardware. This will include the number of ports, size, weight, and appearance.

As stated earlier, the architecture refers to the hardware implementation of the device. The architecture, combined with the type of chassis, delineates the hardware families. The chassis defines how many line cards can exist on the device. The chassis may have slots into which network interface cards can be inserted. Different types of interfaces can be included on each line card.

Cisco updates their product line often. There may be new series by the time this book is published. Your best resource for more information on Cisco products is their Web page, `www.cisco.com`. Cisco also has a useful tool to aid in product selection located at `http://www.cisco.com/pcgi-bin/front.x/corona/prodtool/select.pl`.

Software and Hardware

Before introducing the hardware, it is helpful to understand the different types of software you will encounter while using Cisco products. The software is actually a real-time operating system. This is very similar to the operating system running on your home computer or graphics workstation. For this networking equipment, the software is highly specialized; however, just like your home computer, it has a user interface.

The traditional user interface presents you with a prompt for entering commands. There are two primary types of user interfaces, or software types, used by Cisco equipment. The two types will be referred to as *Internetworking Operating System* (IOS) and the Set Commands. Cisco strives to create a common interface to all their hardware. However, like many other companies, Cisco has purchased technology to augment their product line. Through one such purchase, Cisco acquired the Catalyst series of switches (formerly Crescendo).

The Catalyst hardware already included software that controlled the switch. Cisco left the user interface intact rather than delay product shipment by trying to change the user interface to look like the IOS interface. As products have matured, the Catalyst series from Cisco has maintained, and augmented, the original Catalyst command interface (the Set Commands). By the end of this text, you will be intimately familiar with both interfaces.

Sometimes you have to update the software on your home computer: The same holds true for the software running these switches. Cisco releases software updates to fix bugs, or problems, with the current release. Cisco may also add new features or support for new hardware. Software updates may be free or may require a fee, depending on the type of update and the existence of, or lack thereof, a support contract for your current hardware. The updates or new versions are distributed as large files, referred to as software images. These files contain a complete new operating system. The operating system image and the configuration file are two separate files.

User Interface

As you unpack your new hardware, you are anxious to put your skills to work and power up the equipment. You should understand the common interfaces that all Cisco products support. These include terminal, Telnet, and the Web interface.

Terminal

This is by far the most ubiquitous form of hardware communication and configuration. At the very least, almost all hardware devices from any vendor will require you to connect via a serial cable to initially configure the device. You can certainly use a serial port and a communications package on a *Personal Computer* (PC) rather than a dumb terminal (VT100 or VT220 device). Connecting via a PC can give you the feeling that you are working in modern times; however, as your career expands in networking, you will come to appreciate the simplicity, reliability, and the universal presence of the serial ports on networking hardware.

Telnet

After a device is configured, operational, and attached to a network, you should be able to manage it remotely. Cisco gives you the ability to use standard Telnet to communicate with their devices. Telnet is a TCP/IP application; it comes standard with most all desktop operating systems. After connecting, you will be presented with the same user interface that is on the standard serial console port, an 80 column by 24 row terminal screen.

Web Browser

When a device is on the network, many more options become instantly available, including communicating with the device via a Web browser. Your Web browser is also a TCP/IP application. It works by communicating with a Web server. This is not usually enabled by default on the device and must be enabled before use. When it is enabled, you are starting a built-in Web server on the device. The Web server presents the user interface via a Web page and translates your link selections into commands to control the device. Cisco's Web interface maps closely to the commands available in the CLI. We are confident you will be comfortable with the Web interface after you understand the CLI. This text will concentrate on the CLI, both Cisco IOS and the Set Commands.

Cisco IOS

Cisco's IOS is a highly feature-packed network device operating system. IOS has a command line interface and a Web interface built in. IOS has many features, and you can select the feature set when choosing a version of IOS for your devices. After you've identified the correct IOS version for your hardware, the feature set selected will affect the cost and memory requirements of your hardware.

IOS offers nearly 80 feature sets, but they can be classified into the following groups:

- IP and IP Routing
- Connectivity and Scaleability
- Enterprise
- Extended Management Features
- Extended Features for Specialized Hardware

IP and IP routing includes basic IP functionality. This includes basic IP routing, including static routes, and protocols like RIP, IGRP, and EIGRP.

Connectivity and scaleability includes advanced routing protocols. These protocols include OSPF and PIM.

Enterprise includes support for many legacy protocols. These protocols include DECNet, SNA, and APPN.

Extended management features include support for Cisco's ClickStart management software and Web-based management.

Extended features for specialized hardware includes support for interfaces such as *Integrated Services Digital Network* (ISDN) or *Plain Old Telephone Service* (POTS).

Set Commands

Many of the Layer 2-only switching devices use the Set Commands. The Set Command software does not include feature set distinctions as IOS does, but is usually separated into a standard version and enterprise version. The latest software release for a particular hardware series is shipped with the hardware when purchased. You should periodically check Cisco's Web site for updates. Cisco will have new releases as the product's life cycle evolves.

Product Lines

The following describes each family of products. The descriptions will be a useful reference as you make hardware selections for your campus network deployments.

1900 Series

The 1900 series is a group of entry-level switches. The series offers Layer 2 forwarding capability only. It is available in two configurations, 12 and 24, 10Mbps ports for desktop machines, and two 100Mbps Fast Ethernet ports. Though the 1900 series is considered entry level, the architecture is hardly sub-par.

Architecture   The switch architecture is non-blocking with an available bandwidth of 370Mbps. The 1900 switches can forward at wire-speed on all ports. With this impressive architecture comes a modest set of available hardware options.

Hardware Configuration   The 1900 series is a fixed-configuration chassis; it does not accept any line cards. The series comes in two hardware configurations: 12 ports (Catalyst 1912) and 24 ports (Catalyst 1924). In addition, the 100Mbps ports can be two *unshielded twisted pair* (UTP) or one fiber and one UTP. All ports support half-duplex and full-duplex operation. The 1900's also have an *Attachment Unit Interface* (AUI) port to allow connection to legacy networks.

The footprint is small: only 1.73 × 17.5 × 8.25 inches (4.39 × 44.45 × 21 cm). It is also lightweight at seven pounds (3.2 kg). All Cisco equipment is steel blue in color.

In addition to network interfaces, the series also supports the addition of a Cisco redundant AC power system. The 1900 series also has a couple of software options.

Software Features   The user interface for the 1900 series is unique. The standard firmware neither uses IOS nor the Set Commands. The standard 1900 series user interface is menu-driven. If you upgrade to the enterprise version of the firmware, you can choose between either the menu version or an IOS CLI. You may upgrade to the enterprise software version at any time; no change at the hardware level occurs.

The menu-driven software comes standard with many features. The features include

- Enhanced congestion control to assure packets are not dropped
- Support for IEEE 802.3 and 802.3x for back-pressure and flow control on 10Mbps and 100Mbps ports respectively
- Broadcast storm control on a per-port basis
- Choice of switching operations: cut-through for performance (receives only destination hardware address before forwarding), or store-and-forward for error-checking (receives entire frame before forwarding)
- *Spanning-Tree Protocol* (STP) for redundancy. (This is covered later in more detail.)
- Shared memory pool for hardware address table (1,024 addresses)
- Support for network/drain port to allow unlimited hardware addresses on the uplink port
- *Simple Network Management Protocol* (SNMP) and RMON support for remote management and monitoring via a *network management system* (NMS), such as CiscoWorks

The 1900 series is a feature-packed entry level switch. We recommend upgrading to the enterprise software package to gain the benefit of a consistent user interface across all of Cisco's product line.

2926 Series

The 2926 series, also Layer 2 only, is the next step up from the 1900's. The 2926 series contains a single product offering, the Catalyst 2926 switch. While offering many of the same features available in the 1900's, it also offers a much higher bandwidth back-plane.

Architecture   The 2926 architecture is modeled after the 5000 series, Cisco's flagship multilayer switch. The 2926 series sports a 1.2Gbps back-plane capable of more than one million *packets-per-second* (pps), or twice the throughput of the 1900 series. The increased back-plane capacity affords more hardware options as well.

Hardware Configuration   The 2926 series is once again a fixed-configuration chassis. Each model has 24 10/100Mbps ports and a choice of interfaces for the two uplink ports. Your choices include 100Mbps UTP or fiber ports, 100Mbps *Media Independent Interface* (MII), or 1Gbps UTP or fiber ports.

The Catalyst 2926 is considerably larger than the 1900's. Its dimensions are 5.75 × 17 × 18 inches (14.6 × 43.2 × 45.7 cm.) and weighs in at a hefty 35 pounds (15.9 kg). Models with Gigabit ports weigh 40 pounds (18.14 kg).

In addition to the greater number of hardware options, more software features are available also.

Software Features   Cisco's Set-Command based software comes standard on the 2926 series. The hardware also supports many of the advanced switching features.

- Broadcast storm control on a per-port basis

- Choice of switching operations: cut-through for performance, or store-and-forward for error checking

- *Spanning-Tree Protocol* (STP) for redundancy. (This is covered later in more detail.)

- *Simple Network Management Protocol* (SNMP) and RMON support for remote management and monitoring via a network management system (NMS), such as CiscoWorks

Advanced features include

- Fast EtherChannel, or the aggregation of two or four ports into logical interfaces with two or four times the capacity

- IEEE 802.1Q *Virtual LAN* (VLAN) trunking. (This is covered later in more detail.)

- *Inter-Switch Link* (ISL) trunking and *dynamic ISL* (DISL) trunking

- Shared memory pool for hardware address table (16,000 addresses)

- *Switched Port Analyzer* (SPAN) functionality for advanced traffic monitoring

- Load balancing and redundancy support for trunks (VLAN, ISL, and DISL)

In addition to more software redundancy, a second power supply is also available. This will enable you to bring full redundancy to this network device.

As you can see, this is a very versatile and powerful switch. The fixed-configuration chassis translates to a lower cost per port. Coupled with the versatile interface options and the high performance back-plane, this series is highly attractive to the network manager.

2900 Series

The 2900 series is the father of the 2926 series. The 2900 series is the first to offer a high-capacity back-plane with a modular chassis. In addition to the larger capacity, a new hardware option is also available: the *Gigabit Interface Converter* (GBIC) interface, which is described in more detail later. The series includes five different chassis options, making it a very versatile hardware option.

The following switches comprise the 2900 series, the first three are fixed configuration chassis, and the last two have expansion slots:

- Catalyst 2912
- Catalyst 2924 XL
- Catalyst 2924C XL
- Catalyst 2924M XL
- Catalyst 2912MF XL

Architecture   The back-plane provides more capacity than the 2926 series. The 2900 series has a 3.2Gbps switch fabric that is capable of wire-speed to all ports at three million *packets-per-second* (pps).

Hardware Configuration   Catalyst 2912 switches offers 12 10Mbps UTP Ethernet ports.

The Catalyst 2924 XL is a 24-port 10/100Mbps *unshielded twisted pair* (UTP) Ethernet switch.

The Catalyst 2924C XL provides 22 ports with 10/100Mbps UTP Ethernet and two ports with 100Mbps Fast Ethernet fiber.

The Catalyst 2912MF XL and Catalyst 2924M XL offer two slots for expansion modules with various interfaces. The Catalyst 2912MF XL has

12 100Mbps fiber Fast Ethernet ports, whereas the Catalyst 2924M XL has 24 10/100Mbps UTP Ethernet ports.

The expansion slots have a variety of available interface cards. With a large capacity back-plane, it should come as no surprise that card options include ATM OC-3 (155Mbps) and Gigabit Ethernet ports, in addition to fiber and UTP Fast Ethernet cards.

The Gigabit Ethernet ports support GBICs.

The IEEE 802.3z Task Force defined GBIC. GBIC provides a layer of abstraction from the Gigabit switching hardware and the physical network interface. This abstraction gives network hardware users flexibility when deploying Gigabit Ethernet. GBIC ports allow the network manager to install the particular Gigabit Ethernet physical interface required for their installation. Several types of physical media are available, including fiber-optic (long wave and short wave) and copper.

The fixed configuration models are $1.75 \times 17.5 \times 14.5$ inches ($4.5 \times 44.5 \times 36.83$ cm.) and weigh seven pounds (3.2 kg). The modular chassis are larger and heavier. The dimensions for the Catalyst 2912MF XL and 2924M XL are $3.46 \times 17.5 \times 12$ inches ($8.8 \times 44.5 \times 30.5$ cm). They weigh 15 pounds (6.8 kg) with two cards installed.

Software Features   The Cisco IOS-based 2900 series offers many of the same software features as on the Catalyst 2926.

The Standard Edition offers many features:

- Broadcast storm control on a per-port basis
- Choice of switching operations: cut-through for performance, or store-and-forward for error checking
- *Spanning-Tree Protocol* (STP) for redundancy. (This is covered later in more detail.)
- *Simple Network Management Protocol* (SNMP) and RMON support for remote management and monitoring via a *network management system* (NMS), such as CiscoWorks

Advanced features include

- Fast EtherChannel, or the aggregation of two or four ports into logical interfaces with two or four times the capacity
- Shared memory pool for hardware address table (2048 addresses or 8192 addresses for the Catalyst 2912MF XL and 2924M XL model)

- *Switched Port Analyzer* (SPAN) functionality for advanced traffic monitoring
- Load balancing and redundancy support for trunks (VLAN, ISL, DISL)
- *Network Time Protocol* (NTP)

Upgrade to the Enterprise Edition and, in addition, you get end-to-end VLAN support as well. Features include

- IEEE 802.1Q *Virtual LAN* (VLAN) trunking. (This is covered later in more detail.)
- *Inter-Switch Link* (ISL) trunking and dynamic ISL (DISL) trunking

The XL Command Software upgrade is another option available. The upgrade gives you the capability of managing a group, or cluster, of switches as a single entity. The cluster may include 2900 XL series, 1900 series, and 3500 series switches.

Offering a Web-based interface, the *Cisco Visual Switch Manager* (CVSM) provides a visual representation for managing and configuring a group of switches.

Furthermore, the interface offers multilevel security to allow specified users to troubleshoot network problems without enabling them to modify the device configuration.

3500 Series

The 3500 series continues the trend with a higher capacity back-plane. In the software options and features area, you won't find anything new.

Architecture   The 3500 series ships with a 10Gbps back-plane and forwarding capability of 6.5 million *packets-per-second* (pps).

Hardware Configuration   The 3500 series contains only three chassis options, two being fixed configurations. The Catalyst 3512 XL and the Catalyst 3524 XL offer 12 and 24 10/100Mbps UTP Ethernet ports, respectively. Additionally, both have two GBIC-based Gigabit Ethernet ports.

The Catalyst 3508G is an interesting chassis. The 3508G chassis contains eight GBIC-based ports. Though not modular in the traditional sense, with slots for cards, the GBIC ports offer flexibility for a variety of Gigabit Ethernet interfaces.

One particular GBIC interface is the GigaStack. The GigaStack is a special GBIC interface for Cisco switches. The interface allows stacking of 3500 series and 2900 series switches. Stacking allows you to manage a stack of switches through one user interface for the entire stack.

The 3500 series packs a lot into a relatively small form-factor. The dimensions are $1.75 \times 17.5 \times 11.8$ inches ($4.4 \times 44.5 \times 30$ cm.) and weigh only 10.25 pounds (4.6 kg).

Software Features With the *Cisco Visual Switch Manager* (CVSM) software, you may manage a stacked group of 2900 and 3500 series switches through a Web-based interface. The software includes the following features:

- Broadcast storm control on a per-port basis
- Choice of switching operations: cut-through for performance, or store-and-forward for error checking
- *Spanning-Tree Protocol* (STP) for redundancy. (This is covered later in more detail.)
- *Simple Network Management Protocol* (SNMP) and RMON support for remote management and monitoring via a *network management system* (NMS), such as CiscoWorks

Advanced features include

- Fast EtherChannel, or the aggregation of two or four ports into logical interfaces with two or four times the capacity
- Switched Port Analyzer (SPAN) functionality for advanced traffic monitoring
- Load balancing and redundancy support for trunks (VLAN, ISL, DISL).
- *Network Time Protocol* (NTP)
- IEEE 802.1Q *Virtual LAN* (VLAN) trunking. (This is covered later in more detail.)
- *Inter-Switch Link* (ISL) trunking, and dynamic ISL (DISL) trunking

4000 Series

The 4000 series is the first to only offer a modular configuration chassis. The 4000 series has a single member, the Catalyst 4003.

Architecture   The 4000 series back-plane provides a 24Gbps-switch fabric with capability of forwarding 18 million *packets-per-second* (pps).

The Catalyst 4003 chassis has three slots. One slot is reserved for the Supervisor module.

The Supervisor module adds the brains to the unit. By itself, the Catalyst 4003 is an empty metal casing. The Supervisor module has the controller processor and provides a console port for configuration. Utilizing a separate module, which contains the system processor, you have the benefit of keeping the same chassis and back-plane, and may upgrade only the Supervisor card as new versions are created.

Hardware Configuration   You will find that modular chassis are much more expensive than fixed configuration models. Flexibility comes at a price, but the advantages are worth it. For instance, you do not have to populate all the slots when purchasing the chassis; you need only purchase the interfaces you need. When new interfaces are available or you simply need more ports, you may purchase the required line card.

The Catalyst 4003 has several line cards, or blades, from which to choose. First, a 48-port 10/100Mbps UTP Ethernet card is available for areas where you have a high concentration of machines. Also, 6 and 18-port Gigabit Ethernet blades are available with GBIC ports.

Two other cards are available, both offering further options for expandability. One is a card with 32-port 10/100Mbps UTP Ethernet ports and two GBIC ports. Also available is a blade with 32 10/100Mbps UTP Ethernet ports and a daughter card slot. The daughter card slot allows you to purchase a four-port 100Mbps-fiber Ethernet card that attaches to the primary line card.

Software Features   The features of the software include

- Broadcast storm control on a per-port basis
- Choice of switching operations: cut-through for performance, or store-and-forward for error checking
- *Spanning-Tree Protocol* (STP) for redundancy. (This is covered later in more detail.)

- *Simple Network Management Protocol* (SNMP) and RMON support for remote management and monitoring via a *network management system* (NMS), such as CiscoWorks

Advanced features include

- Fast EtherChannel, or the aggregation of two or four ports into logical interfaces with two or four times the capacity
- *Switched Port Analyzer* (SPAN) functionality for advanced traffic monitoring
- Load balancing and redundancy support for trunks (VLAN, ISL, DISL)
- *Network Time Protocol* (NTP)
- IEEE 802.1Q *Virtual LAN* (VLAN) trunking. (This is covered later in more detail.)
- *Inter-Switch Link* (ISL) trunking and *dynamic ISL* (DISL) trunking
- Multicast support via *Protocol Independent Multicast* (PIM), *Internet Group Management Protocol* (IGMP), and *Cisco Group Management Protocol* (CGMP)
- *Quality of Service* (QoS) support via *Resource Reservation Protocol* (RSVP)
- Dynamic VLAN services for easy host management

5000 Series

The 5000 series is Cisco's flagship multilayer switch. Supporting cell and frame switching, the high performance switch fabric can easily support Fast Ethernet, Gigabit Ethernet, and *Asynchronous Transfer Mode* (ATM). It is the first product line to support Layer 3 routing.

Architecture   Two architectures exist in the 5000 series. The Catalyst 500X models offer a 12Gbps back-plane. The Catalyst 550X models offer a 50Gbps back-plane and are capable of handling 100 million *packets-per-second* (pps). Both back-planes support packet switching and cell switching for ATM.

The Supervisor module is brain of the unit. By itself, the Catalyst 5000 is a Layer 2-only switch. The Supervisor card manages the back-plane and configuration of each of the modules in the chassis. One special module is the *Route Switch Module* (RSM). The RSM adds Layer 3 and Layer 4 functionality to the switch, including routing and security features.

Having two brains (processors) creates a unique user interface for the network manager. The Layer 2 Supervisor card is running software that uses the Set Commands. The RSM card runs IOS. Of course, you must have the ability to access both user interfaces. Both the Supervisor card and the RSM have console ports to the switch to allow access to the CLI.

Although unique, the dual-interface design may seem overly complicated; however, it provides a lot of flexibility. You can purchase the Catalyst 5000 as a Layer 2-only device and upgrade to more functionality as your network grows. In addition, keeping the same chassis and backplane, you may upgrade only the Supervisor card as new versions are created.

The layered design helps reduce the complexity of the interface. It is easy to remember to use the Set-Command user interface when changing Layer 2 configuration, and the IOS interface when dealing with Layer 3 and above configuration.

Hardware Configuration   The 5000 series offers a lot of flexibility. Couple the architecture options with the five different chassis available and you will have a very adaptable and scaleable networking system. The five chassis options are as follows:

- Catalyst 5002 with 2 slots
- Catalyst 5000 with 5 slots
- Catalyst 5505 with 5 slots
- Catalyst 5509 with 9 slots
- Catalyst 5500 with 13 slots

The chassis do not come standard with any modules. Each module must be purchased separately. One module necessary to operate the device is the Supervisor module. The standard Supervisor module has two 100Mbps FastEthernet ports, so the entire slot is not wasted.

All chassis have the option of redundant power supplies. The Catalyst 5002 comes standard with two power supplies. The 5000 series has full redundancy; in addition to the power supplies, all cards may be hot-swapped.

Software Features   The software features include

- Broadcast storm control on a per-port basis
- Choice of switching operations: cut-through for performance, or store-and-forward for error checking
- *Spanning-Tree Protocol* (STP) for redundancy. (This is covered later in more detail.)
- *Simple Network Management Protocol* (SNMP) and RMON support for remote management and monitoring via a *network management system* (NMS), such as CiscoWorks

Advanced features include

- Fast EtherChannel, or the aggregation of two or four ports into logical interfaces with two or four times the capacity
- *Switched Port Analyzer* (SPAN) functionality for advanced traffic monitoring
- Load balancing and redundancy support for trunks (VLAN, ISL, DISL)
- *Network Time Protocol* (NTP)
- IEEE 802.1Q *Virtual LAN* (VLAN) trunking. (This is covered later in more detail.)
- *Inter-Switch Link* (ISL) trunking and *dynamic ISL* (DISL) trunking
- Multicast support via *Protocol Independent Multicast* (PIM), *Internet Group Management Protocol* (IGMP), and *Cisco Group Management Protocol* (CGMP)
- *Quality of Service* (QoS) support via *Resource Reservation Protocol* (RSVP)
- Dynamic VLAN services for easy host management
- *Hot Standby Routing Protocol* (HSRP) for network redundancy
- Standard Layer 3 routing protocols including *Border Gateway Protocol* (BGP), *Routing Information Protocol* (RIP), and *Open Shortest-Path First* (OSPF)
- Cisco proprietary routing protocols, including IGRP and EIGRP

6000 Series

The 6000 series provides the same features as the 5000 series with the addition of a larger capacity switching back-plane. In addition, the 6000 series shares the same cards/modules as the 5000 and 8500 series.

Architecture   The Catalyst 650X models have a 256Gbps back-plane; the more economical Catalyst 600X models have a 32Gbps back-plane.

Hardware Configuration   The 6000 series comes in two hardware configurations: a six-slot version and a nine-slot version.

Software Features   The software features include

- Broadcast storm control on a per-port basis
- Choice of switching operations: cut-through for performance, or store-and-forward for error checking
- *Spanning-Tree Protocol* (STP) for redundancy. (This is covered later in more detail.)
- *Simple Network Management Protocol* (SNMP) and RMON support for remote management and monitoring via a *network management system* (NMS), such as CiscoWorks

Advanced features include

- Fast EtherChannel, or the aggregation of two or four ports into logical interfaces with two or four times the capacity
- *Switched Port Analyzer* (SPAN) functionality for advanced traffic monitoring
- Load balancing and redundancy support for trunks (VLAN, ISL, DISL)
- *Network Time Protocol* (NTP)
- IEEE 802.1Q *Virtual LAN* (VLAN) trunking. (This is covered later in more detail.)
- *Inter-Switch Link* (ISL) trunking and *dynamic ISL* (DISL) trunking
- Multicast support via *Protocol Independent Multicast* (PIM), *Internet Group Management Protocol* (IGMP), and *Cisco Group Management Protocol* (CGMP)
- *Quality of Service* (QoS) support via *Resource Reservation Protocol* (RSVP)
- Dynamic VLAN services for easy host management
- *Hot Standby Routing Protocol* (HSRP) for network redundancy
- Standard Layer 3 routing protocols including *Border Gateway Protocol* (BGP), *Routing Information Protocol* (RIP), and *Open Shortest-Path First* (OSPF)
- Cisco proprietary routing protocols, including IGRP and EIGRP

8500 Series

The 8500 series is the top-of-the line campus switch offered by Cisco. The series has two switches: the 8510 and the 8540. The 8510 incorporated a previous Cisco product, the Lightstream 1010 cell switch.

Architecture   The Catalyst 8510 has a 10Gbps back-plane and is capable of handling six million *packets-per-second* (pps).

The Catalyst 8540 has a 40Gbps back-plane capable of 24 million pps.

The high-speed back-plane provides bandwidth for many high-speed interfaces including OC3 and OC12. The Catalyst 8540 also provides hardware redundancy via the Cisco IOS *Enhanced High-System Availability* (EHSA) model.

Hardware Configuration   The Catalyst 8510 has slots for five cards and the Catalyst 8540 can hold 13 cards.

Software Features   Features of the software include

- Broadcast storm control on a per-port basis
- Choice of switching operations: cut-through for performance, or store-and-forward for error checking
- *Spanning-Tree Protocol* (STP) for redundancy. (This is covered later in more detail.)
- *Simple Network Management Protocol* (SNMP) and RMON support for remote management and monitoring via a *network management system* (NMS), such as CiscoWorks

Advanced features include

- Fast EtherChannel, or the aggregation of two or four ports into logical interfaces with twice or four times the capacity
- *Switched Port Analyzer* (SPAN) functionality for advanced traffic monitoring
- Load balancing and redundancy support for trunks (VLAN, ISL, DISL)
- *Network Time Protocol* (NTP)
- IEEE 802.1Q *Virtual LAN* (VLAN) trunking. (This is covered later in more detail.)
- *Inter-Switch Link* (ISL) trunking and *dynamic ISL* (DISL) trunking

- Multicast support via *Protocol Independent Multicast* (PIM), *Internet Group Management Protocol* (IGMP), and *Cisco Group Management Protocol* (CGMP)
- *Quality of Service* (QoS) support via *Resource Reservation Protocol* (RSVP)
- Dynamic VLAN services for easy host management
- *Hot Standby Routing Protocol* (HSRP) for network redundancy
- Standard Layer 3 routing protocols including *Border Gateway Protocol* (BGP), *Routing Information Protocol* (RIP), and *Open Shortest-Path First* (OSPF)
- Cisco proprietary routing protocols, including IGRP and EIGRP

Layer Product Selection

Product selection can be a chore. It is a process of identifying

- Current needs
- Future needs
- Budget
- Physical space
- Power requirements

Access Layer

Devices suitable for the access layer depend heavily on the size of the network on the drawing board. We will examine a few scenarios to make application of the hardware.

For a small LAN, where users are sharing relatively small amounts of data at any moment, the 1900 series would be most adequate. Offering 10Mbps per port to the desktop and a 100Mbps uplink to the distribution layer, the 1900 is ideal for the small LAN environment.

Perhaps you have a slightly larger LAN environment that requires more ports and more capacity for handling a local file server all users are accessing. The 2900 series fits the bill nicely. With as many as 48 ports at 10/100Mbps, the 2900 enables you to offer connections to older desktops at

10Mbps and other clients and servers at 100Mbps. Furthermore, depending on your distribution layer, several uplink options are also available. If you need more flexibility, the 3500 series with stacking capability can increase your port density.

The Catalyst 4003 can provide high port density with a high capacity back-plane. With the modular chassis, you are also provided a large selection of available interfaces at the additional costs associated with modular units.

Distribution Layer

As stated earlier, the distribution layer is where Layer 3 routing takes place in the campus area network. The need for routing at the distribution layer defines your starting point for hardware. The 5000 series is the first series to offer full IOS routing capability with the addition of a *Route Switch Module* (RSM).

The Catalyst 5000 is a modular chassis. This allows you to choose the hardware necessary for your network design; however, depending on your needs, you need purchase only the minimal hardware required to complete the network.

If you require more ports or more capacity, the 6000 and 8500 series with the addition of an RSM will provide a high-capacity, scaleable distribution layer.

Core Layer

Core layer devices include the Catalyst 5500, 6500, and 8500 series switches. These devices include a very high capacity back-plane. The core layer does not usually include routing; the switching capacity dictates the qualifications of a core layer device.

Interface Requirements

Modern campus networks actually require only a few network interfaces. The most prevalent are 10Mbps Ethernet, 100Mbps FastEthernet, and 1000Mbps Gigabit Ethernet.

Chapter Summary

This chapter introduces Cisco's multilayer switching hardware. Each hardware line from the Catalyst 1900 series through the Catalyst 8500 series is described in some detail. This includes device architecture, software features, and hardware options.

We looked at the software running on the hardware: the real-time operating system and how it is controlled. Methods of control included

- Terminal
- Network (using Telnet or management software)
- Web browser

We also discussed the different command line interfaces you will encounter as you use a terminal or Telnet to configure the devices. These include

- Catalyst 1900 menu-driven interface
- Set-Command interface
- Cisco's IOS

Later chapters will detail configuration using both Set-Commands and Cisco's IOS.

In addition to software, we looked closely at the hardware and hardware options available in Cisco's product line. First, the chassis types were covered:

- Fixed configuration
- Modular configuration

Fixed configuration has a lower price-point and offers modular configuration, providing scaleability and available upgrade options.

Then, we examined each of the following product lines in detail:

- Catalyst 1900 Series
- Catalyst 2926 Series
- Catalyst 2900 Series
- Catalyst 3500 Series
- Catalyst 4000 Series

- Catalyst 5000 Series
- Catalyst 6000 Series
- Catalyst 8500 Series

The Catalyst 1900 is the entry-level switch. With a fixed configuration and 24 10Mbps ports, it offers an exceptional value for small work-groups.

The Catalyst 2926 is a great value. The Catalyst 2926 has a fixed configuration chassis using the same architecture as the Catalyst 5000 series without the enhanced back-plane performance and modularity. The Catalyst 2926 can be used to serve a cluster of servers, or as an aggregation device for other 2926s or 1900s.

The Catalyst 2900 series offers a mix of fixed and modular chassis. It has many interface options and a modular chassis to provide for future growth. The Catalyst 2900 XL series chassis also provides the group management feature, allowing you to group devices into a single management entity.

The Catalyst 3500 series provides the same flexibility as the 2900 series, but includes a higher capacity back-plane, with additional Gigabit options.

The Catalyst 4000 series can also provide high port density and high capacity. It does not offer group management, but features the same software as its parent, the Catalyst 5000.

The Catalyst 2900, 3500, and 4000 series can provide desktop or server type connections in addition to providing bandwidth necessary to act as network aggregation devices.

The Catalyst 5000 is the first device in the product line to provide Layer 3 functions, making it suitable for the distribution layer. Layer 3 functions are provided by the addition of a *Route Switch Module* (RSM), which runs Cisco's IOS.

The Catalyst 6000 and 8500 series offer the same functionality as the 5000 series, but with more muscle. All three series may be used in the distribution or core layers depending on the need.

Lastly, we examined some of the interfaces offered by these products. Ethernet is the most predominant interface in today's networks. Depending on your application, you may choose 10Mbps, 100Mbps, or 1000Mbps (1Gbps) Ethernet interfaces to include in your network.

Frequently Asked Questions (FAQ)

Question: What is the best switch?

Answer: Strictly depends on network and budget requirements

Question: Which products share the same user interface?

Answer: The Catalyst 2900 and Catalyst 3500 run Cisco IOS. The Catalyst 2926, 4000, 5000, 6000 and 8500 employ the Set-Command interface for Layer 2 configuration. The Catalyst 1900 uses a menu-driven interface. Or, if you have purchased the optional Extended Edition software, you can select an IOS interface. All of the *Route Switch Modules* (RSMs) run Cisco IOS.

Case Study

Objective: The objective in this case study is to map the types of devices specified in Chapter 2, "Multilayer Switching Network Design Basics," to Cisco products. These are the products that you must purchase to deploy the new network for CPI.

The following constraints are given to help you design the network.

- Ten buildings are scattered across 128 acres

- There are five well-defined departments—R&D, Shipping/Receiving, Administration, Manufacturing, and Information Technology.

- Each of the departments is fairly localized with the following exceptions.

  - Administration is scattered throughout the campus.

  - R&D is scattered through the Manufacturing areas.

  - Information Technology houses the centralized storage and processing farms.

Figure 3-1 was developed in Chapter 2 and shows the network topology based on the three main network components: core, distribution, and access.

Figure 3-1
CPI building blocks

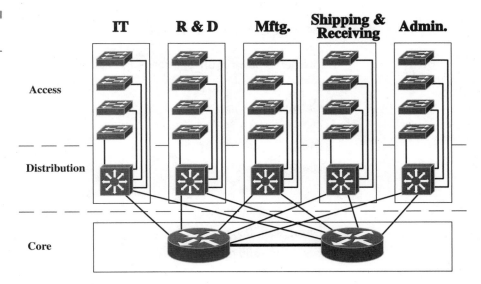

Figure 3-2
CPI department map

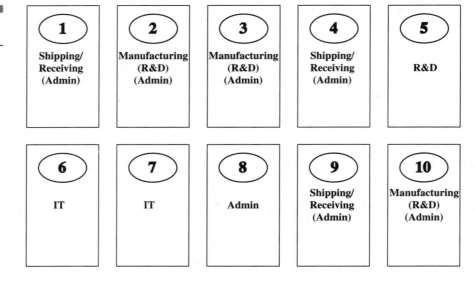

Figure 3-2 is given to help you determine the location of the various departments.

At this point, do not be concerned about how the various departments communicate with each other. This problem will be tackled at a later time.

Required Information

Implementation requires knowledge of the Cisco product lines, including the following:

- Catalyst 1900 Series
- Catalyst 2926 Series
- Catalyst 2900 Series
- Catalyst 3500 Series
- Catalyst 4000 Series
- Catalyst 5000 Series
- Catalyst 6000 Series
- Catalyst 8500 Series

Approach

To achieve the objectives, the following tasks must be completed:

- Identify products for the Core Layer
- Identify products for the Distribution Layer
- Identify products for the Access Layer

Core Layer For the core layer, we must provide high-availability and redundancy to keep the business running smoothly in the event of a system failure. With only five distribution devices, the core switches will not require a high port density. The core must be able to handle the traffic load produced by all departments utilizing centralized services and storage in Information Technologies.

Shown in Figure 3-3, a good choice for a Core Layer switch to meet these needs would be a Catalyst 6506. The six slots, with 100Mbps fiber-optic ports, will provide plenty of interfaces to support the distribution links.

Distribution Layer The Distribution Layer must have many of the same qualities as the core. In addition, the Distribution Layer must provide routing. The distribution switches will have to service approximately two buildings each, or about eight Access Layer switches.

Figure 3-3
CPI network diagram

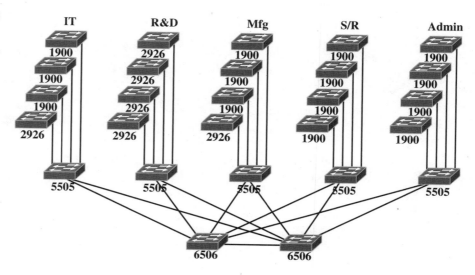

An appropriate choice for Distribution Layer devices is the Catalyst 5505 equipped with a Route Switch Module.

Access Layer   The Access Layer devices will depend on the required connection types and the number of devices. Most users desktop machines will only require 10Mbps Ethernet connections. Servers and high-end workstations will require 100Mbps FastEthernet connections.

To service 10Mbps devices, a Catalyst 1924 is the ideal product. The Catalyst 1924 has 24 10Mbps ports, wire-speed performance, and the lowest price in their line of devices.

For 100Mbps devices, the Catalyst 2926 will provide plenty of 100Mbps ports. The 2926 has exceptional performance and the fixed hardware configuration keeps the price-point down.

Questions

1. How many FastEthernet ports are on a Catalyst 1900 series switch?

    a. 1
    b. 2
    c. 4
    d. 24

2. The Standard Edition software included with a Catalyst 1900 series switch utilizes a _____ based user interface?

    a. Set-Command
    b. Menu-driven
    c. Cisco IOS
    d. Mouse

3. The Catalyst _____ and _____ series switches are stackable and several can be managed as a single group.

    a. 1900, 2900
    b. 2900, 2926
    c. 2900, 3500
    d. 3500, 4000

4. The Catalyst 2926 shares the same switch architecture as what other series?

    a. Catalyst 1900
    b. Catalyst 2900
    c. Catalyst 3500
    d. Catalyst 5000

5. The Catalyst 4000 series includes a single chassis with _____ modules/blades.

    a. 2
    b. 3
    c. 4
    d. 5

6. The Catalyst _____ and _____ series are fixed configuration chassis.

   a. 3500, 4000
   b. 1900, 2926
   c. 2900, 3500
   d. 2926, 3500

7. The Catalyst 2900 is a modular chassis device.

   a. True
   b. False
   c. Both a and b

8. A _____ has an IOS CLI.

   a. RSM
   b. ISL
   c. GBIC
   d. Sup3

9. A switch console may be accessed from

   a. A terminal
   b. *Network Management System* (NMS)
   c. Telnet
   d. Both a and c

10. IOS is _____.

   a. Interconnection Of Switches
   b. Interface Operating System
   c. Internetworking Operating System
   d. Internal Optical Service

11. The console interface of a Catalyst 5000 is

   a. Set-Command
   b. Cisco IOS
   c. Menu Driven
   d. Web-based

12. The console interface of a Catalyst 6000 RSM is

   a. Set-Command
   b. Cisco IOS
   c. Menu-driven
   d. Web-based

13. The console of a Catalyst 4003 Supervisor card is

    a. Set-Command
    b. Cisco IOS
    c. Menu-driven
    d. Web-based

14. Which product series may be used in the access layer?

    a. Catalyst 5000 Series
    b. Catalyst 3500 Series
    c. Catalyst 4000 Series
    d. All the above

15. Which product series may be used in the distribution layer?

    a. Catalyst 1900 Series
    b. Catalyst 5000 Series with RSM
    c. Catalyst 6000 Series with RSM
    d. Both b and c

16. Which product series may be used in the core layer?

    a. Catalyst 3500 Series
    b. Catalyst 4000 Series
    c. Catalyst 5000 Series
    d. All the above

17. Which product series supports IP routing?

    a. Catalyst 2926 Series
    b. Catalyst 6000 Series with RSM
    c. Catalyst 5000 Series with RSM
    d. Both b and c

18. Which product series supports Web-based management?

    a. Catalyst 2926 Series
    b. Catalyst 2900 Series
    c. Catalyst 4000 Series
    d. All the above

19. GBIC is most frequently used to mean
_____.

    a. Gigabit Interface Controller
    b. Gigabit Interface Converters
    c. Gigabit Binary Interface Controller
    d. Gigabit Binary Interface Converter

20. GBIC interfaces are not available for

    a. Catalyst 1900 Series
    b. Catalyst 2926 Series
    c. Catalyst 4000 Series
    d. Both a and b

Answers

1. How many FastEthernet ports are on a Catalyst 1900 series switch?

    b. 2

2. The Standard Edition software included with a Catalyst 1900 series switch utilizes a _____ based user interface?

    b. menu-driven

3. The Catalyst _____ and _____ series switches are stackable and can be several can managed as a single group.

    c. 2900, 3500

4. The Catalyst 2926 shares the same switch architecture as what other series?

    d. Catalyst 5000

5. The Catalyst 4000 series includes a single product with _____ modules/blades.

    b. 3

6. The Catalyst _____ and _____ series are fixed-configuration chassis.

    b. 1900, 2926

7. The Catalyst 2900 is a modular chassis device.

    c. Both a and b

    The Catalyst 2900 series contains several devices, some fixed, some modular.

8. A _____ has an IOS CLI.

    a. RSM

9. A switch console may be accessed from

    d. Both a and c

10. IOS is _____.

    c. Internetworking Operating System

11. The console interface of a Catalyst 5000 is

    a. Set-Command

12. The console interface of a Catalyst 6000 RSM is

    b. Cisco IOS

    All route switch modules run Cisco IOS.

13. The console of a Catalyst 4003 Supervisor card is

    a. Set-Command

    All Supervisor cards use the Set-Command software.

14. Which product series may be used in the access layer?

    d. All the above

    All switches can be utilized in the access layer. A large switch may be necessary where there is a high concentration of connections; for example, a large teaching lab.

15. Which product series may be used in the distribution layer?

    d. Both b and c

    Any series that can have an RSM added can be used in the distribution layer.

16. Which product series may be used in the core layer?

    d. All the above

    Layer 2 switching is all that is required for the core layer.

17. Which product series supports IP routing?

    d. Both b and c

    An RSM must be supported to add Layer 3 functionality.

18. Which product series supports Web-based management?

    d. All the above

19. GBIC is most frequently used to mean _____.

    b. Gigabit Interface Converters

    To be fair, some documentation will refer to them as Gigabit Ethernet Interface Carriers.

20. GBIC interfaces are not available for

    d. Both a and b

Connecting the Campus Network

In the previous chapters, we have covered design concepts of the building blocks of the campus network and the Cisco multilayer switching product line. This chapter will get you started on actually building a campus network by applying your knowledge of network design and Cisco's multilayer switching products. This begins your practical implementation of your design.

Objectives Covered in the Chapter

In this chapter, we will cover the following concepts:

- Ethernet operation
- Network cabling
- Initial switch setup
- Packet formats

The idea behind this chapter is to give you a solid foundation to help you begin to build your campus network. Up to this point, we have covered basic network design concepts and the Cisco switch product line. Now we begin to put the two together to be able to move on to configuration at Layer 2, Layer 3, and Layer 4.

Because this book focuses on Ethernet for the physical layer, the basic principles and operation of Ethernet will be described first. Here you will learn about the underlying protocols that allow Ethernet to be a robust and reliable physical layer protocol. The principles of *Carrier Sense Multiple Access with Collision Detect* (CSMA/CD) will be described.

Next, the details of network cabling will be described. Network cabling is the number one cause of network problems in a production network. It is imperative that you fully understand how Ethernet devices connect. Without this knowledge, configuration at the upper layers is futile.

The different types of physical layers for Ethernet include the following:

- 10Base2
- 10Base5
- 10BaseT

- 100BaseT
- 100BaseFx
- 1000BaseLx/Sx

The types of cabling to connect different network devices using these physical interface types will be described. The wiring of both twisted pair and fiber-optic Ethernet media types will be covered along with a description of the different types of twisted pair and fiber-optic cables.

Making a connection to an Ethernet switch's console port is an important first step to configuring it. This is the interface you will use to begin configuration of the device. This will also be the interface you will use to troubleshoot and reconfigure in the event of a failure that prevents you from reaching the device through the network. The connection to the console port will be covered in this chapter.

After your devices are connected and you have a working connection to the console port, you will need to make a few configuration changes to ease the implementation of more complex concepts as you begin to build the upper-layer configuration of your campus network. These initial configuration elements include the following:

- Password configuration
- Hostname and system name configuration
- Setting up an IP address for the device
- Naming the Ethernet ports
- Configuring the speed and duplex mode for the Ethernet ports
- Testing your initial setup

This list of configuration tasks will give you the necessary setup information to move on to configuring the upper layer protocols in your campus network.

The final topic in this chapter will be describing packet formats. In the previous chapters, we covered the concepts of the communication between layers and how upper layers are placed into the payload of the lower layers. This section will cover the details of how the packets are built by describing the layout of the various fields of the following protocols:

- Ethernet
- IP

- TCP
- UDP

This discussion will provide you with a foundation to understand other protocols in the TCP/IP suite. The other protocols will be related to the IP, TCP and UDP protocols.

Ethernet Operation

Chapter 2, "Multilayer Switching Network Design Basics," introduced basic topological concepts about Ethernet such as bus structure and collisions. Now we will dive deeper into the function of Ethernet to see how it works. Ethernet is known as a *Carrier Sense Multiple Access with Collision Detect* (CSMA/CD) with exponential backoff network. Here are a few examples to explain the meaning of CSMA/CD with exponential backoff.

Consider the following network where several devices are networked together using Ethernet (see Figure 4-1). Notice the bus topology of the network. If host A would like to send a packet to host B, host A listens to the bus and waits for all packets currently being transmitted on the bus to pass. After the bus is quiet, host A begins sending an Ethernet frame onto the bus. All the hosts connected to the bus see the packet being sent from A. Host B sees the packet and recognizes the destination MAC address as its

Figure 4-1
Generic Ethernet LAN

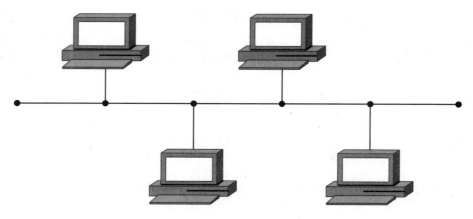

own address and then keeps the packet. The other hosts on the network ignore the packet destined to B. This property of waiting for the bus to be silent is called Carrier Sense. Because there are many devices using the Ethernet bus, it is a Multiple Access network.

Now consider a similar scenario where host A waits for the bus to be silent and begins to transmit a frame the same time that host C begins to send a frame onto the bus. This is called a collision. Because the transmitting hosts listen to the bus while they are transmitting, they can detect a collision. After detecting a collision, the transmitting hosts stop sending their packets and wait for a random period of time before sending the packet again. This random period of time is based on an average wait time. The capability of an Ethernet host to know if another host begins transmitting at the same time is called *collision detection*.

If, after waiting a random period of time, a host experiences another collision, the host will stop transmitting the packet. This time, the host will wait a random length of time based on twice the average wait time after the last collision. Therefore, if succeeding collisions are experienced, the host waits longer and longer to retransmit the packet. This is called *exponential backoff*.

Putting these properties together makes a CSMA/CD with exponential backoff network. It's relatively simple to understand, but there are some behaviors that make Ethernet interesting.

If many stations on an Ethernet all transmit the same number of small *packets per second* (pps), the probability for collisions only enables the bus to be utilized at 30% of its maximum capacity. For a 10Mbps Ethernet connecting many stations, only 3Mbps of the available bandwidth can be used. (For more information, see Appendix D.)

This is pretty dismal performance. Fortunately, switched Ethernet networks can reduce the number of hosts on an Ethernet segment to two. This results in a much greater utilization of the Ethernet segment. To further improve the performance of an Ethernet, network adapters and network equipment now provide full duplex operation. This allows both hosts on a switched Ethernet network segment to transmit at the same time without collisions. Because collisions do not occur in full-duplex switched Ethernet networks, the effective throughput is twice the maximum transmission rate of Ethernet. In other words, the full bandwidth of the Ethernet link can be utilized both to and from an Ethernet host. Note that not all Ethernet hosts and network equipment support full duplex operation.

We used 10Mbps Ethernet as an example, but other Ethernet rates exists. Fast Ethernet operates at 100Mbps and Gigabit Ethernet operates at 1000Mbps.

Network Cabling

Cabling is an important issue in implementing networks. It is often said that 80% of network problems are caused by cabling issues. This subsection will cover the cabling properties of Ethernet.

The Many Names of Ethernet

10Mbps Ethernet has many different types of cabling. It can use thick coax cable, thin coax cable, and twisted pair cable. The most commonly used cabling method for modern 10Mbps Ethernet is twisted pair. This type of Ethernet is called 10BaseT. The "10" in 10BaseT represents the transmission rate of the Ethernet, "Base" signifies that the network carries one signal as opposed to broadband, and T refers to the cabling type—*unshielded twisted pair* (UTP) in this case.

Thick coax Ethernet is called 10Base5 and thin coax Ethernet is called 10Base2. The "5" in 10Base5 refers to the maximum cable distance in hundreds of meters—500 meters in this case. 10Base2 has a maximum distance of 200 meters. 10Base2 and 10Base5 are rarely installed in networks today—inexpensive twisted pair cable makes 10BaseTx the economic choice. 10BaseFx Ethernet uses fiber-optic cabling; thus the "Fx" suffix.

These names are extended to include Fast Ethernet and Gigabit Ethernet. Fast Ethernet typically only uses twisted pair and fiber-optic cabling, 100BaseT and 100BaseFx, respectively. Gigabit Ethernet generally uses fiber-optic cabling and is called 1000BaseLx or 1000BaseSx. The Lx designation refers to a long wavelength optical signal and the Sx designation refers to a short wavelength optical signal. There is also an emerging copper Gigabit Ethernet standard called 1000BaseCx.

Ethernet Cabling

The Category ratings denote the quality of twisted pair cables. These cable quality standards are based on such cable characteristics such as the number of twists per foot, the size of the wires used in the cable, and the quality of the cable jacket.

Category 3 cabling can be found in older buildings and is primarily used for voice circuits, but 10BaseT can use Category 3 cable. Due to higher bandwidth, 100BaseT must use Category 5 cable. Category 5 cable is a higher quality of cable than Category 3 cable and therefore has a higher cost. However, due to price reductions in Category 5 cable and the popularity of higher speed LANs, new installations of Category 3 cable are virtually nonexistent.

Fiber-optic cables can be used for Ethernet wiring. Whether its 10BaseFx, 100BaseFx, or 1000BaseFx, one pair of fibers are needed for one link, where each single strand of fiber carries one direction of the traffic between the Ethernet devices. Two basic types of fiber-optic cables exist—multimode and singlemode.

Multimode fiber-optic cable is typically less expensive than singlemode fiber-optic cable. It can typically transmit up to about 2km in distance depending on the bandwidth of the signal. As the bandwidth of the signal increases, the shorter the maximum distance the fiber-optic cable can carry. Multimode transmitters are typically low cost *Light Emitting Diodes* (LEDs). The color of the multimode fiber-optic jacket is conventionally orange.

Singlemode fiber cable is usually more expensive than multimode fiber cable. Depending on the type of transmitter, it can carry signals 40–80km. Singlemode transmitters use more expensive laser devices, which can be hazardous if pointed toward your eyes. The fiber-optic jacket is typically yellow.

1000BaseLx/Sx Ethernet uses fiber-optic cables due to the high bandwidth of the signals. As noted earlier, a standard is emerging of 1000BaseCx for twisted pair cables.

Ethernet Wiring Standards

Twisted pair Ethernet uses conductors 1, 2, 3, and 6. Conductors 1 and 2 are the transmit side of the link and conductors 3 and 6 are for the receive side of the link.

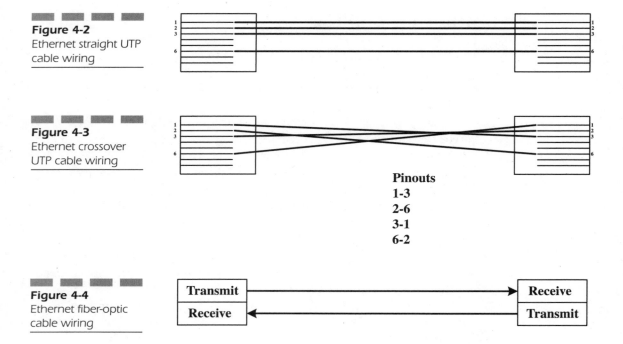

Figure 4-2
Ethernet straight UTP
cable wiring

Figure 4-3
Ethernet crossover
UTP cable wiring

Pinouts
1-3
2-6
3-1
6-2

Figure 4-4
Ethernet fiber-optic
cable wiring

Two types of Ethernet ports—end station ports and network device ports (cross ports)—exist. End station ports and cross ports can be connected with a "straight-through" cable (see Figure 4-2). This cable is wired to from conductor 1 to conductor 1, 2 to 2, 3 to 3, and 6 to 6. If two network devices are connected together or two end stations are connected together, a crossover cable is needed (see Figure 4-3). A crossover cable is wired from conductor 1 to conductor 3, 2 to 6, 3 to 1, and 6 to 2.

Ethernet links that use fiber-optic cable have two fiber strands in the link between two stations (see Figure 4-4). The two strands each carry one unidirectional signal to form a bidirectional link.

Building the Switch Block

In Chapter 2, the concept of a switch block was defined. This section will cover how to connect Cisco switches to begin building the switch block in your network. These concepts will make configuring the Layer 2 and Layer 3 functionality easier and the end result will be a more maintainable network.

Connecting to the Console Port

Cisco Ethernet switches are supplied with the cabling necessary to connect to the console port of the device. The console port is used for configuration, troubleshooting, monitoring, and maintenance of the switch. Connection to the console port is a necessary and fundamental step in implementing your campus network.

For a 1900, 2800, or 2900 switch, the console port is an RJ-45 connector on the rear of the device. A 5500 series switch has an RJ-45 connector on the front of the device. Connect the supplied eight-conductor flat cable to this connector and the other end of the cable into one of the three serial adapters as follows:

- The RJ-45 to DB-9 female DTE adapter for PC connection

- The RJ-45 to DB-25 female DTE adapter for connection to a UNIX workstation

- The RJ-45 to DB-25 male DCE adapter for connection to a modem

A 5000 series switch doesn't have an RJ-45 connector for the console port. Instead, these switches have female DB-25 ports. The only difference in connecting to the console port from the previous instructions is to use an RJ-45 to male DB-25 adapter to connect the switch to the black 8 conductor flat cable.

You may need to attach DB-25 to DB-9 adapters as needed if your terminal equipment varies from the previous descriptions. If the modem or terminal emulation program doesn't work after making the connections, use a serial port breakout box to make sure the RS-232 data and control signals are correctly wired (see Figure 4-5).

Figure 4-5
Serial connection to
Cisco device

Using a null modem cable solves most RS-232 cabling problems. A null modem crosses the transmit and receive signals and some of the control signals, depending on the type of null modem cable. Crossing the transmit and receive signals solves most problems.

Connecting Ethernet Ports

When connecting two Ethernet devices together, use the following rule to determine if you should use a straight-through cable or a crossover cable.

- When connecting a switch to a workstation, servers, and routers use a straight-through cable.
- When connecting a switch to another switch, hub, or repeater, use a crossover cable.

The speed and duplex of the ports on both sides of the link must match. If the speed and duplex doesn't match, the connection will not work or behave poorly at best.

Monitoring Port Status

Set Command To check the status of a port, including speed and duplex settings, you may use the following Set Command:

```
Switch> show port [mod_num[/port_num]]
```

You may specify a specific port using the module/port convention. For example, to view port 3 on module 2, you would enter the following:

```
Switch> show port 2/3
```

Alternatively, you can view all ports for a card. For example, to view all the ports on module 2:

```
Switch> show port 2
```

Or, you can get a summary of all ports on the entire device:

```
Switch> show port
```

Cisco IOS For a Cisco IOS-based device, you must use the command show interface while in enable mode:

```
Switch# show interface [interface]
```

For example, for interface Ethernet 0:

```
Switch# show interface Ethernet0
```

For a summary of all interfaces:

```
Switch# show interface
```

Setting Switch Passwords

Passwords are used to protect switches from being monitored or configured from unauthorized users. Cisco switches use two levels of password protection. One level of password is used for access to the switch and the ability to monitor the switch. The second level of password protection gives the user full administrative access to configure the switch.

To set the access password, you would use the following command for a Set Command-based device:

```
Switch(enable) set password
```

To set the administrator password, use the following command:

```
Switch(enable) set enablepass
```

Both commands will follow with prompts to effect the password change.

```
Enter old password: oldPassword
Enter new password: newPassword
Retype new password: newPassword
Password changed.
```

For a Cisco IOS-based device, you may use the following commands:

```
Switch(config)# enable password level 1 newPassword
Switch(config)# enable password level 15 newPassword
```

Level 1 is the default security level for user access. Level 15 is the security level entered upon typing the `enable` command. IOS has 16 levels (0-15) of security. Although usually unused, they can be helpful in specialized situations.

Setting the Host Name and System Prompt

Setting the system prompt is an important step in beginning to configure a multilayer switch in a large campus network. The system prompt can be used to quickly assess that the configuration commands are being done on the correct device. Finding that the reason the configuration command you just entered didn't work is because you entered it into the wrong device is very frustrating. Not only did you enter the command into the wrong device, you probably just caused more problems. When system uptime and reliability are important to the campus network users, this type of unnecessary downtime should be avoided at all costs. Take the time to modify the system prompt.

To configure the prompt on a Set-Command based device, enter the following:

```
Switch(enable) set prompt name
```

On a Cisco IOS-based device, use the `hostname` command.

```
Switch(config)# hostname name
```

In both cases, the device will respond by changing the system prompt to the specified name.

Setting the IP Address for Network Accessibility

Until now, the only method of configuration has been through the serial port. After the IP address is set on the switch, a network administrator can access the same commands by using the Telnet application from an end station that has connectivity to the IP address of the switch.

We will cover IP addressing in much more detail in a later chapter, but for now, understand that IP addresses follow a XXX.XXX.XXX.XXX format, where XXX is a decimal number representing eight bits of the 32-bit IP address.

The following commands may be used to configure the IP address for your devices.

For a Set-Command based system, use the following:

```
Switch(enable) set interface sc0 ip-address netmask broadcast
```

The broadcast address may be omitted: The system will calculate it using the supplied IP address and netmask.

Unless otherwise specified, your switch will default to membership in VLAN 1. To specify a different VLAN, enter the following:

```
Switch(enable) set interface sc0 vlan-id
```

You can optionally verify these settings using the show interface command.

```
Switch(enable) show interface
```

You can set the IP address of a Cisco IOS-based device as follows:

```
Switch(config)# ip address ip-address netmask
```

If you need to verify the IP address, use this command:

```
Switch(config)# show ip
```

Naming Ports

Much like setting the prompt for the switch helps reduce unnecessary downtime caused by configuring the wrong device, naming the physical ports on your switch can reduce the chance of monitoring or configuring the wrong port.

For Set Command-based devices, you may set the description for each port by specifying the module and port number.

```
Switch(enable) set port name mod-num/port-num [description]
```

The description may be up to 21 characters in length, including spaces. To clear the description for a port, enter the same command but without the description.

```
Switch(enable) set port name mod-num/port-num
```

If your device is Cisco-IOS based, use the following interface level command:

```
Switch(config-if)# description description
```

You may use the `no description` command to clear the description for an interface. To include spaces in the description, you must enclose the description in quotation marks.

Setting Link Speed and Duplex Mode

As mentioned before, it is important to have the speed and duplex mode of both sides of an Ethernet link set identically. Otherwise, the link could perform miserably or even completely fail.

The speed and duplex can be administratively set for both ports on the Ethernet link to auto-negotiate. When auto-negotiation is enabled on a port, the port sends negotiation impulses to let the other device on the link know what its capabilities are. Auto-negotiation then finds the highest possible combination of speed and duplex mode to optimize the configuration of the link.

Note, however, that devices with fixed speed and duplex settings or with no auto-negotiation features will not be compatible with a device that has auto-negotiation enabled. Also, auto-negotiation may have compatibility problems between different vendors' equipment. This could result in less than optimal link settings or a link failure. Always check for the actual operational speed and duplex mode after the devices are configured and connected to see that auto-negotiation succeeded. Or, you can avoid problems with auto-negotiation by forcing both speed and duplex settings for every port. Configuration mismatches with duplex mode and speed for Ethernet ports on the same link are the source of many network problems.

To configure ports on a Set Command-based device, do the following:

```
Switch(enable) set port speed mod-num/port-num {10 | 100 | auto}
Switch(enable) set port duplex mod-num/port-num {full | half}
```

To verify settings, use the `show port` command.

For a Cisco IOS-based device, use the following interface commands:

```
Switch(config-if)# duplex {auto | full | full-flow-control | half}
```

To verify the port/interface settings, use the `show interface` command.

Testing Connectivity

A useful tool called ping exists in the IP protocol suite to help troubleshoot connectivity between IP devices. In testing the IP connectivity between two hosts, it also tests the physical links between the hosts. For most ping implementations, the resulting information is a packet by packet round-trip latency measurement and a percentage of successful ping attempts.

On a trivial note, there is a never-ending argument over the origin of the name "ping." Some say PING stands for *Packet INternet Groper*. The author of ping says ping is simply analogous to the sonar sound *ping* and the name "Packet INternet Groper" was added later.

PING is an invaluable tool as you build your network. As with the implementation of any complex system, it's best to move slowly and make sure that each step is successfully completed. As your network is being built, use ping often to insure that your network has connectivity between devices.

The ping function is analogous to a sonar ping. A signal is sent out. When it returns after reflecting off its destination, information can be derived such as whether the destination object exists and the distance in milliseconds from the transmitter. Similar to the sonar ping, an IP hosts sends an *Internet Control Message Protocol* (ICMP) request packet to the destination host. The packet includes the destination IP address and an IP protocol type field that specifies that the packet is an ICMP request. The destination receives the ICMP request and sends back an ICMP reply to the sender.

The use of ping to verify connectivity is the same for both Set Command and Cisco IOS-based command devices.

You may use ping by specifying a destination IP address where the packet will be directed. Output is similar to the following:

```
Switch> ping dest-ip-address
Sending 5, 100-byte ICMP Echos to dest-ip-address, time out is 2
seconds:
!!!!!
Success rate is 100 percent (5/5), round-trip min/avg/max 0/2/10 ms
```

It's alive! You will not always be that fortunate. The ! means a response was received. A period or dot (.) denotes that a response was never received. Other possible PING results include

- Destination not responding
- Unknown host
- Destination unreachable
- Network unreachable

Destination not responding means no answer was received from the target host.

The message Unknown host may be received when you optionally specify a host name instead of an IP address, and the host name is not recognized or cannot be translated to an IP address.

You may receive a Destination unreachable message if the default gateway cannot reach the specified network.

A Network unreachable message will be returned if the device does not have a valid route to get to the specified network.

Packet Formats

In Chapter 2, we covered the concept of nesting protocols inside the payload of other protocols. This makes layered communication possible. In this section, we'll give the details of the packet formats for the Ethernet protocol, IP, TCP, and UDP. This will give enough of a foundation to find out how the other protocols we will cover in the remainder of the book relate to each other.

Ethernet Packet Format

Figure 4-6 shows the packet format for an Ethernet version 2 packet.

The Preamble field is an eight-byte field that specifies the beginning of an Ethernet packet.

The Source and Destination Address fields are each six bytes long. These fields hold the MAC addresses of the hosts.

The following specifies the two-byte EtherType field Length/Type. If the value of this field is less than or equal to 1500, the Length/Type field indi-

Figure 4-6
Ethernet packet format

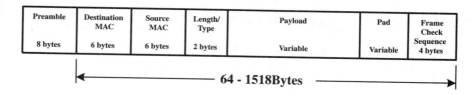

Preamble	Destination MAC	Source MAC	Length/ Type	Payload	Pad	Frame Check Sequence
8 bytes	6 bytes	6 bytes	2 bytes	Variable	Variable	4 bytes

64 - 1518Bytes

Figure 4-7
IP packet format

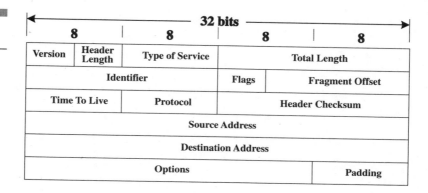

cates the number of bytes in the payload. If the value of this field is greater than or equal to 1536, the Length/Type field indicates the protocol in the payload. For example, a type field value of 0x0800 specifies that the payload is IP. The data field is variable in length and holds the payload of the Ethernet packet.

The *Frame Check Sequence* (FCS) is a four-byte *Cyclic Redundancy Check* (CRC) used for error detection and correction.

IP Packet Format

The IP header follows the format shown in Figure 4-7.

The four-bit Version field identifies what version of IP is being used. The most prevalent version of IP is version 4. Table 4-1 lists the valid version numbers.

The four-bit Header Length field gives the length of the IP header. The header is variable in length depending on the length of the options field described below. The minimum IP header length is 20 bytes and the maximum IP header length is 24 bytes (depending on the Options field length).

Table 4-1

IP version numbers

Number	Version
0	Reserved
1–3	Unassigned
4	*Internet Protocol* (IP)
5	ST Datagram Mode
6	*Simple Internet Protocol* (SIP)
7	TP/IX
8	*P Internet Protocol* (PIP)
9	*TCP and UDP over Bigger Address* (TUBA)
10–14	Unassigned
15	Reserved

Table 4-2

ToS bits

Bits	Field	Value
0–2	Precedence	See Precedence bit table
3	Delay	0 = normal 1 = minimize
4	Throughput	0 = normal 1 = maximize
5	Reliability	0 = normal 1 = maximize
6	Monetary Cost	0 = normal 1 = minimize
7	Reserved	Always 0

The eight-bit *Type of Service* (ToS) field defines the priority of a packet. This field is generally not used. However, emerging standards in differentiated services is generating new interest in the ToS field. Table 4-2 lists the significance of the eight ToS bits.

Table 4-3 lists the values for the precedence field in the ToS field.

The Total Length field is a 16-bit field that specifies the total length of the packet. The length of the payload can be found by subtracting the Header Length field from the Total Length field.

Table 4-3

Precedence bits

Value	Meaning
000	Routine
001	Priority
010	Immediate
011	Flash
100	Flash Override
101	CRITIC/ECP
110	Internetwork Control
111	Network Control

The Identifier field is a 16-bit field used to identify an IP fragment. IP packets can be fragmented to fit inside a Layer 2 packet or frame.

The Flags field is a three-bit field. The first bit position is unused. The second bit position is a *Don't Fragment* (DF) bit. If this bit is set to one, the router will not be allowed to fragment the frame. If the router must fragment the frame to forward it, the packet will be dropped and an error message will be sent to the source. The third bit is a *More Fragments* (MF) bit. If a router fragments a packet, this bit is set for all fragments except for the last.

The Fragment Offset is a 13-bit field that specifies the offset of the fragment from the header. This allows fragments to be sent out of order and reassembled in the correct order.

The *Time to Live* (TTL) field is an eight-bit field that is decremented each time the packet passes through a router. If the TTL field reaches zero, the packet will be dropped. This provides a mechanism for packets to be removed if they are caught in a routing loop.

The Protocol field specifies the protocol that is embedded in the payload of the IP packet. Table 4-4 lists some of the frequently used protocols.

The Header Checksum field is a 16-bit field to provide error correction. It is a one's complement checksum that covers the entire IP header, but not the IP payload.

The Source and Destination Addresses are a 32-bit IP address specifying the IP source and destination for the packet.

Table 4-4

Common IP
protocol field
values

Number	Protocol
1	*Internet Control Message Protocol* (ICMP)
2	*Internet Group Management Protocol* (IGMP)
3	Gateway to Gateway Protocol
4	IP in IP
6	*Transmission Control Protocol* (TCP)
8	*Exterior Gateway Protocol* (EGP)
17	*User Datagram Protocol* (UDP)
35	*Inter-Domain Policy Routing Protocol* (IDPR)
45	*Inter-Domain Routing Protocol* (IDRP)
46	*Resource Reservation Protocol* (RSVP)
47	*Generic Routing Encapsulation* (GRE)
54	NBMA *Next Hop Resolution Protocol* (NHRP)
88	Cisco *Internet Gateway Routing Protocol* (IGRP)
89	*Open Shortest Path First* (OSPF)

The Options field is variable in length and optional. The values for the options field are outside the scope of this book.

The Padding field adds zeros to the end of the header to make sure that the header ends on a 32-bit boundary.

Transmission Control Protocol (TCP) Packet Format

The *Transmission Control Protocol* (TCP) provides guaranteed communication between devices. Guaranteed communication means that the packets that are accepted by the receiving device are guaranteed to be correct. This is achieved at the cost of increased complexity compared to other protocols that do not support guaranteed communication.

The TCP packet format is shown in Figure 4-8.

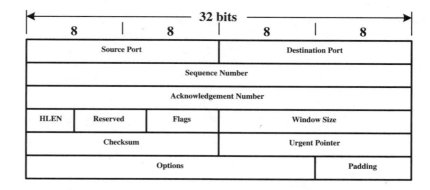

Figure 4-8
TCP packet format

The Source and Destination Port fields are each 16 bits long. They specify the applications on both sides of the TCP session. RFC 1700 describes the commonly used port numbers.

The Sequence Number field is a 32-bit long number that specifies the order of TCP packets. Because packets can be received out of order, this field provides a mechanism to reassemble the packets in proper order. The sequence number is incremented by the number of bytes in the TCP payload.

The Acknowledgment Number is a 32-bit field that determines the next sequence number to be received. If the sequence number received is different than the sequence number expected, the destination knows how many packets were lost.

The Header Length field is a 4-bit field that specifies the length of the TCP header in 32-bit words. This is necessary because the Options field length is variable.

The 6-bit Reserved field is always set to 0.

The 6-bit Flags field is used for flow and connection control. The values are shown in Table 4-5.

The Window Size is a 16-bit field used for flow control. This field specifies the number of bytes that the receiver can accept from the sender before an acknowledgment. The number of bytes is specified from the Acknowledgment Number field.

The Checksum field is a 16-bit CRC that covers the header and the payload.

The Urgent pointer is a 16-bit field that is only used when the URG flag is set. The number represented by this pointer value is added to the Sequence Number to indicate the end of the urgent data.

Table 4-5

Flag bits

Flag Bit	Meaning
1	*Urgent* (URG)
2	*Acknowledgment* (ACK)
3	*Push* (PSH)
4	*Reset* (RST)
5	*Synchronize* (SYN)
6	*Final* (FIN)

Figure 4-9
UDP packet format

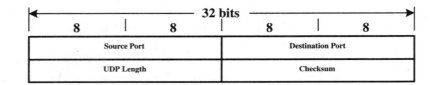

The variable length Options field is an optional field required by the Sender's TCP process. The remainder of this field is padded with zeros to fill out the header to a 32-bit boundary.

User Datagram Protocol (UDP) Packet Format

The *User Datagram Protocol* (UDP) is not a guaranteed communication protocol like TCP. In other words, no mechanism guarantees that the packets destined for a receiving device made it to their destination. This is analogous to sending first class mail through the postal service. The sender addresses the piece of mail and places the mail in a mail receptacle with high hopes, but no guarantees, that it will reach its destination. The advantage is the reduced complexity of UDP compared to TCP.

The UDP packet format is displayed in the Figure 4-9.

The Source and Destination fields are 16-bit application addresses that specify the application at both ends of the UDP session.

The UDP length is a 16-bit number that represents the length of the entire segment in bytes.

The 16-bit Checksum covers the entire segment. The Checksum is optional. If it is not used, the field is set to zeros.

Chapter Summary

This chapter gives you the background information you need to begin building campus networks with Cisco multilayer switching equipment. The following topics are covered:

- Ethernet (CSMA/CD) operation
- Network cabling
- Initial switch setup
- Packet formats

We described both the Ethernet protocol and cabling in detail. This helps you understand the behavior of the Ethernet links and shared networks across your campus network. The cabling standards used in each of the physical interface types were described to help you set up and troubleshoot the cabling system of your network.

We covered initial multilayer switch setup. These setup items lay a foundation for the upper layer configurations to implement the features of your campus network. The following setup items were covered:

- Password configuration
- Hostname and system prompt configuration
- Setting up an IP address for the device
- Naming the Ethernet ports
- Configuring the speed and duplex mode for the Ethernet ports
- Verifying link integrity and testing your initial setup with PING

Now you are equipped to learn to configure the upper layers of your campus network. Chapter 5, "Layer 2 Configuration," describes the details of Layer 2 networking and how to configure Layer 2 in your network. We will discuss techniques to help you improve network performance and provide fault tolerance.

Frequently Asked Questions (FAQ)

Question: How long can I run my Ethernet cables?

Answer: It depends on the cable type. Cable types and their associated maximum lengths are as follows:

- 10Base2—200m
- 10Base5—500m
- 10BaseT—100m
- 100BaseT—100m
- 10BaseFx/100BaseFx (multimode)—2km
- 10BaseFx/100BaseFx (singlemode)—10km
- 1000BaseLX (long wavelength) and 1000BaseSX (short wavelength) —1000m.

Question: Why not always use Ethernet auto-negotiation?

Answer: Ethernet auto-negotiation works well in certain instances, but you should be aware of the following issues:

- Multivendor interoperability of Ethernet auto-negotiation should never be trusted without testing its operation first. In some cases, auto-negotiation doesn't work at all, leaving the ports not configured identically. In some cases, auto-negotiation may appear to work, but the port speed or duplex mode may not be optimally set.

- Auto-negotiation will not work if one port has auto-negotiation enabled and the other port is manually set. The port that is manually set will not transmit the negotiation impulses. The result is the port with auto-negotiation enabled will not receive the impulses and will not be configured.

Case Study

Objective: *Cubby Products International* (CPI) has a plan and budget for implementing a multilayer switching campus network with Cisco equipment. The topology and equipment list has been defined. Figure 4-10 shows the topology and equipment placement for the initial design of their campus network.

Your objective is to define the connections between the switches in the initial design and connect the switches. After the connections have been made, properly configure the interface and verify their operation. Next, define and configure the IP addresses for each of the switches and verify IP connectivity. The last thing to do is to set the hostname, system prompt, and port names for each of the switches.

Required Equipment

The following equipment is required to implement CPI's campus network:

- (14) Cisco 1900's
- (6) Cisco 2926's
- (5) Cisco 5505's
- (2) Cisco 6506's

Figure 4-10
CPI campus network
topology

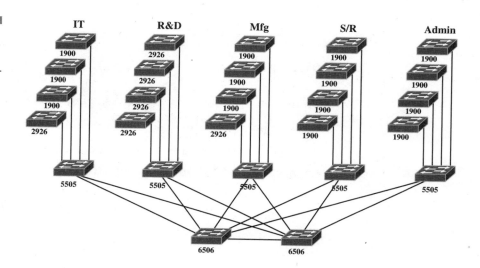

A naming convention should be defined to help keep track of the switches. The following naming convention will be used throughout this case study:

```
<switch/core block name >-<number of switch in switch/core
block>-<access|distribution if not core>-<switch type>
```

Table 4-6 lists the switch names throughout the CPI network.

Required Information

You must understand the following concepts to implement the objective:

- Ethernet cabling
- Connecting to the console port
- Connecting Ethernet ports
- Monitoring port status
- Setting switch passwords
- Setting the switch hostname and system prompt
- Setting the switch IP address
- Naming the switch ports
- Setting the switch Ethernet interface link speed and duplex mode
- Testing the initial setup

Approach

You must complete the following tasks to implement the objective:

- Connect to the switch console port
- Define the interface types between the network switches
- Connect the network interfaces together
- Configure the interface speed and duplex mode
- Verify that the ports are connected
- Set the switch password

Table 4-6

CPI campus network switch names

Switch/Core Block Name	Model	Switch Name
IT	5505	IT-1-dist-5505
IT	2926	IT-2-access-2926
IT	1900	IT-3-access-1900
IT	1900	IT-4-access-1900
IT	1900	IT-5-access-1900
RD	5505	RD-1-dist-5505
RD	2926	RD-2-access-2926
RD	1900	RD-3-access-1900
RD	1900	RD-4-access-1900
RD	1900	RD-5-access-1900
Mfg	5505	Mfg-1-dist-5505
Mfg	2926	Mfg-2-access-2926
Mfg	1900	Mfg-3-access-1900
Mfg	1900	Mfg-4-access-1900
Mfg	1900	Mfg-5-access-1900
SR	5505	SR-1-dist-5505
SR	1900	SR-2-access-2926
SR	1900	SR-3-access-1900
SR	1900	SR-4-access-1900
SR	1900	SR-5-access-1900
Admin	5505	Admin-1-dist-5505
Admin	1900	Admin-2-access-2926
Admin	1900	Admin-3-access-1900
Admin	1900	Admin-4-access-1900
Admin	1900	Admin-5-access-1900
Backbone	6506	Backbone-1-core-6506
Backbone	6506	Backbone-2-core-6506

- Set the switch host name and system prompt
- Name the switch ports
- Set the switch IP address
- Verify the IP connectivity of the switch

Connect to the Switch Console Port

The first thing to do when building a network with Cisco switches is to gain access to the switch after the cards are inserted into its chassis (if applicable) and the switch is powered up.

The details on connecting to the console port will be covered by switch type.

6506/5505 Console Port Connection   The 6506 and 5505 switches have supervisor cards with female DB-25 RS-232 serial ports. Connect to this port with a male DB-25 cable. The other end of the cable will connect to a terminal device—either a serial terminal or a PC running Hyperterminal or another piece of terminal emulation software. To connect between a Cisco 6506 or 5505 and a terminal, use a straight-through serial cable.

At this point, type <return> to ensure that the console connection works.

2926/1900 Console Port Connection   The Cisco 2926 and 1900 switches have RJ-45 sockets for the console port. Plug the 8-conductor flat cable that is supplied with the switch into this port. Use the 9-pin female to RJ-45 adapter supplied with the switch to connect to the terminal if the terminal has a 9-pin male serial port. If the terminal device has a 25-pin connector, use the 25-pin to RJ-45 adapter marked "terminal" that is supplied with the switch.

Type <return> to verify that the console connection works.

General Comments   If the console connection does not work after following the previous instructions, try using a null modem adapter.

In some cases, the gender of the serial connectors may not be compatible. Use a "gender-mender" to correct this situation. "Gender-menders" are adapters with two female or two male connectors. They come in all combinations of 9-pin and 25-pin connectors.

Define the Interface Types Between the Network Switches

There are several things to consider when defining the interfaces:

- Bandwidth needed on the link
- Distance between devices on a link
- Supported interfaces on a device

We may find that after the network is implemented, a lot of bandwidth is needed between the core switches and the distribution switches. Gigabit Ethernet is a consideration, but may be cost-prohibitive. We will learn in the next chapter how to increase the bandwidth of inter-switch connections without using Gigabit Ethernet. For now, we will use 100Mbps Ethernet.

CPI's network must cover all 10 of its buildings over 128 acres. The distance rules out twisted pair between buildings. Therefore, we must use fiber-optic cables between buildings. There is an added benefit to using fiber-optic cables. The fiber-optic cable cannot conduct electricity, which could cause potential grounding problems or a path for lightning strikes. Also, fiber-optic cables are not susceptible to *Electromagnetic Interference* (EMI) or *Radio Frequency Interference* (RFI).

The two core switches will be placed in separate buildings to give some degree of fault tolerance if power goes out in one of the buildings. The distribution switches will be placed in five of the ten buildings where the highest concentration of connections are located.

Because the distribution and core switches won't be configured often after the network is implemented, the speed and duplex mode between the core and distribution switches will be forced to 100Mbps and full duplex operation. Auto-negotiation will not be enabled on these interfaces. The access to distribution switch device connections will have auto-negotiation enabled because these connections may change as the network evolves.

The connections from the hosts to the access switches will have auto-negotiation enabled because the hosts have a good chance of being moved, added, or removed. Because auto-negotiation raises interoperability issues, all types of devices to be connected to the network must be adequately tested before and after being added to the network.

Connect the Network Interfaces Together

Now that the link design of the network has been defined, the devices can be physically connected. The network has two media types—100BaseT and 100BaseFx.

The 100BaseFx connections are made with two strand fiber-optic cables. When two 100BaseFx ports are connected, the transmitter of one interface must be connected to the receiver of the other interface.

The 100BaseT connections between switches must be made with cross-over cables because the interface types between the two switches are the same.

Set the Switch Host Name and System Prompt

To reduce confusion while administering the campus switches, first set the switch's host name and system prompt. Each of the user interface types will be covered individually. Use the switch names in the name table defined earlier.

6506/5505/2926 Host Name and System Prompt Configuration   To set the prompt for the Catalyst 6506, Catalyst 5505, and Catalyst 2926 devices, you must use the following command:

```
Switch(enable) set prompt IT-1-dist-5505
```

Repeat the command for all the Set Command based devices.

1900 Host Name and System Prompt Configuration   To set the prompt on the Catalyst 1900, you must use the following Cisco IOS command:

```
Switch(config)# hostname IT-3-access-1900
```

Cisco IOS will use the devices hostname as the text for the system prompt. Repeat the command for all other Catalyst 1900s.

Configure the Interface Speed and Duplex Mode

From the diagram in Figure 4-10, the speed and duplex mode parameters can be configured. Each of the switch types will be covered individually. Due to the symmetry of the network, each of the devices of the same type has identical interface configurations.

Due to the redundant links in this network, the Spanning Tree Protocol must be enabled. The Spanning Tree Protocol is enabled by default. The operation and configuration of the Spanning Tree Protocol is covered in Chapter 5.

6506 Ethernet Interface Configuration   The 6506s have a connection between themselves and a connection to each of the distribution switches. There are six Ethernet interfaces in all. Each of these interfaces are 100BaseFx and should be configured for 100Mbps full duplex operation. Ethernet auto-negotiation should be disabled.

To accomplish this task, enter the following:

```
Backbone-1-core-6506(enable) set port enable 2/1-6
Backbone-1-core-6506(enable) set port duplex 2/1-6 full

Backbone-2-core-6506(enable) set port enable 2/1-6
Backbone-2-core-6506(enable) set port duplex 2/1-6 full
```

5505 Ethernet Interface Configuration   The 5505s all have connections to their associated access switches and to both of the core switches. The connections to the access switches and core switches will be via 100BaseFx.

The links to the core switches will have auto-negotiation disabled and will be configured for 100Mbps and full duplex. The links to the access switches will have auto-negotiation enabled. All the physical configurations of the 5505s in the CPI campus network are identical.

To configure the ports, you would enter the following:

```
IT-1-dist-5505(enable) set port enable 2/1-6
IT-1-dist-5505(enable) set port duplex 2/1-2 full
IT-1-dist-5505(enable) set port duplex 2/3-6 auto

RD-1-dist-5505(enable) set port enable 2/1-6
RD-1-dist-5505(enable) set port duplex 2/1-2 full
RD-1-dist-5505(enable) set port duplex 2/3-6 auto

Mfg-1-dist-5505(enable) set port enable 2/1-6
Mfg-1-dist-5505(enable) set port duplex 2/1-2 full
Mfg-1-dist-5505(enable) set port duplex 2/3-6 auto

SR-1-dist-5505(enable) set port enable 2/1-6
SR-1-dist-5505(enable) set port duplex 2/1-2 full
SR-1-dist-5505(enable) set port duplex 2/3-6 auto

Admin-1-dist-5505(enable) set port enable 2/1-6
Admin-1-dist-5505(enable) set port duplex 2/1-2 full
Admin-1-dist-5505(enable) set port duplex 2/3-6 auto
```

For each 5505 distribution switch, ports 1 and 2 will connect to the backbone 6506s. Ports 3 through 6 will connect to the access devices.

2926 Ethernet Interface Configuration   The 2926 access switches use auto-negotiation on all ports. The connection to the 5505 distribution switch will be via 100BaseFx. The connections to the end stations will be via 10/100BaseT in full or half duplex depending on the auto-negotiated configuration.

Performing the configuration will require the following commands:

```
IT-2-access-2926(enable) set port enable 1/1
IT-2-access-2926(enable) set port duplex 1/1 auto
IT-2-access-2926(enable) set port duplex 2/1-24 auto
IT-2-access-2926(enable) set port speed 2/1-24 auto

RD-2-access-2926(enable) set port enable 1/1
RD-2-access-2926(enable) set port duplex 1/1 auto
RD-2-access-2926(enable) set port duplex 2/1-24 auto
RD-2-access-2926(enable) set port speed 2/1-24 auto

Mfg-2-access-2926(enable) set port enable 1/1
Mfg-2-access-2926(enable) set port duplex 1/1 auto
Mfg-2-access-2926(enable) set port duplex 2/1-24 auto
Mfg-2-access-2926(enable) set port speed 2/1-24 auto

SR-2-access-2926(enable) set port enable 1/1
SR-2-access-2926(enable) set port duplex 1/1 auto
SR-2-access-2926(enable) set port duplex 2/1-24 auto
SR-2-access-2926(enable) set port speed 2/1-24 auto

Admin-2-access-2926(enable) set port enable 1/1
Admin-2-access-2926(enable) set port duplex 1/1 auto
```

```
Admin-2-access-2926(enable) set port duplex 2/1-24 auto
Admin-2-access-2926(enable) set port speed 2/1-24 auto
```

Slot 1 of the 2926 has two 100BaseFx ports and slot 2 has 24 10/100BaseTx ports.

1900 Ethernet Interface Configuration   The 1900 configuration is similar to the 2926 configuration in that all ports have auto-negotiation enabled and 100BaseFx will be used to connect to the 5505 distribution switch.
   To configure your switches, use the following Cisco IOS commands.

```
Switch-access-1900# configure terminal
Switch-access-1900(config)# interface fastethernet 0/25
Switch-access-1900(config-if)# duplex auto
Switch-access-1900(config-if)# interface ethernet 0/1
Switch-access-1900(config-if)# duplex auto
Switch-access-1900(config-if)# interface ethernet 0/2
Switch-access-1900(config-if)# duplex auto
. . .
Switch-access-1900(config-if)# interface ethernet 0/23
Switch-access-1900(config-if)# duplex auto
Switch-access-1900(config-if)# interface ethernet 0/24
Switch-access-1900(config-if)# duplex auto
```

Repeat those commands for all your Catalyst 1900 access switches.

Verify That the Ports Are Connected

Now that all the ports have been connected and configured, verify that the interfaces are up and in a proper state. Each user interface type is covered individually.

6506/5505/2926 Interface Verification   For the Set Command-based devices, use the following command:

```
Switch(enable) show port
```

1900 Interface Verification   For the Cisco IOS-based 1900, use the following:

```
Switch# show interface
```

Set the Switch Password

Now that you have assured that all the switches and their interfaces are up and operating properly by checking the link indicator lights on the devices, the switch's password must be set. This will be covered by user interface type.

The access passwords will all be the same: c1sc0rulz

The enable passwords will be set according to the following convention:

```
<switch/core block name>+<core/switch block switch number>
```

Table 4-7 lists the access and enable passwords for all the switches.

6506/5505/2926 Password Configuration For the Set Command-based devices, use the following command. Repeat it for all devices in your network.

First, set the access level password:

```
Admin-2-access-2926(enable) set password
Enter old password: cisco
Enter new password: c1sc0rulz
Retype new password: c1sc0rulz
Password changed.
```

Next, set the administrative level password:

```
Admin-2-access-2926(enable) set enablepass
Enter old password: cisco
Enter new password: Admin+2
Retype new password: Admin+2
Password changed.
```

1900 Password Configuration For the Cisco IOS-based Catalyst 1900, set the access level password:

```
Admin-3-access-1900(config)# enable password level 1 c1sc0rulz
```

Next, set the administrative level password:

```
Admin-3-access-1900(config)# enable password level 15 Admin+3
```

Repeat for all Catalyst 1900 access layer switches.

Table 4-7

CPI switch password list

Switch Name	Access Password	Enable Password
IT-1-dist-5505	c1sc0rulz	IT+1
IT-2-access-2926	c1sc0rulz	IT+2
IT-3-access-1900	c1sc0rulz	IT+3
IT-4-access-1900	c1sc0rulz	IT+4
IT-5-access-1900	c1sc0rulz	IT+5
RD-1-dist-5505	c1sc0rulz	RD+1
RD-2-access-2926	c1sc0rulz	RD+2
RD-3-access-1900	c1sc0rulz	RD+3
RD-4-access-1900	c1sc0rulz	RD+4
RD-5-access-1900	c1sc0rulz	RD+5
Mfg-1-dist-5505	c1sc0rulz	Mfg+1
Mfg-2-access-2926	c1sc0rulz	Mfg+2
Mfg-3-access-1900	c1sc0rulz	Mfg+3
Mfg-4-access-1900	c1sc0rulz	Mfg+4
Mfg-5-access-1900	c1sc0rulz	Mfg+5
SR-1-dist-5505	c1sc0rulz	SR+1
SR-2-access-2926	c1sc0rulz	SR+2
SR-3-access-1900	c1sc0rulz	SR+3
SR-4-access-1900	c1sc0rulz	SR+4
SR-5-access-1900	c1sc0rulz	SR+5
Admin-1-dist-5505	c1sc0rulz	Admin+1
Admin-2-access-2926	c1sc0rulz	Admin+2
Admin-3-access-1900	c1sc0rulz	Admin+3
Admin-4-access-1900	c1sc0rulz	Admin+4
Admin-5-access-1900	c1sc0rulz	Admin+5
Backbone-1-core-6506	c1sc0rulz	Backbone+1
Backbone-2-core-6506	c1sc0rulz	Backbone+2

Name the Switch Ports

Though a tedious task, naming the switch ports can be a great time-saver in the long run. It will help prevent configuring the wrong port and make it easier to decide which port to configure. Each of the user interface types will be covered individually.

The name of the port will be the name of the device that is connected to the port.

6506/5505/2926 Port Naming   For Set-Command based devices, use the following to set the port name:

```
IT-1-dist-5505(enable) set port name 2/1 Backbone-1-core-6506
IT-1-dist-5505(enable) set port name 2/2 Backbone-2-core-6506
IT-1-dist-5505(enable) set port name 2/3 IT-2-access-2926
IT-1-dist-5505(enable) set port name 2/4 IT-3-access-1900
IT-1-dist-5505(enable) set port name 2/5 IT-4-access-1900
IT-1-dist-5505(enable) set port name 2/6 IT-5-access-1900
```

Following the previous example, repeat the commands for the rest of the devices in the network.

1900 Port Naming   For Cisco IOS-based 1900s, enter a description for each interface:

```
IT-3-access-1900(config)# interface fastethernet 0/25
IT-3-access-1900)(config-if)# description IT-1-dist-5505
```

Repeat for all other Catalyst 1900s.

Set the Switch IP Address

Now that the access and enable passwords and the host names and system prompts have been set, the IP address of the switch can be set so the switches can be configured over the network instead of through the console port.

For this case, we will obtain a subnet with at least 64 addresses to allow all the switches to be in the same subnet and to allow for additional switches in the future. The following subnet will be used for switch administration and access:

```
100.1.1.0 with subnet mask of 255.255.255.192
```

The first ten addresses will be reserved for administrative use. Table 4-8 lists the IP addresses of the switches.

The IP address configuration for each of the switches will be covered for each user interface type individually.

6506/5505/2926 IP Address Configuration   Set the IP address using the following Set Command:

```
IT-1-dist-5505(enable) set interface sc0 100.1.1.11 255.255.255.192
```

Repeat the command for all other Set Command-based devices.

1900 IP Address Configuration   Set the IP address using the following Cisco IOS command:

```
IT-3-access-1900(config)# ip address 100.1.1.13 255.255.255.192
```

Again, repeat for all other IOS-based devices.

Verify the IP Connectivity of the Switch

Now that everything is connected and configured with an IP address, verify IP connectivity with ping. This will also give an absolute verification of the individual links.

You can verify proper configuration and cabling by using ping from a single device and attempting to reach all other devices. (Command syntax is the same for all devices.)

```
IT-1-distribution-5505(enable) ping 100.1.1.12
IT-1-distribution-5505(enable) ping 100.1.1.13
IT-1-distribution-5505(enable) ping 100.1.1.14
IT-1-distribution-5505(enable) ping 100.1.1.15
. . .
IT-1-distribution-5505(enable) ping 100.1.1.36
IT-1-distribution-5505(enable) ping 100.1.1.37
```

NOTE: The first ping packet may fail because the device does not have the MAC address of the destination device. The first ping packet will prompt the device to ARP for the hardware address. Issuing the ping *command again should result in no packets lost.*

Table 4-8

CPI switch IP address list

Switch Name	IP Address
IT-1-dist-5505	100.1.1.11
IT-2-access-2926	100.1.1.12
IT-3-access-1900	100.1.1.13
IT-4-access-1900	100.1.1.14
IT-5-access-1900	100.1.1.15
RD-1-dist-5505	100.1.1.16
RD-2-access-2926	100.1.1.17
RD-3-access-1900	100.1.1.18
RD-4-access-1900	100.1.1.19
RD-5-access-1900	100.1.1.20
Mfg-1-dist-5505	100.1.1.21
Mfg-2-access-2926	100.1.1.22
Mfg-3-access-1900	100.1.1.23
Mfg-4-access-1900	100.1.1.24
Mfg-5-access-1900	100.1.1.25
SR-1-dist-5505	100.1.1.26
SR-2-access-2926	100.1.1.27
SR-3-access-1900	100.1.1.28
SR-4-access-1900	100.1.1.29
SR-5-access-1900	100.1.1.30
Admin-1-dist-5505	100.1.1.31
Admin-2-access-2926	100.1.1.32
Admin-3-access-1900	100.1.1.33
Admin-4-access-1900	100.1.1.34
Admin-5-access-1900	100.1.1.35
Backbone-1-core-6506	100.1.1.36
Backbone-2-core-6506	100.1.1.37

If you are lacking in connectivity, you may try issuing the pings from another device.

If problems persist, reverify your configuration. You should use the `show port` Set Command or `show interface` IOS command.

Case Study Summary

This case study has taken our network design from a rough network design with product selection to a working network with IP connectivity for management through the network.

To get to this point, we took the following steps:

■ Define the building blocks of the campus network.

■ Select the products to implement the building blocks.

■ Define the interface media types in the network.

■ Configure the physical layer operation of the interfaces.

■ Define passwords for the network devices.

■ Give names to the devices and their ports.

■ Define and configure IP addresses for all the devices.

■ Verify the connections and IP connectivity.

The next step in building this network is to define the operation and configuration of Layer 2 features. This will be covered in Chapter 5.

At this point, you should have a good foundation of how to connect together your campus network at the physical layer.

Questions

1. What is the maximum Ethernet frame size?

   a. 1024B
   b. 4500B
   c. 1500B
   d. 1518B

2. What is the transmission rate of 10BaseTx?

   a. 10MBps
   b. 10Mbps
   c. 100MBps
   d. 100Mbps

3. What type of cable is used for 1000BaseFx?

   a. fiber-optic
   b. unshielded twisted pair
   c. coax
   d. twinax

4. How many bidirectional communications channels are there in 10Base2?

   a. 1
   b. 2
   c. 5
   d. 10

5. What is the approximate average utilization of a shared Ethernet with 100 devices that are always ready to transmit?

   a. 10%
   b. 30%
   c. 80%
   d. 100%

6. How many fiber strands are needed for one 10BaseFx link?

   a. 1
   b. 2
   c. 4
   d. 10

7. Collisions _____ occur on a half duplex 100BaseT link.

   a. can
   b. often
   c. always
   d. never

8. Collisions _____ occur on a full duplex 100BaseT link.

   a. can
   b. often
   c. always
   d. never

9. When two transmitting Ethernet stations sense a collision, they

   a. stop and wait for the other to transmit
   b. continue transmitting
   c. continue transmitting until one stops
   d. stop transmitting and wait a random time period until retransmission

10. When an Ethernet station encounters a collision while retransmitting a packet after a collision, it

    a. tries harder
    b. stops transmitting
    c. waits to get a signal from the Ethernet to retransmit
    d. doubles the average random wait time before retransmission

11. Ethernet has a _____ topology

    a. star
    b. point-to-point
    c. bus
    d. crossbar fabric

12. Cisco switches use which of the following for administrative access security?

    a. firewall
    b. license server
    c. password
    d. none of the above

13. How many access levels does a Cisco switch have?

    a. 1
    b. 2
    c. 4
    d. 7

14. While in _____ mode, you can monitor Ethernet interfaces.

    a. access
    b. enable
    c. access and enable
    d. none of the above

15. While in _____ mode, you can configure Ethernet interfaces.

    a. access
    b. enable
    c. access and enable
    d. none of the above

16. Ping gives you the following information.

    a. number of packets sent from the pinging device
    b. average round-trip times for successful ping request/replies
    c. both a and b
    d. none of the above

17. Ethernet Auto-negotiation can set the following on a 100BaseT link.

    a. port speed only
    b. duplex mode only
    c. port speed and duplex mode
    d. port speed, duplex, and packet rate

18. You must use a _____ cable to connect two switches via 10BaseT.

    a. straight
    b. crossover
    c. null modem
    d. none of the above

19. You must use a _____ cable to connect a switch and a PC via 10BaseT.

    a. straight
    b. crossover
    c. null modem
    d. none of the above

20. You must use a _____ cable to connect a switch and router via 10BaseT.

    a. straight
    b. crossover
    c. null modem
    d. none of the above

Answers

1. What is the maximum Ethernet frame size?

   d. 1518B

2. What is the transmission rate of 10BaseTx?

   b. 10Mbps

   The 10 in 10BaseTx refers to the transmission rate in Mbits/second.

3. What type of cable is used for 1000BaseFx?

   a. fiber-optic

   The Fx in 1000BaseFx refers to the Ethernet media type. Fx is a fiber-optic interface.

4. How many bidirectional communications channels are there in 10Base2?

   a. 1

   "Base" in 10Base2 means there is only one communications channel in the link.

5. What is the approximate average utilization of a shared Ethernet with 100 devices that are always ready to transmit?

   b. 30%

   The theoretical maximum throughput of a shared Ethernet with many talkative devices is about 30% of the transmission rate.

6. How many fiber strands are needed for one 10BaseFx link?

   b. 2

   Two fibers strands are needed. One strand is needed for each of the bidirectional links in an Ethernet connection.

7. Collisions _____ occur on a half duplex 100BaseT link.

   a. can

   A half duplex Ethernet 100BaseT link has the potential for collisions, but they will only occur if both hosts on the link try to communicate at the same time.

8. Collisions _____ occur on a full duplex 100BaseT link.

   d. Never

   In a full duplex Ethernet link, no chance exists that a collision can occur because both stations on the Ethernet link can send and receive at the same time.

9. When two transmitting Ethernet stations sense a collision, they

   d. stop transmitting and wait a random time period until retransmission

   This behavior describes the Collision Detection (CD) capability of CSMA/CD.

10. When an Ethernet station encounters a collisions while retransmitting a packet after a collision, it

    d. doubles the average random wait time before retransmission.

    This describes the exponential backoff behavior of Ethernet. Ethernet is Carrier Sense Multiple Access with Collision Detect and exponential backoff.

11. Ethernet has a _____ topology

    c. bus

    Ethernet is a bus topology. Each host has equal access to the common communications medium, much like a two-way radio and a radio frequency.

12. Cisco switches use which of the following for administrative access security?

    c. password

13. How many administrative access levels does a Cisco switch have?

    b. 2

    A Cisco switch has two administrative access levels—access mode and enable mode. Access mode has basic interface and table monitoring capability, whereas the enable mode has full administrative capability to configure the device.

14. While in _____ mode, you can monitor Ethernet interfaces.

    c. access and enable

    Both access and enable modes give the user the ability to monitor Ethernet interfaces.

15. While in _____ mode, you can configure Ethernet interfaces.

    b. enable

    Only enable mode gives the user the ability to configure device interfaces.

16. PING gives you the following information.

    c. both a and b

    Ping returns the number of packets sent, the number of packets received, and the round trip times for all packets in milliseconds.

17. Ethernet auto-negotiation can set the following on a 100BaseT link.

    c. port speed and duplex mode

    Both the transmission rate and the duplex mode can be automatically set using auto-negotiation. The packet rate is not set with Ethernet auto-negotiation.

18. You must use a _____ cable to connect two switches via 10BaseT.

    b. crossover

    When connecting two twisted pair Ethernet interfaces of the same type (host/straight to host/straight or hub/cross to hub/cross), you must use an Ethernet crossover cable to properly connect the transmit and receive signals of the interfaces.

19. You must use a _____ cable to connect a switch and a PC via 10BaseT.

    a. straight

    When connecting two twisted pair Ethernet interfaces of different types (host/straight to hub/cross), you must use an Ethernet straight cable. A switch has hub interfaces and a PC has host interfaces.

20. You must use a _____ cable to connect a switch and router via 10BaseT.

    a. straight

    When connecting two twisted pair Ethernet interfaces of different types (host/straight to hub/cross), you must use an Ethernet straight cable. In most cases, a standalone router interface has a host Ethernet interface. However, in most cases, a switch with routing functions has hub ports.

Layer 2
Configuration

In the previous chapter, we covered how to initially setup a Cisco multilayer switch. We also laid the framework for understanding the packet formats for Ethernet, IP, TCP, and UDP. This chapter will concentrate on the switch block. We will discuss Layer 2 network configuration of the broadcast domains, operation and configuration of multilayer switch features, and Layer 2 optimization.

In this chapter, we will cover the following topics.

- VLAN operation
- Static and Dynamic VLAN configuration
- VLAN trunking
- *VLAN Trunking Protocol* (VTP)
- 802.1q tagging
- ISL tagging
- 802.1q and ISL auto-negotiation
- VLAN trunk configuration
- Spanning Tree operation
- Spanning Tree convergence
- Spanning Tree over VLANs
- Spanning Tree optimization features
- Link aggregation

Objectives Covered in the Chapter

This chapter will cover the following objectives:

- The implementation of workgroups using *Virtual LANs* (VLANs)
- How to design a VLAN
- How to connect the same VLAN in separate parts of the campus network
- How to eliminate bridge loops with the *Spanning Tree Protocol* (STP)
- How to optimize STP for your campus network

In Chapter 2, "Multilayer Switching Network Design Basics," we discussed the problems with scaling broadcast domains to include a large number of hosts. We discovered that topologically distant hosts cannot be included in the same broadcast domain without increasing the impact of broadcast storms.

This chapter will provide a solution to this problem. The answer is *Virtual LANs* (VLANs). VLANs, when designed properly, provide the ability to group hosts together to form workgroups that have a common set of features, functions, and services. Access to services can be managed more efficiently without being bound to a geographical location or topology. This level of abstraction provides the network architect and administrator with a powerful set of tools to build highly efficient and effective networks.

We also discussed in Chapter 2 the detrimental effects of bridging loops and that *Spanning Tree Protocol* (STP) eliminates the occurrence of these bridging loops. This chapter will describe the elegant operation of STP. Specifically, we will explore how it works to eliminate the chance of a bridging loop, which can bring a broadcast domain to a halt.

After understanding the operation of STP, we will discuss some of the inherent disadvantages of STP and how to reduce the effects of these disadvantages by optimizing the configuration of STP in your network.

This chapter will equip you with the ability to design a solid Layer 2 network to implement the access layer of your switch block. This knowledge will help you optimize the host concentration layer of your campus network.

This chapter will close by providing you with a case study of a network that should implement VLANs and STP. This case study will show you how to apply the principles covered in this chapter to a practical network design and configuration problem.

Common Workgroups with Virtual LANs (VLANs)

In Chapter 2, we covered the significance of proper broadcast domain design through switch blocks. At one time, the only way to configure such a network was to connect Layer 2 devices together to form the broadcast domain (see Figure 5-1). The physical collection of Layer 2 devices was also

Figure 5-1
Classical broadcast
domain

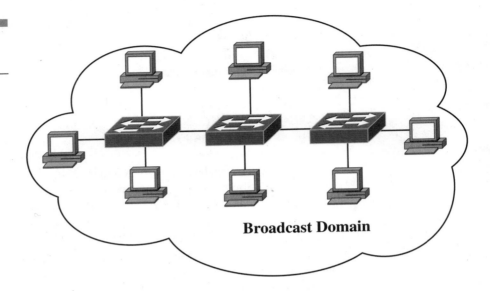

Broadcast Domain

the broadcast domain. With modern broadcast domains, this topological dependence (that is, physical adjacency) is no longer a limitation.

Modern broadcast domains make use of a concept known as *Virtual LANs* (VLANs) (see Figure 5-2). With VLAN-enabled Layer 2 switches, each switch or group of switches can now have multiple VLANs. This enables the network designer and administrator to group hosts together logically instead of geographically. Logical grouping allows for more control and flexibility to the network administrator to design and maintain a network by function instead of topology.

Virtual LANs (VLANs) Overview

VLANs have a number of favorable characteristics:

- Configurable broadcast domains
- Logical groupings instead of geographical groupings
- Security configuration
- Load balancing over multiple paths
- Problem containment

■■■ ■■ ■■ ■

Figure 5-2
Broadcast domains
defined by VLANs

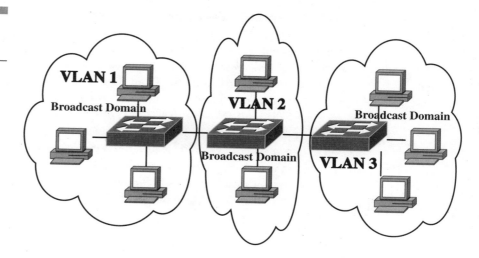

The concept of broadcast domains is covered in previous chapters. In a broadcast domain, all devices can see the broadcast packets being sent by any device. Broadcasting is a necessary part of networking, as we will see later in the book. The problem with broadcast domains is that they don't scale very well.

However, broadcasting isn't the only necessary feature of a modern network. Today's networking workgroups are becoming less based on physical adjacency and more based on logical grouping. In other words, the network must have a way to include distant devices in the same broadcast domain.

The simple answer to this is to make the campus network one large broadcast domain. This may work in very small networks, but not in large, campus area networks. Broadcast storms can consume a significant chunk of bandwidth, affecting performance and efficiency. Virtual LANs provide a way to group hosts into the same broadcast domain in a scalable manner regardless of their geographical location.

After the network is divided into several logical broadcast domains, the domains are connected by a routing function. This routing function can provide an opportunity to enable security features such as packet filtering and access lists.

Normally, redundant links would create a problem for the network. Because the broadcast domains are connected with Layer 3 switching functions, Layer 3 routing protocols can be used to manage traffic across the redundant links without causing routing loops. Depending on the routing protocol, the traffic can be load balanced over the links.

In a conventional network, dividing the broadcast domains into smaller groups is difficult. Now, with VLANs, broadcast domains can be reduced in size to contain problems. Typically, broadcast domains propagate problems such as over-talkative devices and bridging loops. If the broadcast domains are large, a large number of network hosts are affected by the problem. With a smaller number of hosts for each broadcast domain, problems can be contained to a reduced broadcast domain, which in turn affects a smaller number of hosts.

VLAN Design

The design and sizing of a VLAN can be based on the following:

- IP addressing scheme employed
- Number of devices to be placed in the VLAN
- Physical location of the devices to be grouped together

The IP addressing scheme can be a constraint on the number hosts that can be placed in a VLAN. We will cover IP addressing in Chapter 6, "Unicast Layer 3 Configuration," but suffice it to say that the maximum size of the IP subnet is determined by how the IP addressing is set up.

Sometimes the hosts to be placed in a VLAN are in relatively distant locations on the network. At other times, hosts in a VLAN are all on the same floor or in the same building. The location of the hosts to be placed on a common VLAN will determine if the VLANs will be placed into one of the following types of VLANs:

- End-to-End VLANs—(80/20 rule)
- Local VLANs—(20/80 rule)

End-to-end VLANs consist of hosts that are geographically distant. The path between two hosts in an end-to-end VLAN may cross several switches. The rule of thumb for designing end-to-end VLANs is to make sure that 80% of the traffic remains in the VLAN and only 20% of the traffic goes outside of it. This rule helps optimize the usage of the resources used to form the VLAN.

Hosts on a local VLAN are geographically close. They could all be connected to the same switch or the same group of switches on a particular floor or a building. Typically, the traffic patterns in a local VLAN follow the new 20/80 rule: 20% of the traffic remains on the VLAN and 80% of the traffic leaves the VLAN. Local VLANs are typically easier to maintain and manage due to the simplicity of the configuration.

Creating a VLAN

A VLAN can be created by grouping hosts together by switch port or by MAC address. VLANs grouped by switch port are called Static VLANs (see Figure 5-3), whereas VLANs grouped by MAC address are called Dynamic VLANs.

Static VLANs are called static because the devices connected to a particular port will always be members of a particular VLAN. This makes for a simple configuration. You do not need to track the MAC address for this type of VLAN. The disadvantage is that if a host is moved to a different port on a switch, the network must be reconfigured to incorporate the new port into the VLAN.

Figure 5-3
Static VLAN
architecture

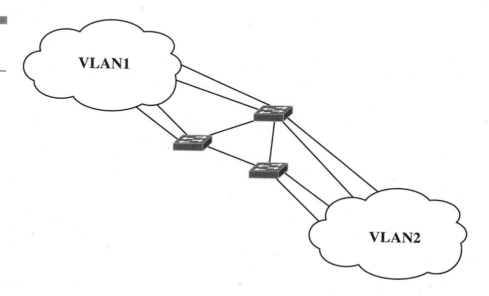

With static VLANs, ports can be grouped together into a broadcast domain. The host doesn't have to know that it is in a VLAN. The network handles the grouping of hosts by port. As with any VLAN (or LAN), interconnection of static VLANs must be by a Layer 3 forwarding device.

The performance of Static VLANs is very good. The host and the network do not interact to define its VLAN. The switch simply follows simple groupings of ports to VLANs. The VLAN grouping function is performed in hardware to maximize the performance.

The configuration of Static VLANs is very simple, easy to manage and maintain. It must be assumed that moves and changes within a network are infrequent to reduce the manual configuration of the Static VLAN.

With Dynamic VLANs, VLAN assignment is based on a host's MAC address (see Figure 5-4). If the host is to move to a different port, the host is still a member of the same VLAN. The disadvantage with Dynamic VLANs is the amount of configuration that must be done to place all hosts into a VLAN. Configuration of Dynamic VLANs is done through Cisco-Works 2000 or *CiscoWorks for Switched Internetworks* (CWSI). When a new host wants to join a VLAN, the switch must query a database to find out to which VLAN the host belongs.

Configuration of Dynamic VLANs is beyond the scope of this book. Please refer to the CiscoWorks 2000 or *CiscoWorks for Switched Internetworks* (CWSI) documentation for more information.

Figure 5-4
Dynamic VLAN
architecture

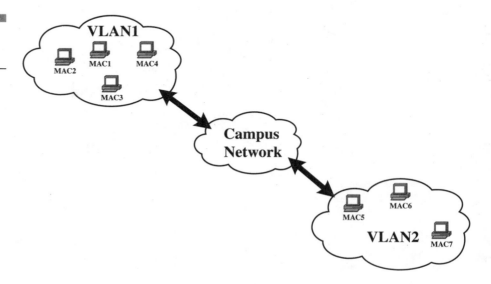

Configuring Static VLANs

You can use a couple of different methods to configure a static VLAN.

Set Commands   To create a Static VLAN, you would use the following Set Command:

```
Switch(enable) set vlan vlan_num mod_num/port_list
```

To create a VLAN numbered 101 that encompasses ports 1–4 on module 2, use the following command:

```
Switch(enable) set vlan 101 2/1-4
```

Cisco IOS   Creating a static VLAN using Cisco IOS is very similar, but requires a two-step process.

First, you must create the VLAN:

```
Switch(config)# vlan vlan_num
```

Next, you must place the desired interface into the defined VLAN:

```
Switch(config)# interface interface
Switch(config-if)# vlan-membership static vlan_num
```

VLAN Link Types

A VLAN has two types of links: access links and trunk links. Access links are links that carry the traffic of one VLAN. Trunk links can carry the traffic of many VLANs.

Access links are simple to implement, and the packets that cross them do not require special labeling or tagging to denote the VLAN to which the packets belong. Packet tagging is not needed because it can be assumed that all the packets crossing the access link are from one particular VLAN. The VLAN crossing an access link is known as the native VLAN (see Figure 5-5).

Trunk links can carry packets from multiple VLANs (see Figure 5-6); therefore, trunk links are used to connect switches to switches or switches to routers. To distinguish to what VLANs the packets belong, the packets

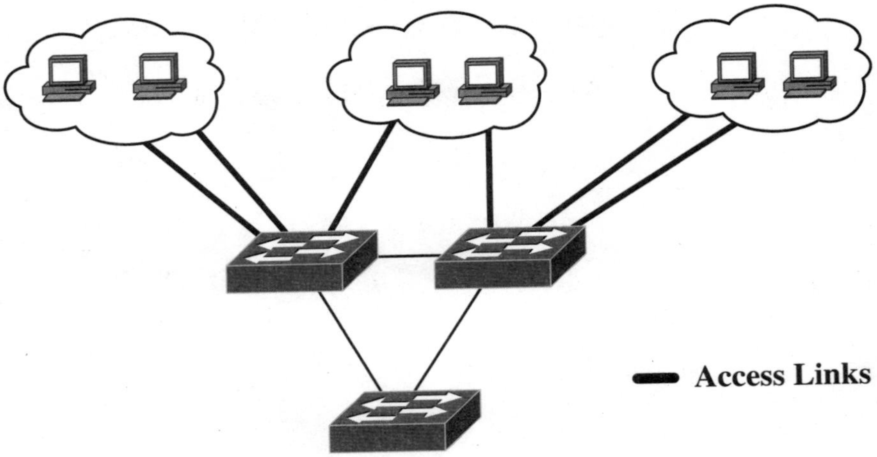

Figure 5-5
VLAN access links

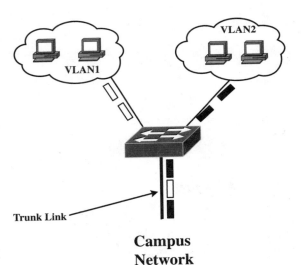

Access Links

Figure 5-6
VLAN trunk links

VLAN2

VLAN1

Trunk Link

**Campus
Network**

must be labeled or tagged. Packets can be tagged by one of two methods—
Cisco *Inter Switch Link* (ISL) or IEEE 802.1q standard. The following sections cover Cisco ISL and IEEE 802.1q tagging.

VLAN trunk links are supported on Fast Ethernet and Gigabit Ethernet links.

Cisco Inter Switch Link (ISL) Tagging

Inter Switch Link (ISL) tagging is a Cisco proprietary protocol for VLAN tagging between Cisco switches. This is the default method for VLAN tagging in Cisco products.

ISL encapsulates an Ethernet frame with a 26-byte header that includes a 10-bit VLAN ID. A four-byte CRC trailer is appended to the Ethernet frame to facilitate error checking. This header and trailer is added before forwarding any packet from an access link to a trunk link and is removed before forwarding a packet from a trunk link to an access link. The header remains intact when forwarding a packet from a trunk link to another trunk link.

IEEE 802.1q Tagging

IEEE 802.1q is a standards-based method of tagging packets with VLAN ID information. This method is interoperable with other devices that are compatible with the standard.

The IEEE 802.1q information is embedded in the standard Ethernet header. It includes a two-byte field called the *tag protocol identifier* (TPID), which indicates that the Ethernet frame is encoded with 802.1q information. The header also includes a two-byte *tag control information* (TCI) field.

The TCI field is made up of a three-bit user priority field, a one-bit canonical format indicator, and a 12-bit *VLAN identifier* (VID).

VLAN Tagging Method Negotiation

Cisco implements *Dynamic Trunking Protocol* (DTP) to determine which method of VLAN tagging is to be used on a trunk link. It supports the negotiation between two trunking ports to decide whether to use ISL or 802.1q tagging.

During dynamic trunk negotiation, the Spanning Tree Protocol is disabled. The Spanning Tree Protocol will be covered in detail later in this chapter.

Configuring Trunks

Several different commands may be used to configure a trunk.

Set Commands   To create a trunk using the Set Commands you utilize the `set trunk` command. The options are as follows:

```
Switch(enable) set trunk mod_num/port_num [on | off | desirable |
auto | nonegotiate][vlan_range] [isl | dot1q | dot10 | lane |
negotiate]
```

To create an ISL trunk using ports 1–2 on module 1 for VLANs 1 through 10, use the following command:

```
Switch(enable) set trunk 1/1-2 on 1-10 isl
```

To utilize 802.1q, use the following command:

```
Switch(enable) set trunk 1/1-2 on 1-10 dot1q
```

Cisco IOS   Enabling trunking for Cisco IOS-based devices involves two commands.

First, enable trunking:

```
Switch(config)# interface interface
Switch(config-if)# trunk [on | off | desirable | auto |
nonegotiate]
```

The options are as follows:

- `on`—Enables port trunk mode.
- `off`—Disables port trunk mode.
- `desirable`—Enables trunking if available on connected device. The port negotiates to a trunk port if the connected device is either in the On, Desirable, or Auto state. Otherwise, the port becomes a non-trunk port.
- `auto`—Enables trunking only if the connected device has the trunk state set to On or Desirable.
- `nonegotiate`—Enables port trunk mode and disables trunk negotiation with connected device.

Next, you can optionally specify the VLANs known by the trunk.

```
Switch(config-if)# trunk-vlan vlan-list
```

Using the previous example:

```
Switch(config-if)# trunk on
Switch(config-if)# trunk-vlan 1-10
```

VLAN Trunk Protocol (VTP)

The implementation of VLANs throughout the campus network is tedious and difficult to correctly configure. If this situation is complicated with multiple changes in the VLAN configuration, keeping up with the campus network configurations could overwhelm network administration staff.

To help alleviate this problem, Cisco developed a *VLAN Trunk Protocol* (VTP). VTP makes sure that the VLAN configuration across the campus network is consistent.

VTP provides the following features:

- VLAN configuration consistency across the campus network
- A method for configuring VLANs that cross different media types such as ATM, FDDI, and Ethernet
- A way to track and monitor VLANs
- A way to detect new VLANs added to another switch
- A way to add new VLANs from one switch

VTP is a protocol that allows switches to communicate together to exchange their VLAN information. A VTP management domain bounds this communication. All switches that have the same VTP domain name define the VTP management domain. The following pieces of information are exchanged between switches.

- Management domain name
- Configuration revision number
- Known VLANs with their configuration information

A switch can be configured in secure mode where the VTP management domain requires a password. The password must be configured and identical on all the switches in a VTP management domain. By default, Cisco switches are configured in non-secure mode where no password is required.

The switches use the configuration revision number to determine if the current switch internal database should be changed to reflect the information in the received VTP update. If the configuration revision number of the received VTP update is the same or less than the configuration revision number of the internal database, the update is ignored. Otherwise, the internal VLAN database information is updated.

VTP Modes of Operation   VTP operation has three modes. Switches can be configured to operate in any one of the following three modes:

- Server mode
- Client mode
- Transparent mode

A switch in VTP Server Mode can create, delete, or modify global VLAN information. The switch will update internal information based on received VTP updates and will send VTP updates.

A switch configured to operate in Client mode will receive VTP updates and change internal VLAN information if necessary. The switch in Client Mode cannot create, delete, or modify global VLAN information.

A switch configured to Transparent mode will not listen to VTP updates. The switch will forward these updates on to the trunk ports so other switches will get the information. The switch will not update any internal database information with received VTP updates, nor will it transmit VTP updates (see Figure 5-7). However, the switch can create, delete, and modify VLANs local to that switch.

Adding Switches to a VLAN with VTP   Adding new switches to a VLAN can be tricky. The problem is that you cannot be sure that the current revision number of the switch is lower than that of the network without first clearing the configuration and then power cycling the switch. Clearing the configuration will clear out all VLAN information that may

Figure 5-7
VTP architecture

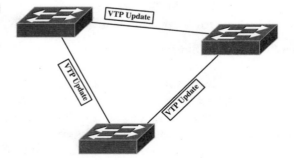

conflict with the network's understanding of the network VLAN configuration. Power-cycling the switch after clearing the configuration will reset the configuration revision number to 0.

Power-cycling the switch after clearing the configuration will ensure that connecting a switch to the network will not disturb the VLAN Trunking Protocol information on the network.

WARNING: *If the configuration is cleared but the configuration revision number is not reset by a power cycle and the configuration revision number is higher than the other switches on the network, all the other switches on the network will delete their VLANs.*

VTP Updates   The VTP update protocol is very simple. A switch requests an update and a server replies back with current known VLAN information and configuration revision number. All the updates are sent on a multicast address over trunk links.

These are the three types of VTP messages:

- Update requests from clients
- Summary updates that are sent from servers every 300 seconds or when a change occurs
- Subset updates from servers that contain VLAN details

All updates include the following data:

- Management domain name
- Configuration revision number
- MD5 digest key
- Update sender ID

If the switch is configured with a different management domain name from the management domain name in the update, the update is ignored. If the received update has a higher configuration revision number than the internal VLAN database configuration revision number, the internal VLAN information is updated with the data in the received VTP update.

The MD5 digest is a key that is associated with a VTP management domain in secure mode. If the key doesn't match the receiving switch key, the update is ignored. The update sender ID is the ID of the switch that is sending the update.

The following information is transmitted on a VTP subset update:

- VLAN ID from ISL or 802.1q
- VTP management domain name
- VTP configuration revision number
- VLAN configuration that includes a maximum transmission unit value for each VLAN
- Frame format

If a switch receives a summary update with a configuration revision number that is higher than the switch's internal configuration revision number, the switch will request a subset update. The switch will update its internal VLAN database information with the information from the subset update from the server.

VTP Version   Two versions of VTP exist. By default, version 1 is configured when VTP is enabled. Version 2 of VTP provides the following features in addition to the features of version 1:

- Support for Token Ring switching VLANs
- Unrecognized Type-Length Value (TLV) support
- Version-dependent transparent mode
- VLAN consistency checks

Version 2 VTP still forwards updates if its TLV is not recognized. Version 2 forwards updates in transparent mode even if the version number doesn't match.

If all switches in a VTP management domain are capable of running VTP version 2, only one switch has to have version 2 turned on. This information will propagate through the network and all the switches will run version 2 of VTP.

VTP Pruning   VTP pruning allows the network of switches in a VTP management domain to only send broadcasts to the ports that are members of the same VLAN. By default, VTP pruning is disabled.

In a network where VTP pruning is disabled, broadcasts and flooded traffic from one VLAN will appear on all trunk links in the VTP management domain. If all switches in the VTP management domain do not have ports that are members of the VLAN, the switches will have to forward unnecessary traffic between trunk ports.

VTP pruning insures that broadcast and flooded traffic is only sent to trunk ports of switches that have ports that are members of a particular VLAN.

Configuring VTP

You may use one of a few different methods to configure VTP.

Set Commands To configure VTP using the Set Commands, use the following command:

```
Switch(enable) set vtp [domain domain_name] [mode {client | server
| transparent}] [passwd passwd] [pruning {enable | disable}] [v2
{enable | disable}]
```

To enable a device as a VTP version 2 client for the SALES domain with pruning enabled to optimize broadcast traffic, try the following command:

```
Switch(enable) set vtp domain SALES mode client pruning enable v2
enable
```

To define which VLANs pruning applies, you may use the following command:

```
Switch(enable) set vtp pruneeligible vlans
```

To allow pruning for VLANs 1 through 10, do the following:

```
Switch(enable) set vtp pruneeligible 1-10
```

Cisco IOS Commands To configure VTP using the Cisco IOS commands, use the following command:

```
Switch(config)# vtp [server | transparent][domain domain-name][trap
{enable | disable}] [password password] [pruning {enable |
disable}]
```

VTP aids in the management VLANs. Let's look at how the Spanning Tree Protocol aids in the management of redundant links.

Managing Redundant Links with the Spanning Tree Protocol

As we discussed in Chapter 2, when more than one Layer 2 switch is connected in a network with redundant links, a potential for Layer 2 switching loops can occur. A Layer 2 switching loop will cause the network to be fully saturated with one packet as it is forwarded between switches as fast as the devices or network can sustain. This brings networks to a halt. The only way to rectify the situation is to shut down the switches or disconnect the redundant links. Redundant links can be very difficult to find in a complex network. *Spanning Tree Protocol* (STP) aids with this problem.

Before discussing STP, let's review a couple of concepts that will come up in the discussion. Recall from Chapter 2 that a Layer 2 switch is identical in operation to a bridge. "Bridge" and "switch" are terms that can be used interchangeably. We will refer to the devices as Layer 2 switches; however, STP is defined in terms of a bridge by convention. A bridge has a bridge table. On a switch, the corresponding table is called a *Content Addressable Memory* (CAM) table. The bridge table, or CAM table, is the mapping of MAC addresses to switch ports. The switch learns where hosts are located by examining the source MAC address in the packets received on each port. The MAC address and port comprise an entry to the CAM table. The switch uses the CAM table information to make Layer 2 switching decisions based on the destination MAC address of packets received on each port (see Figure 5-8).

The Spanning Tree Protocol runs in each Layer 2 switch and senses redundant links in the switched network. When a redundant link is detected, the corresponding ports are shut down, which eliminates the chance for switching loops. It sounds very simple, but the underlying algorithms are complex. The following sections explain how the Spanning Tree Protocol works.

Spanning Tree Operation

Layer 2 switches running the Spanning Tree Protocol send *Bridge Protocol Data Unit* (BPDU) frames out onto the network. These BPDUs contain information necessary for calculating a Spanning Tree graph of the network. This Spanning Tree that each switch calculates is free from any redundant links. All ports that aren't associated with the Spanning Tree aren't allowed to send frames other than BPDUs.

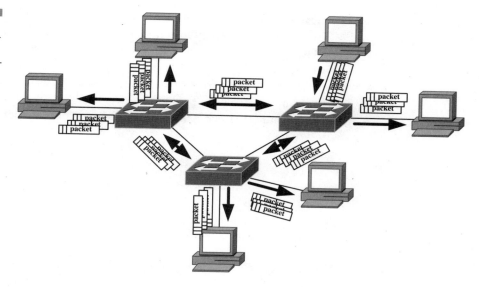

Figure 5-8
Network with a Layer
2 switch loop

The following operations are executed to perform the Spanning Tree algorithm:

- Root Bridge selection
- Root association
- Spanning Tree recalculation

Root Bridge Selection   When the Spanning Tree Protocol starts, a Root Bridge is elected. The election is simple. Each Layer 2 switch has a bridge ID that is formed by a two-byte priority field and a six-byte switch MAC address. The priority field is configurable by the administrator and the MAC address is, of course, fixed. The switch with the lowest bridge ID is elected as the Root Bridge. This Layer 2 switch becomes the root of the Spanning Tree.

Root Association   For Ethernet segments with multiple Layer 2 switches, one of the switches is elected as the Designated Bridge. This Layer 2 switch typically has the fewest number of hops to the Root Bridge. The number of hops from a particular Layer 2 switch to the Root Bridge is defined by the number of Layer 2 switches between the particular switch and the root. Each port that is connected to the Designated Bridge is defined as a designated bridge port.

Each Layer 2 switch in the network defines one port as the root port. This port has the fewest number of hops from the switch to the Root Bridge.

After all these elements are defined, the root ports and designated bridge ports are included in the Spanning Tree. These ports are enabled to forward packets. All other ports not included in the Spanning Tree are not allowed to send or receive data packets.

Note that the Root Bridge forms the root of the Spanning Tree graph of the Layer 2 switch network and the Designated Bridges form the branch nodes of the network (see Figure 5-9).

All ports on the Root Bridge are part of the Spanning Tree unless some of the ports on the Root Bridge are connected together.

The cost of a path to the root is calculated by factoring together the number of hops to the Root Bridge and the bandwidth of the links. A higher bandwidth link translates to a lower cost path.

Spanning Tree Recalculation   The Spanning Tree will be recalculated when a Layer 2 switch is added or removed from the network or if a link fails. A switch detects these conditions when a BPDU is not received within a certain amount of time. A timer called the maximum age timer defines this length of time. When the Layer 2 switch updates its stored information, the maximum age timer begins to count down. Every time the switch receives a BPDU that matches its stored information, the maximum age timer is reset.

Figure 5-9
Spanning Tree graph
of the physical
network

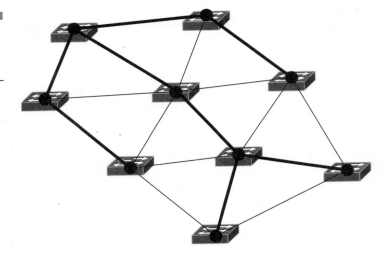

Spanning Tree Convergence

BPDUs are formed by the Layer 2 switches and contain the following information:

- The bridge ID of the assumed Root Bridge
- Root path cost to the assumed Root Bridge
- The bridge ID of the Layer 2 switch sending the BPDU

A Layer 2 switch receives BPDUs and compares the information in the packet with its understanding of the root and how far away it is. If the switch receives a BPDU with a lower bridge ID for the Root Bridge or a lower root path cost to the root, the Layer 2 switch's Spanning Tree information is updated.

Eventually, all the Layer 2 switches in the network will have the same information. This is called convergence.

The selection of the Designated Bridge works in a similar fashion. Layer 2 switches compare the information in the received BPDU with their stored information. If the stored root path cost is less than the root path cost in the received BPDU, the Layer 2 switch is the Designated Bridge.

The Root Bridge sends hello packets every two seconds by default. This frequency is controlled by a Hello Timer which is configurable by the switch administrator. When a Layer 2 switch receives a BPDU, it sends its own BPDU. The Root Bridge also sends the maximum age timer via hello packets. This value is propagated through the other Layer 2 switches in the network. The maximum age timer is configurable, but is typically set to 20 seconds.

Spanning Tree States

Spanning Tree has five port states after powering up the bridging and starting the Spanning Tree algorithm (see Figure 5-10). These states are listed as follows:

- Blocking
- Listening
- Learning

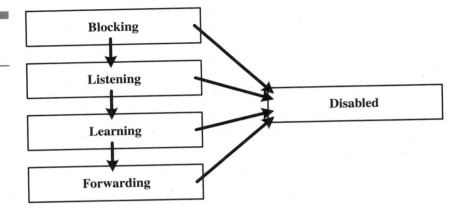

Figure 5-10
Spanning Tree state diagram

- Forwarding
- Disabled

  A port moves through the states as follows:

- Blocking to Listening or to Disabled
- Listening to Learning or to Disabled
- Learning to Forwarding or to Disabled
- Forwarding to Disabled

Power-on Initialization   After all power-up routines are completed, the switch begins by placing all ports in the Blocking state.

Blocking State   In the Blocking state, the port does not participate in frame forwarding. At this point, the switch assumes that it is the root. If no other switches are connected to it, the forwarding delay timer will expire and it will move on to the Listening State. If other switches are connected to this port, the root election process will continue until the forwarding delay timer expires.

The following lists the function of ports in the Blocking state.

- Throw away all data frames received
- Throw away all data frames to be sent out this port
- No addresses are added to its CAM table

- Receive BPDUs
- Do not send BPDUs
- Receive and send responses to network management requests

Listening State   A port enters the Listening state after leaving the Blocking state. The Listening state is similar to the Blocking state except that the port in Listening state sends BPDUs. The following is a list of functions of a port in the Listening state:

- Throw away all data frames received
- Throw away all data frames to be sent out this port
- No addresses are added to its CAM table
- Receive and process BPDUs
- Send BPDUs
- Receive and send responses to network management requests

Learning State   A port enters the Learning state after leaving the Listening state. The Learning state is similar to the Listening state except that in the Learning state, the port updates its CAM table with MAC addresses. The following is a list of functions of a port in the Learning state:

- Throw away all data frames received
- Throw away all data frames to be sent from this port
- Add addresses to the CAM table
- Receive and process BPDUs
- Send BPDUs
- Receive and send responses to network management requests

Forwarding State   A port enters the Forwarding state from the Learning state. In this state, the port forwards packets to and from other ports. The following is a list of functions of a port in the Forwarding state.

- Forward received frames
- Transmit frames from other ports
- Add addresses to the CAM table

- Receive and process BPDUs
- Send BPDUs
- Receive and respond to network management requests

Disabled State   A port can enter the Disabled state from any of the states. The following is a list of functions of a port in the Disabled state:

- Throw away received frames
- Throw away frames from other ports
- Do not update addresses to the CAM table
- Receive BPDUs
- Do not send BPDUs
- Receive and respond to network management requests

Spanning Tree Timers

Three timers are necessary for the operation of Spanning Tree. The following is a discussion of each of the timers. The Spanning Tree timers are as follows:

- Hello timer
- Forward Delay timer
- Maximum Age timer

The Hello timer determines the frequency of the transmission of Hello messages. The Forward Delay timer determines the amount of time a port will stay in the Listening state and Learning state before moving to the Forwarding state.

The Maximum Age timer determines how long the internal Spanning Tree information is kept, which defines how long the switch remains in the Blocking state.

The Root Bridge propagates the values for these timers. The network administrator can configure these values. The default values for the timers are as follows:

- Hello timer—2 seconds
- Maximum Age timer—20 seconds
- Forward Delay timer—15 seconds

These defaults are based on a Hello timer of two seconds and a maximum of seven hops from the Root Bridge. The Root Bridge counts as one hop. The minimum setting for the Forward Delay timer is four seconds. This defines two as the minimum number of hops from the Root Bridge to the outside of the network.

Cisco recommends that the number of hops from the Root Bridge to the outside of your network be seven or less. If this is not possible, slowly increase the timer values to stabilize the network. Cisco recommends that the Spanning Tree timers be increased, not decreased, from the default values.

Spanning Tree and VLANs

Using the Spanning Tree protocol over VLANs raises interesting problems relating to scaleability and interoperability. Three solutions are provided for handling different situations:

- IEEE *Common Spanning Tree* (CST)
- Cisco *Per VLAN Spanning Tree* (PVST)
- Cisco *Per VLAN Spanning Tree with CST* (PVST+)

CST is the IEEE solution for running Spanning Tree with VLANs. CST defines that one instance of Spanning Tree must exist for all VLANs implemented throughout the Layer 2 switch network. This instance of Spanning Tree runs on VLAN1.

PVST is a Cisco proprietary solution that handles Spanning Tree over VLANs. PVST runs a separate instance of Spanning Tree for each VLAN. PVST requires that Cisco's *Inter Switch Link* (ISL) run on trunk links between switches.

PVST+ is another Cisco proprietary solution for handling Spanning Tree over VLANs. PVST+ allows CST information to be passed to PVST for interoperating with other vendors Spanning Tree over VLAN implementations.

Common Spanning Tree (CST)   CST is an IEEE-specified method of handling Spanning Tree over VLANs. IEEE specifies that Spanning Tree runs on VLAN1. All Layer 2 switches in the network that contain multiple VLANs form one Spanning Tree graph with one Root Bridge and one set of Designated Bridges.

With this implementation of Spanning Tree over VLANs, the placement of the Root Bridge cannot be optimized to best serve all the VLANs because the topology of the VLANs can differ significantly. Also, all ports of all the Layer 2 switches in the switched network must be a part of the single Spanning Tree implementation. This does not scale well as the network grows larger. Fortunately, only one instance of Spanning Tree exists for all switches in the network. Therefore, the switch processor isn't overly burdened with Spanning Tree operations and the amount of BPDUs is kept to a minimum.

CST can be summarized as follows:

- Minimal amount of BPDU traffic
- Switch processing is kept to a minimum
- Less than optimum placement of the Root Bridge for all VLANs
- Longer convergence times—the Spanning Tree must cover all ports of all switches

Per VLAN Spanning Tree (PVST)   To handle some of the scaleability issues with Common Spanning Tree, Cisco devised *Per VLAN Spanning Tree* (PVST). Here, one instance of Spanning Tree runs on each VLAN. This configuration reduces the amount of convergence time because each of the Spanning Tree graphs that map to each VLAN are smaller than a Spanning Tree graph for the entire network.

The scaleability problem is pushed into a different area with PVST, however. With Cisco Catalyst 2820 and Catalyst 1900 switches, Spanning Tree can only be run on 64 VLANs. Even with this limitation, most networks can operate within this range.

PVST must have ISL enabled on all trunk links in the network.

PVST can be summarized as follows:

- PVST is more scalable than CST for large switched networks.
- PVST has a lower convergence time than that of CST.

- PVST causes a higher processor utilization in switches.
- Where Catalyst 2820s and Catalyst 1900s are used, the number of VLANs must be no greater than 64.

Per VLAN Spanning Tree with CST (PVST+)   *Per VLAN Spanning Tree with CST* (PVST+) allows interoperability with other switches that do not implement PVST as well as switches that do implement it. This allows a connection between Cisco and other vendors' switches in a VLAN environment.

This provides a way for Cisco switches to enable PVST in the presence of CST switches and maintain a network wide STP graph. A PVST+ enabled switch has no special commands for PVST+. The switch simply recognizes both CST and PVST in the network and allows bridging of the information carried by both methods across the network.

IEEE 802.1q must be enabled on the links between the CST network and the PVST network.

Spanning Tree Optimization

The network administrator can do a few things to optimize the operation of Spanning Tree. These items are listed below:

- Specify the Root Bridge
- Modify the port cost
- Modify the Spanning Tree timers
- Optimize the Spanning Tree convergence time through special features

The first three items have been introduced in the above sections. Cisco gives the network administrator the ability to change the Spanning Tree operating parameters to optimize Spanning Tree operation. The last item in the above list, optimizing the Spanning Tree convergence time, is implemented by using an enhanced Spanning Tree operation parameters defined by Cisco.

Specifying the Root Bridge   Recall from the above sections that the Root Bridge is elected by selecting the switch with the lowest Bridge ID.

The Bridge ID is an eight-byte value defined by the bridge priority followed by the switch MAC address. Simply setting a low value for bridge priority selects the Root Bridge. Cisco sets this value to 0x2000 when a switch is set to be the Root Bridge. If more than one switch is defined as the Root Bridge, the switch with the lowest MAC address becomes the Root Bridge.

To configure the Spanning Tree Root Bridge, you use the following Set Command:

```
Switch(enable) set spantree root [secondary] [vlan_list] [dia
network_diameter] [hello hello_time]
```

To configure a device as the Root Bridge, use the following command:

```
Switch(enable) set spantree root
```

Cisco also allows the network administrator to set a switch to be the secondary bridge. A switch configured to be the secondary bridge gets a bridge priority of 0x4000. The secondary bridge would get the Root Bridge designation if there were no operational bridges defined as the Root Bridge.

To configure a device as a secondary Root Bridge, the following command is used:

```
Switch(enable) set spantree root secondary
```

The default value for the bridge priority is 0x8000.

The Root Bridge should be placed near the center of the network so the path costs will be nearly equal for all switches in the same topological layer. This helps optimize the convergence time by reducing the number of hops from the Root Bridge to the most distant Layer 2 switch in the network.

Placement of the Root Bridge has the largest effect on Spanning Tree performance and should be chosen carefully.

Modifying the Port Cost   The port cost is used to find the least cost path to the Layer 2 switch. The path cost is used to define the Designated Bridges on the network. The path cost is the sum of all the port costs for each hop to the Root Bridge.

If the path cost is equal for more than one path, Spanning Tree breaks the tie by choosing the port with the lowest port ID. The port ID can be changed on Cisco switches. This parameter is called the port priority.

To specify the port priority, the following Set Command is used:

```
Switch(enable) set spantree portpri {mod_num/port_num | trcrf}
[priority | trcrf_priority]
```

Or use the following Cisco IOS command:

```
Switch(config-if)# spantree priority priority-value
```

To change the port ID to 10 for port 3 on module 2 using the Set Commands, do the following:

```
Switch(enable) set spantree portpri 2/3 10
```

Cisco recommends that the port ID be changed only in specific instances where network performance is greatly enhanced. This is a rare case. Cisco recommends optimizing your Spanning Tree network by careful placement of the Root Bridge.

The port cost is typically 1000 divided by the media transmission rate in Mbps. This value may be modified on Cisco switches. The higher the bandwidth the lower the port cost. The range of configurable port costs is 1 to 65535.

To change the port cost, use the following Set Command:

```
Switch(enable) set spantree portcost {mod_num/port_num | trcf} cost
```

Or if you are using Cisco IOS:

```
Switch(config-if)# spantree cost cost-value
```

To change the port cost of port 4 on module 2, which is a 100Mbps Fast Ethernet link, from the default value of 10 (1000/100 = 10) to 12, do the following:

```
Switch(enable) set spantree portcost 2/4 12
```

Modifying the Spanning Tree Timers   Three timers are necessary for Spanning Tree stability—Hello, Forward Delay, and Maximum Age timers.

The timers may be modified using the following Set Commands:

```
Switch(enable) set spantree fwddelay delay [vlan]
Switch(enable) set spantree hello interval [vlan]
Switch(enable) set spantree maxage agingtime [vlan]
```

Cisco IOS uses the `spantree-template` command to change the timers.

Note that the timers can be changed on a per VLAN basis.

Optimizing the Spanning Tree Convergence Time Through Special Features Cisco makes three features available to shorten the convergence time of Spanning Tree:

- PortFast
- UplinkFast
- BackboneFast

PortFast is used on ports of switches that have one device connected to them. The idea is that no switch is connected to the port, so including the port in the Spanning Tree graph is not necessary. The fewer ports in the Spanning Tree, the shorter the convergence time.

Using the following Set Command will enable PortFast:

```
Switch(enable) set spantree portfast mod_num/port_num {enable |
disable}
```

The Cisco IOS command for enabling PortFast is not as straightforward.

```
Switch(config-if)# spantree start-forwarding
```

UplinkFast is used on access layer switches that have redundant links into the distribution layer. Typically these connections are the only connections to other switches. Because the distribution layer usually has only two connections for redundancy, a switch with UplinkFast enabled will quickly failover to the redundant link when the link in forwarding state fails. This failover can happen in three to four seconds without waiting on the Maximum Age timer to expire. This greatly reduces the amount of time it takes for Spanning Tree to converge.

The UplinkFast feature is automatically disabled if the switch is the Root Bridge.

To enable UplinkFast, use the following Set Command:

```
Switch(enable) set spantree uplinkfast enable [rate
station_update_rate] [all-protocols {off | on}]
```

To disable:

```
Switch(enable) set spantree uplinkfast disable
```

Cisco IOS uses a similar command:

```
Switch(config)# uplink-fast
```

BackboneFast is a Cisco proprietary Spanning Tree enhancement that changes how switches interact with each other using Spanning Tree. If the BackboneFast feature is enabled in the network, the feature becomes active when the switch receives an inferior BPDU. An inferior BPDU is one that advertises one switch to be the Root Bridge and the Designated Bridge. This indicates that a failure on the path between the Designated Bridge and the Root Bridge has occurred.

Normally the switches ignore inferior BPDUs for the duration of the maximum age timer. Cisco has devised a way to shorten this convergence time by sending a special BPDU called a *root link query PDU* (RLQ PDU) on the blocked ports when an inferior BPDU is received. If an alternate path to the Root Bridge is found, the Maximum Age timer is expired and the ports that can connect to the Root Bridge are moved out of the Blocking State. If no path to the Root Bridge can be found, the Maximum Age timer for the alternate ports are expired.

To enable or disable BackboneFast operation, the following Set Command may be used:

```
Switch(enable) set spantree backbonefast {enable | disable}
```

Cisco IOS does not have a BackboneFast command.

Link Aggregation

In addition to VLANs, another great addition to Layer 2 functionality is the capability of grouping ports together into a single logical link to increase bandwidth. Cisco provides a mechanism to bundle up to four Fast Ethernet or Gigabit Ethernet ports together into one logical link. This is called *Fast*

EtherChannel (FEC) or *Giga EtherChannel* (GEC). In the case of Fast Ethernet, FEC can provide up to 800Mbps of bandwidth for the logical link. The logical link consists of four full duplex Fast Ethernet ports. Three positive characteristics result from this feature:

- Bandwidth scaling
- Fault tolerance
- Load balancing

Fast EtherChannel provides bandwidth scaling by providing one logical link between two switches that is up to four times the maximum bandwidth of one port. Some routing techniques can provide the same performance, but Fast EtherChannel operates at Layer 2, which greatly simplifies the configuration and decreases the forwarding latency.

When one link in a Fast EtherChannel bundle fails, the rest of the links in the bundle still carry traffic. The worst outcome is that the overall bandwidth of the bundle decreases, but the logical link is still operational. This method of fault tolerance requires much less time for recovery. Fault recovery is localized to only the ports that make up the bundle. No convergence time is necessary as in Spanning Tree.

The traffic that flows over the Fast EtherChannel links is equally divided between the links that form the bundle. Therefore, no link will carry more traffic than the other links in the bundle.

Cisco has devised a protocol called *Port Aggregation Protocol* (PAgP) to aid in automating the configuration of Fast EtherChannel links. If PAgP discovers a neighboring switch that is connected by multiple ports, it will automatically configure the switch to put these ports into a Fast EtherChannel bundle.

Here are a few guidelines to consider when configuring Fast EtherChannel links:

- All the ports in the Fast EtherChannel link must be members of the same VLAN or must be trunk ports.
- If the ports in a Fast EtherChannel link are trunk ports, they all must be configured with the same trunk mode and the ports must have same VLAN range.
- All the ports in the Fast EtherChannel link must have the same speed and duplex mode settings.

- Fast EtherChannel links do not work with dynamic VLANs. The VLAN must be the same for all ports in the bundle.
- All ports in the bundle must be enabled for all the links to come up in the bundle.

To enable Fast EtherChannel, use the following Set Command:

```
Switch(enable) set port channel port_list [admin_group]
Switch(enable) set port channel port_list mode {on | off |
desirable | auto} [silent | non-silent]
```

With Cisco IOS, use the following commands to create a virtual port channel interface on the switch:

```
Switch(config)# port-channel mode [on | off | desirable | auto]
Switch(config)# interface port-channel channel_number
```

With Fast EtherChannel enabled, you may specify which ports participate in the channel using the following interface command:

```
Switch(config-if)# channel-group channel_number
```

The channel number may be 1 through 4 and must be the same as specified in the `interface port-channel` command.

Chapter Summary

In this chapter, we covered the following topics:

- VLAN operation
- Static and Dynamic VLAN configuration
- VLAN trunking
- VLAN Trunking Protocol (VTP)
- 802.1q tagging
- ISL tagging
- 802.1q and ISL auto-negotiation
- VLAN trunk configuration

- Spanning Tree operation
- Spanning Tree convergence
- Spanning Tree over VLANs
- Spanning Tree Optimization Features
- Link Aggregation

These topics help you gain an understanding of classical broadcast domains, a foundation of distributed broadcast domains through VLANs, and how to handle multiple VLAN traffic through the campus network using VLAN trunking.

VLAN network configuration through VLAN trunking is cumbersome. The solution is *VLAN Trunking Protocol* (VTP). VTP allows you to make VLAN changes to one switch in the network and have the new VLAN information propagate automatically through to the other switches in the network.

After covering VLAN networking, this chapter introduces you to redundant link management (bridge loop avoidance) through the *Spanning Tree Protocol* (STP). After you learned about STP and its convergent problems, you discovered how to optimize your STP configuration.

Another Layer 2 configuration option called Fast EtherChannel is covered in this chapter. This feature provides bandwidth scaling, fault tolerance, and load balancing.

Coverage of these topics and the discussion of a practical case study equip you with the knowledge to design, configure, and manage your broadcast domains throughout your network. The following chapters will cover how to connect broadcast domains with Layer 3 functionality. These principles will then give you the ability to implement your distribution topology layer design and be well on your way to creating an efficient and feature-rich campus network.

Frequently Asked Questions (FAQ)

Question: Where do I find more information on Cisco VLANs?

Answer: Search www.cisco.com. If you have an account with Cisco, you can create a login for the Cisco Web site based on your account number. Depending on your account type, this may give you access to detailed information on the operation and configuration of VLANs on Cisco multilayer switches.

Question: Where do I find more information on the Spanning Tree Protocol?

Answer: Search the Web for Spanning Tree Protocol. Many good resources are available on STP. Also try www.cisco.com, where you may find Cisco-specific information on STP. Radia Perlman, the creator of the STP protocol, has written a book called *Interconnections* (see the bibliography). The STP protocol operation is covered in great detail in this book.

Question: Is Cisco's STP interoperable with other vendors' products?

Answer: STP is standard, very mature, and has been successfully implemented in multivendor networks. However, some quirky traits may cause problems with certain combinations of vendors. Always make sure that you test and stage multivendor STP before deploying it into your campus network.

Question: Are Cisco VLANs interoperable with other vendor's VLAN implementations?

Answer: If the other vendor complies with 802.1q, the VLANs will probably interoperate across trunk links. Always test the interoperability of VLANs before deploying multivendor VLANs in your campus network.

Question: What happens when I configure ISL on a port that connects to a switch that doesn't support ISL?

Answer: Very bad things. If the switch connected to a port with ISL enabled doesn't support ISL, it will see invalid Ethernet packets. In this case, it could see oversized (giant) packets. Some networking equipment will actually shut down a port after seeing large amounts of invalid packets. Regardless, the switch wouldn't know what to do with the Ethernet packets encapsulated with ISL. At best, the result would be lost packets. Be careful with ISL configuration.

Question: Can I operate my network without STP?

Answer: Yes, but be very careful that loops do not exist in your broadcast domains. Realize that inadvertently creating a loop when making topological changes in your network could render your broadcast domain useless. Finding loops after they are created is not always easy. The advantage to not running STP is marginal performance increase.

Case Study

Objective: The objective in this case study is to create a scaleable and optimum Layer 2 configuration. This configuration must provide good performance and minimize possible network bottlenecks. This case study builds on the CPI network discussed in the previous chapters.

The following constraints are given to help you design the network:

■ 10 buildings are scattered across 128 acres.

■ Five well-defined departments exist: Research and Development, Shipping/Receiving, Administration, Manufacturing, and Information Technology.

■ Each of the departments is fairly localized, with the following exceptions:

   ▪ Administration is scattered throughout the campus.

   ▪ Research and Development is scattered through the Manufacturing areas.

■ Information Technology houses the centralized storage and processing farms.

Figure 5-11 will help you determine the location of the various departments.

Figure 5-12 shows a current network design and topology.

At this point, you do not need to be concerned about how the various departments communicate together. This problem will be tackled at a later time. Assume that all communications will be intradepartmental.

Required Information

Implementation of this configuration requires knowledge of the following:

■ VLAN implementation

■ Spanning Tree configuration and optimization

■ Link Aggregation

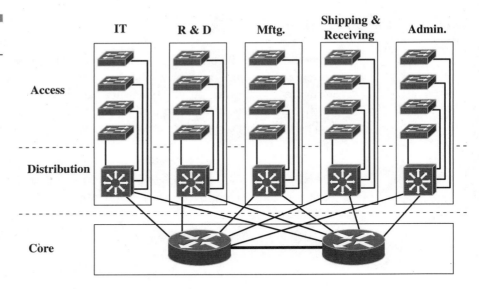

Figure 5-11
CPI department map

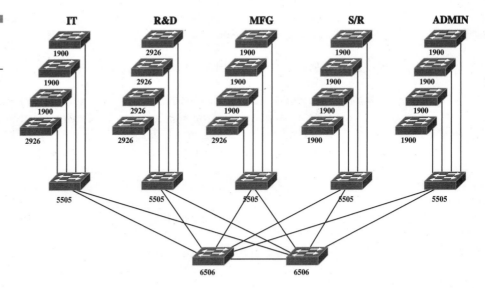

Figure 5-12
Current CPI network topology

Approach

To achieve the objectives, the following items must be completed in sequential order:

1. Define which hosts are in which VLAN
2. Determine the Trunking Links and the VLAN tagging method
3. Evaluate and implement trunk link negotiation and *VLAN Trunking Protocol* (VTP)
4. Determine how Spanning Tree will be implemented
5. Optimize Spanning Tree convergence
6. Evaluate and implement link aggregation

VLAN Evaluation and Implementation

CPI has five departments. Therefore, five VLANs should be implemented. The five departments are Shipping/Receiving, Administration, Research and Development, Manufacturing, and Information Technologies.

Administration is scattered throughout the campus—Research and Development is scattered throughout the Manufacturing areas. The other departments, Information Technologies, Manufacturing, and Shipping/Receiving, are in their own buildings.

The first thing to do is to place the Catalyst 1900 and Catalyst 2926 switches appropriately through the campus. Table 5-1 shows the distribution of hosts through the campus buildings.

With this information, we can distribute the switches throughout the buildings. The buildings are small enough to have the switches in one central closet in each building, so all the hosts can be connected to the access switches with twisted pair cable. The following rules dictate how the switches are placed.

■ If a department has enough hosts to fill half the ports on a switch in a particular building, that switch is dedicated to that department.

■ If the number of hosts for a department in a building is less than half the number of ports on a switch, the department will be put on a switch that belongs to another switch block.

Table 5-1

Distribution of
hosts throughout
CPI campus

Building	#S/R	#IT	#Mfg	#Admin	#R&D
1	15	0	0	5	0
2	0	0	15	5	15
3	0	0	15	5	15
4	15	0	0	5	0
5	0	0	0	0	30
6	0	30	0	5	0
7	0	30	0	5	0
8	0	0	0	50	0
9	20	0	0	15	0
10	0	0	25	5	0

■ The distribution switches go in the building with the most access switches from its switch block.

■ The two core switches were placed in the two IT buildings.

Table 5-2 lists the switches by name and in which building they are to be placed.

Next, we define a VLAN for the localized departments. Table 5-3 lists the number of ports for each VLAN for each switch. Note that we are using static VLANs because we assume that hosts will not move often.

Each of the VLANs need an ID. Table 5-4 lists the VLAN IDs for each VLAN.

Most of the access switch VLAN configuration is fairly straightforward because they are dedicated to one VLAN. The other switches have their ports split over several VLANs.

Here are the VLAN configurations for each of the switches.

First, the IT devices:

```
[IT-2-access-2926]
IT-2-access-2926(enable) set vlan 5 2/1-24
[IT-3-access-1900]
IT-3-access-1900(config)# interface 0/1
```

Table 5-2

CPI campus switch placement

Switch Name	Building
IT-1-dist-5505	6
IT-2-access-2926	6
IT-3-access-1900	6
IT-4-access-1900	7
IT-5-access-1900	7
RD-1-dist-5505	5
RD-2-access-2926	5
RD-3-access-2926	5
RD-4-access-2926	3
RD-5-access-2926	2
Mfg-1-dist-5505	10
Mfg-2-access-2926	2
Mfg-3-access-1900	3
Mfg-4-access-1900	10
Mfg-5-access-1900	10
SR-1-dist-5505	9
SR-2-access-1900	1
SR-3-access-1900	4
SR-4-access-1900	9
SR-5-access-1900	9
Admin-1-dist-5505	8
Admin-2-access-1900	8
Admin-3-access-1900	8
Admin-4-access-1900	8
Admin-5-access-1900	9
Backbone-1-core-6506	6
Backbone-2-core-6506	7

Table 5-3

VLAN port
distribution

Switch Name	R&D VLAN	Mfg VLAN	S/R VLAN	Admin VLAN	IT VLAN
IT-2-access-2926	–	–	–	–	All
IT-3-access-1900	–	–	–	5 ports	15 ports
IT-4-access-1900	–	–	–	–	All
IT-5-access-1900	–	–	–	5 ports	15 ports
RD-2-access-2926	All	–	–	–	–
RD-3-access-2926	All	–	–	–	–
RD-4-access-2926	All	–	–	–	–
RD-5-access-2926	All	–	–	–	–
Mfg-2-access-2926	–	15 ports	–	5 ports	–
Mfg-3-access-1900	–	15 ports	–	5 ports	–
Mfg-4-access-1900	–	All	–	–	–
Mfg-5-access-1900	–	15 ports	–	5 ports	–
SR-2-access-1900	–	–	15 ports	5 ports	–
SR-3-access-1900	–	–	15 ports	5 ports	–
SR-4-access-1900	–	–	All	–	–
SR-5-access-1900	–	–	All	–	–
Admin-2-access-1900	–	–	–	All	–
Admin-3-access-1900	–	–	–	All	–
Admin-4-access-1900	–	–	–	All	–
Admin-5-access-1900	–	–	–	All	–

```
IT-3-access-1900(config-if)# vlan 5
IT-3-access-1900(config)# interface 0/2
IT-3-access-1900(config-if)# vlan 5
. . .
IT-3-access-1900(config)# interface 0/14
IT-3-access-1900(config-if)# vlan 5
IT-3-access-1900(config)# interface 0/15
IT-3-access-1900(config-if)# vlan 5
```

Table 5-4

VLAN IDs

VLAN	VLAN ID
R&D	1
Mfg	2
SR	3
Admin	4
IT	5

```
IT-3-access-1900(config)# interface 0/16
IT-3-access-1900(config-if)# vlan 4
IT-3-access-1900(config)# interface 0/17
IT-3-access-1900(config-if)# vlan 4
. . .
IT-3-access-1900(config)# interface 0/19
IT-3-access-1900(config-if)# vlan 4
IT-3-access-1900(config)# interface 0/20
IT-3-access-1900(config-if)# vlan 4
[IT-4-access-1900]
IT-4-access-1900(config)# interface 0/1
IT-4-access-1900(config-if)# vlan 5
IT-4-access-1900(config)# interface 0/2
IT-4-access-1900(config-if)# vlan 5
. . .
IT-4-access-1900(config)# interface 0/23
IT-4-access-1900(config-if)# vlan 5
IT-4-access-1900(config)# interface 0/24
IT-4-access-1900(config-if)# vlan 5
[IT-5-access-1900]
IT-5-access-1900(config)# interface 0/1
IT-5-access-1900(config-if)# vlan 5
IT-5-access-1900(config)# interface 0/2
IT-5-access-1900(config-if)# vlan 5
. . .
IT-5-access-1900(config)# interface 0/14
IT-5-access-1900(config-if)# vlan 5
IT-5-access-1900(config)# interface 0/15
IT-5-access-1900(config-if)# vlan 5

IT-5-access-1900(config)# interface 0/16
IT-5-access-1900(config-if)# vlan 4
IT-5-access-1900(config)# interface 0/17
IT-5-access-1900(config-if)# vlan 4
. . .
IT-5-access-1900(config)# interface 0/19
IT-5-access-1900(config-if)# vlan 4
IT-5-access-1900(config)# interface 0/20
IT-5-access-1900(config-if)# vlan 4
```

Next, the RD devices:

```
[RD-2-access-2926]
RD-2-access-2926(enable) set vlan 1 2/1-24
[RD-3-access-2926]
RD-3-access-2926(enable) set vlan 1 2/1-24
[RD-4-access-2926]
RD-4-access-2926(enable) set vlan 1 2/1-24
[RD-5-access-2926]
RD-5-access-2926(enable) set vlan 1 2/1-24
```

Next, the Mfg devices:

```
[Mfg-2-access-2926]
Mfg-2-access-2926(enable) set vlan 2 2/1-15
Mfg-2-access-2926(enable) set vlan 4 2/16-20
[Mfg-3-access-1900]
Mfg-3-access-1900(config)# interface 0/1
Mfg-3-access-1900(config-if)# vlan 2
Mfg-3-access-1900(config)# interface 0/2
Mfg-3-access-1900(config-if)# vlan 2
. . .
Mfg-3-access-1900(config)# interface 0/14
Mfg-3-access-1900(config-if)# vlan 2
Mfg-3-access-1900(config)# interface 0/15
Mfg-3-access-1900(config-if)# vlan 2

Mfg-3-access-1900(config)# interface 0/16
Mfg-3-access-1900(config-if)# vlan 4
Mfg-3-access-1900(config)# interface 0/17
Mfg-3-access-1900(config-if)# vlan 4
. . .
Mfg-3-access-1900(config)# interface 0/19
Mfg-3-access-1900(config-if)# vlan 4
Mfg-3-access-1900(config)# interface 0/20
Mfg-3-access-1900(config-if)# vlan 4
[Mfg-4-access-1900]
Mfg-4-access-1900(config)# interface 0/1
Mfg-4-access-1900(config-if)# vlan 2
Mfg-4-access-1900(config)# interface 0/2
Mfg-4-access-1900(config-if)# vlan 2
. . .
Mfg-4-access-1900(config)# interface 0/23
Mfg-4-access-1900(config-if)# vlan 2
Mfg-4-access-1900(config)# interface 0/24
Mfg-4-access-1900(config-if)# vlan 2
[Mfg-5-access-1900]
Mfg-5-access-1900(config)# interface 0/1
Mfg-5-access-1900(config-if)# vlan 2
Mfg-5-access-1900(config)# interface 0/2
Mfg-5-access-1900(config-if)# vlan 2
. . .
Mfg-5-access-1900(config)# interface 0/14
Mfg-5-access-1900(config-if)# vlan 2
Mfg-5-access-1900(config)# interface 0/15
Mfg-5-access-1900(config-if)# vlan 2
```

```
Mfg-5-access-1900(config)# interface 0/16
Mfg-5-access-1900(config-if)# vlan 4
Mfg-5-access-1900(config)# interface 0/17
Mfg-5-access-1900(config-if)# vlan 4
. . .
Mfg-5-access-1900(config)# interface 0/19
Mfg-5-access-1900(config-if)# vlan 4
Mfg-5-access-1900(config)# interface 0/20
Mfg-5-access-1900(config-if)# vlan 4
```

Next the SR devices:

```
[SR-2-access-1900]
SR-2-access-1900(config)# interface 0/1
SR-2-access-1900(config-if)# vlan 3
SR-2-access-1900(config)# interface 0/2
SR-2-access-1900(config-if)# vlan 3
. . .
SR-2-access-1900(config)# interface 0/14
SR-2-access-1900(config-if)# vlan 3
SR-2-access-1900(config)# interface 0/15
SR-2-access-1900(config-if)# vlan 3

SR-2-access-1900(config)# interface 0/16
SR-2-access-1900(config-if)# vlan 4
SR-2-access-1900(config)# interface 0/17
SR-2-access-1900(config-if)# vlan 4
. . .
SR-2-access-1900(config)# interface 0/19
SR-2-access-1900(config-if)# vlan 4
SR-2-access-1900(config)# interface 0/20
SR-2-access-1900(config-if)# vlan 4
[SR-3-access-1900]
SR-3-access-1900(config)# interface 0/1
SR-3-access-1900(config-if)# vlan 3
SR-3-access-1900(config)# interface 0/2
SR-3-access-1900(config-if)# vlan 3
. . .
SR-3-access-1900(config)# interface 0/14
SR-3-access-1900(config-if)# vlan 3
SR-3-access-1900(config)# interface 0/15
SR-3-access-1900(config-if)# vlan 3

SR-3-access-1900(config)# interface 0/16
SR-3-access-1900(config-if)# vlan 4
SR-3-access-1900(config)# interface 0/17
SR-3-access-1900(config-if)# vlan 4
. . .
SR-3-access-1900(config)# interface 0/19
SR-3-access-1900(config-if)# vlan 4
SR-3-access-1900(config)# interface 0/20
SR-3-access-1900(config-if)# vlan 4
[SR-4-access-1900]
SR-4-access-1900(config)# interface 0/1
SR-4-access-1900(config-if)# vlan 3
SR-4-access-1900(config)# interface 0/2
```

```
SR-4-access-1900(config-if)# vlan 3
. . .
SR-4-access-1900(config)# interface 0/23
SR-4-access-1900(config-if)# vlan 3
SR-4-access-1900(config)# interface 0/24
SR-4-access-1900(config-if)# vlan 3
[SR-5-access-1900]
SR-5-access-1900(config)# interface 0/1
SR-5-access-1900(config-if)# vlan 3
SR-5-access-1900(config)# interface 0/2
SR-5-access-1900(config-if)# vlan 3
. . .
SR-5-access-1900(config)# interface 0/23
SR-5-access-1900(config-if)# vlan 3
SR-5-access-1900(config)# interface 0/24
SR-5-access-1900(config-if)# vlan 3
```

Next, the Admin devices:

```
[ADMIN-2-access-1900]
ADMIN-2-access-1900(config)# interface 0/1
ADMIN-2-access-1900(config-if)# vlan 4
ADMIN-2-access-1900(config)# interface 0/2
ADMIN-2-access-1900(config-if)# vlan 4
. . .
ADMIN-2-access-1900(config)# interface 0/23
ADMIN-2-access-1900(config-if)# vlan 4
ADMIN-2-access-1900(config)# interface 0/24
ADMIN-2-access-1900(config-if)# vlan 4
[ADMIN-3-access-1900]
ADMIN-3-access-1900(config)# interface 0/1
ADMIN-3-access-1900(config-if)# vlan 4
ADMIN-3-access-1900(config)# interface 0/2
ADMIN-3-access-1900(config-if)# vlan 4
. . .
ADMIN-3-access-1900(config)# interface 0/23
ADMIN-3-access-1900(config-if)# vlan 4
ADMIN-3-access-1900(config)# interface 0/24
ADMIN-3-access-1900(config-if)# vlan 4
[ADMIN-4-access-1900]
ADMIN-4-access-1900(config)# interface 0/1
ADMIN-4-access-1900(config-if)# vlan 4
ADMIN-4-access-1900(config)# interface 0/2
ADMIN-4-access-1900(config-if)# vlan 4
. . .
ADMIN-4-access-1900(config)# interface 0/23
ADMIN-4-access-1900(config-if)# vlan 4
ADMIN-4-access-1900(config)# interface 0/24
ADMIN-4-access-1900(config-if)# vlan 4
[ADMIN-5-access-1900]
ADMIN-5-access-1900(config)# interface 0/1
ADMIN-5-access-1900(config-if)# vlan 4
ADMIN-5-access-1900(config)# interface 0/2
ADMIN-5-access-1900(config-if)# vlan 4
. . .
ADMIN-5-access-1900(config)# interface 0/23
```

```
ADMIN-5-access-1900(config-if)# vlan 4
ADMIN-5-access-1900(config)# interface 0/24
ADMIN-5-access-1900(config-if)# vlan 4
```

VLAN Trunking and Tagging

Now that we have fully defined the access links and VLANs, we will move on to the trunk links. All the interswitch links are trunk links. The question is whether to use 802.1q or ISL. Because we have implemented five VLANs in this campus network, it would greatly improve the performance of Spanning Tree if we could implement a separate Spanning Tree for each VLAN. Considering this, using ISL would give us the benefit of running PVST instead of CST.

For each of the Catalyst 2926 access switches, enter the following:

```
Switch-access-2926(enable) set trunk 1/1 on isl
```

For the Catalyst 1900 access switches, use the following command:

```
Switch-access-1900(config)# interface fastethernet 0/25
Switch-access-1900(config-if)# trunk on
```

Repeat for all access switches.

Trunk Link Negotiation and VLAN Trunking Protocol (VTP)

Because all the trunk links will implement ISL, *Dynamic Trunking Protocol* (DTP) does not need to negotiate the VLAN tagging method for the trunk links.

The use of VLAN Trunking Protocol would ease the addition and removal of VLANs in the future. To enable VTP, we issue the following commands:
For the Set Command-based devices:

```
Switch(enable) set vtp domain CPI mode server pruning enable
```

For the Cisco IOS-based Catalyst 1900, use the following:

```
Switch(config)# vtp server domain CPI pruning enable
```

We have enabled all devices to be servers, allowing all to create and remove VLANs as required.

Spanning Tree Implementation

To improve the performance of the *Spanning Tree Protocol* (STP), we will use Cisco's *Per VLAN Spanning Tree* (PVST) feature. This allows the creation of one Spanning Tree per VLAN.

NOTE: Cisco will use PVST by default when an ISL trunk link exists.

Spanning Tree Optimization

These steps can optimize Spanning Tree operation:

- Specify the Root Bridge
- Modify the port costs
- Modify the Spanning Tree timers
- Use the PortFast, UplinkFast, and BackboneFast features

We'll consider each of these steps in order.

Specify the Root Bridge   The Root Bridge for each of the VLANs should be the 5505 switches in each of the switch blocks. Table 5-5 lists the Root Bridge switches for each of the VLANs.

Because all the Root Bridges are 5505s, the command is the same for all Root Bridges. Use the following command to implement a Root Bridge for each of the 5505s:

```
RD-1-dist-5505(enable) set spantree root vlan-id
```

For each Root Bridge, substitute the correct VLAN ID from the previous table.

Modify the Port Costs   Modification of the port costs is recommended by Cisco only in rare cases. Because the CPI campus network is not

Table 5-5

Root Bridges by VLAN

VLAN	VLAN ID	Root Bridge Switch
R&D	1	RD-1-dist-5505
Mfg	2	Mfg-1-dist-5505
SR	3	SR-1-dist-5505
Admin	4	Admin-1-dist-5505
IT	5	IT-1-dist-5505

extremely large, modifying this parameter is not necessary at this point. This change should only be considered when needed.

Modify the Spanning Tree Timers   Because the default Spanning Tree timer values are based on a maximum hop count of seven from the Root Bridge, increasing the timer values is absolutely not necessary. In the case of CPI's campus network, the only change that would make sense would be to decrease the timer values. Cisco warns against doing this because it could lead to network instability. We choose not to modify the Spanning Tree timers.

Use PortFast, UplinkFast, and BackboneFast Features   The Port-Fast, UplinkFast, and BackboneFast features can go a long way to reduce the convergence time of Spanning Tree in the CPI network.

PortFast allows us to remove the ports that have hosts connected to them from the Spanning Tree calculation. All the access switch ports with the exception of the ports that connect to the 5505 switches should have Port-Fast enabled. The following commands enable PortFast on the 1900 and 2926 switches. Enter the commands on all access switches.

For the Catalyst 1900, use the following interface sub-command:

```
Switch-access-1900(config-if)# spantree start-forwarding
```

For the Catalyst 2926, use the following Set Command:

```
Switch-access-2926(enable) set spantree portfast 2/1-24 enable
```

UplinkFast is only used in access switches that have redundant connections to the distribution layer. Only single links are used from the access switches to the distribution layer in CPI's campus network. Therefore, UplinkFast will not be of use to us.

BackBoneFast is a feature that allows faster convergence when the switch detects an inferior BPDU. Hopefully, this occurrence is rare, but still a chance that it might happen exists. With the hardware selected, we will not be able to use BackboneFast in CPI's network. The Catalyst 1900 runs Cisco IOS, which, at the time of this writing, does not support BackboneFast operation.

Link Aggregation

To increase the bandwidth between switch blocks, we will use Fast Ether-Channel. The best place to implement Fast EtherChannel is on the links between the 5505s and the 6506s. Using four Fast Ethernet links between all the 5505s and all the 6506s is unnecessary. The most need for the bandwidth will be in and out of the IT switch block due to the centralized storage and processing located in the IT switch block. The connections between the IT 5505 and the 6506s will use four Fast Ethernet links in one Fast EtherChannel link. The rest of the connections between the 5505s and the 6506s will be two Fast Ethernet links configured as one Fast EtherChannel link.

To ease the configuration of the Fast EtherChannel links, we will make use of the *Port Aggregation Protocol* (PAgP) to automatically set up the links. All the ports are configured as trunk ports, forced to 100Mbps and full duplex operation, and are enabled. All we have to do is plug in the links to begin aggregating the links into one Fast EtherChannel link.

First, configure the Catalyst 5505 ports for connection to the core.

```
IT-1-dist-5505(enable) set port channel 3/1-4 mode auto
IT-1-dist-5505(enable) set port name 3/1-4 Backbone-1-core-6506
IT-1-dist-5505(enable) set port channel 3/5-8 mode auto
IT-1-dist-5505(enable) set port name 3/5-8 Backbone-2-core-6506

Admin-1-dist-5505(enable) set port channel 3/1-2 mode auto
Admin-1-dist-5505(enable) set port name 3/1-2 Backbone-1-core-6506
Admin-1-dist-5505(enable) set port channel 3/3-4 mode auto
Admin-1-dist-5505(enable) set port name 3/3-4 Backbone-2-core-6506

SR-1-dist-5505(enable) set port channel 3/1-2 mode auto
SR-1-dist-5505(enable) set port name 3/1-2 Backbone-1-core-6506
SR-1-dist-5505(enable) set port channel 3/3-4 mode auto
SR-1-dist-5505(enable) set port name 3/3-4 Backbone-2-core-6506
```

```
Mfg-1-dist-5505(enable) set port channel 3/1-2 mode auto
Mfg-1-dist-5505(enable) set port name 3/1-2 Backbone-1-core-6506
Mfg-1-dist-5505(enable) set port channel 3/3-4 mode auto
Mfg-1-dist-5505(enable) set port name 3/3-4 Backbone-2-core-6506

RD-1-dist-5505(enable) set port channel 3/1-2 mode auto
RD-1-dist-5505(enable) set port name 3/1-2 Backbone-1-core-6506
RD-1-dist-5505(enable) set port channel 3/3-4 mode auto
RD-1-dist-5505(enable) set port name 3/3-4 Backbone-2-core-6506
```

Next, configure the Catalyst 6506s for connection to the distribution layer.

```
Backbone-1-core-6506(enable) set port channel 2/1-4 mode auto
Backbone-1-core-6506(enable) set port name 2/1-4 IT-1-dist-5505
Backbone-1-core-6506(enable) set port channel 2/5-6 mode auto
Backbone-1-core-6506(enable) set port name 2/5-6 Admin-1-dist-5505
Backbone-1-core-6506(enable) set port channel 2/7-8 mode auto
Backbone-1-core-6506(enable) set port name 2/7-8 SR-1-dist-5505
Backbone-1-core-6506(enable) set port channel 2/9-10 mode auto
Backbone-1-core-6506(enable) set port name 2/9-10 Mfg-1-dist-5505
Backbone-1-core-6506(enable) set port channel 2/11-12 mode auto
Backbone-1-core-6506(enable) set port name 2/11-12 RD-1-dist-5505

Backbone-2-core-6506(enable) set port channel 2/1-4 mode auto
Backbone-2-core-6506(enable) set port name 2/1-4 IT-1-dist-5505
Backbone-2-core-6506(enable) set port channel 2/5-6 mode auto
Backbone-2-core-6506(enable) set port name 2/5-6 Admin-1-dist-5505
Backbone-2-core-6506(enable) set port channel 2/7-8 mode auto
Backbone-2-core-6506(enable) set port name 2/7-8 SR-1-dist-5505
Backbone-2-core-6506(enable) set port channel 2/9-10 mode auto
Backbone-2-core-6506(enable) set port name 2/9-10 Mfg-1-dist-5505
Backbone-2-core-6506(enable) set port channel 2/11-12 mode auto
Backbone-2-core-6506(enable) set port name 2/11-12 RD-1-dist-5505
```

Notice the value in port naming.

Case Study Summary

This case study has brought our network from a group of switches with passwords and IP connectivity to a well-defined and well-configured bridging network. To get to this point, we had to complete the following steps:

- Define which hosts are in which VLAN
- Determine the Trunking Links and the VLAN tagging method
- Evaluate and implement trunk link negotiation and *VLAN Trunking Protocol* (VTP)

- Determine how Spanning Tree will be implemented
- Optimize Spanning Tree convergence
- Evaluate and implement link aggregation

This configuration doesn't address the ability to communicate between VLANs. All the VLANs are separate networks that are unable to communicate together. The next chapter will cover the functionality to implement interVLAN communication.

Currently CPI's network is unable to implement centralized storage and processing unless all the hosts in the IT center are equipped with one network interface per VLAN. This would prove to be a management problem as well as a waste of money. Chapter 6 will give you the tools to build functionality into CPI's network to efficiently implement centralized storage, centralized processing, and interVLAN communication.

Questions

1. Which best describes the broadcast behavior of VLANs?

   a. All VLANs see all broadcast traffic.

   b. VLANs only see their own broadcast traffic.

   c. Broadcast traffic in VLANs increase as the number of VLANs increase.

   d. A router forwards broadcast traffic between VLANs.

2. With VLANs, Layer 2 hosts need not be grouped _____.

   a. logically

   b. geographically

   c. carefully

   d. manually

3. Static VLANs group hosts by _____.

   a. MAC address

   b. location

   c. port

   d. IP address

4. Dynamic VLANs group hosts by _____.

   a. MAC address

   b. location

   c. port

   d. IP address

5. Access links can support VLAN traffic from _____ VLAN(s).

   a. 0

   b. 1

   c. 16

   d. 1024

6. Trunk links carry traffic from _____.

   a. one VLAN to another

   b. one VLAN

   c. many VLANs

   d. one subnet to another

7. Which of the following is true about InterSwitch Link (ISL)?

    a. ISL is used on access links.

    b. ISL is used between switches of different vendors.

    c. ISL can create invalid Ethernet frames.

    d. ISL is any link between switches.

8. How many VLANs can be uniquely identified with IEEE 802.1q?

    a. 1

    b. 1024

    c. $10^{12}-1$

    d. $10^{16}-1$

9. VLAN Trunk Protocol (VTP) provides _____.

    a. a way for many VLANs to be tagged over a trunk link

    b. VLAN security

    c. a way for VLANs to be monitored from a management station

    d. a method for VLANs to be configured over the whole campus network from one switch

10. VTP pruning is a way to _____.

    a. remove VLANs

    b. diminish the amount of broadcast and flooded traffic on trunk ports

    c. diminish the amount of VTP traffic

    d. diminish the number of trunk ports

11. Which of the following best describes the Spanning Tree Protocol (STP)?

    a. STP creates a Layer 2 forwarding table

    b. STP removes bridging loops

    c. STP removes routing loops

    d. STP creates a Layer 3 forwarding table

12. The Root Bridge is declared by _____.

    a. vote

    b. election

    c. default

    d. size

13. How many Root Bridges does STP support?

    a. 1

    b. 2

    c. 4

    d. 16

14. A Bridge Protocol Data Unit is used to _____.

    a. forward packets
    b. implement STP operation
    c. manage switches
    d. advertise bridge forwarding tables

15. How many Spanning Trees can Cisco's *Per VLAN Spanning Tree* (PVST) support?

    a. an infinite number
    b. 64, if 1900 or 2820 switches are in the network
    c. zero
    d. PVST doesn't support Spanning Tree

16. *Common Spanning Tree* (CST) supports

    a. one Spanning Tree per VLAN
    b. one Spanning Tree per campus network
    c. one Spanning Tree per subnet
    d. one VLAN per Spanning Tree

17. Which of the following is true about Cisco's PVST+?

    a. It won't interoperate with other vendors' switches.
    b. It will interoperate with other vendors' switches.
    c. It was created by a multivendor committee.
    d. It can support more Spanning Trees than PVST.

18. Spanning Tree optimization is

    a. not recommended
    b. always necessary
    c. a waste of time
    d. enhanced by PortFast

19. How many links can be aggregated with Fast EtherChannel?

    a. 0
    b. 2
    c. 4
    d. 8

20. Which of the following media types can be grouped with Fast Ether-Channel?

    a. 10BaseT but not 100BaseT

    b. 100BaseFx but not 1000BaseFx

    c. 100BaseTx, 100BaseFx, and 1000BaseFx

    d. 1000BaseFx but not 100BaseFx

Answers

1. Which best describes the broadcast behavior of VLANs?

   b.   VLANs only see their own broadcast traffic.

   This is the beauty of VLANs. The Layer 2 network can grow without increasing impact of broadcast storms.

2. With VLANs, Layer 2 hosts need not be grouped _____.

   b.   geographically

   Now Layer 2 hosts can be grouped regardless of location using VLANs.

3. Static VLANs group hosts by _____.

   c.   port

4. Dynamic VLANs group hosts by _____.

   a.   MAC address

5. Access links can support VLAN traffic from _____ VLAN(s).

   b.   1

   Access links are links that are not connected to other switches. They are connected to hosts. A host can only join one VLAN.

6. Trunk links carry traffic from _____.

   c.   many VLANs

   Trunk links connect switches that implement more than one VLAN.

7. Which of the following is true about *InterSwitch Link* (ISL)?

   c.   ISL can create invalid Ethernet frames

   ISL encapsulates an Ethernet frame with a 26-byte header and 4-byte checksum, creating the potential for frames that are larger than the largest allowable Ethernet frame size.

8. How many VLANs can be uniquely identified with IEEE 802.1q?

   c. 10^{12}-1

   The VLAN identifier field is 12 bits long.

9. *VLAN Trunk Protocol* (VTP) provides _____.

   d.   a method for VLANs to be configured over the whole campus network from one switch

10. VTP pruning is a way to _____.

    b.   diminish the amount of broadcast and flooded traffic on trunk ports

11. Which of the following best describes the *Spanning Tree Protocol* (STP)?

b.   STP removes bridging loops.

12. The root bridge is declared by _____.

b.   Election

The bridge with the largest bridge ID becomes the root bridge. This process is known as election.

13. How many root bridges does STP support?

a.   1

There is only one root bridge in STP.

14. A Bridge Protocol Data Unit is used to _____.

b.   implement STP operation

15. How many Spanning Trees can Cisco's *Per VLAN Spanning Tree* (PVST) support?

b.   64, if 1900 or 2820 switches are in the network

PVST is limited to one Spanning Tree for 64 VLANs if 1900 or 2820 switches are on the network.

16. *Common Spanning Tree* (CST) supports

b.   one Spanning Tree per campus network

This standard solution only allows one Spanning Tree per Layer 2 network regardless of the number of VLANs implemented.

17. Which of the following is true about Cisco's PVST+?

b.   it will interoperate with other vendors' switches

PVST+ is PVST with CST. CST is interoperable with other vendors' switches.

18. Spanning Tree optimization is

d.   enhanced by PortFast

PortFast removes access links from the Spanning Tree calculation, which improves the Spanning Tree convergence time.

19. How many links can be aggregated with Fast EtherChannel?

c.   4

20. Which of the following media types can be grouped with Fast Ether-Channel?

c.   100BaseTX, 100BaseFx, and 1000BaseFx

Unicast Layer 3 Configuration

The last chapter was devoted to developing Layer 2 networks within your campus network. The benefits of Virtual LANs and the Spanning Tree Protocol were covered in great detail. We also covered how to span VLANs across your campus network and how to implement Spanning Tree over the VLANs.

Now that you know how to build and implement these Layer 2 networks in your campus network, what's the next step? These Layer 2 networks are unable to intercommunicate. Without connection at a higher layer, the Layer 2 VLANs cannot communicate together. They are simply disjointed network segments that can only provide connectivity between hosts inside the VLAN. This is where Layer 3 forwarding, also known as routing, comes into play. Layer 3 forwarding mechanisms allow Layer 2 networks to intercommunicate.

Objectives Covered in the Chapter

The following topics will be covered in this chapter:

- IP addressing
- Routing basics
- Routing between VLANs
- Optimizing routing through multilayer switching
- Fault tolerant routing with *Hot Standby Routing Protocol* (HSRP)

So far we have covered Layer 2 concepts with bridging and Spanning Tree Protocol. Recall from Chapter 2 that bridging networks do not scale well because of an increasing broadcast domain. The more hosts on a bridged network, the more broadcasts that will occur. These broadcast packets can begin to utilize a significant portion of network bandwidth, leaving less and less bandwidth for unicast traffic.

The only solution is to break up the broadcast domain into smaller broadcast domains. Now that multiple broadcast domains exist, they must be connected to allow the devices in the broadcast domains to communicate. To connect individual broadcast domains, an addressing scheme must be used that allows a hierarchical organization so devices within a broadcast domain can be logically grouped. The Internet Protocol addressing scheme does just that. This book will concentrate on *Internet Protocol* (IP) routing because it is the most prevalent Layer 3 protocol. This section describes the operation and implementation of IP routing, the vehicle to interconnect the Layer 2 broadcast domains.

After the VLAN discussion from Chapter 5, "Layer 2 Configuration," the complexity of implementing VLANs in your campus network should be obvious. *Inter Switch Link* (ISL) makes the maintenance of VLANs feasible. ISL comes into play again with routing between VLANs. The implementation of VLAN routing will be covered in this chapter.

Cisco has implemented a method to improve the performance of inter-VLAN routing by providing a method for cut-through routing. This technology allows the switch to cache the routing information gathered from the routing engine. This configuration allows for routing to happen at virtually the same speed as Layer 2 switching.

To round out the introduction to routing, we will cover *Hot Standby Routing Protocol* (HSRP). This protocol enables the distribution layer to have redundant routers to provide failover redundancy in the event of a router failure.

These topics will provide you with a strong foundation for understanding the basics of routing in your campus network. The information in this and previous chapters will give you the tools necessary to fully implement an IP unicast network.

Routing Issues

A router simply forwards a packet from one Layer 2 network to another using Layer 3 addressing. In other words, a router forwards packets at Layer 3. Several issues arise from the ability to route, especially when combined with VLANs:

- How can VLANs communicate together when their job is to isolate traffic?

- How does a router know how to route?

- How do you route on a link carrying multiple VLANs?

- How does a packet associate a Layer 2 address with a Layer 3 address?

Let's look at each of these issues individually.

InterVLAN Connectivity   VLANs by nature isolate traffic into separate broadcast domains. This is by design so networks can grow without being burdened by broadcast storms. Therefore, VLANs must rely on another mechanism to connect them together. They require that another device handle the forwarding of packets from one VLAN to another.

Each of the hosts in a particular VLAN must be a part of a unique set of Layer 3 addresses in the network. These groups of addresses are called Layer 3 subnets (see Figure 6-1). The routers in the campus network know the location of these subnets so packets can be forwarded from one VLAN to another.

The result is connectivity between VLANs. Now VLANs can provide a separation of broadcast domains and have a path for packets to flow between them.

The particular Layer 3 protocol that will be covered in this book is the *Internet Protocol* (IP). IP provides a method for dividing a large group of addresses into smaller subnets. The details of IP will be covered in a later section.

How a Router Routes   Here are some of the issues to consider in exploring how a router is able to forward at Layer 3:

- How does a host know how to forward packets out of the VLAN?
- How does a router know how to forward packets from one VLAN to another?

Figure 6-1
IP subnets

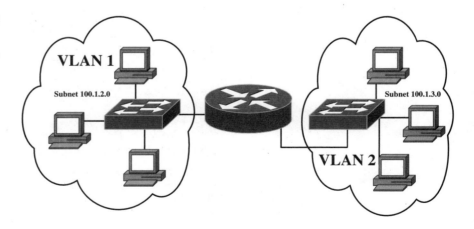

A host can send traffic outside a VLAN by directing a packet to its default router. A default router must be configured in the host so it knows where to send packets outside its own subnet. If the host must communicate outside its subnet, packets are directed to a default gateway (see Figure 6-2).

Because the packet must be directed to the default gateway for forwarding outside the VLAN, it stands to reason that the default gateway must be inside the same VLAN. The host simply sends the packet to a Layer 2 MAC address that happens to be a router with the capability to forward the packet to another subnet.

When the router gets the packet, it looks at the Layer 3 address and decides to which subnet it should be forwarded. It makes this decision by looking through a table that associates what interface goes with a particular subnet.

VLANs and Routing   We looked at the details of implementing many VLANs across a campus network and learned that the traffic from many VLANs can be carried by one link. This poses a problem for routers. The most obvious way to handle the problem is to set up an individual link between the VLAN and the router. However, this doesn't scale well because the number of links needed between each VLAN and router increases as the number of VLANs increase (see Figure 6-3).

The more elegant method of handling this problem is to use Cisco's ISL protocol between the Cisco switches implementing the VLANs and the

Figure 6-2
Default gateway

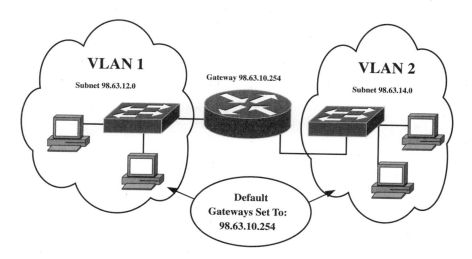

Figure 6-3
InterVLAN routing
with multiple links

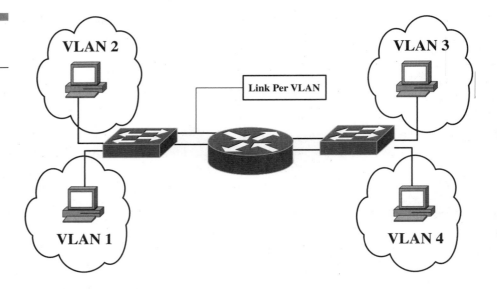

Cisco router that will provide routing between the VLANs (see Figure 6-4). ISL tags the packets with information about what VLAN they are associated with. The router looks at the destination IP subnet that the packet is destined for and changes the ISL tag information so the packet now is destined for the appropriate VLAN.

Layer 2 Address to Layer 3 Address Mapping   Layer 2 and Layer 3 addresses on their own are completely unrelated. Addressing at Layer 3 has no knowledge of Layer 2 addressing. This creates a problem because routers and hosts need to eventually send packets to the destination host. In the case of IP over Ethernet, an Ethernet host has an Ethernet MAC address and an IP address that is assigned to it.

When a packet is destined for a particular IP address, the router may have no idea of the destination MAC address of the host. In this case, the router must ask all the hosts in the broadcast domain what the MAC address is for a particular host. If any host knows the MAC address associated with a particular IP address, the host will reply to the broadcasted request and provide the requested MAC address. This is called address resolution. In the case of IP and Ethernet, a protocol called *Address Resolution Protocol* (ARP) maps Layer 2 addresses to Layer 3 addresses. The hosts

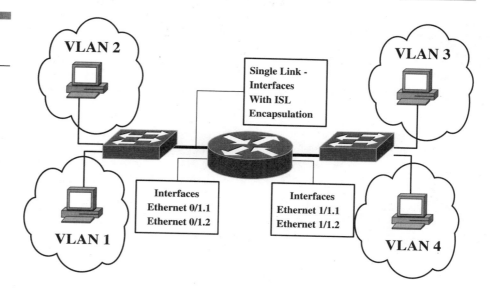

Figure 6-4
InterVLAN routing with ISL

using this protocol keep a table that associates all known Layer 2 to Layer 3 address mappings. These entries age over time because the IP address can be changed on a host. If the entry ages out of the table, the host will simply use ARP to find the appropriate MAC address.

Before we go into the details of IP routing, we will discuss the fundamentals of IP addressing.

IP Addressing

We mentioned previously that IP addressing has a hierarchical structure; now let's examine how IP addressing works. (Any mention of IP in this book refers to IP version 4.)

IP addresses are 32 bits long. Typically these 32-bit addresses are written in dotted-decimal with the form XXX.XXX.XXX.XXX. The four groupings of decimal numbers between the dots represent eight bits of the IP address. Therefore, none of the three-digit decimal numbers can be greater than 255.

Figure 6-5
IP address fields

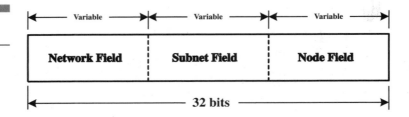

Table 6-1

IP address classes

Class	Most Significant Bits	Length of Network Field	Use
A	0	8	Unicast
B	10	16	Unicast
C	110	24	Unicast
D	1110	—	Multicast
E	11110	—	Reserved

The IP address is made up of three fields: network, subnet, and node (see Figure 6-5). The lengths of the fields are variable.

The network field is determined by the first few bits of the address according to Table 6-1.

As shown in the above table, IP addresses are divided into classes determined by the most significant bits of the address. Classes A, B, and C are used only for unicast addressing, whereas Class D is used for multicast addressing. Class E is reserved for future use. The network field length of Class A is 8 bits, Class B 16 bits, and Class C 24 bits.

After the length of the network field is known, the subnet mask determines the length of the subnet field. A subnet mask is a 32-bit binary number that is formed by contiguous 1s, starting with the most significant bit. For example, a valid subnet mask would be 11111111111111111111111100000000. For clarity, the subnet masks are written in dotted-decimal form like IP addresses. The above mask is written in dotted-decimal form as 255.255.255.0.

Here is an example of how IP addresses and subnet masks work. Consider an IP address of 128.1.1.1 with a subnet mask of 255.255.255.0. In binary form, the IP address would be 10000000000000010000000100000001 and the subnet mask would be 11111111111111111111111100000000. Because the subnet mask contains eight zeros, the node field contains eight bits. Because the first bits in IP address are 10, it is a Class B address and has a 16-bit network field length. With 16 bits in the network field and eight bits in the node field, that leaves eight bits for the subnet field.

The fields of an IP address allow for a hierarchical address structure. For example, one network field number can have many subnets and one subnet within a network field can have many nodes. Changing the length of the network and subnet fields determines the number of nodes per subnet and subnets per network.

IP Addresses and MAC Addresses

Layer 2 and Layer 3 addresses are associated together by the use of *Address Resolution Protocol* (ARP). Hosts maintain a table that associates an IP address with a MAC address. This table is built by using ARP to find the MAC address of the host with a particular IP address. The protocol works by broadcasting an ARP request packet to the network. The ARP request has IP address of the host with an unknown MAC address. All the devices in the broadcast domain see the request. The host that has the IP address in the ARP request sends a packet back to the ARP request's source MAC address with its MAC address (see Table 6-2). The host that originated the ARP request sees the ARP reply and updates its ARP table with the new information.

ARP is very important because this protocol is the glue between Layer 2 and Layer 3 addressing. Remember that Ethernet devices must address their packets to Ethernet MAC addresses. ARP provides the translation between Layer 2 and Layer 3 addresses.

Table 6-2

Sample ARP table

IP Address	MAC Address
100.1.100.3	00-00-2b-3e-45-23
100.1.100.254	00-00-c0-4f-25-96
152.1.32.2	00-00-c0-4f-25-96
100.1.100.10	08-00-20-4a-c4-21

IP Communication

If an IP host wishes to communicate with another IP host, the transmitting IP source must determine if the destination IP address is in the same subnet or not. If the destination is in the same subnet, the host must simply ARP for the MAC address of the destination if the destination MAC address isn't already in its ARP table (see Table 6-2). If the destination is not in the same subnet as the source, the source must send the packet to the MAC address of the gateway for that subnet. Most IP hosts have one IP address to send its packets to if they are destined for any subnet other than its own. This is called the default gateway or default router address. The user configures the default gateway address.

After the default gateway (router) gets the packet and sees that the packet is destined for its own MAC address and at the same time destined for another IP host, the router knows that it must forward the packet to another interface to move the packet closer to its destination.

The mechanism for determining if the destination IP host is in the same subnet is as follows. The subnet mask is bitwise AND'd with both the source IP address and the destination IP address. The result of these two functions are exclusively OR'd. If this final result is not zero, then the destination IP address is in another subnet.

Here is an example of determining if the destination address is in the same subnet as the host.

Source IP address:	$(100.1.43.1)_{\text{dotted-decimal}}$
	$(01100100.00000001.00101011.00000001)_{\text{binary}}$
Subnet mask:	$(255.255.255.0)_{\text{dotted-decimal}}$
	$(11111111.11111111.11111111.$
	$00000000)_{\text{binary}}$
Destination IP address:	$(100.1.44.2)_{\text{dotted-decimal}}$
	$(01100100.00000001.00101100.00000010)_{\text{binary}}$
Source IP address AND'd with subnet mask:	

01100100.00000001.00101011.00000001
<u>11111111.11111111.11111111.00000000</u>
01100100.00000001.00101011.00000000

Destination IP address
AND'd with subnet
mask: 01100100.00000001.00101100.00000010
            <u>11111111.11111111.11111111.00000000</u>
            01100100.00000001.00101100.00000000

The two results XOR'd: 01100100.00000001.00101011.00000000
            <u>01100100.00000001.00101100.00000000</u>
            00000000.00000000.00000111.00000000

The result of the XOR function is not zero. Therefore, the destination IP address is in another subnet than the source and the packet must be sent to the default gateway for Layer 3 forwarding.

Router Operation

When the router gets a packet to be forwarded to another subnet, the router must manipulate the Ethernet and IP header fields to ensure that the packet is forwarded toward its destination.

Three things must happen when the router forwards the packet at Layer 3.

- Determine the port to forward the packet to.
- Update the destination MAC address.
- Decrement the IP *Time To Live* (TTL) field.

The port that the packet is forwarded to is determined by looking through the route table that the router maintains. This route table associates a route with a physical port.

The destination MAC address must be updated with the MAC address of the destination IP host if the host is directly connected. If the destination host is not directly connected to one of the ports of the router, the router must forward the packet to the next router to continue the packet toward the destination IP host. In either case, if the router doesn't know the MAC address of the next hop toward the destination, it must ARP for the MAC address.

The IP TTL field is decremented. This field provides a mechanism for the packet to be removed from the network if it gets caught in a loop. Without such a mechanism, the packet may be forwarded for as long as the routing loop is active. The packet is removed by a router if its TTL field is zero.

Maintaining Routes

The two methods for defining routes in a router are

- Static Routes
- Dynamic Routes

Static routes are routes that are entered manually in the router (see Figure 6-6). A typical static route statement that defines how to get to a particular subnet would include the netmask of the subnet to define the span of the subnet and the router interface address to get to this subnet. As the number of routes (subnets) that need to be interconnected in a network increase, manually adding each of the routes is not feasible.

Figure 6-6
Static route
architecture

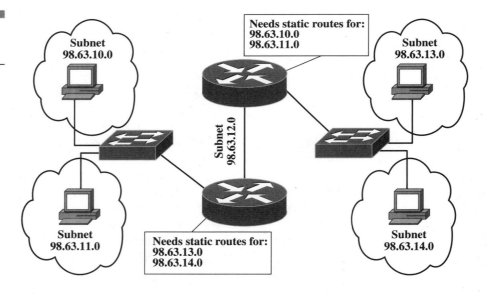

The solution to maintaining a router's route table in a large network is to use dynamic routing protocols. A protocol is needed for the routers in a network to advertise and update their route tables automatically. This increases the configuration complexity of the network, but the benefits of not having to manually configure these routes greatly outweigh this disadvantage.

In a routing protocol environment, only the Layer 3 addresses for the local interfaces must be configured (see Figure 6-7). Once the routing protocol is enabled and configured properly, the router will periodically advertise its known routes to the network and listen to the network to obtain routes from other routers.

This defines the function of a router. The mechanism for building a router's routing table is discussed in a later section.

Distribution Layer Topology

In Chapter 2 "Multilayer Switching Network Design Basics," the concept of a three-layer topological campus network model was introduced. This model consists of the access, distribution, and core layers. The access layer

Figure 6-7
Routing protocol architecture

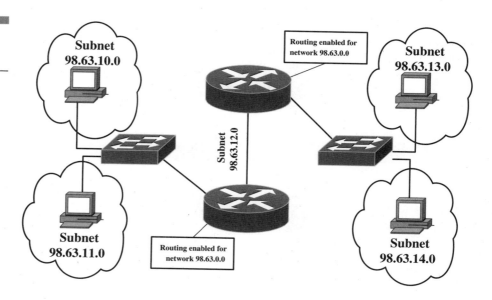

is made up of switches and shared hubs that connect hosts to the campus network. Typically, the access layer implements some combination of Spanning Tree and VLANs.

The distribution layer is where routing happens. The access layer defines the individual broadcast domains and the distribution layer connects these broadcast domains together through routing. Routing in multilayer switches takes place in a route processor.

The two basic physical topologies for routing in the distribution layer are

- External Route Processor Topology
- Internal Route Processor Topology

External Route Processor Topology   An External Route Processor Topology has the router outside of the distribution layer switch. This is achieved by connecting a Cisco router to the distribution switch via a Layer 2 connection with *Inter Switch Link* (ISL) protocol enabled. (see Figure 6-8).

A *Netflow Feature Card* (NFFC) or NFFC II card is needed in a Catalyst 5000 series switch to implement the external route processor topology. The Cisco routers that can be used as the external route are the Cisco 7500, 7200, 4500, and 4700 routers. They must have the *MultiLayer Switch Pro-*

Figure 6-8
External Route
Processor Topology

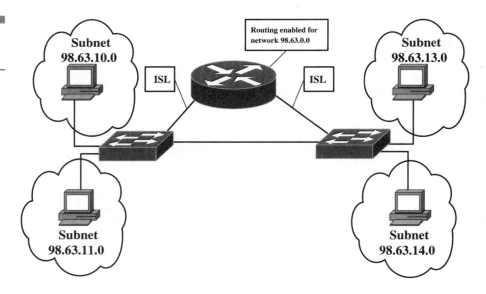

Routing enabled for network 98.63.0.0

Subnet 98.63.10.0

ISL

ISL

Subnet 98.63.13.0

Subnet 98.63.11.0

Subnet 98.63.14.0

tocol (MLSP) software and Cisco IOS 11.3.4 or later software image to implement the external route processor functionality.

The connection from the multilayer switch to the external router can be either with a separate Ethernet connection per VLAN or by one ISL link.

Internal Route Processor Topology   The route processor resides inside the multilayer switch in the Internal Route Processor Topology (see Figure 6-9). This topology can be implemented as follows.

- Catalyst 5000 family switch with a *Route Switch Module* (RSM)
- Catalyst 5000 family switch with a *Route Switch Feature Card* (RSFC)
- Catalyst 6000 or 6500 switch with a *Multilayer Switch Module* (MSM)

The RSM runs Cisco IOS software and plugs into the Catalyst 5000 family switch. From the user interface, the RSM is a module with one trunk port having a single MAC address.

The RSFC is a daughter card addition to the supervisor module of the Catalyst 5000 family switches. This daughter card works with either the Supervisor Engine II G or Supervisor Engine III G modules.

Figure 6-9

Internal route processor topology

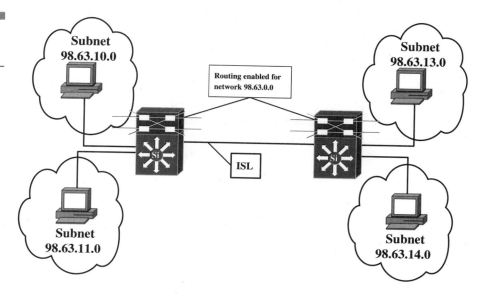

The MSM is installed into the chassis of the Catalyst 6000 or 6500. Four Gigabit Ethernet interfaces connect it to the switching bus. These interfaces can be individual connections or a Gigabit EtherChannel interface. If one interface is used and several VLANs have been implemented, ISL can be used to allow routing between the VLANs. 802.1Q can also be used if one interface is used to connect the MSM to the switching bus and multiple VLANs are present. After the connection is made between the MSM and the switching bus, individual sub-interfaces are set up for each VLAN to allow routing between the VLANs.

Configuring InterVLAN Routing

The following describes the steps necessary to configure interVLAN routing on a Catalyst series switch with a *Route Switch Module* (RSM) installed.

One way to connect to the RSM console is to physically plug into the console port on the module. The alternative and less resource-consuming method is to use the `session` command to communicate with the RSM. To do the latter, you first must identify the module in which your RSM is located.

Instead of physically looking at the device to determine the location of the RSM module, do the following:

```
Switch(enable) show module [mod_num]
```

The `show module` command, when given no arguments, will display the contents of all modules in the system. Providing an optional module number will give additional information about that specific module.

Upon listing all the modules, you should see a Module-Type of `Route Switch` along with the module number to the far left. Using the module number, you can initiate a connection to the RSM using the `session` command.

```
Switch(enable) session mod_num
```

At this point, you will be connected to the RSM and IOS will prompt you for a password, just as if you were on the serial console.

```
Switch(enable) session 3
Enter Password: cisco
Router>
```

After you are logged into the RSM, you must enter privileged mode in order to modify the device configuration.

```
Router> enable
Enable Password: cisco
Router#
```

Notice that your prompt changes when you are in privileged mode just like the switch interface. That is, of course, to warn you that you have the capability to do major damage to your network.

The first step in configuration is to assign your RSM a unique name. This enables you to better manage your network and makes it a little more personal. The name assigned is considered to be the hostname and is displayed on the prompt. This also helps you to identify which device you are configuring and minimize confusion.

```
Router# configure terminal
Router(config)# hostname SANDY
SANDY(config)# exit
SANDY#
```

Now that you have made friends with your RSM, you can enable inter-VLAN routing. Here, you must make a decision regarding which routing protocol to implement. If you already have a network in place, you will want to use the same routing protocol currently in use. Here we will use IGRP (discussed in later chapters) and enable routing for the 10.0.0.0 network.

```
SANDY# configure terminal
SANDY(config)# ip routing
SANDY(config)# router igrp
SANDY(config-router)# network 10.0.0.0
SANDY(config-router)# exit
SANDY(config)# exit
SANDY# show running-config
```

The last command will enable you to view the RSM configuration file. It will look similar to the following:

```
Building configuration...
Current configuration:
! This is a comment marker
hostname SANDY
! (text deleted)
router igrp 1
   network 10.0.0.0
! (text deleted)
end
```

You will notice the extra parameter at the end of the `router igrp` statement you entered. You should not be concerned; the `router` command starts a routing process on the RSM and Cisco IOS labels each router process with a unique identifier. IOS allows you to run multiple routing processes, even for the same protocol. For clarity, you may specify the process identifier when configuring routing:

```
SANDY(config)# router igrp 1
```

Specifying a new process identifier will start another routing process for that protocol. In general, you will never want more than one routing process for a given routing protocol.

When enabling IP routing, you should always define a default route for your device. The default route (or gateway) specifies where to send packets that are not destined for a local network or, in the case of a router, a more specific route does not exist.

On a Cisco IOS-based device, issue the following command:

```
SANDY(config)# ip default-gateway gateway-ip-address
```

For the switch configuration (Set Commands), use the following:

```
Switch(enable) set ip route default gateway-ip-address metric
```

In both cases, the gateway IP address is the address of the next-hop router. In the latter case, metric is usually 1, meaning remote destination. A metric of 0 means the gateway is the device itself.

Internal Route Processor Configuration   Internal Route Processor configuration involves two steps:

1. Creating and configuring VLANs on the switch interface, including mapping switch ports to VLANs.
2. Creating and configuring VLAN interfaces on the RSM. This includes an interface per VLAN.

Step 1 was covered in detail in Chapter 5, "Layer 2 Configuration." Step 2 involves creating the VLAN interfaces on the RSM. This process is very straightforward.

When creating VLAN interfaces for the first time, you must remember three steps:

1. Create the virtual interface.
2. Assign the interface an IP address, supplying an appropriate subnet mask.
3. Turn on the interface.

Configuration goes as follows:

```
SANDY(config)# interface vlan-interface-number
SANDY(config-if)# ip address ip-address subnet-mask
SANDY(config-if)# no shutdown
```

By default, when created, interfaces are shutdown; however, an interface will remain enabled until it is forcibly shutdown again.

```
SANDY(config)# interface vlan 10
SANDY(config-if)# ip address 10.1.1.1 255.255.255.0
SANDY(config-if)# no shutdown
SANDY(config-if)# exit
SANDY(config)# interface vlan 11
SANDY(config-if)# ip address 10.1.2.1 255.255.255.0
SANDY(config-if)# no shutdown
```

Let's see what we have thus far.

```
SANDY# show running-config
Building configuration...
Current configuration:
!
version 12.0
! (text deleted)
hostname SANDY
!
enable password cisco
! (text deleted)
router igrp 1
   network 10.0.0.0
!
interface Vlan10
   ip address 10.1.1.1 255.255.255.0
!
interface Vlan11
   ip address 10.1.2.1 255.255.255.0
!
ip default-gateway 11.1.1.1
! (text deleted)
end
```

Let's see how External Route Processor configuration differs from Internal Route Processor configuration.

External Route Processor Configuration The External Route Processor configuration is similar in many respects to the Internal Route Processor. The process is as follows:

1. Create a virtual sub-interface.
2. Enable VLAN encapsulation.
3. Assign the interface an IP address, supplying an appropriate subnet mask.
4. Turn on the interface.

The only major difference is the encapsulation. In the Internal Route Processor case, the encapsulation is handled internally and is hidden from the user interface. In this case, we must explicitly tell the interface to perform encapsulation. Encapsulation refers to the addition and removal of the ISL header information from the packets sent and received on the interface.

Configuration would proceed as follows:

```
SANDY(config)# interface interface-type slot-umber/port-
number.subinterface-number
SANDY(config-if)# encapsulation isl vlan-number
SANDY(config-if)# ip address ip-address subnet-mask
SANDY(config-if)# no shutdown
```

By default, when created, interfaces are shutdown; however, an interface will remain enabled until it is forcibly shutdown again.

```
SANDY(config)# interface FastEthernet 0/1.1
SANDY(config-if)# encapsulation isl 10
SANDY(config-if)# ip address 10.1.1.1 255.255.255.0
SANDY(config-if)# no shutdown
SANDY(config-if)# exit
SANDY(config)# interface FastEthernet 0/1.2
SANDY(config-if)# encapsulation isl 11
SANDY(config-if)# ip address 10.1.2.1 255.255.255.0
SANDY(config-if)# no shutdown
```

Let's see what we have thus far.

```
SANDY# show running-config
Building configuration...
Current configuration:
!
version 12.0
! (text deleted)
hostname SANDY
!
enable password cisco
```

```
! (text deleted)
router igrp 1
   network 10.0.0.0
!
interface FastEthernet0/1.1
   encapsulation isl 10
   ip address 10.1.1.1 255.255.255.0
!
interface FastEthernet0/1.2
   encapsulation isl 11
   ip address 10.1.2.1 255.255.255.0
!
ip default-gateway 11.1.1.1
! (text deleted)
end
```

As you can see, Internal versus External Route Processor configuration is not all that different.

Multilayer Switching (MLS)

Now that you have a firm grasp on the concepts of routing, we can look at how to optimize routing performance using *Multilayer Switching* (MLS) features.

Multilayer Switching (MLS) Overview

The external router or internal route module makes routing decisions. A packet entering the switch must be forwarded to the router so the packet fields can be changed for the packet to be forwarded on to the destination by the switch. This is a roundabout process that can take a lot of time, thereby adding significant delay. Fortunately, the traffic patterns of the campus network can be used as an advantage to improve the performance of routing at the distribution layer.

This is achieved by defining flows within the network (see Figure 6-10). A flow is a string of packets associated with an application from a source to a destination. After the router and switch combination detects a flow, functions that a router normally performs are moved to the switching hardware. Functions such as packet forwarding, IP header changes, and Ethernet header changes are now done with MLS enabled.

After the routing functions are moved to the switch for a particular flow, subsequent packets in the flow do not have to go through the router because

Figure 6-10
MLS architecture

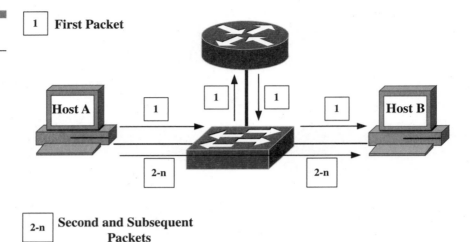

the switch will intercept the flow before it ever gets to the router. This results in faster forwarding at Layer 3.

Flows

A flow is a relatively new concept in networking. IP is a connectionless protocol, meaning that the traffic to and from an IP device does not have to follow a predefined circuit. The network decides the path that a packet should take. This gives a great deal of flexibility to the network design because the network can adapt to changes within the network.

Connection-oriented protocols must have a circuit defined to send traffic. An example would be a phone call. Before the "traffic," in this case a voice signal, can be sent through the network, an end-to-end circuit must be set up. If a change happens within the network that affects this particular circuit, the circuit must be reestablished before the voice signal can continue to be sent.

Regardless of the connectionless nature of IP, a source and destination pair can have many end-to-end traffic streams, known as *flows*. Some flows can involve lots of packets, like *File Transfer Protocol* (FTP) transactions. Other flows only have a few packets, like *Domain Name Services* (DNS) lookups. Some flows can last a long time, but only send a few packets, like Telnet sessions. *Hypertext Transfer Protocol* (HTTP), used for Web transactions, can form flows that last a long time and involve lots of packets. Therefore, the nature of flows can be somewhat characterized by the type of application that forms them.

Multilayer Switching (MLS) Requirements

MLS has different requirements depending on the MLS architecture. The following sections list the requirements for both an internal route processor topology and an external route processor topology.

Internal Route Processor Requirements   To implement an internal route processor distribution layer topology, the following requirements are necessary:

- Catalyst 2926G, 5000, or 6000 family switch
- Firmware release 5.1 or later
- *Route Switch Module* (RSM) or *Route Switch Feature Card* (RSFC)
- Cisco IOS release 12.0(3c)W5(8) or later

External Route Processor Requirements   The following requirements are necessary for building an external route processor distribution layer topology:

- Cisco 8500, 7500, 7200, 4700, 4500, or 3600 series router
- Cisco IOS release 12.0(3c)W5(8) or later

The connection between the switch and the router must be either one link for each VLAN or one link with *Inter Switch Link* (ISL) enabled.

Multilayer Switching (MLS) Operation

This section describes the logical components (and their operation) that are used to implement *Multilayer Switching* (MLS).

Components   The following components are needed for implementing MLS:

■ *Multilayer Switching Switch Engine* (MLS-SE)

■ *Multilayer Switching Route Processor* (MLS-RP)

■ *Multilayer Switching Protocol* (MLSP)

The *Multilayer Switching Switch Engine* (MLS-SE) is the component that forwards packets from one interface to another. If certain fields of the packet must be changed in this forwarding process, the MLS-SE will make the necessary changes. The MLS-SE is implemented in a *NetFlow Feature Card* (NFFC) on the Supervisor Engine III in a Catalyst switch.

The *Multilayer Switching Route Processor* (MLS-RP) is the component that makes the decision where a packet should be routed. The MLS-RP is implemented on a RSM or MSM in a Catalyst switch or on an externally connected router depending on the distribution layer topology you chose.

The *Multilayer Switching Protocol* (MLSP) is a protocol that operates between the MLS-SE and the MLS-RP. The MLSP is used to advertise routes and routing changes from the MLS-RP to the MLS-SE. VLAN information and MAC address information are also exchanged using this protocol.

MLS-RP Advertisement   The MLS-RP sends out multicast hello messages every 15 seconds. These hellos are sent to every switch on the network. These messages contain the following information.

■ The MAC addresses of the MLS-RP interfaces that are participating in MLS

■ Access list information

■ Route changes

The MLSP hello messages are sent to the *Cisco Group Management Protocol* (CGMP) multicast address. CGMP will be covered in more detail in a later chapter, but for the purposes of MLSP, CGMP is simply the transport protocol for the MLSP hello messages.

All Cisco switches receive MLSP hello messages, but only Cisco switches with Layer 3-capability process them. Cisco switches without Layer 3 capability simply flood the MLSP hello packets through the switch. When an MLS-SE sees the MLSP hellos, it extracts the MAC address for the MLS-RP and its associated VLAN ID and puts it in a table on the switch.

A one-byte identifier called an XTAG followed by its MAC address designates an MLS-RP. Because multiple routers can be connected to one switch, the XTAG ID is necessary to fully distinguish a particular MLS-RP. All the MAC addresses learned from a particular MLS-RP get the same XTAG.

MLS Cache Operation   The MLS-SE maintains a cache for determining the route for a particular flow. All packets are compared to this cache to determine the route for a packet. If the packet doesn't match a cache entry, it is sent to the MLS-RP. The process for maintaining the MLS cache is relatively complex.

The process of determining if a received packet is part of a flow is detailed below. In this example, the flow of the received packet is not in the MLS cache.

1. A packet enters the switch and the switch looks at the destination MAC address.

2. The switch compares the destination MAC address with the *Content Addressable Memory* (CAM) table and finds that the packet is destined for a route processor.

3. The switch looks in the MLS cache to see if the packet is part of a flow. The packet does not match any flows in the cache.

4. The packet is forwarded on to the route processor.

When flow for a packet is not found in the MLS cache and is forwarded to a route processor, the flow information for the packet is entered in the MLS cache and is labeled a candidate entry.

The following steps illustrate what happens when the MLS-RP receives the packet.

1. The MLS-RP receives the packet from the MLS-SE and looks to its routing table to see if it has a route to the packet's destination subnet.

2. The MLS-RP finds a route to the packet's destination IP address and modifies the packet's Layer 2 header. The Layer 2 source MAC address becomes the MLS-RP's MAC address and the destination MAC address becomes the next hop in the packet's path.

3. The packet is then forwarded back to the MLS-SE.

So far, the packet has entered the MLS-SE and was forwarded to the MLS-RP to determine the route to the destination and was forwarded back to the MLS-SE. The following steps show what happens when the packet is received on the MLS-SE again.

1. The MLS-SE sees the frame from the MLS-RP. The switch knows which port the packet should be forwarded on after a lookup in its

CAM table. The MLS-SE also looks at the source MAC address and recognizes it as the MAC address for the MLS-RP.

2. The MLS-SE looks to see if the MLS cache has any candidate entries. The MLS-SE finds that the flow has been entered as a candidate flow in the MLS cache. The flow is updated in the MLS cache as an enable entry.

The enable entry in the MLS cache is what allows the MLS-SE to route the packet on its own without having to consult the MLS-RP. The following steps describe what happens when the MLS-SE receives a packet that matches an enable entry in the MLS cache.

1. The MLS-SE receives a frame. The source and destination IP addresses are in the MLS cache as an enable entry.

2. The MLS-SE takes the destination MAC address for the flow entry and updates the packet's destination MAC address. The MAC address for MLS-RP for the flow is used for the packet's updated source MAC address.

The previous steps show the process for routing the flow without having to forward packets to the MLS-RP. This greatly improves the throughput and latency of packets in a flow.

Commands Incompatible with MLS   Four commands will disable MLS:

- `no ip routing`—This command turns off routing on the MLS-RP and therefore disables MLS.
- `ip security`
- `ip tcp compression-connections`
- `ip tcp header-compression`

Note that using `clear ip-route` clears the MLS cache, which erases all the MLS entries used for improving routing performance. This is a momentary condition and will be corrected over time by using the MLS feature.

Flow Masks

A flow mask is used to determine the criteria for comparing packets with the MLS cache. A particular MLS-SE only supports one flow mask for all MLS-RPs that it supports. The MLS-SE learns about the flow mask from

MLSP messages. Whenever the flow mask changes, the MLS cache is cleared.

The three modes of operation for defining flows are

- Destination IP
- Source and Destination IP
- IP Flow

The flow mask modes are defined as follows. The Destination IP flow mask is the default mode. For this mode, the MLS-SE keeps one MLS cache entry for each known IP destination address. There must not be any access lists defined on any of the MLS-RPs supported by the MLS-SE.

While using the Source and Destination IP flow mask mode, the MLS cache keeps an entry for each source and destination IP pair. These flows disregard any Layer 4 port addresses. The mode is compatible with standard IP access lists on any of the supported MLS-RP interfaces.

The IP Flow flow mask mode is the most specific flow mask mode. In this mode, the MLS cache maintains an entry for each IP source and destination pair and source and destination port address. This flow mask mode is used if any of the MLS-RPs are configured with an extended IP access list.

Configuring the Multilayer Switching Switch Engine

In Chapter 5, we covered configuring VTP on the switch using the Set-Commands. MLS requires configuring VTP in addition to the MLS configuration.

To enable an MLS-SE, you need only use the following command:

```
Switch(enable) set mls enable
```

The switch will then listen for MLSP messages from the RSM. In the event that the MLS-RP is an external router, you have to tell the switch to implicitly listen for MLSP messages from that router by specifying its IP address.

```
Switch(enable) set mls include ip-addr
```

Now that you have the switch listening for MLSP messages from the MLS-RP, you have more configuration options. From the MLS-SE perspective, you have a couple of options for increasing the performance of MLS.

The MLS-SE has two timers. The first is a cache aging timer. The cache aging time specifies how long the switch will keep an MLS flow entry in the cache. The default value is 256 seconds, but may vary from 8 to 2032 seconds (in eight-second increments). You may modify the cache aging time as follows:

```
Switch(enable) set mls agingtime aging-time
```

The cache may be increased in low-traffic VLANs or decreased in high-traffic VLANs to optimize cache memory usage.

The second parameter also relates to cache aging, but is for very specific flow types. Short flows can quickly create many cache entries that will stay around until they expire per the aging time specified above. To better handle short flows, another parameter exists:

```
Switch(enable) set mls agingtime fast fast-agingtime pkt-threshold
```

The default values for fast aging time and packet threshold are zero seconds.

The two parameters combined enable you to specify how many packets must arrive in the supplied interval for the entry to remain in the cache. The allowable fast aging time values are 32, 64, 96, or 128 seconds. The packet threshold may be 1, 3, 7, 15, 31, or 63 packets.

One example is

```
Switch(enable) set mls agingtime fast 64 15
```

This specifies that the switch must see 15 packets in a 64-second period, or the cache entry expires. As you can see, this can significantly impact your cache management by optimizing for short flows.

Finally, verifying your MLS configuration is a good idea. You can do this using the following command:

```
Switch(enable) show mls
```

This will let you view the configured parameters and cache statistics for MLS flows. In addition, you can view the details for each configured MLS-RP.

First, to view the list of MLS-RPs, use the following command:

```
Switch(enable) show mls include
```

Next, specify the MLS-RP you want information about:

```
Switch(enable) show mls rp ip-address
```

After verifying proper configuration, examining the MLS cache to verify operation is helpful. To examine the cache details, enter the following:

```
Switch(enable) show mls entry
```

To clear a specified entry from the cache, use the following command:

```
Switch(enable) clear mls entry ip [destination ip_addr_spec]
[source ip_addr_spec] [flow protocol src_port dst_port] [all]
```

Configuring the Multilayer Switching Route Processor

Enabling MLS on a route processor (MLS-RP) is a simple four-step process.

1. Enable MLS on the route processor.
2. Assign an MLS interface to a VTP domain.
3. Enable MLS on an interface.
4. Specify MLS management interface.

Enabling MLS requires turning on MLS in the global configuration. You may do that by entering the following:

```
SHERRY(config)# mls rp ip
```

Next, assign the interface to a VTP domain using the following command:

```
Router(config-if)# mls rp vtp-domain domain-name
```

For our example, we'll configure the VLAN 13 interface to be a part of the ADMIN VTP domain. Three cases may arise:

- Router is acting as an Internal Route Processor
- Router is acting as an External Route Processor with ISL
- Router is acting as an External Route Processor without ISL

The first two cases require only adding the `mls rp vtp-domain` command to the interface or sub-interface and enabling MLS.

```
SHERRY(config)# interface Vlan13
SHERRY(config-if)# mls rp vtp-domain ADMIN
SHERRY(config-if)# mls rp ip
```

The last case requires that the interface know the VLAN ID. As discussed earlier, ISL encapsulation includes the VLAN ID in the header information. The Internal Route Processor uses ISL internally; furthermore, an interface with ISL encapsulation would also have the VLAN ID available. For an interface that does not use ISL, you must specify the VLAN ID. The following Cisco IOS command is used.

```
Router(config-if)# mls rp vlan-id vlan-id-number
```

For example, if VLAN 13 was connected to an Ethernet interface on a router acting as an External Route Processor:

```
JOCKO(config)# interface Ethernet 0/1
JOCKO(config-if)# mls rp vlan-id 13
JOCKO(config-if)# mls rp vtp-domain ADMIN
JOCKO(config-if)# mls rp ip
```

The last step is to specify one interface to send MLSP messages; you may specify more than one, but this procedure is not recommended. To specify the interface, use the following command.

```
Router(config-if)# mls rp management-interface
```

Using the first example, we can make VLAN 13 the management interface also.

```
SHERRY(config)# interface Vlan13
SHERRY(config-if)# mls rp management-interface
```

Here is what the final configuration will resemble:

```
SHERRY# show running-config
Building configuration...
Current configuration:
!
version 12.0
! (text deleted)
hostname SHERRY
!
enable password cisco
! (text deleted)
router igrp 1
   network 12.0.0.0
!
interface Vlan13
   mls rp vtp-domain ADMIN
   mls rp management-interface
   mls rp ip
   ip address 12.1.1.1 255.255.255.0
!
ip default-gateway 11.1.1.1
! (text deleted)
end
```

With the configuration parameters verified, you can verify the MLS status for a VLAN using the `show mls rp interface` command.

```
Router# show mls rp interface interface-number
```

For the previous example:

```
SHERRY# show mls rp interface Vlan13
```

The output will verify if MLS is active, check the MLS domain, and denote if the interface is the MLSP management interface.

As discussed earlier, you can further optimize MLS performance by utilizing flow masks. For router configuration, flow masks are applied if access lists are present on the MLS interface. No access list denotes a flow mask of destination IP address. Using a standard IP access list will force the MLS-SE to use a source and destination IP address flow mask. An extended IP access list will force the MLS-SE to create an entry for every IP flow. Access lists in this context refer to outbound IP access lists. Inbound IP access lists disable MLS on an interface. Access lists will be examined in great detail later; however, to enable MLS to work properly with an inbound IP access list, you must explicitly allow input access lists on an MLS-RP interface.

```
Router(config)# mls rp ip input-acl
```

Fault-Tolerant Routing with Hot Standby Routing Protocol

The router is a critical point in the campus network. If the router fails, many paths within the network could fail. If this is not acceptable, fault tolerance in the routing layer must be implemented. The Hot Standby Routing Protocol is one choice for implementing fault tolerance for routing.

Other solutions using standard routing protocols exist. Implementing routing fault tolerance with standard routing protocols raises some interesting issues. The most important issue to acknowledge is route convergence time. When a router fails, it takes time for the network to discover the change and adapt to it. Using standard routing protocols can create significant route convergence times. The Cisco proprietary *Hot Standby Routing Protocol* (HSRP) minimizes the convergence time of the routing network.

For fault-tolerant routing networks to exist, redundant links must occur inside the distribution layer. Dealing with routing in the presence of redundant paths is a difficult task. Either the network or all the end stations must know about the alternate default gateway to forward packets in the event of a failure of the primary router. The following examples describe the need for a fault-tolerant routing protocol.

In the case of one-hop routing networks, Proxy ARP is often used. It is a simple way to implement routing in this particular environment. In fact, two routers can be interconnected between each other and all their interfaces to provide dual paths between all networks. The addition of the second router will give a failover path if the first router were to fail. In the case of a failure, the end stations must all ARP again for the default gateway. This isn't an instantaneous result because the end station keeps an ARP table that ages very slowly. The ARP entry must age out before another ARP request is sent for the new router. The ARP aging time would result in end stations not being able to find a default gateway for a long period of time. This is unacceptable.

Introduction to Hot Standby Routing Protocol (HSRP)

With HSRP, a group of routers can be configured to appear as one router. If one of the routers in the group fails, another router in the group will take over the routing operation. The result is that routing still takes place and the hosts have no idea that the router has changed.

The HSRP standby group is made of the following components:

- One active router
- One standby router
- One virtual router

One router may be a member of several HSRP virtual groups. One standby group can emulate one router. There may be as many as 255 standby groups on a LAN.

In the case of VLANs, a router failure could be catastrophic. Fortunately, HSRP will work in a multiple VLAN environment using *Inter-Switch Links* (ISL). Several routers can be added to the multiple VLAN architecture to provide fault tolerance. Each router can be a backup router for multiple VLANs.

Hot Standby Routing Protocol (HSRP) Operation

The virtual router is made up of several routers (see Figure 6-11). Only one of the routers may be the active router. The active router does all the routing function of the virtual router. The active router responds to ARP requests, forwards packets on to other subnets, and changes the MAC source, MAC destination, and TTL fields.

The router that has the highest standby priority is elected to be the active router. This value is configurable by the network administrator. If two routers have an equal priority, the router with the higher IP address becomes the active router. When a router becomes the active router, it services all the routing needs of the virtual router. The active router routes packets destined for the virtual router MAC address. This MAC address is used for the new source MAC address of the routed packet.

Active and Standby Router Communication   The active router handles all the routing functions of the virtual router. Another router in the group becomes the standby router. Both the active router and standby router send HSRP hello messages to advertise their active and standby

Figure 6-11
HSRP architecture

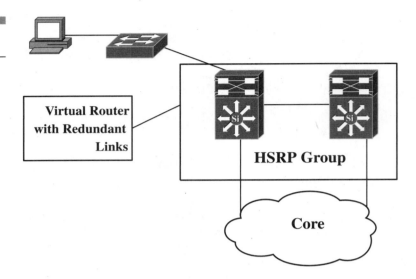

router status. Only the Active and Standby routers send HSRP messages after they have been elected.

The standby router monitors the hello messages sent from the active router to determine whether the active router is capable of forwarding packets. As soon as the standby router determines that the active router has failed, the standby router assumes the role of the active router.

Other routers in the standby group monitor the HSRP hello messages from the active and standby routers. As long as these routers determine that the active or the standby routers are operational, they do nothing. When both the active and standby routers have failed, the remaining routers in the standby group contend for active and standby router status.

When the standby router assumes the role of the active router, the hosts on the network see no difference because the new active router uses the MAC address and IP address of the virtual router. The time it takes for the standby router to fully assume the role of the active router can be measured in seconds. HSRP's fast and seamless operation is very desirable when building redundancy into a routing network.

Hot Standby Routing Protocol (HSRP) Messages   HSRP packets are UDP packets using port 1985. The destination IP address is a well-known multicast address called the "all router" address. The Time to Live field is set to a value of one. The following list shows the fields in the HSRP packet (UDP payload).

- HSRP Version
- Op Code
- State
- Hello Time
- Hold Time
- Priority
- Group
- Authentication Data
- Virtual IP Address

The HSRP Version field displays the version of HSRP. The Op Code field describes the type of HSRP message. An HSRP message can be one of three types:

- *Hello Message*   Advertises that a router is operational and is able to become an active or standby router.
- *Coup Message*   Advertises that a router wishes to become an active router
- *Resign Message*   Advertises that a router wants to stop being the active router

The State field describes the state of the router in the standby group. The HSRP states are described in a following subsection.

The Hello Time field contains the period of hello message transmission in seconds. This field is only applicable to hello messages.

The Hold Time field displays the length of time that a hello message is valid in seconds. This field is only applicable to hello messages.

The Priority field contains the priority of the router. This field is used in the election of the active and standby routers.

The Group field contains the ID of the standby group. This value can be from 0 through 255.

The Authentication field contains a password for the standby group. This password is transmitted in clear text.

The Virtual IP Address field contains the IP address of the virtual router.

Hot Standby Routing Protocol (HSRP) States   The six HSRP states are

- Initial State
- Learn State

- Listen State
- Speak State
- Standby State
- Active State

The Initial State is the first state that a router enters before beginning HSRP operation. No HSRP messages are sent while the router is in this state.

While in the Learn State, the router waits to receive an HSRP message from the active router. The router knows nothing about the standby group while in this state.

When a router is in the Listen State, it has learned the Virtual Router IP address, but is not the active or standby router. The router listens for HSRP hello messages while in this state.

From the Listen State, the router enters the Speak State. While in the Speak State, the router actively participates in the election of the active and standby routers. Because the router entered the Speak State from the Listen State, it knows the Virtual Router IP address.

When a router enters the Standby State from the Listen State, it is a candidate for becoming the active router. It sends periodic HSRP hellos to the network.

When a router enters the Active State from the Standby State, it is the active router. This means that this router is conducting the routing function of the virtual router.

Configuring Hot Standby Routing Protocol (HSRP)

To enable a router to participate as a Hot Standby group member, you must enable HSRP for the interface you wish to participate in the group. HSRP is enabled on an interface by issuing the following command:

```
Router(config-if)# standby group-number ip ip-address
```

The group number must be the same for all interfaces that wish to participate as a Hot Standby interface for a given group. The IP address specifies the virtual address of the HSRP router. This is the IP address that the interface will respond to (in addition to the other interface addresses) if this interface becomes the active Hot Standby interface.

Configuring Hot Standby Routing Protocol (HSRP) Standby Priority In addition to adding an interface to an HSRP group, you can specify the priority of the interface in the group. This gives you the flexibility to fully specify the order of the interfaces if fail-over occurs. Though not necessary, as discussed in Chapter 2, knowing deterministically what can happen in your network is valuable.

To specify the priority, you do the following:

```
Router(config-if)# standby group-number priority priority-value
```

The priority can be any number in the range 0 to 255. The default value is 100.

Configuring Hot Standby Routing Protocol (HSRP) Standby Preempt Further desiring the deterministic quality in your network, you can specify what happens when a failed link/interface returns to service. By default, HSRP will let the current active interface remain active. However, assuming you went through the trouble to specify the HSRP interface group priorities, you would also want the interfaces to return to their original status and priorities when all is functioning normally.

To enable an interface to always become the primary interface, you can use the following command:

```
Router(config-if)# standby group-number preempt
```

Configuring Hot Standby Routing Protocol (HSRP) Hello Message Timers The default timer values will work in many networks; however, it may become necessary to modify these values if the hello packets need to pass through networks that become congested at times.

```
Router(config-if)# standby group-number timers hello-interval
hold-time
```

The hello interval by default is three seconds, but may range from 1 to 255 seconds. The hold time should be at least three times the hello interval. The default hold time is 10 seconds.

If you have a congested network, three hello packets may not successfully make it within the 10-second hold time. This could lead to HSRP fail-over even though no problem exists. Increasing the hello interval and hold time can prevent accidental fail-over; however, it has the side effect of increasing the time necessary for fail-over to occur in the event of a hardware or link failure.

Viewing the Virtual Router MAC Address   You can view the virtual MAC address in use for a specific HSRP standby group by using the following command:

```
Router# show standby interface group-number
```

Interface refers to the specific interface in the HSRP group, and group number is the HSRP standby group number identifier.

Monitoring a Hot Standby Routing Protocol (HSRP) Interface   To monitor the HSRP group and interface status, you may use the following commands:

```
Router# show standby interface group-number brief
```

where *interface* refers to the specific interface in the HSRP group, and *group-number* is the HSRP standby group number identifier. The brief option will only output the current status.

Alternatively, you can list the status for all groups and interfaces on the router that are configured for HSRP.

```
Router# show standby brief
```

Chapter Summary

This chapter covers the following topics:

- Routing issues
- IP addressing
- Router operation
- Maintaining routes
- InterVLAN routing
- *Multilayer Switching* (MLS)
- Fault-tolerant routing with Hot Standby Routing Protocol

First, routing issues are covered to describe why routing is necessary. A discussion of IP addressing and IP communication basics follows. Topics such as subnet masks and the *Address Resolution Protocol* (ARP) are covered. These topics lay the foundation for a discussion of router operation. This chapter also covers the classical concepts of routing.

After discussing routing basics, we moved on to the concept of a route and how to configure it. We examined default routes as a method for manually implementing a route table. We also mentioned the concept of dynamic route table maintenance through routing protocols.

The topics until this point build a platform to bring together the concepts of VLANs and routing. Here, we discussed interVLAN routing and how to implement it. We recalled the concept of *InterSwitch Links* (ISLs) and how to implement ISL to route between multiple VLANs on one link.

Next, we improved on the concepts of InterVLAN routing by discussing *multilayer switching* (MLS). Here we learned of a method for pushing the routing decisions out to the switch after making an initial route decision at the route processor. This concept of caching routing information in the switch results in much faster routing.

After we have gained a full grasp of basic routing, routing between VLANs, and *multilayer switching* (MLS), we cover fault tolerant routing. Fault tolerance is a necessary component in a mission-critical campus network design. The implementation of this technology raises several issues. Cisco has created a protocol called *Hot Standby Routing Protocol* (HSRP) to provide a solution to the issues raised with providing fault tolerance in a campus network architecture. We learned that this protocol provides fast and seamless failover protection in the event of a router failure.

Now we are ready to cover the concepts of multicast routing. Up until this point, our Layer 3 discussions have been focused on unicast concepts. Multicast provides a good method for communicating from one device to many others on the network. The implementation of this feature raises a number of issues to be dealt with. This will be covered in a subsequent chapter.

Frequently Asked Questions (FAQ)

Question: Where can I learn more about InterVLAN routing and HSRP?

Answer: Visit www.cisco.com.

Question: Can I use HSRP with other vendors' router products?

Answer: Most likely, no. HSRP is a Cisco proprietary means to provide fault-tolerant routing. The other vendor would have to implement HSRP, which is unlikely.

Question: Why not always use proxy ARP for routing?

Answer: Proxy ARP provides a simple and easy-to-manage routing function in a one-router environment. Proxy ARP will not work through more than one router hop. In multiple router environments, you must use a routing protocol or use static routes.

Question: Is HSRP a routing protocol?

Answer: No. HSRP is a way to implement failover-based fault tolerance in the event of a router failure. In multiple router environments, you would still need a routing protocol or manually enter static routes to build the route tables in the routers. Even if a router is part of a virtual router and can provide fault tolerance, the router must have a valid routing table.

Case Study

Objective: From the last chapter, we built the *Cubby Products International* (CPI) campus network to have VLANs, an optimal Spanning Tree configuration and aggregated links. Now we need communication between VLANs so everyone has access to centralized storage and processing in the IT VLAN. Your job is to implement Layer 3 switching in CPI's campus network. This includes setting up IP addresses, defining a default gateway for all hosts, configuring routes in the switches, and implementing MLS and HSRP if appropriate (see Figure 6-12)

Approach

The following items must be completed in order:

1. Define IP addressing for all VLANs
2. Define the default gateway for all hosts
3. Define a method for building the routing table
4. Explore optimizing routing performance with MLS
5. Explore fault-tolerant routing

Figure 6-12
CPI campus network topology

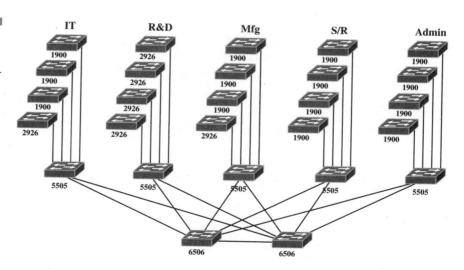

Define IP Addressing for All VLANs

We have defined an IP subnet for remote management of all the switches in the case study from Chapter 4. This is the first subnet available for the campus network. The other VLANs will use subsequent subnets using the same network number. The IP subnets are defined in Table 6-3. All subnets will have a subnet mask of 255.255.255.0. This will give 256 addresses per subnet, which should leave plenty of room for future growth.

Define IP Addressing and Default Gateway for All Hosts

Now that the IP subnets and subnet masks have been defined, we will define the default gateways for each of the subnets. Each of the hosts will have these values manually set its configuration.

The convention for default gateway addresses and host addresses will be to use the last valid IP address in the subnet as the default gateway address. The first IP addresses in the subnet will be for the hosts in the subnet. Table 6-4 shows the default gateway addresses for each subnet. Note that the last IP address in the subnet is a broadcast address for the subnet.

Other hosts on the subnet will get IP node address 1–253. Each of the hosts on the network can now be configured with a valid IP address.

Configure the switches with the appropriate VLAN IP addresses.

5505 IP Address Configuration   For each Catalyst 5505, perform the following configuration on the RSM.

Table 6-3

IP subnets by VLAN

VLAN	VLAN ID	IP Subnet
Management		100.1.1.0
R&D	1	100.1.2.0
Mfg	2	100.1.3.0
SR	3	100.1.4.0
Admin	4	100.1.5.0
IT	5	100.1.6.0

Table 6-4

IP default gateway addresses by VLAN

VLAN	VLAN ID	IP Subnet	Default Gateway
Management		100.1.1.0	100.1.1.254
R&D	1	100.1.2.0	100.1.2.254
Mfg	2	100.1.3.0	100.1.3.254
SR	3	100.1.4.0	100.1.4.254
Admin	4	100.1.5.0	100.1.5.254
IT	5	100.1.6.0	100.1.6.254

Recall, to get to the RSM for a device, you may do the following:

```
RD-1-dist-5505(enable) session 5
```

In this case, the RSM is in module 5 of the Catalyst 5505. You can use the `show module` command to locate the RSM.

After you have logged into the RSM, you should configure the hostname appropriately:

```
Router# configure terminal
Router(config)# hostname RD-1-dist-5505
```

After the host name is configured, your prompt will show the device name. Perform the steps for setting the host name for each device. You may also configure the interfaces at the same time.

The following commands set the appropriate IP address for the VLAN interfaces per Table 6-4.

```
RD-1-dist-5505(config)# interface Vlan1
RD-1-dist-5505(config-if)# ip address 100.1.2.254 255.255.255.0
RD-1-dist-5505(config-if)# no shutdown

Mfg-1-dist-5505(config)# interface Vlan2
Mfg-1-dist-5505(config-if)# ip address 100.1.3.254 255.255.255.0
Mfg-1-dist-5505(config-if)# no shutdown

SR-1-dist-5505(config)# interface Vlan3
SR-1-dist-5505(config-if)# ip address 100.1.4.254 255.255.255.0
SR-1-dist-5505(config-if)# no shutdown

Admin-1-dist-5505(config)# interface Vlan4
Admin-1-dist-5505(config-if)# ip address 100.1.5.254 255.255.255.0
Admin-1-dist-5505(config-if)# no shutdown
```

```
IT-1-dist-5505(config)# interface Vlan5
IT-1-dist-5505(config-if)# ip address 100.1.6.254 255.255.255.0
IT-1-dist-5505(config-if)# no shutdown
```

Notice that we went ahead and enabled the interface. They are shutdown by default.

Define a Method for Building the Routing Tables

Due to the moderate complexity of the CPI network, static routes are not practical to maintain. If any change occurs in the routing architecture of the campus network, all the switches would have to be changed to reflect the routing change.

Instead, we will use a routing protocol to automatically learn routes from the network. We choose *Cisco's Interior Group Routing Protocol* (IGRP). The configuration is simple and easy to maintain. The following lists the commands to set up routing in the 5505s. Note that the 5505s are the only devices that perform routing. IGRP is covered in detail in Chapter 10.

Configuring IGRP in 5505s   Enabling routing is the same for each of the Catalyst 5505s. For example:

```
IT-1-dist-5505(config)# ip routing
IT-1-dist-5505(config)# router igrp
IT-1-dist-5505(config-router)# network 100.0.0.0
```

With routing enabled, your Catalyst 5505 will now perform interVLAN routing. Repeat the commands for each Catalyst 5505.

Optimizing Routing Performance

All traffic between VLANs has to go through the RSMs. This could create a bottleneck in the network as the amount of interVLAN traffic increases. The answer to this problem is to implement *Multilayer Switching* (MLS) features in the 5505s. The following lists the configuration needed in the 5505s to implement MLS.

MLS Configuration in the 5505s   First, you must enable the MLS-SE.

```
IT-1-dist-5505(enable) set mls enable
```

No other commands are necessary for the MLS-SE. Because we will be using the RSM as the MLS-RP, you do not have to specify an MLS-RP using the `set mls include` command. Repeat the command on all Catalyst 5505s.

Next, you must configure the MLS-RP. Use the `session` command to connect to the RSM and enter the following commands:

```
IT-1-dist-5505(config)# mls rp ip
IT-1-dist-5505(config)# interface VlanX
IT-1-dist-5505(config-if)# mls rp vtp-domain CPI
IT-1-dist-5505(config-if)# mls rp ip
IT-1-dist-5505(config-if)# mls rp management-interface
```

This will enable MLS on the router and enable and configure MLS on the VLAN interface. Repeat the commands for all Catalyst 5505s in the network. Recall that only one management interface should be enabled per device.

Fault-Tolerant Routing

Fault-tolerant routing is not applicable in this network because only one path exists to the MLS-RP from the hosts. In other words, no redundant path to the distribution layer from the access layer exists.

If a redundant path existed from the access layer to the distribution layer, HSRP could be implemented. This is a possibility for a future upgrade to the CPI network. This would require more ports in the distribution layer to implement HSRP. Due to funding issues, we must choose either path redundancy between the access layer and distribution layer or between the distribution layer and the core layer. Redundancy in the core layer is more important.

Case Study Summary

The CPI campus network is now to a point where interVLAN communication can take place. Now centralized storage and processing can be implemented in the IT department. This will go a long way in saving money on

IT functions and give CPI a more efficient way to implement their information technologies.

The following steps were completed to get to this point. We started with an optimal Layer 2 configuration.

1. Define IP addressing for all VLANs.
2. Define default gateway for all hosts and define host IP addresses.
3. Configured 5505 IP addresses.
4. Implemented IGRP routing protocol in all the 5505s.
5. Implemented MLS in 5505s.
6. Decided not to implement HSRP.

CPI's network is now configured to handle unicast IP routing between VLANs in an optimal fashion. Later chapters will explore how to implement routing features optimized for multicast transmission. Security and traffic access issues will be covered in a later chapter also.

Questions

1. How many node addresses are there in an IP subnet that has a host with an IP address of 153.12.53.2 and an IP subnet mask of 255.255.248.0?

   a. 256
   b. 512
   c. 1024
   d. 2046

2. Which of the following are valid IP subnet masks?

   a. 152.12.53.2
   b. 255.255.248.255
   c. 255.255.0.0
   d. 0.0.255.255

3. What is the broadcast address for the subnet having an IP address of 153.12.53.2 and a subnet mask of 255.255.248.0?

   a. 153.12.53.2
   b. 153.12.53.255
   c. 153.12.54.255
   d. 153.12.55.255

4. IP is a _____ layer protocol.

   a. physical
   b. data link
   c. network
   d. transport

5. The *Address Resolution Protocol* (ARP) links _____.

   a. a MAC address to an IP address
   b. an IP address to a MAC address
   c. two VLANs
   d. two subnets

6. What two fields does a router modify when forwarding a packet at Layer 3?

   a. source MAC address and destination IP address
   b. source MAC address and source IP address
   c. destination MAC address and TTL
   d. destination MAC address and source IP address

7. A host must forward a packet to the _____ if it is destined for a different subnet than the host's.

   a. switch
   b. destination host
   c. standby router
   d. default router

8. A host's default gateway must be in the same _____ as the host.

   a. link
   b. broadcast domain
   c. department
   d. IP subnet

9. When not using a routing protocol, _____.

   a. the router can't forward packets at Layer 3
   b. static routes or a default route must be configured
   c. dynamic routes must be configured
   d. the router responds with "destination route unknown"

10. Which of the following can describe a flow?

   a. a string of packets
   b. a group of TCP sessions
   c. a list of routes
   d. packets with the same IP source and destination

11. The *multilayer switching route processor* (MLS-RP) _____.

   a. is the MLS component that forwards packets at Layer 3
   b. must be internal to the switch
   c. makes routing decisions in a MLS architecture
   d. is unnecessary

12. An *MLS switch engine* (MLS-SE) _____.

   a. is the MLS component that forwards packets at Layer 3
   b. must be internal to the switch
   c. makes routing decisions in a MLS architecture
   d. is unnecessary

13. What does the MLS cache hold?

   a. the MAC address of the MLS-RP
   b. the MAC address of the MLS-SE
   c. flow information
   d. routes

14. With MLS, _____.

    a. all packets must be processed by the MLS-RP
    b. all packets must appear in the MLS cache
    c. all packets are forwarded at Layer 3
    d. all packets do not have to be processed by the MLS-RP

15. Which of the following is not a valid flow mask?

    a. destination IP address
    b. source and destination IP address and source and destination port address
    c. source IP address
    d. source and destination IP address

16. *Hot Standby Routing Protocol* (HSRP) provides _____.

    a. load balancing between routers
    b. failover router redundancy
    c. new routes to unknown subnets
    d. security

17. HSRP replaces _____ of some routing protocols.

    a. scaleability
    b. security
    c. fault tolerance
    d. the routes

18. The _____ router is the logical router entity for HSRP.

    a. active
    b. standby
    c. virtual
    d. default

19. The _____ router is what is currently forwarding packets at Layer 3 in an HSRP implementation.

    a. active
    b. standby
    c. virtual
    d. default

20. The active router assumes the MAC address of the _____ router.

   a. standby

   b. default

   c. next

   d. virtual

Answers

1. How many node addresses are in an IP subnet that has a host with an IP address of 153.12.53.2 and an IP subnet mask of 255.255.248.0?

   d. 2046

   255.255.248.0 in binary is 11111111.11111111.11111000.00000000. Therefore, the node field has 11 bits, creating 2^{11} or 2048 addresses. Recall that the first and last addresses, 0 and 255, are not available.

2. Which of the following is a valid IP subnet mask?

   c. 255.255.0.0

   Subnet masks must have contiguous 1s starting from the most significant bit.

3. What is the broadcast address for the subnet having an IP address of 153.12.53.2 and a subnet mask of 255.255.248.0?

   d. 153.12.55.255

   The broadcast address is the address corresponding to all 1s in the node field.

4. IP is a _____ layer protocol.

   c. network

5. The Address Resolution Protocol (ARP) links _____.

   a. IP address to a MAC address

6. What two fields does a router modify when forwarding a packet at Layer 3?

   c. destination MAC address and TTL

7. A host must forward a packet to the _____ if it is destined for a different subnet than the host's.

   d. default router

8. Host's default gateway must be in the same _____ as the host.

   d. IP subnet

   A router would not be needed if the host can forward to a different subnet.

9. When not using a routing protocol, _____.

   b. static routes or a default route must be configured

   Otherwise, the router has no way of learning routes from the network.

10. Which of the following can describe a flow?

    d.   packets with the same IP source and destination

11. The multilayer switching route processor (MLS-RP) _____.

    c.   makes routing decisions in a MLS architecture

    The MLS-RP does forward packets at Layer 3, but only back to the MLS-SE. The MLS-SE actually does the forwarding.

12. A MLS switch engine (MLS-SE) _____.

    a.   is the MLS component that forwards packets at Layer 3

13. What does the MLS cache hold?

    c.   flow information

14. With MLS, _____.

    d.   all packets do not have to be processed by the MLS-RP

    After the flow is registered in the MLS cache, the MLS-SE can do the forwarding.

15. Which of the following is not a valid flow mask?

    c.   source IP address

16. Hot Standby Routing Protocol (HSRP) provides _____.

    b.   failover router redundancy

17. HSRP replaces _____ of some routing protocols.

    c.   fault tolerance

18. The _____ router is the logical router entity for HSRP.

    c.   virtual

19. The _____ router is currently forwarding packets at Layer 3 in an HSRP implementation.

    a.   active

20. The active router assumes the MAC address of the _____ router.

    d.   virtual

IP Multicast
Configuration

Introduction

The previous chapters have discussed in great detail the methods of transmitting unicast and broadcast streams through the campus network. This chapter will explore the need for multicast and the mechanisms for carrying multicast traffic.

Objectives Covered in the Chapter

The following topics will be covered in this chapter:

- Network transmission models
- Multicast addressing
- Multicast group maintenance

The first subject to be covered in multicasting is the need for multicasting. The approach will be to build on the network transmission models that have been discussed in previous chapters. Here, we will review unicast and broadcast transmission models and see where multicast fits in.

After we understand the need for multicasting, we will delve into multicast addressing schemes. This discussion will be based on IP multicasting due to its prevalence in modern networking. Here we will cover the concept of an IP multicast group address and how it maps to Ethernet MAC addresses.

With an understanding of IP multicast group addressing, we will explore the ways to manage an IP multicast group. This is accomplished via an IP multicast group management protocol. This protocol will handle the management tasks of a host joining and leaving an IP multicast group.

Network Transmission Models

This section helps define the need for multicast in the campus network. This discussion begins by discussing the three basic network transmission models. These models are as follows:

- Unicast
- Broadcast
- Multicast

The number of transmitters (sources) and receivers (destinations) delineate the different transmission models. The models will be covered in more detail in the following text. Some of these will sound very familiar.

Unicast Transmission

We have covered unicast routing and switching in great detail in the previous chapters. Unicast traffic streams have one transmitter and one receiver (see Figure 7-1). This traffic model is the foundation for the other types of traffic patterns. This is what TCP does well. In TCP, there is an IP/port pair that defines a flow. The unicast flow is the fundamental building block found in all networks.

Broadcast Transmission

Broadcasting is another fundamental network transmission model. We have seen this model in operation in some of our previous discussions (see

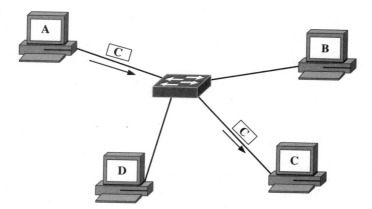

Figure 7-1
Unicast transmission model

Figure 7-2
Broadcast
transmission model

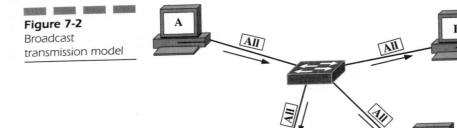

Figure 7-2). Broadcasting is simply one host transmitting to all hosts. In the case of Ethernet, broadcast traffic is bound to all the hosts in a broadcast domain. In IP, a broadcast is bound to an IP subnet.

As we have seen, broadcasting can cause problems due to its global nature. Because all broadcast packets are sent to all hosts, probably not all the hosts need to receive the packet. This global transmission can lead to unnecessary traffic.

An example of broadcasting is the *Address Resolution Protocol* (ARP) request. ARPs are sent to all hosts to find a host that knows the MAC address associated with a particular IP address. More than one host may have the information, but in other cases only one may have it. This situation requires the use of the broadcast transmission model.

Multicast Transmission

Multicasting is similar to broadcasting in that there is a one-to-many traffic pattern. The difference is the receiving hosts are a subset of all the hosts. Already, we can see that multicasting can increase the efficiency of the network by reducing the amount of unnecessary network traffic.

Creating many unicast streams can mimic multicasting (see Figure 7-3). Each of these streams will have the same originating host and each stream will terminate to a different host in the multicast group. However, using many unicast streams to implement one multicast stream is inefficient across a large internetwork.

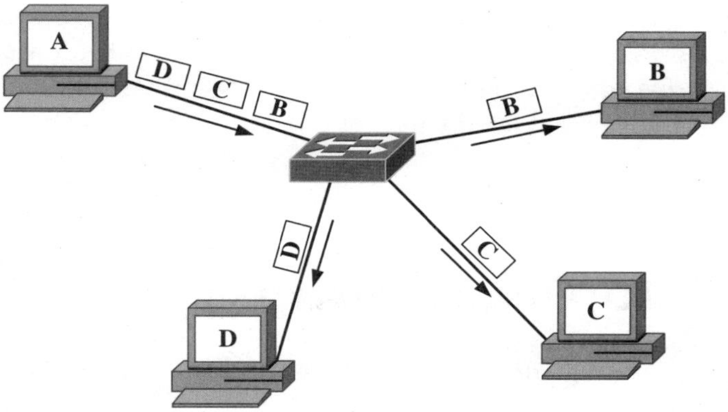

Figure 7-3
Many unicast streams

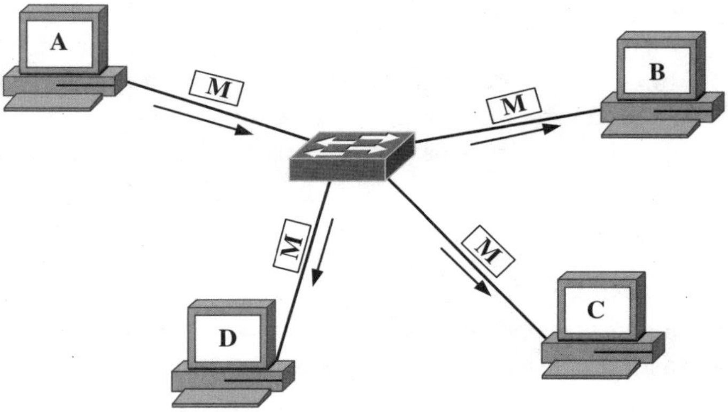

Figure 7-4
One multicast stream

If many unicast streams originate from the same source and each terminates to a different user and carries the same traffic, the intermediate links could be burdened with lots of redundant traffic. The solution is to create a group of hosts and an addressing scheme for the group and let the network decide how to replicate the source stream to all receivers. The traffic stream will then be sent to the multicast address (see Figure 7-4). The network is left to decide how to organize traffic over its links to best utilize available bandwidth.

Multicasting can be deployed for a number of applications. The most obvious application is video transmission over the campus network. In this case, the same traffic is sent from one source to many hosts. Video traffic can be very bandwidth-intensive. Duplicating the traffic to many hosts can be detrimental to a network, if not impossible. Multicasting helps alleviate this problem by having the source send one stream to a multicast group address and let the network decide what links should carry the multicast traffic.

Multicast Addressing

Multicast addressing involves both Layer 2 and Layer 3 addressing. The IP layer specifies the IP multicast group address. The Layer 2 MAC address is changed according to the Layer 3 IP multicast address. The Layer 2 MAC addresses are derived from the Layer 3 multicast address so multicast ARPs are not needed.

Note that implementing multicast ARP could be a horrendous task. Imagine if a multicast group address exists and a host needs to send a packet to the multicast group. After the IP header is addressed with the IP multicast address as the destination IP addresses, the host needs to determine the MAC addresses of all the hosts in the multicast group. In most cases, this would be nearly impossible because the multicast address can span multiple broadcast domains. Therefore this imaginary multicast ARP would have to trasverse all subnets, VLANs, and broadcast domains. After multicast becomes a staple for a campus network, the network could come to a standstill just from a multicast ARP transaction using this method.

Both Layer 3 and Layer 2 multicast addressing is discussed in the following sections.

IP Multicast Addressing

Multicast IP addressing uses class D IP addresses. Recall from Chapter 6, "Unicast Layer 3 Configuration," that class D addresses start with the bit pattern 1110. Therefore, the first four bits of an IP multicast address are fixed. The following 28 bits of the IP multicast address can be anything, so the range of IP multicast addresses starts with 224.0.0.0 and ends with 239.255.255.255. The bit pattern of the IP multicast following the initial byte has no structure. There are some well-known IP multicast addresses, however. The *Internet Assigned Numbers Authority* (IANA) defines these well-known IP multicast addresses. Table 7-1 lists a few.

	IP Multicast Address	Description
Table 7-1	224.0.0.1	All hosts on a subnet
Well-known IP multicast addresses	224.0.0.2	All routers on a subnet
	224.0.0.4	All Distance Vector Multicast Routing Protocol (DVMRP) routers
	224.0.0.5	All Open Shortest Path First (OSPF) routers
	224.0.0.6	All OSPF designated routers
	224.0.0.9	All Routing Information Protocol v2 (RIP2) routers
	224.0.0.13	All Protocol Independent Multicast (PIM) routers

Ethernet Multicast Addressing

Ethernet multicast addressing is a little trickier. As discussed previously, the Layer 2 multicast MAC address is derived from the Layer 3 IP multicast address. The process is as follows.

IANA has defined that all Ethernet multicast addresses always begin with the hex values "01 00 5E" in the first three bytes. The next bit of the address is "0." That takes care of 25 of the 48 bits in the Ethernet MAC address (see Figure 7-5). The remaining 23 bits are derived from the lowest order 23 bits from the IP Multicast address.

Here is an example of how this Ethernet multicast-addressing scheme works. For the multicast address 224.0.1.1, the resulting Ethernet MAC address is derived as follows.

$$1\,224.0.1.1\,2^{10} = 11100000.00000000.00000001.00000001$$

The lowest 23 bits of the IP multicast address are as follows.

$$0000000.00000001.00000001$$

Because all multicast Ethernet MAC addresses always begin with $(01\text{-}00\text{-}5e)^{16}$, this defines the Ethernet Multicast address as

$$00000001-00000000-01011110-00000000-00000001-00000001$$

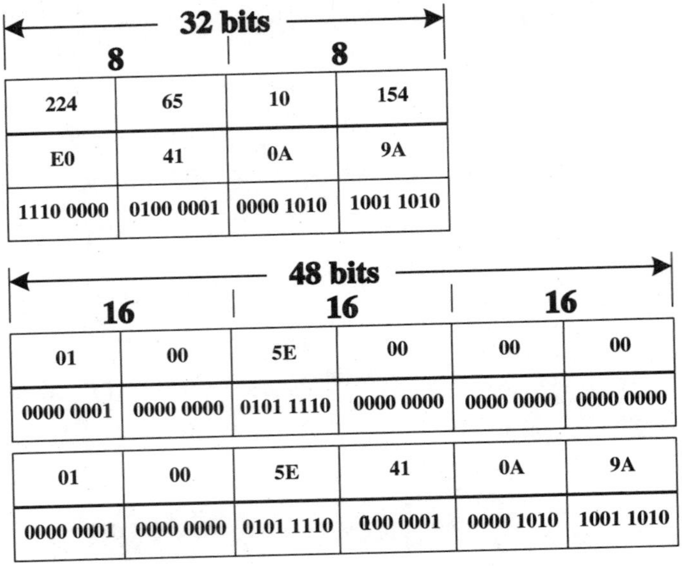

Figure 7-5
IP multicast to
Ethernet MAC
address mapping

32 bits			
8		8	
224	65	10	154
E0	41	0A	9A
1110 0000	0100 0001	0000 1010	1001 1010

48 bits					
16		16		16	
01	00	5E	00	00	00
0000 0001	0000 0000	0101 1110	0000 0000	0000 0000	0000 0000

01	00	5E	41	0A	9A
0000 0001	0000 0000	0101 1110	0100 0001	0000 1010	1001 1010

Note that because 23 bits of a 32-bit IP multicast address are mapped to a MAC multicast address, a chance exists that two different IP multicast groups can have the same multicast MAC address.

For example, map the following IP Multicast addresses to multicast MAC addresses: 224.1.1.1 and 225.1.1.1.

For the case of 224.1.1.1:

$$224.1.1.1 = 11100000.00000001.00000001.00000001$$

The resulting multicast MAC address is

$$00000001-00000000-01011110-00000001-00000001-00000001$$
$$\text{or } 01-00-5e-01-01-01.$$

For the case of 225.1.1.1:

$$225.1.1.1 = 11100001.00000001.00000001.00000001$$

The resulting multicast MAC address is

$$00000001-00000000-01011110-00000001-00000001-00000001$$
$$\text{or } 01-00-5e-01-01-01.$$

Both of the MAC addresses are identical for different IP multicast addresses.

Note that applications typically use UDP port numbers in multicasting to distinguish what stream belongs to a particular application on a host. A host would not be able to distinguish two multicast streams with identical destination MAC addresses and identical UDP port addresses. Fortunately, this is an unlikely case.

Multicast Group Management

Multicast traffic management works by forwarding multicast traffic onto a particular port if at least one device on the port is a member of the multicast group to which the multicast traffic corresponds. If no hosts connected to a port are members of that particular multicast group, no multicast packets are forwarded to that port for that group.

If more than one host on a port is a member of a particular multicast group, all the hosts will receive the multicast group traffic because all the hosts have the same multicast MAC address.

This operation makes group management a necessity. This section describes three mechanisms for managing multicast group management. These mechanisms are as follows:

- *Internet Group Management Protocol, Version 1* (IGMPv1)
- *Internet Group Management Protocol, Version 2* (IGMPv2)
- *Cisco Group Management Protocol* (CGMP)

Internet Group Management Protocol Version 1 (IGMPv1)

IGMPv1 is encapsulated in an IP packet with a protocol identifier of 2.

IGMP Version 1 Packet Format   The packet format for IGMP Version 1 is shown in Figure 7-6.

The version field is a four-bit value that is always set to 1 because the version 2 packet format is different.

Figure 7-6
IGMP version 1
packet format

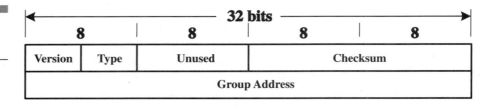

Table 7-2

IGMP v1 type
field values

Value	Description
1	Host Membership Query
2	Host Membership Report

The Type field is a four-bit field that specifies the type of IGMP message the packet represents. The valid values for this field are shown in the Table 7-2.

The next byte of the IGMPv1 packet is unused and set to all zeros. The receiver ignores this field.

The checksum field is two bytes long and is a 16-bit complement of the entire IGMPv1 message.

The Group Address field holds a four-byte IP multicast address of the multicast group that a host is a member of. The use of this field is explained in more detail later. This field is used for a Host Membership Report only. This field is set to all zeros if the packet is a Host Membership Query message.

IGMPv1 Operation   The operation of IGMPv1 is very simple. The router sends Host Membership Queries and the hosts respond with Host Membership Reports. The idea is for the router to keep up with what group traffic must be forwarded to each of its interfaces. The following discussion describes the details of IGMPv1 operation.

A router sends an IGMP Host Membership Query to determine the group membership information for all the multicasting hosts on each of its interfaces. If any host responds, the router must send all traffic for that group to the interface. IGMP Host Membership Queries are sent to an IP multicast address of 224.0.0.1, which is the All Hosts well-known IP multicast address. The TTL value in the IP header is set to 1.

The host responds with one or more Host Membership Report packets to let the router know what groups it is a member of. The host places the multicast group address of the group it has joined in the Group Address field in the IGMPv1 packet.

Close examination shows us that this type of operation could cause a flooding problem. When the router sends a Host Membership Query, all multicast enabled hosts can respond to the query with a Host Membership Report packet for each group of which the host is a member.

Multicast hosts do two things to diminish the effects of Host Membership Report flooding:

■ Implement a Host Membership Report timer

■ Implement a selective Host Membership Report scheme

A Host Membership Report timer is used to reduce the frequency of the reports from a particular multicast host. This timer can be configurable by the user.

Because the router only needs to know that one host is a member of a particular group for an interface, the router doesn't need to see multiple Host Membership Reports for any multicast group. To reduce the occurrence of multiple Host Membership Reports, the hosts can implement the Host Membership Timer and listen for Host Membership Reports for other hosts on the network that are members of the same groups. If the host sees a Multicast Host Membership Report from another host that is a member of the same group, the host no longer needs to send the report. If all multicast hosts implement the Host Membership Timer, the amount of bandwidth consumed with Host Membership Report packets is greatly reduced.

IGMPv1 States   Figure 7-7 shows the state diagram of a multicast host with IGMPv1 enabled.

Three states for each IGMPv1 multicast host are in each multicast group:

■ Non-member

■ Delaying member

■ Idle member

A host in the non-member State is not a member of the particular multicast group.

Figure 7-7
IGMPv1 state

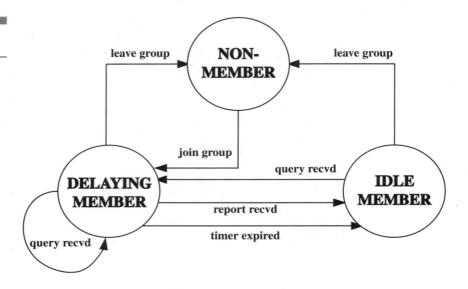

A host in the Delaying Member State has received a Host Membership Query from the router and has started its Host Membership timer. The host will not send the Host Membership Report until its Host Membership timer has expired.

A host enters the Idle State when the Host Membership Report is sent or it has seen a Host Membership Query from another host.

The following events cause the host's transition between states:

■ A host joins a group

■ A host leaves a group

■ A Host Membership Query is received

■ A Host Membership Report is received from another host

■ The Host Membership timer expires

Joining and Leaving Multicast Groups   A host joins a multicast group by simply sending a Host Membership Report message. The host does not need to wait for a Host Membership Query from the router.

A host leaves a group by not sending any Host Membership Reports. The router knows to stop forwarding packets to a group when no more Host

Membership Reports are received in response to its Host Membership Queries.

Configuring IGMPv1   To enable IGMP on a router, use the following global Cisco IOS command:

```
Router(config)# ip multicast-routing
```

By default the router will then enable IGMPv2 on all interfaces. To specify IGMPv1, enter the following interface sub-command:

```
Router(config-int)# ip igmp version 1
```

To verify the IGMP version on a particular interface, enter the following:

```
Router# show ip igmp interface [interface]
```

Without specifying a particular interface, it will display information for all interfaces. To verify proper IGMP operation after you have hosts attached, you may view the requested groups using the following:

```
Router# show ip igmp groups
```

Now that you have an active router sending Host Membership Queries, you must enable IGMP on your switches to keep multicast under control on each network segment.

To enable IGMP on a Set-Command based switch, use the following:

```
Switch(enable) set igmp enable
```

To turn off IGMP, use the disable form of the command.

```
Switch(enable) set igmp disable
```

To verify operation, enter the following:

```
Switch(enable) show igmp statistics [vlan_id]
```

Note that switches using Cisco IOS do not include IGMP operation. With an understanding of IGMPv1, let us look at the improvements in Version 2.

Internet Group Management Protocol Version 2 (IGMPv2)

IGMPv2 is fully specified in RFC 2236.

IGMPv2 Packet Format Figure 7-8 shows the packet format for an IGMPv2 packet. The format is very similar to the IGMPv1 packet format.

The type field represents the type of IGMPv2 message. Table 7-3 lists the possible values.

The Membership Query message can be either a general query or a group-specific query. The general query is used to determine which groups have active members. The group-specific query is used to determine if a particular multicast group has active members. The group address field is the way to distinguish between a general query and a specific query. A general

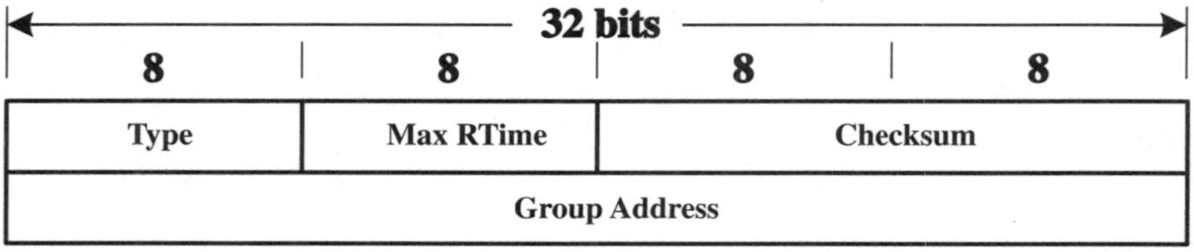

Figure 7-8
IGMPv2 packet format

32 bits			
8	8	8	8
Type	Max RTime	Checksum	
Group Address			

Table 7-3

IGMPv2 type field values

Type Field Value	Description
0x11	Membership Query
0x16	Version 2 Membership Report
0x17	Leave Group
0x12	Version 1 Membership Report

query will have zeros in the group address field and the group-specific query will have a valid IP multicast address.

The Max RTime is an eight-bit field that specifies the maximum amount of time a host can wait before responding to a Membership Query message. This field is only applicable to Membership Query messages. The Maximum Response time is represented in tenths of seconds.

The checksum field is identical to the two-byte checksum field in an IGMPv1 packet. The checksum is a 16-bit complement of the entire IGMPv2 message.

The Group Address is a four-byte IP multicast address.

The Querier Router   IGMPv2 handles the case of multiple routers on a multiple access network. All routers begin in a querier state. Routers will transition from a querier state to a non-querier state when they receive a membership query from another router with a lower IP address. Therefore, only one router eventually remains in the querier state. This router has the lowest IP address of all the multicast routers on the network.

IGMPv2 also handles the situation when the querier router fails. The non-querier routers maintain an Other Querier Present Interval timer. This timer is reset every time the router receives a Membership Query message. If the timer expires, the router begins sending Query messages and the querier router elections begin.

The querier router must send periodic Membership Query requests to make sure that other routers on the network understand that the querier router is still operational. To do this, the querier router maintains a Query Interval timer. This timer is reset when a Membership Query message is sent. When the Query Interval Timer reaches zero or out of necessity, the querier router sends another Membership Query.

Multicast Router Initialization   When the router first comes up, it sends a number of General Query messages to see which multicast groups should be forwarded on a particular interface. The number of General query messages a router sends is based on the Startup Query Count value configured in the router. The amount of time between the initial General Query messages is defined by the Startup Query Interval value.

IGMPv2 Host Operation   The host sets a delay timer when a General Query message is received. This value is set to a random number between

1 and the Maximum Response Time for each multicast group of which the host is a member. When any of these delay timers reach zero before the host receives a Membership Report for any of its groups, the host sends a Membership Query report.

If the host receives a Membership Report, the delay timer for that group is reset and the Membership Report is canceled. When the host receives a Membership Query for a group that has a delay timer that hasn't expired, the host will reset the timer only if the time remaining on the delay timer is greater than the Maximum Response Time in the Membership Query packet.

Joining and Leaving a Multicast Group When a host intends to join a multicast group, it sends a Membership Report for the group it wants to join. The host waits a predetermined amount of time and sends another Membership Report. The host sends two Membership Reports to lessen the possibility of the Membership Report not making it to the router. The length of time between the Membership Reports is called the Unsolicited Report Interval.

To leave a group, the host that sent the last Membership Report for a group sends a leave message to the all router multicast address, 224.0.0.2. If a host intends to leave a group, but wasn't the last host to send a Membership Report for the group, it is not necessary for the host to send a leave message. In either case, a host can send a leave message. The use of the leave message in IGMPv2 is different than in IGMPv1 where the group eventually times out.

When the querier router receives a leave message, it must send a Group-Specific Membership Query to find out if the host is the last to leave the group. The router sends a number of these messages before stopping to forward packets for that group. This number is equal to the Last Member Query Count. The router sends more than one Group-Specific Membership Query to make sure there are no more members in that group. These queries are sent every Last Member Query Interval seconds to pace the queries. When no responses are received for the queries, the router stops forwarding multicast traffic for this group address on that particular interface.

IGMPv2 Timers Table 7-4 summarizes the timers and counters discussed above in describing IGMPv2 operation.

Table 7-4

IGMPv2 timers and counters

Variable	Default Value
Query Interval (QI)	125 seconds
Query Response Interval (QRI)	10 seconds
Startup Query Interval	0.25(Query Interval)=31 seconds
Startup Query Count (SQC)	2
Other Querier Present Interval	(SQC*QI)+QRI/2=255 seconds
Group Membership Interval	(SQC*QI)+QRI=260 seconds
Last Member Query Interval	1 second
Last Member Query Count	SQC
Unsolicited Report Interval	10 seconds
Version 1 Router Preset Timeout	400 seconds

IGMPv2 State Diagrams Figure 7-9 illustrates the host state diagram for IGMPv2.

Note that the host can be in one of three states—Non-Member, Delaying Member, or Idle Member. This state diagram is kept for all groups. A host in a Non-Member State is not a member of the multicast group. A host in the Delaying Member State has just tried to join the multicast group. A host in the Idle Member State has either an expired timer or has received a Membership Report for the group from another host. If a query is received for the group, the host returns to the Delaying Member State.

Multicast hosts keep up with the version of IGMP routers on the network according to Figure 7-10.

Figure 7-11 summarizes the querier router election process.

The router can be either a querier router or a non-querier router (see Figures 7-12 and 7-13).

Configuring IGMPv2 To enable IGMP on a router, use the following global Cisco IOS command:

```
Router(config)# ip multicast-routing
```

Figure 7-9
IGMPv2 host state

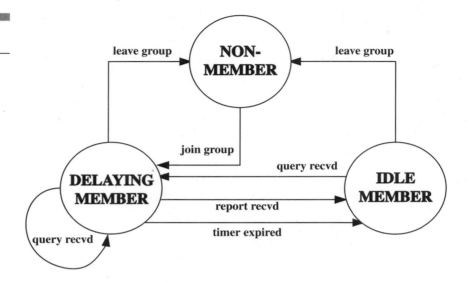

Figure 7-10
IGMPv1 and IGMPv2
interoperability state

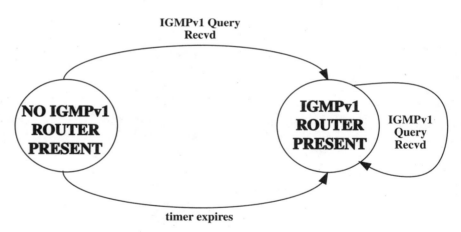

By default, the router will then enable IGMPv2 on all interfaces. However, if you need to specify IGMPv2, enter the following interface sub-command:

```
Router(config-int)# ip igmp version 2
```

To verify the IGMP version on a particular interface, enter the following:

```
Router# show ip igmp interface [interface]
```

Figure 7-11
Querier and non-querier router state

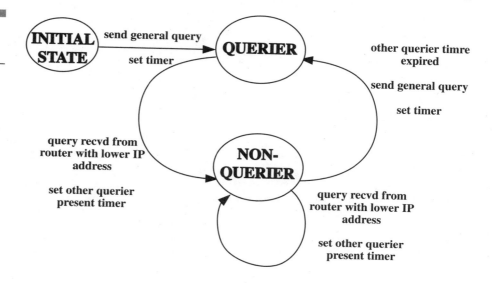

Figure 7-12
Querier router state

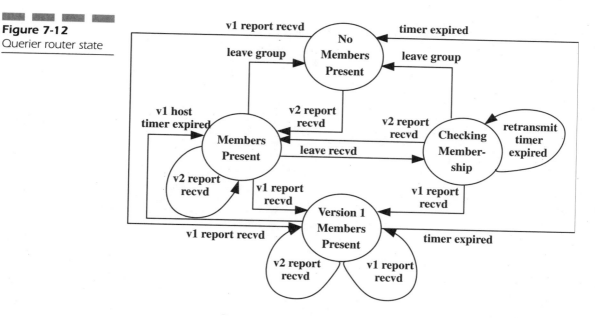

Figure 7-13
Non-querier router
state

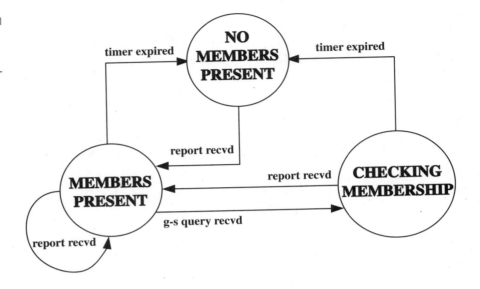

The following shows an example output of the command. You can see the status and version information.

```
Router#show ip igmp interface
Vlan1 is up, line protocol is up
  Internet address is 100.1.1.7/24
  IGMP is enabled on interface
  Current IGMP version is 2
  CGMP is enabled on interface
  IGMP query interval is 60 seconds
  IGMP querier timeout is 120 seconds
  IGMP max query response time is 10 seconds
  Inbound IGMP access group is not set
  IGMP activity: 19 joins, 13 leaves
  Multicast routing is enabled on interface
  Multicast TTL threshold is 0
  Multicast designated router (DR) is 100.1.1.233
  IGMP querying router is 100.1.1.1
  Multicast groups joined (number of users):
      224.2.127.254(1)   239.255.255.255(1)   224.0.1.40(1)
```

Without specifying a particular interface, it will display information for all interfaces. To verify proper IGMP operation after you have hosts attached, you may view the requested groups using the following:

```
Router# show ip igmp groups
```

The following shows an example output from the command:

```
Router# show ip igmp groups
IGMP Connected Group Membership
Group Address    Interface    Uptime      Expires      Last Reporter
239.255.255.255  Vlan1        3d20h       never        100.1.1.7
239.255.255.253  Vlan116      21:41:44    00:02:47     100.1.121.125
239.255.255.253  Vlan114      2d19h       00:02:08     100.1.11.71
239.255.255.253  Vlan109      3d20h       00:02:45     100.1.76.22
224.2.127.255    Vlan113      3d20h       00:02:51     100.1.193.55
```

Now that you have an active router sending Host Membership Queries, you must enable IGMP on your switches to keep multicast under control on each network segment.

To enable IGMP on a Set-Command based switch, use the following:

```
Switch(enable) set igmp enable
```

To turn off IGMP, use the disable form of the command.

```
Switch(enable) set igmp disable
```

To verify operation, enter the following:

```
Switch(enable) show igmp statistics [vlan_id]
```

For IGMPv2, you can also enable fastleave. This feature, when enabled, decreases the delay between receiving a Leave Group packet and disabling forwarding of multicast to the port for that specific group. The default timer value is the Group Membership Interval (default, 260 seconds). Enabling IGMP fastleave reduces this value to the Query Response Interval (default 10 seconds). This works based on the assumption that the querier router will send a Group-Specific Membership Query when a Leave Group packet is received from a host. The Group-Specific Membership Query would force other hosts receiving that group to respond with a Membership Report packet. If a Membership Report packet is received for the same group the Leave Group packet specified, multicast for that group is not interrupted. If the timer expires, traffic is no longer forwarded to the port for the specified multicast group.

```
Switch(enable) set igmp fastleave {enable | disable}
```

IGMP is supported, although not in the Catalyst 1900 series. Cisco Systems' CGMP is their multicast management protocol of choice and is fully supported across the entire product line.

Cisco Group Management Protocol (CGMP)

CGMP Overview So far, we have covered how a host can communicate with a router to enable a multicast flow onto the host's broadcast domain. As mentioned before, the router needs to know only that one host on an interface needs traffic from a particular multicast group to turn on multicast traffic for that group. IGMPv1 and IGMPv2 both handle the communication between the host and the router to turn on this multicast flow.

Let's look a little deeper into the multicast network. A host wants to join a multicast group and uses IGMPv2 to let the router know that it needs that particular multicast traffic. The router begins to forward the multicast traffic onto the same interface to which the host is connected. Note that the broadcast domain to which the router's interface is connected is flooded with the multicast group's traffic. Every host in the broadcast domain sees the traffic because all the switches in the broadcast domain know to flood packets to all ports that are destined for a multicast MAC address.

This is not an ideal situation. It would be better if there was a way to let the switches know what interfaces need to forward multicast traffic. The *Cisco Group Management Protocol* (CGMP) provides this functionality. Note that CGMP is a Cisco proprietary protocol and it does not interoperate with other vendors' switches.

Figure 7-14 shows the interaction between IGMP and CGMP.

Figure 7-14
IGMP and CGMP
interaction

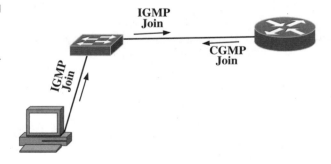

The hosts send IGMP messages that the routers receive and process. The routers in turn communicate with the Layer 2 switches on the network via CGMP. This communication between the routers and switches gives the switches the information they need to know to forward multicast traffic.

CGMP Packet Format   Figure 7-15 shows the CGMP packet format.

The version field is a four-bit field that gives the CGMP version number. CGMP has only one version. This field always has a 0x1 value.

The type field is a four-bit field that describes the CGMP message type. The valid values are 0x0 for Join or 0x1 for Leave.

The reserved field is 16 bits long and is set to all zeros. This field is not currently used.

The count field is an eight-bit field that gives the number of group destination address and unicast source address pairs in the rest of the message.

The *Group Destination Address* (GDA) field is six bytes long. It holds the multicast group destination address.

The *Unicast Source Address* (USA) field is a 6-byte field that contains the MAC address of a host.

CGMP Operation   The router sends a CGMP Join message to the switches on the network to let them know which of their ports is connected to the router. The CGMP packet is formatted as a Join message with the GDA as all zeros and the USA as the router's MAC address.

To notify all the switches that a particular group is no longer active, the router sends a Leave message to the switches with the GDA of the inactive group and the USA field all zeros. The switches then know to delete all the

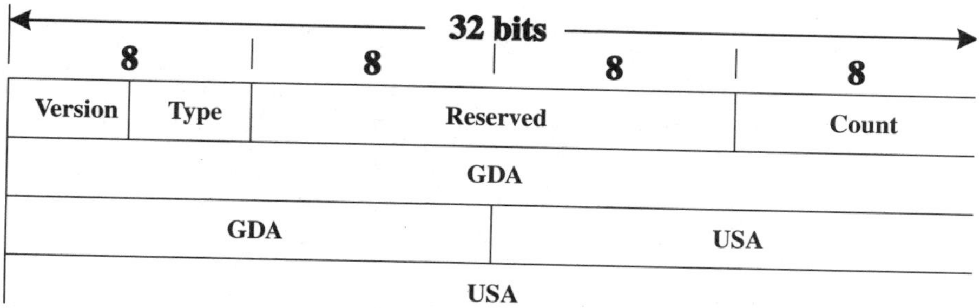

Figure 7-15
CGMP packet format

entries associated with that particular group. If no groups are active, the router sends a Leave message with both the GDA and USA fields set to zero. When a switch receives an all-group leave packet, the switch begins flooding all multicast traffic as if CGMP is disabled.

After a router receives an IGMP join message, it then sends a CGMP Join message to the switches on the same interface. The switches respond by setting their forwarding tables appropriately to only forward multicast traffic for the group listed in the CGMP message to the host listed in the CGMP message. IGMPv2 leave messages received by the router are followed by CGMP leave messages from the router to the switches.

Configuring CGMP   To enable CGMP on a router, you use the following global Cisco IOS command:

```
Router(config)# ip multicast-routing
```

By default, the router will then enable IGMPv2 on all interfaces. In addition to IGMP, you must also specifically enable CGMP. To enable CGMP, enter the following interface sub-command.

```
Router(config-int)# ip cgmp
```

To verify CGMP operation on a particular interface, enter the following:

```
Router# show ip igmp interface [interface]
```

Without specifying a particular interface, it will display information for all interfaces. To verify proper IGMP operation after you have hosts attached, you may view the requested groups using the following:

```
Router# show ip igmp groups
```

Now that you have an active router sending IGMP Host Membership Queries and sending CGMP Join messages on the network, you must enable CGMP on your switches to keep multicast under control on each network segment.

To enable CGMP on a Set-Command based switch, use the following:

```
Switch(enable) set cgmp enable
```

On a switch, you may only enable IGMP or CGMP, not both. To turn off CGMP, use the `disable` form of the command.

```
Switch(enable) set cgmp disable
```

To verify operation, enter the following:

```
Switch(enable) show cgmp statistics [vlan_id]
```

For CGMP, you can also enable IGMPv2 leave processing. This feature, when enabled, decreases the delay between receiving a Leave Group packet and disabling forwarding of multicast to the port for that specific group. When a Leave Group packet is received, the switch sets a Query Response timer (default 10 seconds). If the timer expires before receiving a CGMP Join message, traffic is no longer forwarded to the port for the specified multicast group. By default, with IGMPv2 leave processing disabled, the switch will wait for the CGMP Hold Timer to expire (default 300 seconds) before halting multicast traffic forwarding to the port.

```
Switch(enable) set cgmp leave {enable | disable}
```

To view CGMP leave statistical information, use the command

```
Switch(enable) show cgmp leave
```

To enable CGMP on Cisco IOS-based devices, you would use the following global command:

```
Switch(config)# cgmp
```

To verify CGMP operation, use the following command:

```
Switch# show cgmp
```

Chapter Summary

As we have seen in this chapter, multicast traffic management is quite different from unicast traffic management. IP multicast addressing spans the entire Internet and can not be subnetted like unicast IP addressing.

IGMPv1, IGMPv2, and CGMP exist simply to manage the flow of multicast traffic into and within a broadcast domain because unbridled multicast traffic can bring a campus network to its knees.

In summary, the following topics were covered in this chapter:

- Multicast traffic overview
- IP Multicast Addressing
- *Internet Group Management Protocol Version 1* (IGMPv1)
- *Internet Group Management Protocol Version 2* (IGMPv2)
- *Cisco Group Management Protocol* (CGMP)

Multicast is an important type of traffic in the campus network. Multicast traffic can be achieved by having multiple unicast streams in the network, but the redundant packets are an inefficient use of bandwidth. Multicast traffic provides a mechanism for one host to send one stream to multiple destinations.

IP multicast addressing uses the class D IP address space. All the addresses are in one subnet. In other words, there is no concept of a subnet mask in IP multicasting. An IP multicast address represents a group of destination hosts. The multicast MAC addresses are generated by mapping part of the IP multicast address into part of the MAC address and vice versa.

IGMPv1 and IGMPv2 exist to restrict the flow of multicast traffic to broadcast domains that need the multicast traffic. This goes a long way to thin out unneeded multicast traffic to optimize the use of bandwidth. These protocols operate between the hosts and their routers on the network.

CGMP exists to restrict the flow of multicast traffic within a broadcast domain. This helps restrict multicast traffic to only be forwarded to the Layer 2 switch ports that need multicast traffic. CGMP operates between the router and the switches in a broadcast domain.

At this point, you are equipped to implement IP multicasting in your broadcast domains on your campus network. You are able to efficiently manage the multicast traffic throughout the broadcast domains in your campus network to make good use of available bandwidth.

When you review and thoroughly understand the concepts of IP multicasting and how to apply them to the broadcast domains in your campus network, you are ready to move on to managing the multicast traffic between your broadcast domains with IP multicast routing. These principles will allow you to efficiently route and manage IP multicast streams throughout your entire campus network.

Frequently Asked Questions (FAQ)

Question: Why is there no "multicast ARP" mechanism?

Answer: On the surface, it would make sense to design a protocol to resolve a multicast address to the MAC addresses associated with it. Because multicast groups can span the Internet, one simple "multicast ARP" could be flooded to all Internet connected hosts. The other problem is how to cache the potentially large number of MAC addresses that could be members of a particular multicast group. Therefore, a "multicast ARP" mechanism isn't feasible.

Question: How do other vendors typically manage multicast on the network?

Answer: Other vendors implement IGMP on the switch and the router. When a host sources an IGMP request, the router uses the IGMP request to start forwarding multicast packets for the group. The switch uses the request to set a filter for the port to allow only the requested multicast group traffic to that port.

Case Study

Objective: CPI management has decided to build a video conferencing system to allow employees to meet without having to constantly move from one building to another. Studies have shown that CPI managers consume countless hours traveling between meetings across CPI's large campus.

You are to prepare for the coming application by implementing IP multicast traffic management in each of the VLANs before multicast traffic is turned on across the entire campus network.

Approach

The following tasks must be completed to achieve your objective:

- Decide where multicast traffic will be used throughout the campus network
- Decide how to handle multicast traffic within the broadcast domains in CPI's network
- Implement your multicast traffic management design within the CPI campus network

Where Is Multicast Traffic Needed?

Multicast will be required on the Administrative, Information Technologies, and Research and Development VLANs. The employees of those departments spend the most time going to meetings.

Table 7-5 shows the VLAN identifiers that are in place.

Table 7-6 lists the device names and their IP addresses.

Multicast Traffic Management in the Broadcast Domains

For each VLAN, a multicast management protocol is required to prevent multicast traffic from disturbing other users. Because our network is comprised entirely of Cisco Systems equipment, we will implement CGMP.

Table 7-5

VLANs and their identifiers

VLAN	VLAN ID
Management	
R&D	1
Mfg	2
SR	3
Admin	4
IT	5

Table 7-6

Switch names and IP addresses

Switch Name	IP Address
IT-1-dist-5505	100.1.1.11
IT-2-access-2926	100.1.1.12
IT-3-access-1900	100.1.1.13
IT-4-access-1900	100.1.1.14
IT-5-access-1900	100.1.1.15
RD-1-dist-5505	100.1.1.16
RD-2-access-2926	100.1.1.17
RD-3-access-1900	100.1.1.18
RD-4-access-1900	100.1.1.19
RD-5-access-1900	100.1.1.20
Admin-1-dist-5505	100.1.1.31
Admin-2-access-2926	100.1.1.32
Admin-3-access-1900	100.1.1.33
Admin-4-access-1900	100.1.1.34
Admin-5-access-1900	100.1.1.35

Implementing Multicast Traffic Management in the Broadcast Domains

Implementation will begin with enabling CGMP on the routers.
First, the Administrative router:

```
Admin-1-dist-5505(config)# ip multicast-routing
Admin-1-dist-5505(config)# interface Vlan4
Admin-1-dist-5505(config-if)# ip cgmp
```

Repeat for the Information Technologies and Research and Development routers, substituting the appropriate VLAN identifier.

```
IT-1-dist-5505(config)# ip multicast-routing
IT-1-dist-5505(config)# interface Vlan5
IT-1-dist-5505(config-if)# ip cgmp
```

```
RD-1-dist-5505(config)# ip multicast-routing
RD-1-dist-5505(config)# interface Vlan1
RD-1-dist-5505(config-if)# ip cgmp
```

Next, CGMP must be enabled on all access layer switches.
For the Catalyst 2926 series, use the following commands:

```
Admin-2-access-2926(enable) set cgmp enable
```

Also, enable CGMP leave processing:

```
Admin-2-access-2926(enable) set cgmp leave enable
```

Repeat for the other Catalyst 2926 switches.
For the Catalyst 1900's, enter the following command:

```
Admin-3-access-1900(config)# cgmp
```

Repeat for the rest of the Catalyst 1900s. Recall that the Catalyst 1900 does not support CGMP leave processing.

Case Study Summary

The CPI campus network now supports multicast applications on the Administrative, Information Technologies, and Research and Development VLANs. Now those departments may utilize video conference software to help minimize travel requirements to attend meetings. This will help save money by cutting staff down time.

The following steps were completed to get to this point. We started with an optimal Layer 2 and Layer 3 configuration and then

- Defined where multicast traffic will be used throughout the campus network
- Defined protocol to be used to handle multicast traffic within the broadcast domains in CPI's network
- Implemented multicast traffic management design within the CPI campus network

CPI's network is now configured to handle multicast traffic within the three VLANs in an optimal fashion. Later chapters will explore how to implement routing features optimized for multicast transmission.

Questions

1. _____ can be used to implement IP multicast transmissions.

   a. unicast
   b. multicast
   c. broadcast
   d. none of the above

2. The IP multicast address 236.43.5.1 is translated to which of the following Ethernet MAC addresses?

   a. 01-00-5e-43-05-01
   b. 01-00-5e-2b-05-01
   c. 00-00-5e-2b-05-01
   d. none of the above

3. The IP address 224.43.5.1 is translated to which of the following Ethernet MAC addresses?

   a. 01-00-5e-43-05-01
   b. 01-00-5e-2b-05-01
   c. 00-00-5e-2b-05-01
   d. none of the above

4. Using the conventional Ethernet MAC to IP multicast address mappings, the resulting multicast addresses are _____.

   a. unique
   b. not unique
   c. inverted
   d. six bytes long

5. IGMPv1 is not supported on the Catalyst _____.

   a. 2926
   b. 5505
   c. 1900
   d. 6513

6. IGMPv2 is not supported on the Catalyst _____.

   a. 2926
   b. 5505
   c. 1900
   d. 6513

7. IGMP is a _____ _____ protocol.

   a. group management
   b. host management
   c. multicast routing
   d. Internet routing

8. IGMPv2 is IGMPv1 with the addition of _____.

   a. leave-support
   b. one
   c. routing
   d. CGMP

9. IGMPv2 can support _____ querier routers.

   a. 10
   b. 125
   c. 400
   d. infinite

10. Which of the following does not describe a multicast application?

    a. one sender, many receivers
    b. many senders, many receivers
    c. video conference
    d. telephone

11. CGMP was developed by _____ _____.

    a. 3Com Corporation
    b. Cisco Systems
    c. Nortel Networks
    d. CG and MP

12. CGMP is a replacement for

    a. IGMPv1
    b. IGMPv2
    c. Both a and b
    d. Neither a or b

13. CGMP defines communication between

    a. hosts and switches
    b. hosts and routers
    c. switches and routers
    d. switches and switches

14. Using Cisco IOS, `ip multicast-routing` must be enabled for

    a. IGMPv1
    b. IGMPv2
    c. CGMP
    d. all the above

15. With `cgmp` and `cgmp leave` enabled on a switch and `ip cgmp` enabled on a router, which device(s) receive and process IGMP requests?

    a. both switch and router
    b. only router
    c. neither switch nor router
    d. only switch

16. When configured for IGMPv2 operation, a router will also listen for _____ packets.

    a. SDR
    b. CGMP
    c. NTP
    d. IGMPv1

17. CGMP consists of two types of packets:

    a. request/reply
    b. send/receive
    c. join/leave
    d. forward/reply

18. The all router IP multicast address is _____.

    a. 224.0.0.1
    b. 224.0.0.2
    c. 224.0.0.3
    d. 239.255.255.255

19. IGMPv2 handles multiple routers on a single network by designating a _____ router.

    a. querier
    b. standby
    c. active
    d. default

20. CGMP uses _____ to communicate multicast group joins/leaves between routers and switches.

   a. unicast

   b. multicast

   c. broadcast

   d. simulcast

Answers

1. _____ can be used to implement multicast transmissions.

   a. unicast

   Multicast transmissions can be implemented with many unicast streams. This is not recommended because sending multiple unicast streams is less efficient than one multicast stream.

2. The IP address 236.43.5.1 is translated to which of the following Ethernet MAC addresses?

   b. 01-00-5e-2b-05-01

   All Ethernet MAC address begin with 01-00-5e and a "0" in the next bit position. The last 23 bits of the MAC address are the last 23 bits of the multicast IP address.

3. The IP address 224.43.5.1 is translated to which of the following Ethernet MAC addresses?

   b. 01-00-5e-2b-05-01

   All Ethernet MAC address begin with 01-00-5e and a "0" in the next bit position. The last 23 bits of the MAC address are the last 23 bits of the multicast IP address.

4. Using the conventional Ethernet MAC to IP multicast address mappings, the resulting multicast addresses are _____.

   b. not unique

   Because the last 23 bits of the multicast IP address are used for the MAC address, this address mapping technique between multicast IP and multicast Ethernet MAC addresses is not a one-to-one mapping.

5. IGMPv1 is not supported on the Catalyst _____.

   c. 1900

6. IGMPv2 is not supported on the Catalyst _____.

   c. 1900

7. IGMP is a _____ _____ protocol.

   a. group management

8. IGMPv2 is IGMPv1 with the addition of _____.

   a. leave-support

9. IGMPv2 can support _____ querier routers.

   d.   infinite

10. Which of the following does not describe a multicast application?

   d.   telephone

A telephone call is a one-to-one (point-to-point) connection. A multicast transmission is a one-to-many transmission.

11. CGMP was developed by _____ _____.

   b.   Cisco systems

12. CGMP is a replacement for

   c.   Both a and b (IGMPv1 and IGMPv2)

13. CGMP defines communication between

   c.   switches and routers

IGMP acts as a mechanism to handle multicast group maintenance. With IGMP, hosts communicate group maintenance information to routers. CGMP is a protocol to communicate the group maintenance information to switches in Layer 2 networks.

14. Using Cisco IOS, `IP multicast-routing` must be enabled for

   d.   all of the above

IGMPv1, IGMPv2, CGMP

15. With `CGMP` and `CGMP` leave enabled on a switch and IP CGMP enabled on a router, which device(s) receive and process IGMP requests?

   a.   both switch and router

16. When configured for IGMPv2 operation, a router will also listen for _____ packets.

   d.   IGMPv1

IGMPv2 is backwardly compatible with IGMPv1

17. CGMP consists of two types of packets:

   c.   Join/Leave

18. The all router IP multicast address is _____.

   b.   224.0.0.2

19. IGMPv2 handles multiple routers on a single network by designating a _____ router.

    a. querier

20. CGMP uses _____ to communicate multicast group joins/leaves between routers and switches.

    b. multicast

IP Multicast Routing Configuration

The preceding chapter laid the foundation for handling IP multicast in the broadcast domains of your campus network. Now we will cover the concepts required to carry multicast traffic throughout your entire campus network in an efficient manner.

Objectives Covered in This Chapter

The following topics are covered in this chapter.

- IP Multicast Routing Basics
- *Distance Vector Multicast Routing Protocol* (DVMRP)
- *Multicast Open Shortest Path First* (MOSPF)
- *Protocol Independent Multicast–Dense Mode* (PIM–DM)
- *Core Based Trees* (CBT)
- *Protocol Independent Multicast–Sparse Mode* (PIM–SM)

Multicast Routing Basics

Multicast routing is a difficult problem to address in a network. This capability requires complex and sometimes cumbersome protocols. In this section, we will look at the issues associated with multicast routing.

In the last chapter, we discussed host communication that notifies routers of the need for multicast traffic in the broadcast domain. This chapter covers the methods that routers use to pass multicast traffic from one router to another.

Unicast Routing versus Multicast Routing

Unicast routing is based on forwarding a packet from one source to one destination. Both the source and destination have unique IP addresses to specify their locations. These hosts belong in well-specified subnets. The next hop locations of the subnets from a given point are called *routes*. Unicast routers use routing protocols to pass the route information between the routers so that each one has adequate knowledge of the network.

Multicast routing differs from unicast routing in several ways. First, multicast addresses refer to a group of destinations. Second, no notion of subnets exists in multicast routing. Therefore, no concept of localized addressing is associated with IP multicasting; however, this can be accomplished with filters. Filters are covered in Chapter 9.

One of the most perplexing problems is how to let the network know the location of each destination for each group. This is very difficult, because a group member can exist anywhere in the network, and the group can span the entire network. Consider the following network of four routers in Figure 8-1.

Note that each router has a host connected that is a member of a multicast group. The group has one member that sources the multicast data stream. Each host communicates with the directly connected router using IGMP to let the router know that it wants to join the multicast group. The router now knows that traffic for that particular multicast group can be forwarded to this interface.

When the source sends a multicast packet to its router, the router forwards the packet on to the next router in the network. This router, in turn, forwards the packet to the interface to which the destination host is connected and forwards the packet on to the next router. The next hop router operates in a similar fashion. The result is that each of the hosts sees the traffic from the multicast source.

But what if the third and fourth routers did not have any attached hosts that had joined the multicast group? The second router has no way of knowing not to forward the packets on to the remaining routers. This is one of the functions of a multicast routing protocol. Some multicast routing protocols have the capability to create multicast trees to determine the span of the multicast traffic so that links within the campus network are not used to carry unnecessary traffic.

Figure 8-1
Multicast forwarding

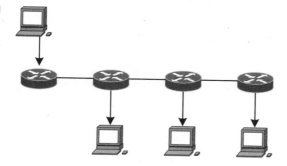

Figure 8-2
Multicast routing
loop

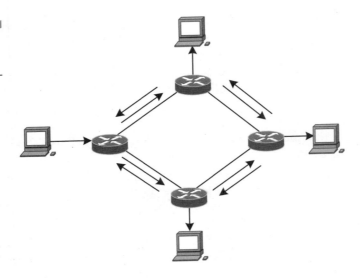

Let's look at another fundamental problem of multicast routing. Consider the network of four routers in Figure 8-2. Assume that the routers forward multicast traffic to all interfaces with a router or device that needs the multicast traffic, except for the interface on which the traffic was received.

The result is a multicast routing loop. The bandwidth of the links will be completely consumed with traffic until the *time-to-live* (TTL) field of the IP packet is decremented to 0. Much traffic, which serves no purpose, is generated. Multicast routing protocols remedy this situation.

Distribution Trees

A distribution tree is a tree structure formed to connect all the members of a multicast group. This structure finds a route from the source to all the destination hosts and solves the problem of multicast routing loops.

Hosts can join and leave multicast groups at any time. The associated tree structure for a group must change to match the current state of the group. When hosts join and leave groups, a logical change is made to the multicast tree structure. The act of adding and taking away branches of the multicast distribution trees is called *grafting and pruning*.

Two methods for creating multicast distribution trees exist—*source-specific trees* and *shared trees*. Shared trees are also called center-specific trees.

Source-specific or source trees find the shortest path from the source to each potential destination. This generates many trees for each group. The trees are generated using a method called *Reverse Path Forwarding* (RPF). This method is covered in greater detail later in this chapter. The basic idea behind RPF is to construct the shortest path back to the source from each destination. Multicast packets are forwarded on all interfaces except the incoming interface. If a multicast packet arrives on an interface that is not the shortest path back to the source, the packet is discarded.

Shared trees form one multicast tree for a particular group. This results in a much smaller overhead at the cost of an optimal end-to-end delay. All traffic for a particular multicast group is carried over one tree regardless of the source.

Multicast Scoping

Scoping is the ability to limit the bounds of a particular traffic stream. In the case of multicast, a stream's scope is defined by the TTL of the packet. In IP unicast, the IP TTL field is used to kill a packet if it gets caught in an endless loop. In IP multicast, the IP TTL field is used to define the scope of a group.

Multicast-enabled routers have a TTL threshold for each interface. If a packet arrives that has a TTL larger than the interface threshold, the packet can be forwarded. Otherwise, the packet is discarded. Table 8-1 lists

Table 8-1

TTL thresholds

TTL Value	Scope
0	Restricted to the same host; not output by any interface.
1	Restricted to the same broadcast domain; not forwarded by the router.
15	Restricted to the same site, organization, or department.
63	Restricted to the same region.
127	Worldwide.
191	Worldwide, limited bandwidth.
255	Unrestricted in scope, global.

TTL thresholds and their associated scopes. Note that the scopes are arbitrary, but these are the commonly accepted values.

The network administrator designates terms such as department and site. After the router forwards the packet, the TTL field is decremented by one.

Dense Mode and Sparse Mode Multicast Routing Protocols

The two classes of multicast routing protocols are *dense mode* and *sparse mode*. The number of receivers throughout the network defines each of the classes.

Dense mode multicast protocols are used when the following conditions exist:

- Densely distributed receivers
- Plentiful bandwidth
- The majority of routers are forwarding multicast traffic.

In dense mode multicast routing protocols, nearly all of the hosts on the network are members of a multicast group. It is also assumed that bandwidth is plentiful. This assumption makes some routing decisions easier because you do not need to take into consideration the optimum use of bandwidth. The maintenance of the multicast tree is often achieved by periodically flooding the network with multicast traffic. The following are several commonly used dense mode multicast routing protocols:

- *Distance Vector Multicast Routing Protocol* (DVMRP)
- *Multicast Open Shortest Path First* (MOSPF)
- *Protocol Independent Multicast–Dense Mode* (PIM–DM)

Sparse mode multicast routing protocols are used when the following conditions exist:

- Sparsely distributed multicast group members
- Limited bandwidth

Sparse mode multicast routing protocols assume that multicast group members are a minority throughout the network. The bandwidth use of the network is also a consideration for sparse mode routing protocols. Flooding of information used to build the distribution trees is considered wasteful.

Because flooding isn't used to build the multicast distribution trees, sparse mode multicast routing protocols rely on explicit joins for a branch to be added to a multicast distribution tree.

The following protocols are examples of sparse mode multicast routing protocols.

- *Core Based Trees* (CBT)
- *Protocol Independent Multicast–Sparse Mode* (PIM–SM)

In a general sense, sparse mode multicast routing protocols are more suited for WAN environments.

Each of these routing protocols is covered in varying detail in the following sections.

DVMRP Overview

DVMRP is fully specified in RFC 1075. It is the routing protocol used most widely in the Internet MBone. A full implementation of DVMRP is not supported by Cisco. Cisco routers can send multicast traffic to and from a DVMRP neighbor, but Cisco does not use DVMRP to forward packets. Cisco uses PIM to make multicast routing decisions.

DVMRP is a dense mode multicast routing protocol that implements source-based multicast distribution trees. DVMRP uses RPF to make multicast traffic forwarding decisions. If a router does not have any interfaces that need multicast traffic, the router can send a prune message to the distribution tree to shut off multicast traffic from a particular group to conserve bandwidth on a link.

DVMRP uses its own unicast routing protocol to determine the shortest path back to the source. This routing protocol is similar to RIP. Therefore, multicast traffic between two hosts may follow a different path than unicast traffic.

RPF

Recall the earlier discussion of the multicast routing loop. RPF is a method to prevent multicast routing loops. It is a very simple protocol that requires that a unicast routing table exists.

It works like this. When the router receives a multicast packet, it looks to see whether it was received on the interface that has the shortest path back to the source. If not, the packet is discarded. If the multicast packet was received on the interface that has the shortest path back to the source, it is forwarded to the interfaces that either have another router connected or that need the multicast traffic via information from IGMP.

Consider the network with four routers in Figure 8-3. This is the same network that resulted in a routing loop in an earlier discussion. Here, we see that the multicast routing loop is eliminated using RPF.

The following actions occur in the network in Figure 8-3:

1. First, a multicast source sends a packet to Router 1. Then Router 1 forwards the packet to Routers 2 and 3. Router 1 forwards the packet to both routers because it received the multicast packet on an interface that is directly connected to the multicast source.

2. Router 2 determines via its unicast routing table that the packet from Router 1 was received on the interface closest to the source. It then forwards the packet on to the directly connected receiver that has joined the group via IGMP. Router 2 also forwards the packet to Router 4.

3. Router 3, like Router 2, determines via its unicast routing table that the packet from Router 1 was received on the interface closest to the source. It then forwards the packet on to the directly connected receiver

Figure 8-3
Multicast forwarding
with RPF

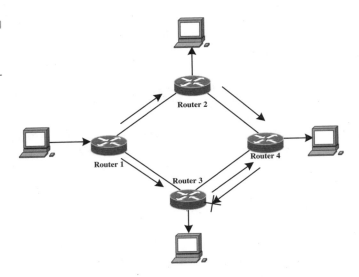

that has joined the group via IGMP. Router 3 also forwards the packet on to Router 4.

4. Router 4 receives multicast packets from Routers 2 and 3. It consults its unicast routing table and determines which interface is closest to the source. Router 4 picks the interface connected to Router 3 even though the interface connected to Router 2 is equally close to the source. Router 4 then forwards the multicast packet to Router 3 and to the directly connected group member.

5. Router 3 receives the multicast packet forwarded from Router 4 and determines that the packet was not received on the interface closest to the multicast source. As a result, the packet is discarded.

This illustrates how RPF works to remove the possibility of multicast routing loops.

DVMRP Operation

The DVMRP protocol works using these four processes:

■ Neighbor discovery

■ Route exchange

■ Pruning

■ Grafting

Each of these processes is discussed in the following sections after first discussing the DVMRP packet formats.

DVMRP Packet Format   DVMRP packets are encapsulated in an IP packet. The IP protocol field is set to 2, which identifies the packet as an IGMP message. In addition the type field is set to 0x13 to denote that the IGMP message is a DVMRP message. The DVMRP header has a code field. The valid values are listed in Table 8-2.

The remainder of the packet definition is covered in the following discussion of the DVMRP processes.

Neighbor Discovery   The DVMRP forwarding process must know whether another DVMRP router is connected to an interface and if a multicast host is a member of a particular group. The multicast host group

Table 8-2

DVMRP code
field values

DVMRP Code Value	Message Description
1	Probe
2	Route Report
5	Ask-Neighbors 2
6	Neighbors 2
7	Prune
8	Graft
9	Graft Acknowledgment

information is obtained from IGMP. The knowledge of a connected router is obtained through DVMRP neighbor discovery.

Neighbor probes are sent on all DVMRP enabled interfaces every 10 seconds. If a previously discovered neighbor doesn't respond within 35 seconds, that neighbor is marked as down. The router then takes the following steps:

- A route learned from the router that is marked as down is put in a hold down state.
- If multicast traffic is forwarded to the router marked as down, the traffic is stopped.
- If the router marked as down was the designated forwarder, a new designated forwarder is elected.
- If the router marked as down is an upstream router, forwarding entries are flushed.
- If grafts from the router marked as down need to be acknowledged, they are cleared. We'll cover grafting later in this chapter.
- If the router marked as down is the last downstream router on the interface and no directly connected hosts are on the router, the interface is pruned.

A packet of the type shown in Figure 8-4 is sent to discover DVMRP neighbors. The packet is addressed to the IP multicast address of 224.0.0.4. This is the well-known address for all DVMRP routers.

The generation ID lets the router know whether the neighbor has been rebooted. When the generation ID changes, the router knows that a reboot

Figure 8-4
DVMRP neighbor
discovery packet
format

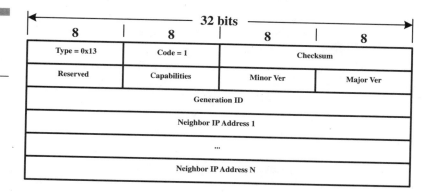

Figure 8-5
Neighboring DVMRP
routers

Figure 8-6
Initial DVMRP
neighbor probe
packet

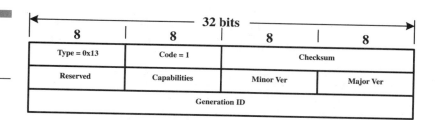

has taken place and flushes any prune information it has concerning the neighbor. Then it sends a copy of the unicast routing table to the neighbor.

Consider the simple network that consists of two DVMRP routers on the same Ethernet in Figure 8-5.

When Router 1 first becomes operational, it sends a DVMRP neighbor probe to the IP multicast address of 224.0.0.4. The packet is formatted as illustrated in Figure 8-6. Notice that no neighbors are listed in the packet.

Router 2 responds with the following DVMRP packet.

Notice that it lists the IP address of Router 1. When Router 1 receives a DVMRP neighbor packet that lists its own source IP address, it has established adjacency with Router 2. Eventually, the same transaction happens with Router 2. This forms a two-way adjacency between Routers 1 and 2.

This adjacency process determines whether an interface is a leaf or a nonleaf interface. A leaf interface is an interface that does not have a DVMRP router attached to it. In this case, the router must receive IGMP messages to know to forward multicast traffic to this interface. A nonleaf interface has a DVMRP router attached to it. The router will receive DVMRP route updates, which build a multicast routing table. The router uses this routing table to decide how to forward multicast traffic for a non-leaf interface.

Route Exchange Figure 8-7 shows the packet format of a DVMRP route report packet. The route list includes a network mask, source network, and metric. Notice that there seems to be no logical explanation for the definition of the source mask, source network, and metric field boundaries in the packet.

The rules used to build the DVMRP route report list are designed to minimize the size of the packet. The following paragraphs describe how the DVMRP route report list is generated.

First, the network mask is assumed to always begin with 255. Therefore, all the mask fields are three bytes long. For example, a network mask of 255.255.0.0 would be represented as 255.0.0. The network is combined with the mask to minimize the length of the network reported by only listing the network that corresponds to the nonzero portion of the network mask. For example, the network 13.0.0.0 with a network mask of 255.0.0.0 would be reported as 13.

The routes to be listed are sorted according to netmask. Table 8-3 shows a valid list of routes, the reported network numbers, and reported network masks.

Figure 8-7
DVMRP route report packet format

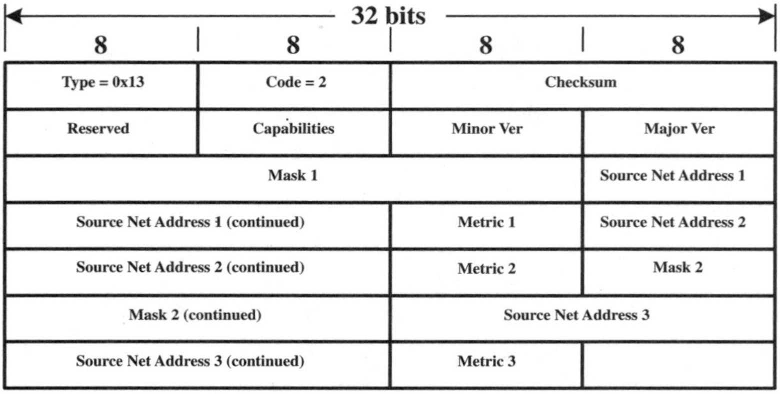

◄─── 32 bits ───►			
8	8	8	8
Type = 0x13	Code = 2	Checksum	
Reserved	Capabilities	Minor Ver	Major Ver
Mask 1			Source Net Address 1
Source Net Address 1 (continued)		Metric 1	Source Net Address 2
Source Net Address 2 (continued)		Metric 2	Mask 2
Mask 2 (continued)		Source Net Address 3	
Source Net Address 3 (continued)		Metric 3	

Table 8-3

Network route list showing reported routes

Network	Network Mask	Reported Network Mask	Metric	Reported Network
13.0.0.0	255.0.0.0	0.0.0	2	13
152.1.34.0	255.255.255.0	255.255.0	4	152.1.34
128.109.0.0	255.255.0.0	255.0.0	3	128.109
156.26.1.0	255.255.255.0	255.255.0	1	156.26.1
130.42.0.0	255.255.255.0	255.255.0	3	130.42.0

Table 8-4

Reported route metrics for network route list

Reported Network	Reported Network Mask	Metric	Reported Network Mask
13	0.0.0	2	2+128=130
152.1.34	255.0.0	4	4
128.109	255.0.0	3	3+128=131
156.26.1	255.255.0	1	1
130.42.0	255.255.0	3	3+128=131

The list of routes in the DVMRP route report packet includes all the routes associated with a particular network mask. To define the end of a list of routes for a particular network mask, the last metric listed has the most significant bit set. This is the equivalent of adding 128 to the metric value. Table 8-4 lists the reported metrics for each of the routes in Table 8-3.

Having defined the route list format, we can look at the following rules for handling a received route list:

1. Routes from established neighbors are accepted, and those from nonneighbors are rejected.

2. If the metric of a route in the report plus the metric of the receiving router is greater than or equal to infinity, the metric is set to infinity. Infinity is represented by the value 32.

3. If the metric of a route in the report is greater than or equal to infinity, no changes are made.

4. If the route is not currently in the routing table and the metric of the route plus the metric of the receiving router is less than or equal to infinity, the route is added to the routing table.

5. If the route is already in the routing table, these rules apply:

   a. If the route's metric is between 32 and 64, the sending router is stating that the receiving router is on the shortest path back to any source on that network. This process is known as *Poison Reverse*. This metric information is important when pruning occurs.

   b. If the metric plus the metric of the receiving router is greater than the metric of the route already in the routing table, then the sending address is checked. If this address is different than the sending address in the route table, the new route is ignored. If the sending address is the same, the metric in the routing table is replaced.

   c. If the metric plus the metric of the receiving router is less than the metric of the route in the routing table, the table is updated. If the sending address of the received route is different than the receiving address in the routing table, the route is Poison Reversed.

   d. The route is refreshed if the metric and the sending address match the routing table entry. If the sending address is different than the one in the routing table, and the received sending address is lower, this neighbor is used as the upstream router.

   e. If the metric of the received route is greater than or equal to 64, the route is ignored.

Pruning   Pruning is necessary for maintaining an optimum use of bandwidth for multicast traffic. If a router finds that all its directly connected multicast hosts have left a group and no downstream routers are dependent on the group traffic, the router sends a prune message upstream to shut off the traffic. The following steps, performed by the DVMRP router, outline the details of the pruning process:

1. If a prune message is received from a router with which it has no adjacency established, the prune is ignored. If the prune message is in an improper format or if the prune message doesn't apply to any known active sources, the prune message is ignored. If the neighbor that sent the prune is not a dependent neighbor, the prune message is ignored.

2. If there is no active prune from this neighbor for the source network and group, the timeout is set using the prune lifetime in the prune message.

3. If all dependent downstream routers have received prune messages and there are no directly connected group members, a prune message is sent to the upstream router.

A DVMRP router does the following when sending a prune message:

1. If the upstream router cannot process prune messages, it is not sent. The ability to process prune messages is communicated in the capabilities and version fields of the DVMRP message from the neighbor.

2. Any outstanding graft messages that require acknowledgement are cancelled.

The prune message contains a prune lifetime value because DVMRP always assumes that multicast traffic should be forwarded to neighboring routers unless a prune message is received. When the prune lifetime expires, the router resumes forwarding the multicast traffic for the group until another prune message is received.

Figure 8-8 shows the format of the DVMRP prune message.

Grafting Grafting is the functional opposite of pruning. When a host sends an IGMP join to a router knowing of a multicast group source, the router sends a DVMRP graft message so that it begins receiving the necessary multicast traffic. Graft messages are sent upstream until they find the distribution tree. The graft messages are acknowledged at every hop.

Figure 8-8
DVMRP prune
message

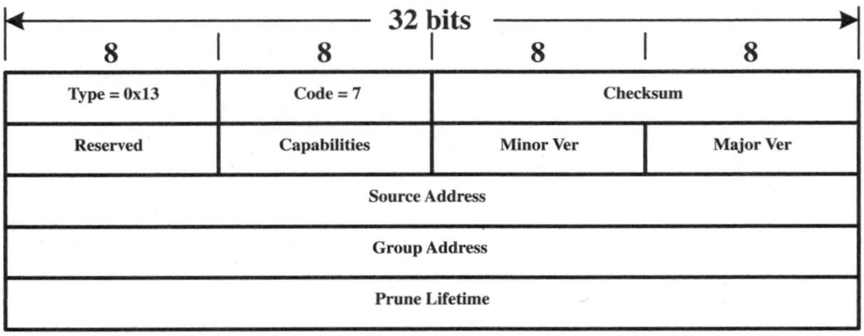

32 bits			
8	8	8	8
Type = 0x13	Code = 7	Checksum	
Reserved	Capabilities	Minor Ver	Major Ver
Source Address			
Group Address			
Prune Lifetime			

Graft messages are sent under the following conditions:

- If a host sends an IGMP join for a group that has been pruned
- If a DVMRP router is enabled on a pruned network and is dependent on the upstream router
- If a DVMRP router is rebooted
- If a graft acknowledgement is not received for a previous graft message

Figure 8-9 displays the format of a DVMRP graft message.

Figure 8-10 shows the packet format of a DVMRP graft acknowledgement message.

DVMRP Limitations

DVMRP is built on the principles of the RIP. RIP is a distance vector unicast routing protocol that, like the DVMRP, has a number of inherent limitations. The following list enumerates some of these limitations:

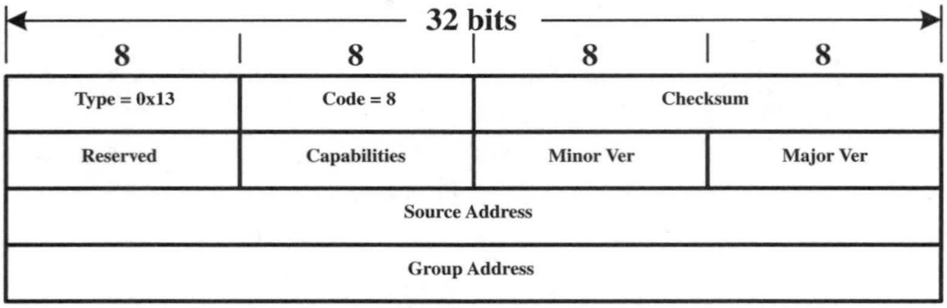

Figure 8-9
DVMRP graft
packet format

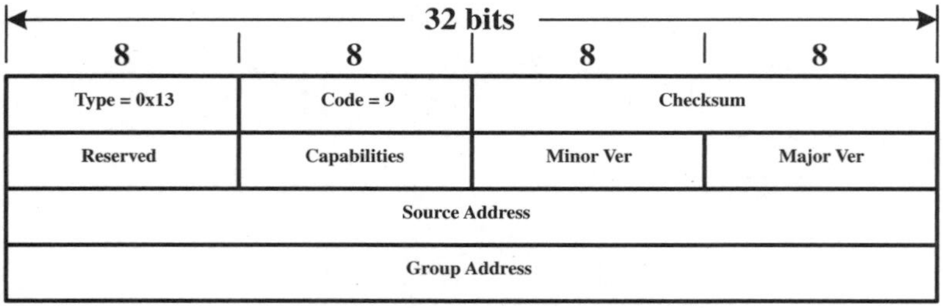

32 bits			
8	8	8	8
Type = 0x13	Code = 8	Checksum	
Reserved	Capabilities	Minor Ver	Major Ver
Source Address			
Group Address			

Figure 8-10
DVMRP graft
acknowledgement
packet format

32 bits			
8	8	8	8
Type = 0x13	Code = 9	Checksum	
Reserved	Capabilities	Minor Ver	Major Ver
Source Address			
Group Address			

- DVMRP has slow convergence time.
- DVMRP has a limited network scope due to the `infinity=32` restriction.
- DVMRP is unable to detect routing loops.
- The only route metric is the hop count. The link transfer rate is not taken into consideration.
- DVMRP picks one route if several possible paths exist. No load balancing exists in DVMRP.

DVMRP Configuration

DVMRP routing is used in three situations. The first is where a DVMRP host is connected to a router. In the second situation, two adjacent routers need to route multicast. The last, and most common, situation is where multicast is received from an MBone tunnel.

A host connected to a router may be running mrouted, a DVMRP implementation that usually runs on UNIX workstations. To interact with mrouted, enable IP multicast on the router and CGMP Proxy on the interface.

```
Router> enable
Router# configure terminal
Router(config)# ip multicast-routing
Router(config)# interface Ethernet 0
Router(config-int)# ip cgmp proxy
```

We want to interact with the DVMRP router, mrouted, so we enable CGMP. In the same fashion that a CGMP-enabled router interacts with IGMP hosts, a CGMP Proxy enabled router will also listen for DVMRP updates and send CGMP join messages to the attached switches. For a full description of CGMP, see Chapter 7, "IP Multicast Configuration."

If we have two adjacent routers wanting to exchange multicast routes, we can enable DVMRP on those interfaces. Suppose that we have two routers connected via Ethernet port 0 on both systems.

```
Router-A(config)# ip multicast-routing
Router-A(config)# interface Ethernet 0
Router-A(config-int)# ip dvmrp unicast-routing
Router-A(config-int)# description Link-to-B
```

```
Router-B(config)# ip multicast-routing
Router-B(config)# interface Ethernet 0
Router-B(config-int)# description Link-to-A
Router-B(config-int)# ip dvmrp unicast-routing
```

This configuration is normally used when connecting PIM and DVMRP based networks. PIM is covered in detail later.

Lastly, connecting to the MBone usually requires connecting via a tunnel to a service provider with a MBone connection.

```
Router(config)# ip multicast-routing
Router(config)# interface tunnel 0
Router(config-int)# ip unnumbered Ethernet 0
Router(config-int)# tunnel source 100.1.1.1
Router(config-int)# tunnel destination 100.2.1.1
Router(config-int)# tunnel mode dvmrp
```

The tunnel interface is a logical, rather than physical, interface. The `interface` command creates the logical tunnel interface. The command `ip unnumbered` specifies that the tunnel will assume the same IP address of the Ethernet 0 interface. We are assuming that the IP address of the Ethernet 0 interface is `100.1.1.1` and `100.2.1.1` is the IP address of the remote tunnel interface.

To verify operation, you can check the contents of the DVMRP routing table.

```
Router# show ip dvmrp route
```

For more detailed information about a specific route:

```
Router# show ip dvmrp route 224.1.220.120
```

The multicast tunnel is the most common use of DVMRP on a network. MOSPF and PIM offer many advantages over DVMRP.

MOSPF

The *Multicast Open Shortest Path First* (MOSPF) multicast routing protocol is a dense mode routing protocol and is fully specified in RFC 1584. It is designed for use within a single routing domain that is controlled by a single organization. Cisco does not support MOSPF in its routing products.

MOSPF uses OSPF unicast routing protocol to define its multicast source-based distribution trees. OSPF is a link state routing protocol that builds its routing information table based on the link states of the routers in the network. OSPF is covered in more detail in Chapter 11.

MOSPF works best in environments with few groups active at any time. This multicast routing protocol does not operate well in networks that have many active multicast groups along with unstable links. This is because MOSPF must recalculate its distribution trees each time a link state changes. Because this is somewhat contradictory to its purpose as a dense mode multicast routing protocol, MOSPF is not used to a great extent throughout the networking industry.

PIM–DM Overview

PIM–DM is very similar in nature to DVMRP. Both are dense mode multicast routing protocols, and both develop source-based trees using RPF. Both assume that multicast traffic is to be forwarded everywhere until a prune message is received on a particular interface. After prune messages time out, the multicast traffic resumes.

The differences between PIM–DM and DVMRP are subtle but fundamental. DVMRP depends on its own routing protocol for building its multicast routing tables; whereas PIM–DM uses an underlying unicast routing protocol to build its multicast routing tables. In the case of Cisco, PIM–DM can use RIP, IGRP, EIGRP, or OSPF for its routing information.

PIM–DM is a bit of a misnomer because the protocol is very much dependent on an underlying unicast routing protocol. "Protocol Independent" simply refers to the fact that PIM–DM is not dependent on a built-in multicast routing protocol.

Because PIM–DM isn't necessarily dependent on a RIP-based multicast routing protocol like DVMRP, PIM–DM does not have the same limitations as DVMRP. Because PIM–DM can use OSPF, the multicast route can follow a path of lowest cost that takes into account the bandwidth of the links as well as the number of hops.

PIM–DM Version 1 Operation

RPF and Source-Based Trees   PIM–DM uses RPF much like DVMRP. See the discussion on RPF in the DVMRP section for a complete view of RPF. To decide whether an interface has the shortest path to the multicast group source, a PIM–DM-enabled multicast router consults its unicast routing table. The router simply looks up the unicast network of the multicast source in the unicast routing table. The routing entry will list the interface to that network. If the interface listed isn't the same as the interface on which the multicast packet was received, the packet is discarded. If the network is not found in the routing table, the router looks for the default route interface.

PIM–DM uses neighbor discovery to detect other attached routers. This operation is very similar to the DVMRP neighbor discovery except there is no neighbor discovery packet in PIM–DM.

PIM–DM Packet Format   Before proceeding further into the protocol, we will look at the PIM–DM packet format. Figure 8-11 shows the layout of the packet.

The PIM–DM packet is encapsulated in an IP packet with a protocol type 0x2, representing an IGMP packet. The IGMP type field contains 0x14, designating that the packet is a PIM–DM Version 1 message. The code field can have one of the values listed in Table 8-5.

PIM–DM Neighbor Discovery   Neighbor discovery is achieved through the use of the PIM–DM query message. Figure 8-12 shows the format of a PIM–DM query message.

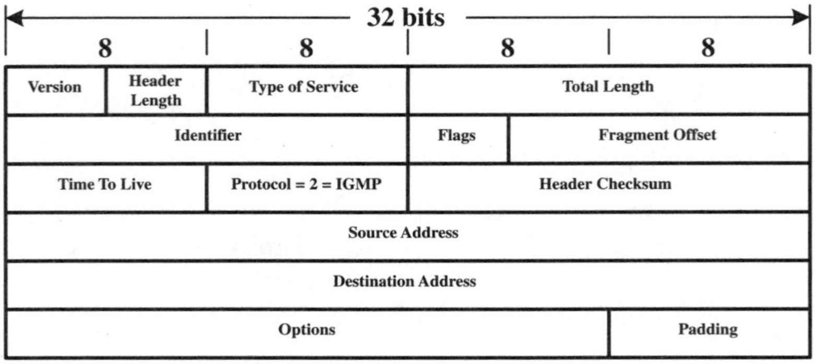

Figure 8-11
PIM–DM packet format

Version	Header Length	Type of Service	Total Length		
Identifier			Flags	Fragment Offset	
Time To Live		Protocol = 2 = IGMP	Header Checksum		
Source Address					
Destination Address					
Options				Padding	

32 bits — 8 | 8 | 8 | 8

Table 8-5

PIM–DM code
field values

PIM–DM Code Value	Description
0	Router Query
1	Register (Sparse Mode)
2	Register-stop (Sparse Mode)
3	Join/Prune
4	RP Reachability (Sparse Mode)
5	Assert
6	Graft
7	Graft Acknowledgement

Figure 8-12
PIM–DM query
message format

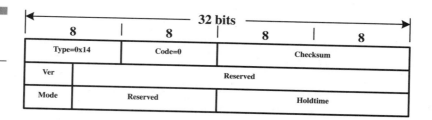

Table 8-6

PIM–DM query
message mode
field values

PIM–DM Query Message Mode Value	Description
0	Dense Mode
1	Sparse Mode
2	Sparse-Dense Mode

The query message can be one of three modes—dense, sparse , or sparse-dense. The values for the mode field of the PIM–DM query message are listed in Table 8-6.

When a PIM–DM-enabled router receives a query message, the router records the IP address of the router. This message isn't acknowledged as in DVMRP discovery messages. The interface on which the query is received is added to an outgoing interface list. This list is consulted when the router needs to forward a multicast packet. Interfaces that receive IGMP join messages are also added to the outgoing interface list. The query message is addressed to the all-routers multicast address—244.0.0.2. This query process acts as the querier router election for IGMP. This process is covered in more detail in Chapter 7, "IP Multicast Configuration."

The query message contains a hold time field. If no other query messages are received within the hold time period from the neighboring router, it is no longer considered a neighbor.

PIM–DM Multicast Packet Forwarding   PIM–DM forwards multicast packets if the packet was received on the RPF interface, in which case the packet is forwarded to all the interfaces in the output interface list.

The output interface list can be in one of three states: null, (*,G), or (S,G). If the output interface list is in the null state, no PIM–DM queries or IGMP joins have been received on any interfaces. If the output interface list is in the (*,G) state, all multicast packets from group G are forwarded to interfaces in the list, regardless of the source. If the output interface list is in the (S,G) state, multicast packets from source S to group G are forwarded to the interfaces in the list.

PIM–DM Pruning   If the output interface list is in the null state, no downstream PIM–DM routers are on the network. This router will send a prune message upstream to a connected PIM–DM router. The upstream router receiving the prune message will disable multicast traffic for the interface that is connected to the downstream router. Figure 8-13 shows the packet format for the prune message.

The PIM–DM prune message contains a list of groups that could be shut off by the downstream router.

The prune message contains a hold time that specifies how long the prune should be in effect. If no more prune messages are received for the groups listed in the prune message, the traffic is, once again, forwarded to the downstream router.

PIM–DM Grafting   If an interface needs to forward multicast traffic before the prune message's hold time timer expires, the router can be grafted to the distribution tree with a PIM–DM graft message. The receiver acknowledges these messages.

Figure 8-14 shows the packet format of a PIM–DM graft message.

Figure 8-15 shows the packet format of a PIM–DM graft acknowledgement message.

Figure 8-13
PIM–DM prune
message

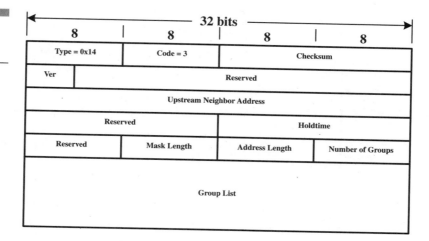

Figure 8-14
PIM–DM graft
message

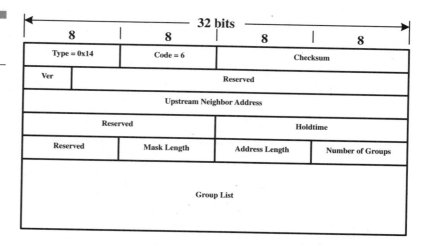

PIM–DM Assert Messages In a multiaccess network like Ethernet where several routers can share one Ethernet segment, multiple copies of multicast packets can be sent to the same router. Consider the following network of four PIM–DM-enabled routers in Figure 8-16.

Router 1 sends multicast traffic to Routers 2 and 3 because both are PIM–DM routers that need that group's multicast traffic. Router 2 forwards the multicast traffic to Router 4. Router 3 likewise forwards the multicast traffic to Router 4. Thus, Router 4 sees the traffic twice. As this is an inefficient use of bandwidth, the PIM–DM assert message fixes this problem.

Figure 8-15
PIM–DM graft
acknowledgement
message

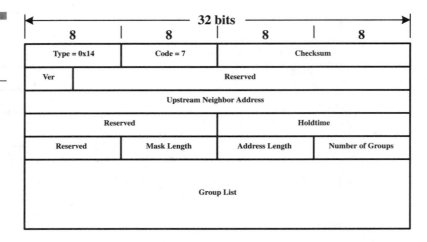

Figure 8-16
PIM–DM in a
multiaccess network

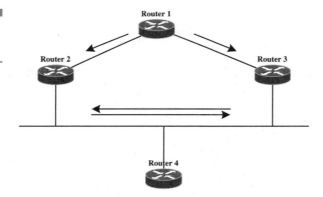

Figure 8-17 shows the PIM–DM assert packet format. The message contains the group address and mask for the source as well as the router's metric back to the source.

Routers 2 and 3 know that both are sending the same multicast packets onto the network. The router with the highest IP address becomes the multicast forwarder for the multiaccess network. The other router prunes the multicast interface from the distribution. The multicast forwarder router then sends Assert messages to let other routers on the network know that it is the router that should be sent prune and graft messages.

Figure 8-17
PIM–DM assert
message

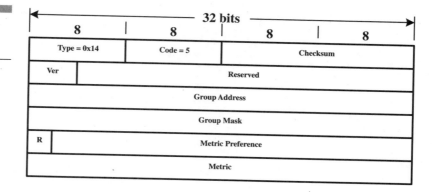

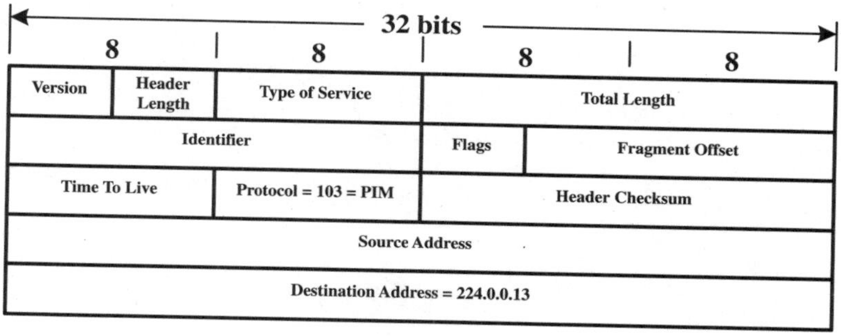

Figure 8-18
PIM–DMv2 packet
format

PIM–DM Version 2

PIM–DM Version 2 differs from PIM–DM Version 1 in the following ways:

- PIM–DMv2 now has an IP protocol number of 103. It is not encapsulated in IGMP packets like PIM–DMv1.
- All PIM–DMv2 messages are sent to the All-PIM routers address of 244.0.0.13.
- The PIM–DMv2 header has been modified from PIM–DMv1. Figure 8-18 shows the packet format for PIM–DMv2. Table 8-7 lists the PIM–DMv2 type codes and their descriptions.
- Instead of a PIM–DM query message, PIM–DMv2 sends a hello message for router discovery.

Table 8-7

PIM–DMv2 code
values

PIM–DM Code Value	Description
0	Router Query
1	Register (Sparse Mode)
2	Register-stop (Sparse Mode)
3	Join/Prune
4	RP Reachability (Sparse Mode)
5	Assert
6	Graft
7	Graft Acknowledgement

- A hold time of 0xFFFF means never time out. This provides a way for prune messages to be permanent.
- The prune message format has changed from PIM–DMv1.

PIM–DM Configuration

Configuring PIM Dense Mode is straightforward. First, enable multicast routing and then enable PIM on the interfaces you want to include in multicast routing.

```
Router(config)# ip multicast-routing
Router(config)# interface Ethernet 0
Router(config-int)# ip pim dense-mode
```

When PIM is enabled, you can use several commands to verify proper operation. First, verify communication with the other PIM-enabled routers.

```
Router# show ip pim neighbor
```

This command will display the list of all known adjacent PIM routers. After you have traffic flowing, you can view the multicast routing table as follows:

```
Router# show ip mroute
```

Make sure to enable CGMP on the interfaces where you expect multicast hosts to reside. PIM–DM will flood and prune regularly for less traffic and processor-intensive route calculations.

CBT

Core Based Tree is a sparse mode multicast routing protocol specified in RFC 2201. CBT builds one distribution tree for each multicast group. This reduces the resources consumed by the router to track the distribution trees.

The CBT distribution tree has a core router that is used to build the tree. Routers that need the multicast traffic for a particular group send a join message to the core router. The router responds by replying with an acknowledgement to the join message. The path taken by the acknowledgement forms the path to the distribution tree. The join message does not need to travel all the way to the core router because any router that is a member of the distribution tree can respond to the join request. Therefore, the router that wants to join the group can connect to the distribution tree without having to send a join request to the core router.

PIM–SM Overview

PIM–SM is similar to PIM–DM in that PIM–SM relies on the underlying unicast routing protocol to make its RPF decisions. PIM–SM, however, assumes that the multicast source and receivers are distant and that the bandwidth between them is not cheap. Therefore, PIM–SM requires an explicit join message from the downstream receivers instead of assuming that all PIM–SM routers and receivers want multicast traffic until a prune is received.

This difference in operation makes PIM–SM more appropriate than PIM–DM for WAN links. However, this does not necessarily mean that PIM–DM is better suited for LAN networks.

PIM–DM uses source-based trees that are dynamically developed using an RPF operation. PIM–SM, on the other hand, builds one shared tree for the entire multicast group. Each member must graft itself to a central point in the tree that is known as a *rendezvous point* (RP). There is only one RP for a multicast group, but there can be as many RPs as there are active multicast groups.

One fundamental difference in the operation of PIM–SM and PIM–DM is that PIM–DM source-based trees create an optimal path from the source to the receivers. The PIM–SM-shared tree is not optimally built in terms of having the shortest path between the source and all receivers. Notice that both use RPF, but create different trees. The PIM–SM tree is built around the RP, the PIM–DM tree from each source. Although not having the shortest path, PIM–SM routers do not have to keep up with as much state information as PIM–DM routers.

Determining the location of the RP can be achieved by statically configuring the address of the RP in each host running PIM–SM or by letting the network determine the RP dynamically. Two methods may be used to dynamically determine the RP. If the routers use PIM–SMv1, the Auto-RP mechanism is used. If the routers are using PIM–SMv2, candidate RP advertisements are used to determine the RP. These methods are covered in detail at the end of this section. For now, assume that the routers know the location of the RP.

PIM–SM Operation

PIM–SM Encapsulation   PIM–SM packets are encapsulated in IGMP packets. The PIM–SM header contains a code field that denotes the PIM–SM message type. Figure 8-19 shows the PIM–SM IGMP encapsulated header.

Figure 8-20 shows the PIM–SM packet format.

Table 8-8 lists the code field values of the PIM–SM packet header. These values denote the type of PIM–SM messages.

Figure 8-19
PIM–SM packet encapsulation

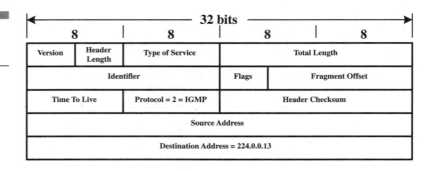

Figure 8-20

PIM–SM packet
format

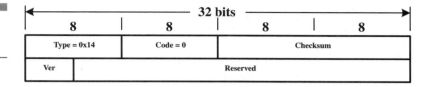

Table 8-8

PIM–SM code
values

Code Value	Description
0	Router Query
1	Register
2	Register-Stop
3	Join/Prune
4	RP Reachability
5	Assert

Figure 8-21

PIM–SM query
message

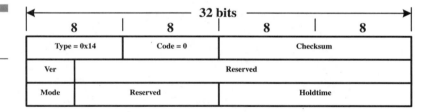

PIM–SM Router Discovery The PIM–SM router discovery process is very similar to that of the PIM–DM, except that the neighbor information is not used to build an output interface list. This is because PIM–SM requires an explicit join message to begin forwarding multicast packets. PIM–SM uses a PIM–SM query message to conduct router discovery. Figure 8-21 and Table 8-9 show the packet format of the PIM–SM router query message and the query message modes.

When a PIM–SM-enabled router receives a query message, the router simply records the IP address of the router. The message isn't acknowledged as with DVMRP discovery messages. The query message is addressed to the all-routers multicast address—244.0.0.2. This query

Table 8-9

PIM–SM query
message type
values

Query Message Mode Value	Description
0	Dense Mode
1	Sparse Mode
2	Sparse-Dense

process acts as the querier router election for IGMP. The IGMP querier router election process is covered in more detail in Chapter 7, "IP Multicast Configuration."

The query message has a hold time field that specifies the length of time that must pass without receiving query messages before the neighboring router is no longer considered a neighbor.

PIM–SM Multicast Packet Forwarding PIM–SM has very simple rules for multicast packet forwarding. Multicast packets are forwarded to interfaces in the output interface list. Directly connected hosts using IGMP join messages or by other PIM–SM routers using an explicit PIM–SM join form this list. Unlike PIM–DM, multicast traffic isn't forwarded to all neighboring routers.

A leaf router will send a (*,G) state join message if the leaf router has received an IGMP join from a directly-connected host. The (*,G) state indicates that packets from any source must be forwarded to group G. The router then forwards the join message to the RP following a unicast route. If a router along the way to the RP isn't in a (*,G) state, the router enters that state and begins forwarding the multicast traffic. If the router is already in the (*,G) state, the router does nothing because the leaf router has reached the shared tree.

PIM–SM uses a registering process to allow multicast packets to be sent from source to the RP. During this process, the router will become part of the distribution tree. When the router first sees a multicast packet from a source, a register packet is sent to the RP and the router immediately begins sending multicast packets to the RP from the source encapsulated in unicast register messages. Figure 8-22 shows the PIM–SM register message packet format.

The RP receives the register packet, begins de-encapsulating the multicast packets, and sends them to the receivers. Then, the RP sends a join

Figure 8-22
PIM–SM register
message packet
format

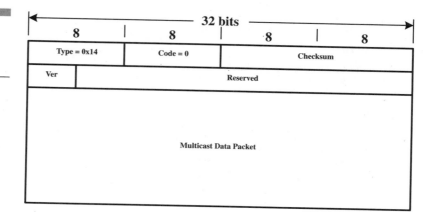

message back to the sender. Following this, the path to the sender becomes the optimal path to the RP. The source begins sending multicast packets directly to the RP using this path. To finish the transaction, the RP sends a register-stop message back to the router that sent the register message. The router then stops encapsulating the multicast packets in register messages to the RP.

PIM–SM Pruning   When a router loses all its directly connected multicast receivers and downstream neighbor routers, the router will send a prune message to the RP. If PIM–SM routers along the way to the RP have lost their downstream and directly-connected member hosts for that particular group, they pass the prune message on to the RP. Otherwise, the intermediate router discards the prune message because that is as far as the distribution tree needs to be pruned.

Figure 8-23 shows the PIM–SM join/prune packet format.

Note that there are no graft messages in PIM–SM. This is because routers forward multicast group packets based on explicit join messages. Also note that prune messages are permanent. The only way for a router to start forwarding multicast packets again for a particular group is to receive a PIM–SM join message.

PIM–SM Assert Mechanism   The PIM–SM assert mechanism works the same as the PIM–DM assert messages. In a multi-access network like Ethernet where several routers can share one Ethernet segment, multiple

Figure 8-23
PIM–SM join/prune
packet format

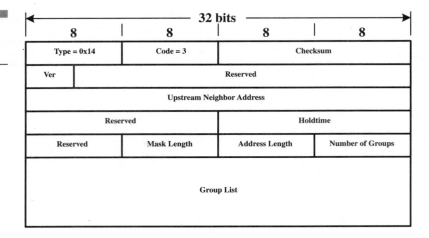

Figure 8-24
PIM–SM in a
Multi-Access Network

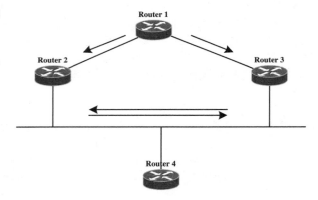

copies of multicast packets can be sent to the same router. Consider the following network of four PIM–SM enabled routers in Figure 8-24.

Router 1 sends multicast traffic to Routers 2 and 3 because both are PIM–SM routers that need that group's multicast traffic. Router 2 forwards the multicast traffic to Router 4. Router 3 likewise forwards the multicast traffic to Router 4. Thus, Router 4 sees the traffic twice. As this is an inefficient use of bandwidth, the PIM–SM assert message fixes this problem.

Figure 8-25 shows the PIM–SM assert packet format. The message contains the group address and mask for the source as well as the router's metric back to the source.

Routers 2 and 3 know that they are both sending the same multicast packets on to the network. The router with the highest IP address becomes

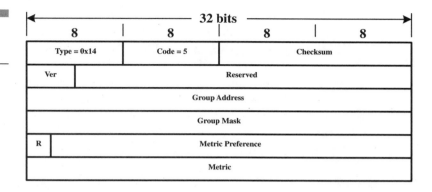

Figure 8-25
PIM–SM assert
message

the multicast forwarder for the multi-access network. The other router prunes the multicast interface from the distribution. The multicast forwarder router then sends assert messages to notify routers on the network that it is the router that should receive prune and graft messages.

PIM–SM Version 2

PIM–SMv2 operates in a manner very similar to PIM–SMv1, although there are some differences between the two versions. PIM–SMv2 is specified in RFC 2362. The following shows the changes to the PIM–SMv2 from PIM–SMv1.

- PIM–SMv2 is encapsulated in IP packets with protocol number 103. Use an IP multicast group destination address of 224.0.0.13.
- Instead of a router query message, a PIM–SM hello message is used. The timeout value of the neighbor can be set to never expire, which shuts off hello messages on pay-by-the-bit link.
- The prune/join message packet format has been changed.

Determining the Location of the Rendezvous Point

Determining the location of the RP can be achieved by statically configuring the address of the RP in each host running PIM–SM or by letting the network determine the RP dynamically. There are two methods of dynamically determining the RP. If the routers use PIM–SMv1, the Auto-RP mechanism is used. If the routers are using PIM–SMv2, candidate RP advertisements are used to determine the RP.

If both static and dynamic methods are used concurrently, the dynamic method takes precedence by default unless the router is configured otherwise.

If the static method for determining the RP is used, all routers are configured with the address of the RP except for the RP. The router that doesn't have an RP address configured will determine that it is the RP. This is a very simple way of defining the RP. However, there are disadvantages to setting a fixed address for the RP. If the RP address were to change, all routers would have to be reconfigured to know the location of the RP.

Cisco routers enabled with PIM–SMv1 use a Cisco proprietary mechanism for determining the RP called Auto-RP. The routers configured as RPs send RP announcements via the PIM–SM-enabled interfaces to the well-known Cisco-RP-Announce multicast group with address 224.0.1.40. All Cisco PIM–SM-enabled routers listen to these announcements to determine the location of the RPs. This protocol works in the presence of multiple RPs in a network by determining that RPs are associated with specific groups.

In PIM–SMv2, the bootstrap messages are used to determine the RPs. A *bootstrap router* (BSR) is elected by bootstrap messages sent by routers configured as bootstrap candidates. The router with the highest BSR priority will win the election. If there is a tie, the router with the highest IP address is elected the BSR.

Candidate RP messages are sent to the BSR. These advertisements contain the address of the advertising candidate RP and the multicast address of groups that the candidate RP can service. The BSR relays the information to all PIM–SM routers.

SPT Switchover

A leaf router can send multicast traffic over the shared tree or a source tree. The source tree is also known as the *Shortest Path Tree* (SPT). By default, a router sends multicast traffic over the SPT. A threshold bandwidth value can be set to determine when the router switches from the shared tree to the source tree. If a threshold of 64kbps is set as the SPT switchover threshold, the router will send the multicast traffic over the shared tree as long as the bandwidth of the session is less than 64kbps. Once the bandwidth of the session becomes greater than 64kbps, the router switches to the SPT.

The SPT typically has a smaller latency than the shared tree. The disadvantage with the SPT is that the router must keep up with more state information to maintain the SPT.

PIM–SM Configuration

Configuring PIM Sparse Mode is straightforward. First, enable multicast routing and then enable PIM on the interfaces you want to participate in multicast routing.

```
Router(config)# ip multicast-routing
Router(config)# ip pim rp-address 10.1.1.1
Router(config)# interface Ethernet 0
Router(config-int)# ip pim sparse-mode
```

When PIM is enabled, you can use several commands to verify proper operation. First, verify communication with the other PIM-enabled routers.

```
Router# show ip pim neighbor
```

That will display the list of all known adjacent PIM routers. In addition, you can view specific RP information.

```
Router# show ip pim rp
```

When you have traffic flowing, you can view the multicast routing table with the following command:

```
Router# show ip mroute
```

Make sure to enable CGMP on the interfaces where you expect multicast hosts to reside. See Chapter 7 for CGMP details.

Chapter Summary

This chapter gives you a broad overview of multicast routing protocols to build on the knowledge gained from Chapter 7, which covers host communication with routers in order to join a multicast group. This chapter discusses router communication for achieving multicast routing.

The following topics are covered in this chapter:

- IP Multicast Routing Basics
- Distance Vector Multicast Routing Protocol
- Protocol Independent Multicast–Dense Mode
- Core Based Trees
- Protocol Independent Multicast–Sparse Mode

IP multicast routing can be a difficult problem to solve because multicast groups can span the entire campus network. Also, it is very easy to generate duplicate packets while forwarding multicast traffic.

This chapter gives you the fundamentals of generating distribution trees to determine the path from a multicast source to the multicast group receivers. There are two basic types of distribution trees—shared trees and source trees.

This chapter covers two source tree multicast routing protocols—DVMRP and PIM–DM. These protocols are also known as dense mode multicast routing protocols because it assumed that there are many multicast group members throughout the network and that bandwidth is cheap. These protocols assume that multicast traffic is to be forwarded on all multicast enabled interfaces unless told to prune the interface. The prune message will eventually time out and the multicast traffic will resume by default. These protocols use RPF to determine where to forward multicast traffic.

DVMRP has a multicast routing protocol built in. PIM–DM relies on the underlying unicast routing protocol to determine the RPF interfaces.

Two sparse mode protocols are covered in this chapter—*Core Based Trees* (CBTs) and *Protocol Independent Multicast–Sparse Mode* (PIM–SM). These protocols use shared multicast distribution trees. Because it is assumed that the number of multicast members is few and bandwidth is expensive, these protocols are attractive for WAN environments.

Frequently Asked Questions (FAQ)

Question: Which multicast routing protocol is best to deploy?

Answer: PIM Sparse Mode. As discussed, PIM–DM uses a flood and prune concept. At three minute intervals, PIM–DM will flood multicast to every interface and wait for prune messages to turn off the traffic. This is less than optimal for any network. Second, PIM–SM is far less processor-intensive. In addition to not having the flurry of packets every three minutes, maintaining a shared tree is far less work than a source-based tree. Lastly, PIM–SM only maintains routing information for active multicast groups.

Question: How do I join the MBone?

Answer: It is best to ask your *Internet Service Provider* (ISP). Otherwise, you can get help on the MBone mailing list, a discussion list for all MBone related issues. For more information, see the mailing list FAQ at `ftp://ftp.isi.edu/mbone/faq.txt`.

Case Study

Objective

CPI management has decided to build a video conferencing system to allow employees to meet without having to leave their buildings. Studies have shown that CPI managers spend countless hours traveling between meetings across CPI's large campus.

With the implementation of IP multicast traffic management on each VLAN, some departments have enjoyed video conferencing for intradepartmental meetings. They now want the same convenience for interdepartmental meetings. You are to implement multicast routing across the entire campus network.

Approach

The following tasks must be completed to achieve your objective.

- Decide where multicast traffic will be used throughout the campus network.
- Decide how to route multicast traffic between VLANs in CPI's network.
- Implement your multicast routing design within the CPI campus network.

Where Is Multicast Traffic Needed?

Multicast will be required on the administrative, information technologies and research and development VLANs. The employees of these departments comprise the majority of those involved in interdepartmental meetings.

Table 8-10 shows the VLAN identifiers and network devices that are in place.

Table 8-11 lists the device names and their IP address.

Table 8-10

VLAN	VLAN ID
Management	
R&D	1
Mfg	2
SR	3
Admin	4
IT	5

Table 8-11

Switch Name	IP Address
IT-1-dist-5505	100.1.1.11
IT-2-access-2926	100.1.1.12
IT-3-access-1900	100.1.1.13
IT-4-access-1900	100.1.1.14
IT-5-access-1900	100.1.1.15
RD-1-dist-5505	100.1.1.16
RD-2-access-2926	100.1.1.17
RD-3-access-1900	100.1.1.18
RD-4-access-1900	100.1.1.19
RD-5-access-1900	100.1.1.20
Admin-1-dist-5505	100.1.1.31
Admin-2-access-2926	100.1.1.32
Admin-3-access-1900	100.1.1.33
Admin-4-access-1900	100.1.1.34
Admin-5-access-1900	100.1.1.35

Selecting a Routing Protocol

Your routing protocol choices are PIM–DM and PIM–SM. Either protocol will solve the problem. Our network has plentiful bandwidth and the multicast usage will be moderate. These characteristics would seem to fit the PIM–DM model; however, multicast flooding every three minutes could impact central storage usage by users across the campus. PIM–SM will eliminate that inconvenience and reduce CPU utilization on your routers.

Implementing Multicast Routing

Implementing PIM–SM consists of enabling multicast routing on the router and then enabling PIM on the interface(s) requiring multicast service.

Because we have previously enabled CGMP for these VLANs, it is not necessary to re-enter the `ip  multicast-routing` command. It is included here for completeness.

An RP must also be selected. The selection is fairly arbitrary, although one could argue that the information technologies router would not be a good first choice. Because the information technologies router must handle more traffic than the others, it would be prudent to use the processing power of one of the other routers. We will make the administrative router the PIM–SM RP.

First the administrative router:

```
Admin-1-dist-5505(config)# ip multicast-routing
Admin-1-dist-5505(config)# interface Vlan4
Admin-1-dist-5505(config-if)# ip pim sparse-mode
```

Repeat for the information technologies and research and development routers, substituting the appropriate VLAN identifier.

```
IT-1-dist-5505(config)# ip multicast-routing
IT-1-dist-5505(config)# ip pim rp-address 100.1.1.31
IT-1-dist-5505(config)# interface Vlan5
IT-1-dist-5505(config-if)# ip pim sparse-mode

RD-1-dist-5505(config)# ip multicast-routing
RD-1-dist-5505(config)# ip pim rp-address 100.1.1.31
```

```
RD-1-dist-5505(config)# interface Vlan1
RD-1-dist-5505(config-if)# ip pim sparse-mode
```

With PIM now enabled on the current multicast interfaces, in addition to CGMP, we must also enable PIM on the backbone links to allow the routers to communicate together.

```
Admin-1-dist-5505(config)# interface Vlan0
Admin-1-dist-5505(config-if)# ip pim sparse-mode

IT-1-dist-5505(config)# interface Vlan0
IT-1-dist-5505(config-if)# ip pim sparse-mode

RD-1-dist-5505(config)# interface Vlan0
RD-1-dist-5505(config-if)# ip pim sparse-mode
```

With PIM–SM enabled on all multicast interfaces, confirm that all routers are communicating properly.

```
Admin-1-dist-5505# show ip pim neighbor
```

You should verify that all three routers are in the neighbor listing. You can also verify RP status.

```
IT-1-dist-5505# show ip pim rp
```

Each router should show the RP as IP address 100.1.1.31. If it does, you have successfully configured multicast routing.

Case Study Summary

The CPI campus network now supports multicast applications on the administrative, information technologies and research and development VLANs. Furthermore, with multicast routing enabled, members of those departments can now participate in interdepartmental meetings via videoconferencing. This will save money by by more efficiently using employees' time.

The following steps were completed to get to this point. We started with multicast enabled only on the VLANs. We then:

- Defined where multicast traffic would be used throughout the campus network.
- Defined a routing protocol for multicast traffic between VLANs in CPI's network.
- Implemented multicast routing within the CPI campus network.

CPI's network is now configured to handle multicast traffic within each VLAN and among all three in an optimal fashion.

Questions

1. RPF is _____ _____ _____.

   a. Reverse Path Forwarding
   b. Reverse Path Filtering
   c. Reverse Polarizing Filter
   d. Run Packet Fast

2. Which protocol uses RPF?

   a. DVMRP
   b. PIM–DM
   c. PIM–SM
   d. All of the above

3. Which protocol uses source-based trees?

   a. DVMRP
   b. PIM–DM
   c. PIM–SM
   d. Both a and b

4. Which protocol uses a shared tree?

   a. DVMRP
   b. PIM–DM
   c. PIM–SM
   d. None of the above

5. Which protocol will always have the smallest multicast routing table?

   a. DVMRP
   b. PIM–DM
   c. PIM–SM
   d. Both b and c

6. Which protocol floods multicast traffic periodically?

   a. DVMRP
   b. PIM–DM
   c. PIM–SM
   d. Both a and b

7. Which protocol interoperates with mrouted software?

   a. DVMRP
   b. PIM–DM
   c. PIM–SM
   d. Both b and c

8. An MBone tunnel requires which protocol?

   a. DVMRP
   b. PIM–DM
   c. PIM–SM
   d. CGMP

9. Which protocol is IGMP-encapsulated?

   a. PIM–SM
   b. PIM–DMv1
   c. PIM–DMv2
   d. Both a and b

10. If you are unsure of the path a multicast packet is traversing, what command will enable you to find out?

    a. `show ip pim rp`
    b. `show ip pim neighbor`
    c. `show ip cgmp`
    d. `show ip rpf`

11. To view the known IP multicast groups, use which command?

    a. `show ip multicast groups`
    b. `show ip mroute`
    c. `show ip route`
    d. `show ip sdr`

12. CBT is _____ _____ _____.

    a. Circular Binary Tree
    b. Circular Bit Tree
    c. Core Binary Tree
    d. Core Based Tree

13. You would use which command to enable CBT:

    a. `ip cbt enable`
    b. `ip cbt`
    c. `set cbt enable`
    d. None of the above

14. Using Cisco IOS, `ip multicast-routing` must be enabled for

    a. DVMRP

    b. PIM–DM

    c. PIM–SM

    d. All the above

15. To prevent redundant multicast packets on the network, PIM uses the

    a. Early Warning System

    b. Alert Mechanism

    c. TTL

    d. Metric

16. When configured for PIM operation, a router will also listen for _____ packets.

    a. IGMP

    b. DVMRP

    c. CBT

    d. Both a and b

17. Multicast tree operations consist of two types:

    a. request/reply

    b. prune/graft

    c. join/leave

    d. forward/reply

18. The all-DVMRP router IP multicast address is _____.

    a. 224.0.0.2

    b. 224.0.0.3

    c. 224.0.0.4

    d. 239.255.255.255

19. PIM–SM creates a shared tree by designating a _____.

    a. STP

    b. SPT

    c. PR

    d. RP

20. MOSPF is a _____ _____ multicast routing protocol.

   a. dense mode

   b. link state

   c. shortest path

   d. Cisco standard

Answers

1. RPF is _____ _____ _____.

    a.   Reverse Path Forwarding

2. Which protocol uses RPF?

    d.   All of the above (DVMRP, PIM–DM, PIM–SM)

3. Which protocol uses source-based trees?

    d.   Both a and b (DVMRP, PIM–DM)

4. Which protocol uses a shared tree?

    c.   PIM–SM

5. Which protocol will always have the smallest multicast routing table?

    c.   PIM–SM

6. Which protocol floods multicast traffic periodically?

    b.   PIM–DM

7. Which protocol interoperates with mrouted software?

    a.   DVMRP

    Mrouted is a multicast routing process used in the Mbone. It uses DVMRP.

8. An MBone tunnel requires which protocol?

    a.   DVMRP

9. Which protocol is IGMP-encapsulated?

    d.   Both a and b (PIM–SM and PIM–DMv1)

10. If you are unsure of the path a multicast packet is traversing, what command will enable you to find out?

    d.   `show ip rpf`

11. To view the known IP multicast groups, use which command?

    b.   `show ip mroute`

12. CBT is _____ _____ _____.

    d.   Core Based Tree

13. You would use which command to enable CBT:

    d.   None of the above

    Cisco doesn't implement CBT.

14. Using Cisco IOS, `ip multicast-routing` must be enabled for:

    d. All the above (DVMRP, PIM–DM, PIM–SM)

15. To prevent redundant multicast packets on the network, PIM uses the

    b. Alert Mechanism

16. When configured for PIM operation, a router will also listen for _____ packets.

    d. Both a and b (IGMP and DVMRP)

17. Multicast tree operations consists of two types:

    b. prune/graft

18. The all-DVMRP router IP multicast address is _____.

    b. `224.0.0.3`

19. PIM–SM creates a shared tree by designating a _____.

    d. RP

    An RP (Rendezvous Point) acts as the core of the shared tree.

20. MOSPF is a _____ _____ multicast routing protocol.

    a. dense mode

Access Control

The previous chapters have discussed many facets of campus area network deployment. First, we covered how to connect devices in a campus network. Next, we moved onto configuring and implementing efficient Layer 2 protocols with *Virtual Local Area Networks* (VLANs) and Spanning Tree. Lastly, we've examined how to configure and implement both unicast and multicast routing architectures.

These principles offer you the means to build a fully functional campus network and achieve the fundamental objectives outlined in Chapter 2, "Multilayer Switching Network Design Basics:"

- Fast convergence
- Deterministic paths
- Deterministic fail-over
- Scalable in size and throughput
- Centralized storage
- The 20/80 rule
- Multi-protocol support
- Multicast support

One important component is still left to be implemented that will help to maintain the quality and reliability of your campus network: *access control*. Access control is the security mechanism necessary to keep out users that could intentionally or unintentionally cause harm to the campus network. Access control also comprises the filtering mechanisms that ensure that traffic flows where it should through your network.

Objectives Covered in the Chapter

The following principles will be covered in this chapter:

- Access policies
- Managing access to network devices
- Policies at the access layer
- Policies at the distribution layer
- Policies at the core layer

A clear definition of an access policy will be given to help you define the standards by which your network operates. This includes how to control management access to network devices, how users access the network, and how traffic flows within the network.

To implement these policies, we will look at each layer of the hierarchical network model to see how each layer plays a part in the access policies. The access layer acts as a mechanism to help ensure that the users that gain access to the network are valid users. Here we will cover the features to implement access policies at this layer.

At the distribution layer, routing is the focus. Here we will cover how IP access lists can be used to implement routing policies and packet filters to control which types of packets flow in various parts of the network. Finally, core layer policies will be considered. Here we will look at the types of policies that are applicable to this layer and why. After completing this chapter, you will be well equipped to implement access control in your network and fulfill the access policies defined for your network.

Access Policies

An access policy is a corporation's documented standard of network access. An access policy can define one or more of the following items:

- Management access to network devices
- User access to the network
- User access to services on the network
- Traffic allowed into and out of the switch block
- Routes seen by the core block and the switch blocks

Management access to network devices is a fundamental and crucial step in defining a corporate access policy. Even with the most elegant and effective access policies, not defining who can access the network devices can create a situation where other policies can be changed without the proper authority. Controlling whom can access and change network device configurations is of utmost importance. Management access is defined through the use of passwords.

Access policies to define a user's access to the network can be implemented with port security and VLAN management. This is of crucial importance and will be covered in more detail later in the chapter.

Access control by a user of network services can be implemented with a combination of access policy mechanisms that will be covered in this chapter. This is a fundamental component of devising a thorough access policy. One method of defining which users have access to which services is through traffic control. This is accomplished by controlling the traffic that is allowed in and out of the switch block. This can be implemented by determining which IP routes that each switch block sees.

Sometimes an access policy defines whether or not a particular service will work. Services are at times limited by the number of hosts they can support. A service that provides for an entire campus network may crash under the traffic load generated from the campus. Filtering this load by setting access policies can alleviate this problem.

Security within the network is another important result of a good access policy. Certain payroll and human resource information is sensitive and only for access by certain individuals. This goes beyond the bounds of network performance and into the realm of privacy. These issues must be protected by your access policy to continue the success of your company or organization.

Recall from earlier chapters the topological layer concept of campus network design. A good access policy considers the policy implementation at the access layer, the distribution layer, and the core layer.

The access layer is the point where all hosts connect to the network. This is the user concentration point of the network. Access policies should be implemented with the use of port security and passwords restricting access to the management interface of the network device.

The distribution layer is where the routing decisions are made within the campus network. This is where the routing policies of the campus network should be implemented. Routing policies can define which subnets are allowed to intercommunicate as well as which paths packets use between networks. One key objective of the distribution layer is to minimize the amount of traffic that traverses the core layer. This is an excellent place to implement access lists.

The core layer should have a fundamental policy to implement as few access lists as possible. This is a consequence of the fact that performance at this layer is of utmost importance. Each policy-routing feature or filtering mechanism used in a switch causes it to slow down from its optimal performance. Therefore, route policies and filters should be avoided at this layer. The core layer depends on the distribution layer to properly implement the route policies and any filtering.

Managing Network Devices

Managing access to network devices is the first step in defining a campus network access policy. We will cover the following topics in this section:

■ Physical security

■ Access passwords

■ Access privilege levels

■ Limiting Telnet access to the network device

■ Limiting *Hypertext Transfer Protocol* (HTTP) access to the network device

The methods for limiting access to the management interfaces of a network device should be implemented at all layers in the campus network including the access layer, the distribution layer, and the core layer.

Physical Security

Almost all network devices have some mechanism to bypass the access password of the switch. If someone knowledgeable in bypassing the access password gains physical access to the network device, they may be able to reconfigure the device. Therefore, physical security is the first and primary step in securing the campus network.

To physically secure the campus network, the following tasks must be accomplished:

■ Devise a configuration and control policy

■ Provide the proper physical environment

- Control direct access to the device
- Secure access to the network links

A configuration control policy should be defined for each device at all hierarchical layers. A security plan details how the network device and its links are to be secured. The proper physical environment includes adequate power, ventilation, and temperature and humidity controls. Also plan for adequate physical security, which can consist of door locks, combinations, and alarms. If possible, lock the racks in which the network device is housed. Set up access passwords for the device and disable any ports, such as the auxiliary port, if they are not used.

Do not overlook the physical security of the wiring closet. A lot of damage can be done in a short amount of time by unauthorized access to a wiring closet. Make sure you define a policy for providing adequate physical security and the necessary physical environment for all wiring closets.

Passwords

We covered setting passwords earlier in Chapter 4, "Connecting the Campus Network." This section provides more details on setting access passwords.

Passwords should be assigned to every management interface access point. These access points can be in-band (through a network port) or out-of-band (through the console or auxiliary ports). The in-band ports are typically used by *Trivial File Transfer Protocol* (TFTP) servers, network management software such as Cisco Works, and virtual terminal ports. The virtual terminal ports are logical ports that emulate terminal access through the console port. These ports are typically accessed via a Telnet session. Five virtual terminal ports are defined by default. These ports are commonly called *vty ports*. More than five vty ports can be created if necessary. Usernames and associated passwords can also be stored locally in the device or in a central authentication server.

The maximum idle time for a session can be specified. This protects the network device if a user logs in and forgets to log out after finishing a session. If there is no timeout in a session, that switch is susceptible to changes in configuration by anyone walking up to a device after a user has logged in to a device and forgotten to log out when finished.

Password Configuration

To set the access password, you would use the following command for a set command-based Cisco device:

```
Switch(enable) set password
```

Setting the administrator password or enable password is as follows:

```
Switch(enable) set enablepass
```

Both commands will follow with prompts to create the password change:

```
Enter old password: oldPassword
Enter new password: newPassword
Retype new password: newPassword
Password changed.
```

For a Cisco IOS-based device, you can use the following command to set the administrator password:

```
Switch(config)# enable password newPassword
```

On Cisco IOS-based devices, the console port has a special name, *line con 0*. To set an access password on the console, you would enter the following:

```
Switch(config)# line con 0
Switch(config-line)# password password
Switch(config-line)# login
```

By default, when a password is set, the password prompt will be displayed upon connection. However, if no password is set, the user will be connected at the default privilege level of 1 and presented with a system prompt. The `login` command will prevent users from connecting if a password is not set. The `login` command should always be included on console and virtual terminal devices to ensure security.

If you have deployed centralized authentication and authorization services such as TACACS, you can specify a line to use that service. Note that full TACACS configuration is beyond the scope of this book, but a complete overview of *Authentication, Authorization, and Accounting* (AAA) services is available on Cisco's Web site.

```
Switch(config)# line con 0
Switch(config-line)# login authentication tacacs+
```

On set command-based devices, TACACS would be enabled for login authentication as follows:

```
Switch(enable) set authentication login tacacs
```

Once you have your authentication mechanism in place, you should further secure the device by adding a timeout that will automatically disconnect the user if left idle for a period of time. For set command-based devices, you may use the following:

```
Switch(enable) set logout minutes
```

For a Cisco IOS-based device, you would use the following commands:

```
Switch(config)# line con 0
Switch(config-line)# exec-timeout minutes [seconds]
```

Using the automatic logout mechanisms helps ensure that if a terminal is left connected after a user is finished, someone else will not be able to abuse it.

Privilege Levels

Cisco enables different levels of user access to the management interface of a device. By default, two levels of access exist: level 1 and level 15. Level 1 access enables the default user EXEC privilege. This lets the user monitor the device but not configure it. Level 15 is the enable mode and gives the user full rights to the device. Enable mode is designated by the # prompt.

Sixteen levels of privilege exist. Level 0 can be used to define a subset of the EXEC level privilege. At other levels of privilege, the commands that can be used must be specified.

Privilege Level Configuration

You can assign passwords for a specified user level when used in conjunction with the *privilege* command and can provide very fine grain access con-

Table 9-1

Privilege command
modes

Mode	Description
configuration	Global configuration
controller	Controller configuration
exec	EXEC
hub	Hub configuration
interface	Interface configuration
ipx-router	IPX router configuration
line	Line configuration
map-class	Map class configuration
map-list	Map list configuration
route-map	Route map configuration
router	Router configuration

trol. For Cisco IOS-based devices, you can use the following command to set the level passwords:

```
Switch(config)# enable password level level newPassword
```

Use the Cisco IOS *privilege* command as follows:

```
Switch(config)# privilege mode level level command
```

Table 9-1 lists the valid modes for the privilege command.

For example, to set a password for a level 3 user, and then enable that user to execute the ping command (which is normally only available to level 15 administrative users), do the following:

```
Switch> enable
Switch# configure terminal
Switch(config)# enable password level 3 marshmello
Switch(config)# privilege exec level 3 ping
Switch(config)# end
```

The resulting configuration file would be as follows:

```
. . .
enable password level 3 marshmello
privilege exec level 3 ping
. . .
```

Banner Messages

A message of the day banner can be set to greet a user. Be careful of the message you use in a device. Do not welcome the user in any way. Hackers have been acquitted in court due to a network administrator "welcoming" them into a system with a message of the day banner.

Banner Message Configuration   Using the set commands, you can set a login banner with the following:

```
Switch(enable) set banner motd delimiter message-text delimiter
```

For the IOS command-based devices, use the following command:

```
Switch(config)# banner motd delimiter message-text delimiter
```

Using *no* before each command will clear the banner message. The delimiter can be nearly any character. The banner message is defined as the text between two delimiter characters. The delimiter cannot be used within the message text. The message itself can be a free-form text message, although including special characters takes some additional keystrokes. An example would be as follows:

```
Switch# show configuration
. . .
banner motd ^C
^M
    Call the helpdesk at 555-3035 if you experience problems.
^M
    Only users with valid accounts may access this device.
^M
^C
. . .
```

The delimiter in the example is ^C, which is the representative of the Control-C key sequence. Furthermore, formatting has been added with the Control-M's. Each of these key sequences cannot be directly entered. Each control key sequence must be prefixed by Control-V as it is entered. The previous banner message is configured by using the following Cisco IOS command:

```
Switch# configure terminal
Switch(config)# banner motd ^V^C^V^M    Call the helpdesk at 555-
3035 if you experience problems.^V^M    Only users with valid
accounts may access this device.^V^M^V^C
```

For users that have access to the console, a banner message is not important. To disable the banner message on a particular line, do the following:

```
Switch(config)# line con 0
Switch(config-line)# no exec-banner
```

Banner messages, if used, should be carefully worded. Ideally, they should neither invite hackers ("Welcome Ya'll!") nor taunt them ("Keep Out! Top Secret!").

Virtual Terminal Access

By default, five virtual terminal lines exist on every Cisco device. More lines can be created if they are needed. If five virtual terminal lines are configured on a Cisco device, five users can access the device simultaneously.

It is good practice to give each of the lines identical access restrictions, because there is no way to determine which line you will use when accessing the device. A list of possible device addresses that can access the network device can be defined.

Configuring virtual terminals is identical to other line-type interfaces. To configure the virtual terminals with a password of "crazytaz" and a time-out of five minutes, enter the following on a Cisco IOS-based device:

```
Switch> enable
Switch# configure terminal
Switch(config)# line vty 0 4
Switch(config-line)# password crazytaz
Switch(config-line)# login
Switch(config-line)# exec-timeout 5 0
Switch(config-line)# end
```

Furthermore, since the virtual terminals are available via Telnet from the network, they should be further secured by using an access list that only permits connections from the local network. Continuing the previous example, we'll add an access list to permit only connections from the 100.1.1.0/24 subnet:

```
Switch(config)# access-list 50 permit 100.1.1.0 0.0.0.255
Switch(config)# line vty 0 4
Switch(config-line)# access-class 50 in
```

The previous configuration would look as follows:

```
Switch# show running-configuration
. . .
access-list 50 permit 100.1.1.0 0.0.0.255
. . .
line vty 0 4
   access-class 50 in
   exec-timeout 5 0
   password crazytaz
   login
. . .
```

More information on the access-list command can be found later in this chapter.

Controlling HTTP Access

Cisco IOS software release 11.0(6) and greater has Web server capabilities for configuring the network device. This makes configuration easier because it can be done graphically and no special client software is needed other than an up-to-date Web browser.

Care must be used when enabling the Web server. It has great advantages, such as the easy-to-use management interface, but you will find security holes in this feature. Access to the Web interface can be restricted similarly to virtual terminal lines.

HTTP Access Configuration

HTTP access, once enabled, should also be secured. To enable the HTTP server for remote configuration and monitoring, the following Cisco IOS command can be used:

```
Switch(config)# ip http server
```

By default, the authentication mechanism used is the administrative or enable password. This is the equivalent of the following Cisco IOS command:

```
Switch(config)# ip http authentication enable
```

As with the virtual terminal lines, remote connections can be limited by specifying an access class that references a network-standard IP access list:

```
Switch(config)# ip http access-class access-list
```

The following will enable the HTTP server, only enable connections from the 100.2.1.1/24 subnet, and use TACACS for authentication:

```
Switch> enable
Switch# configure terminal
Switch(config)# ip http server
Switch(config)# access-list 50 permit 100.2.1.1 0.0.0.255
Switch(config)# ip http access-class 50
Switch(config)# ip http authentication tacacs
Switch(config)# end
```

Access Layer Policy

The access layer is the hierarchical layer of the campus network where any user can connect. Therefore, security is critical since any user can connect from any computer with an Ethernet cable that runs to an access switch. The following precautions should be considered when configuring the access layer:

- VLAN management
- Port security

Port security can be used to limit the *media access control* (MAC) addresses enabled at a particular port on an access switch. This helps prevent unauthorized users from gaining access to the campus network.

The default VLAN of all ports is VLAN1, which is conventionally the management VLAN. Cisco recommends moving the management VLAN to any other VLAN except VLAN1 so that a user is connected to the management VLAN by default if he is connected to an unconfigured port. See the section on VLAN configuration for details on how this is done.

Port Security

Port security is a feature of the Cisco Catalyst switches that enable the switch to block packets that enter a port if the source MAC address does not match the allowed MAC address configured on the port.

Two methods exist for configuring port security on a switch. The allowed MAC address can be configured statically or dynamically. If the MAC address is configured statically, the network administrator enters the MAC address that the port will enable. This is the most deterministic way to configure port security, but it is difficult to manage. Dynamically configured port security learns the first source MAC address that enters the port. This becomes the allowed MAC address for the port. All other source MAC addresses are restricted.

Configuring Port Security

Configuring port security on set command-based devices is straightforward:

```
Switch(enable) set port security mod/ports {enable | disable}
[mac-addr]
```

Supplying the optional MAC address signifies static security configuration; without the MAC address, it signifies a dynamic one. Once configured, you can view the security settings using the following command:

```
Switch(enable) show port security mod/ports [statistics]
```

On Cisco IOS-based devices, port security is available via the following command:

```
Switch(config-int)# port secure [max-mac-count count]
```

Note that static is not an option with Cisco IOS-based devices; only dynamic port security is available. To examine the dynamic port security table, use the following command:

```
Switch# show mac-address-table security [type module/port]
```

Without specifying an interface, all ports are displayed. Specifying an interface will limit data to only that interface.

Distribution Layer Policy

The distribution layer is where the majority of access policies is implemented. It is assumed that the hosts accessing the network are authorized because they can access the network through the access layer with port security enabled and the VLANs properly configured.

The distribution layer helps optimize the traffic flow by ensuring that data entering the core switch block should not stay within it. A good access policy at the distribution layer ensures that the core block is not burdened with unnecessary traffic.

Access policies at the distribution layer can be categorized into the following groups:

- *Access lists*, which define the traffic that is to be passed between VLANs and from the switch block to the core. Access lists are applied to interfaces to filter traffic.

- *Distribution lists*, which define which routes the core block and the switch blocks can see. Distribution lists are applied to prevent certain routes to be advertised to the core block.

- *Service control*, which determines which services are to be advertised to the whole network.

IP Access Lists

IP access lists are defined to restrict traffic from entering or leaving an interface. Two types of IP access lists exist:

- Standard
- Extended

Both of these types of access lists define a filter that permits or denies packets based on a set of criteria. Standard IP access lists filter packets by only looking at the source IP address. This type of access list uses the least amount of system resources on the router.

Extended IP access lists enable more complex packet filtering criteria to be defined. With extended access lists, the source and destination IP addresses can be used in the filter criteria along with the protocol type and port number. Extended access lists offer the most flexibility of the two access list types, but this can be a burden on the router.

Access lists can be used for a number of applications. The following list describes some of these applications:

■ The access list can be applied to a particular layer-3 protocol to manage traffic by filtering on the layer-3 address. This usage of an access list is implemented through the *protocol access-group* command.

■ Access lists can be used for restricting access to a *vty* line. As shown earlier, this can be implemented using the *access-class* command.

■ Routing update information can be managed by a distribution list that defines which routes can be learned by the router and which routes the router can advertise. Distribution lists are implemented by the *distribution-list* command.

■ Service advertisements can be controlled with access lists. An example of this usage is the *ipx output-sap-filter* command to filter IPX *Service Advertisement Protocol* (SAP) messages.

Standard IP Access Lists

The following list defines the rules of usage for standard IP access lists:

■ The match criteria are based on the source IP address only.

■ Standard IP access lists must be assigned a number from 1 to 99.

■ Access lists are processed from the top down until a match is found. When a match is found, the processing of the access list stops.

■ An implicit deny can be found at the end of an access list. If no match is found there, the packet is implicitly denied.

■ Access lists must be applied before they take effect.

■ Access lists can be applied inbound or outbound. Inbound access lists apply to packets entering a port from the wire and outbound access lists apply to packets leaving a port after being routed.

Configuring Standard IP Access Lists

As referenced in earlier examples, standard IP access lists take the following form:

```
Switch(config)# access-list {1-99} {permit | deny} src-network
match-mask
```

As noted previously, the standard IP access list is applied on source addresses only. The best way to understand the arguments for the access list is to remember that you are specifying a fixed address and then specifying wildcard bits. The fixed address is the portion of the source address that *must* match, and the match-mask is the portion that *may* match. Thus, the match-mask is not a subnet mask, but you can use the subnet mask to quickly determine the match-mask.

To create an access list that would enable the Class C subnet address 100.1.2.0/24, you would use the following access list:

```
Switch(config)# access-list 10 permit 100.1.2.0 0.0.0.255
```

The first argument, *10*, is an arbitrary list number that identifies the standard IP access list we are manipulating. The next argument, *permit*, says to allow the address. The source network is *100.1.2.0*. Because we want all the hosts in the subnet to be included, we specify a match-mask of *0.0.0.255*. For the packet to be permitted, it must match *all* the bits in the source network and must match *one* bit in the match-mask.

Because you know the subnet mask of the subnet you want to permit or deny, the match-mask can be quickly calculated as follows:

```
All 1's Mask - Subnet Mask = Match Mask
```

For a Class C subnet, it is as follows:

```
255.255.255.255 - 255.255.255.0 = 0.0.0.255
```

The other common need that comes up is a single host. The match-mask would be *0.0.0.0*.

To apply an access list to an interface to put the list in use, you must use the *ip access-group* command:

```
Switch(config-int)# ip access-group list-number {in | out}
```

To apply the previous access list on the Ethernet 0 interface and filter inbound packets, enter the following:

```
Switch(config)# interface Ethernet 0
Switch(config-int)# ip access-group 10 in
```

Often a standard IP access list does not provide enough flexibility for some complex filtering needs. Extended IP access lists assist with these types of problems.

Extended IP Access Lists

Extended IP access lists are similar to standard IP access lists and must adhere to the following rules:

- The extended access lists are processed from the top down. When a match is made, the processing of the access list stops.
- Extended IP access lists must be numbered from 100 to 199.
- The filtering criteria include the protocol type, source address, destination address, application port, and session layer information.
- If none of the criteria is matched, the packet is implicitly denied.
- The access list must be applied before it takes effect.

Configuring Extended IP Access Lists

Extended IP access lists can become complex, and the following is the general syntax of the command:

```
Switch(config)# access-list list-number {deny | permit} {protocol |
protocol-keyword} {source source-wildcard | any} {destination
destination-wildcard | any} [precedence precedence] [tos tos] [log]
```

In addition to specifying the protocol as a decimal value from 1 to 255, it can also be specified using a protocol keyword. These protocol keywords include the following:

- ip
- tcp
- udp
- icmp
- igmp
- gre

- igrp
- eigrp
- ipinip
- ospf
- nos

Using the protocol keyword *ip*, any IP will be matched. It is important to note that specifying the tcp, udp, igmp, or icmp protocol keyword changes the syntax of the command to accommodate special parameters for those protocols.

Although the extended IP access list enables one to filter by precedence and by the *type of service* (TOS), these parameters are rarely used. The optional *log* keyword enables the logging of packets that match the access list. Logging should only be used temporarily for debugging or if you need to log matches for security purposes. Unnecessary logging uses precious processing power of the network device.

A common need is to filter a TCP or UDP stream based on a source or destination address. An example would be filtering unwanted FTP traffic that originates outside of your network. An FTP stream begins with a source host attempting a TCP connection on port 21 to the destination host. First, it would be helpful to see the full syntax when using the tcp protocol keyword:

```
Switch(config)# access-list {100-199} {deny | permit} tcp {source
source-wildcard | any} [source port] {destination destination-
wildcard | any} [destination port] [precedence precedence] [tos
tos] [log] [established]
```

Therefore, an access list to deny the FTP stream would be created as follows:

```
Switch(config)# access-list 101 deny tcp any any eq 21
Switch(config)# access-list 101 permit tcp any any
```

The command syntax eq 21 specifies TCP port numbers equal to 21. To make the access list complete, we add a permit line so only that stream would be denied.

To apply an access list to an interface to put the list in use, you must use the *ip access-group* command:

```
Switch(config-int)# ip access-group list-number {in | out}
```

To apply the previous access list on the Ethernet 0 interface and filter inbound packets, enter the following:

```
Switch(config)# interface Ethernet 0
Switch(config-int)# ip access-group 101 in
```

Access lists can be difficult, so always be careful when adding or changing an access list.

Controlling Routing Update Traffic

Controlling the routing update traffic in the campus network can accomplish the following tasks:

- Reduce the size of the routing tables in the core block
- Prevent users from accessing networks without a default route
- Prevent incorrect routes from traversing the network

Routing update traffic can be controlled by the following means:

- *Route summarization*, which is implemented through the configuration of certain routing protocols. Route summarization is beyond the scope of this book.
- *Distribution lists*, which implement routing update filters to restrict the routes that are seen by the core block. This can reduce the size of the routing table in the core block, which in turn reduces the amount of processing in the routers within the core block. Remember maximum throughput with minimum latency and redundancy is the goal of the core block.

Configuring Route Filtering

A route filter can be implemented by defining an access list. The steps to define a route filter are as follows:

1. Identify the network addresses you want to filter and define a standard IP access list.

2. Determine whether the routing protocol should be filtered entering the interface or leaving the interface.

3. Assign the access filter to the routing updates.

In combination with the access list, you would use the following Cisco IOS commands to implement route filtering. The first is the command to filter incoming routes:

```
Switch(config-router)# distribute-list {list-number | name} in
[interface-name]
```

The specified access list, by name or number, is applied to the routes being received. In addition, an optional interface can be supplied to limit the filtering operation to the specified interface. As an example, if we want to disregard the routes for subnet 100.10.1.0/24, assuming the router is running the *Interior Gateway Routing Protocol* (IGRP) as its routing protocol, one would use the following series of commands:

```
Switch> enable
Switch# configure terminal
Switch(config)# access-list 11 deny 100.10.1.0 0.0.0.255
Switch(config)# access-list 11 permit 0.0.0.0 255.255.255.255
Switch(config)# router igrp 81
Switch(config-router)# distribute-list 11 in
```

Outgoing route filtering works the same way, only you have a couple of different options for how the filter is applied. The syntax for the Cisco IOS command is as follows:

```
Switch(config-router)# distribute-list {list-number | name} out
[interface-name | routing-process | autonomous-system-number]
```

If we want to prevent IGRP routing process number 81 from distributing a route to 100.1.50.0/24 for any other devices, we could use the following:

```
Switch> enable
Switch# configure terminal
Switch(config)# access-list 12 deny 100.1.50.0 0.0.0.255
Switch(config)# access-list 12 permit 0.0.0.0 255.255.255.255
Switch(config)# router igrp
Switch(config-router)# distribute-list 12 out 81
```

In both of the earlier examples, a permit entry was added following the deny entry in the access list. Without the permit entry, all routes would have been denied. The default access list action is to deny all.

Core Layer Policy

The core layer is designed to run with maximum throughput and minimum latency. Enabling access policies at this layer is not recommended. The only instance when filtering is advisable at the core layer is when policies are set to define behavior during congestion. This behavior defines a concept known as *quality of service* (QoS). QoS can define which packets are discarded during congestion or which packets should be discarded to avoid congestion. QoS can be implemented in many ways and is beyond the scope of this book.

Chapter Summary

This chapter has covered the following topics:

- Access policies
- Managing network devices
- Physical security
- Passwords
- Privilege levels
- Banner messages
- Virtual terminal access
- Controlling HTTP access
- Access layer policy
- Port security
- Distribution layer policy
- IP access lists
- Standard IP access lists
- Extended IP access list

- Controlling routing update traffic
- Core layer policy

Access policies are your campus network's rules of engagement. It defines who can access your network and which services they can access. The key to defining an access policy is ensuring the security of the network. Each device should have a password. Along with the access and enable passwords are user accounts, privilege levels, and access control features to improve the security and manageability of your devices. Don't forget the importance of defining physical security so that physical access can be limited to network administrators. This physical security should be applied both to the wiring closet and the equipment closet if they are separate.

Each hierarchical layer should have a policy defined. The access layer should restrict network access to known users. The distribution layer has the capability to define which traffic is allowed to get to the core layer and other switch blocks. Access lists provide the needed mechanisms to implement access policies at the distribution layer. The core layer should have minimal access policies to maximize the performance of the core layer devices.

This chapter has laid the foundation of knowledge for you to build a secure and well-managed campus network.

Frequently Asked Questions (FAQ)

Question: Why is physical security so important?

Answer: In addition to keeping equipment from growing legs and walking away, it is also important for network device security. Anyone with physical access to a network device has the ability to bypass all security. Once security is breached, an intruder can disrupt network services (in addition to ripping out cables) or monitor network traffic. The latter could include stealing passwords and gaining access to sensitive data.

Case Study

From the last chapter, we built the *Cubby Products International* (CPI) campus network to support multicasts in special areas of the network. With a fully complete network, the only task left at hand is to enhance site security.

Objective

In an earlier chapter, we assigned passwords to all the devices. Your goal is to further enhance security by restricting access to the virtual terminals on the routers. The following tables provide information on the VLANs and switches you'll use.

VLAN	VLAN ID	IP Subnet
Management	0	100.1.1.0
R&D	1	100.1.2.0
Mfg	2	100.1.3.0
SR	3	100.1.4.0
Admin	4	100.1.5.0
IT	5	100.1.6.0

Switch Name	IP Address
IT-1-dist-5505	100.1.1.11
RD-1-dist-5505	100.1.1.16
Mfg-1-dist-5505	100.1.1.21
SR-1-dist-5505	100.1.1.26
Admin-1-dist-5505	100.1.1.31

Approach

In order to reach the objective, we need to examine three steps. First, we must identify who should be restricted. Second, we must determine the proper filter to apply to achieve the objective. Last, we must verify proper access list operation.

Determine Access Policy

In order to determine who should have access to a device, it is best to refer to documented security policies. Security policies are beyond the scope of this book, but for our case study, it is safe to assume that only specified *information technologies* (IT) personnel have passwords to network devices. Furthermore, because only IT staff have device passwords, it follows that only machines used by IT staff should be allowed to Telnet to the distribution-layer devices.

Applying Security Measures

From the information supplied, we know all IT staff reside on the 100.1.6.0 subnet. With this information, we can construct an access list and then apply it to the appropriate virtual terminal lines.

We want to only allow subnet 100.1.6.0 and deny all other IP addresses. The subnet has a 24-bit netmask (255.255.255.0). Using this we can quickly construct the access list. The most difficult part is determining the match-mask.

```
255.255.255.255 - 255.255.255.0 = 0.0.0.255
```

So, our match-mask is 0.0.0.255. Let's create the list:

```
IT-1-dist-5505> enable
IT-1-dist-5505# configure terminal
IT-1-dist-5505(config)# access-list 99 permit 100.1.6.0 0.0.0.255
```

Once constructed, we can apply it to the virtual terminal lines:

```
IT-1-dist-5505(config)# line vty 0 4
IT-1-dist-5505(config-line)# access-class 99 in
```

```
IT-1-dist-5505(config-line)# exec-timeout 10 0
IT-1-dist-5505(config-line)# end
```

The access list number can be any number that has not already been used on the device. We recommend choosing access list numbers carefully in order to keep consistency throughout the network. Here we will always know that access list 99 determines management access to the device. Since there is an implicit deny at the end of all access lists, adding the statement is not necessary. In addition, an exec-timeout is added. This prevents staff from staying needlessly logged in to a device. Recall that only five users (vty 0 through 4) can connect at a time by default.

Confirm the configuration and it should look similar to the following:

```
IT-1-dist-5505# show running-configuration
. . .
access-list 99 permit 100.1.6.0 0.0.0.255
. . .
line vty 0 4
   access-class 99 in
   exec-timeout 10 0
   password password
   login
end
```

Testing One, Two, Three . . . Er, 100.1.X.0

It is imperative that you test the access list once it has been applied. If you have made the configuration modification over a Telnet session, you must be particularly careful. Once completed, you should verify that the filter is working properly by attempting to Telnet to the device from an IT-based machine and without disconnecting yourself. If you disconnect yourself from the Telnet session and try to reconnect, you could be in for a surprise and an unwelcome trip to the device console to fix your mistake.

Once you have verified that IT hosts can connect, try it from a non-IT host to confirm that access will be denied. After confirming all works as expected, implement the same configuration on all other Cisco 5500s.

Case Study Summary

Beyond passwords, access lists provide another barrier to hinder perspective intruders. To implement the access lists, we proceeded through three steps:

1. Identify who should be restricted (access policy).

2. Determine the proper filter to apply.

3. Verify proper access list operation.

The last step is important. Verification is critical to implementing security policy, which should drive implementation. The SANS organization has a lot of information available online to help organizations with their security policies.

Once a security policy is in place, your network is fully functional and now you have the opportunity to monitor the network while it is in production. Network monitoring helps you fully understand what is happening and will be invaluable as you plan to upgrade your network infrastructure.

This concludes the case study that began in Chapter 2. The last two chapters of this book delve deeper into IP routing, which we skimmed over in Chapter 6, "Unicast Layer 3 Configuration." The case study in Chapter 6 implemented IGRP as a routing protocol. Chapter 10, "Classful Interior Routing Protocols," and Chapter 11, "Classless Interior Routing Protocols," will look closer at routing protocols, including IGRP, and the case studies will help you make wise decisions regarding the routing protocol you choose to deploy. The information covered in Chapter 10 and Chapter 11 is not part of the BCMSN curriculum.

Questions

1. The most important access policy to implement is
   - **a.** management access to network devices
   - **b.** user access to the network
   - **c.** advertised routes
   - **d.** user access to services on the network

2. User access to network services refers to
   - **a.** connecting hosts to network devices
   - **b.** connecting hosts to wall jacks
   - **c.** accessing file or print services
   - **d.** using a Web browser

3. Management access to network devices refers to
   - **a.** passwords for network devices
   - **b.** restricting access to virtual terminals
   - **c.** restricting access to the device's Web server
   - **d.** all of the above

4. The administrative password is the _____ password.
   - **a.** login
   - **b.** enable
   - **c.** line
   - **d.** console

5. The default access level upon login to a Cisco device is ____.
   - **a.** 0
   - **b.** 1
   - **c.** 5
   - **d.** 15

6. Using the enable command changes which access level by default?
   - **a.** 5
   - **b.** 10
   - **c.** 15
   - **d.** 16

7. A banner message should be used to

    a. welcome users to the system
    b. tell users who to contact in case of problems
    c. warn about unauthorized access
    d. both b and c

8. An exec-timeout should be used to

    a. automatically log out inactive users
    b. limit how long users can use the system
    c. limit how many commands can be entered
    d. all the above

9. TACACS is

    a. an authentication service
    b. an authorization service
    c. an accounting service
    d. all the above

10. The privilege command is used to

    a. change privilege levels for users
    a. change privilege levels for commands
    a. restrict login access to a device
    a. allow users access to the network

11. The two types of IP access lists are _____ and
    _____.

    a. local, remote
    b. standard, extended
    c. standard, long
    d. Telnet, Web

12. Port security provides

    a. Web security
    b. login control
    c. host-based access control
    d. ship docking control

13. Standard IP access lists are numbered from ___ to ___.

    a. 1, 10
    b. 0, 10
    c. 1, 99
    d. 1, 100

14. Extended IP access lists are numbered from ___ to ___.

    a. 1, 200

    b. 100, 200

    c. 101, 200

    d. 100, 199

15. The commands access-class and distribute-list require a(n) _____ to be defined.

    a. user

    b. interface

    c. access list

    d. login

16. Which access list will permit only a single host (a.b.c.d) access?

    a. access-list 1 permit a.b.c.d 0.0.0.0

    b. access-list 2 permit a.b.c.d 255.255.255.255

    c. access-list 3 permit host a.b.c.d

    d. access-list 4 deny any except a.b.c.d

17. Which access list will deny only a single host (a.b.c.d) access?

    a. access-list 1 deny a.b.c.d 0.0.0.0

    b. access-list 2 permit 0.0.0.0 255.255.255.255/access-list 2 deny a.b.c.d 0.0.0.0

    c. access-list 3 deny a.b.c.d 0.0.0.0/access-list 3 permit 0.0.0.0 255.255.255.255

    d. access-list 4 deny all except host a.b.c.d

18. Which match-mask will match an entire Class B subnet?

    a. 0.0.0.255

    b. 0.0.255.0

    c. 255.255.0.0

    d. 0.0.255.255

19. Which match-mask will match an entire Class C subnet?

    a. 0.0.0.255

    b. 255.0.0.0

    c. 0.0.255.0

    d. 192.255.255.255

20. Which match-mask will match only the first six hosts of a subnet?

    a. 0.0.0.255

    b. 0.0.0.192

    c. 0.0.0.7

    d. 255.255.255.254

Answers

1. The most important access policy to implement is

   a. Management access to network devices

   Since device configuration implements a policy, it is critical that management access be implemented first.

2. User access to network services refers to

   c. Accessing file or print services

   File and print services are the most common. Other services may include mail, application servers, or Web services.

3. Management access to network devices refers to

   d. all of the above

   Any type of access control to the devices.

4. The administrative password is the _____ password.

   b. enable

   Entering the enable password changes from the default privilege level of 1 to 15.

5. The default access level upon login to a Cisco device is ____.

   b. 1

6. Using the enable command changes which access level by default?

   c. 15

7. A banner message should be used to

   d. both b and c

   Remember, never welcome a user to a system.

8. An exec-timeout should be used to

   a. automatically log out inactive users

9. TACACS is

   d. all the above

   AAA refers to authentication, authorization, and accounting.

10. The privilege command is used to

    b. change privilege levels for commands

11. The two types of IP access lists are _____ and _____.

b. standard, extended

12. Port security provides

c. host-based access control

Port security is based on Ethernet hardware addresses.

13. Standard IP access lists are numbered from ___ to ___.

c. 1, 99

14. Extended IP access lists are numbered from ___ to ___.

d. 100, 199

15. The commands access-class and distribute-list require a(n) _____ be defined.

c. access-list

Both commands take an access list number as an argument.

16. Which access list will permit only a single host (a.b.c.d) access?

a. access-list 1 permit a.b.c.d 0.0.0.0

The 0.0.0.0 specifies no wildcard bits, so the address must match exactly.

17. Which access list will deny only a single host (a.b.c.d) access?

c. access-list 3 deny a.b.c.d 0.0.0.0/access-list 3 permit 0.0.0.0 255.255.255.255

The 0.0.0.0 specifies no wildcard bits, so the address must match exactly. In addition, 255.255.255.255 says all bits are wildcards and will match any address. The permit line is needed since everything is denied by default.

18. Which match-mask will match an entire Class B subnet?

d. 0.0.255.255

A Class B subnet has 16 bits for the host portion of the IP address.

19. Which match-mask will match an entire Class C subnet?

    a.   0.0.0.255

A Class C subnet has eight bits for the host portion of the IP address.

20. Which match-mask will match only the first six hosts of a subnet?

    c.   0.0.0.7

Recall that a host cannot have a 0 as the last byte of the IP address.

Classful Interior Routing Protocols

The previous chapters in this book cover the material in the Building Cisco MultiLayer Switched Networks course to prepare you for the certification exam. To give you a more thorough understanding of the material, we have included this chapter to provide an overview of unicast routing protocols. This chapter is outside the scope of the course, but the information is necessary for you to successfully build a routed IP campus network.

Recall the notion of communicating routes between routers from Chapter 6. The network must propagate the location of all subnets within the network so routers will know how to forward packets to their destination. One way of propagating routes through the network is by manually configuring static routes on every router throughout the network as shown in Figure 10-1.

Figure 10-1
Static routes in a
campus network

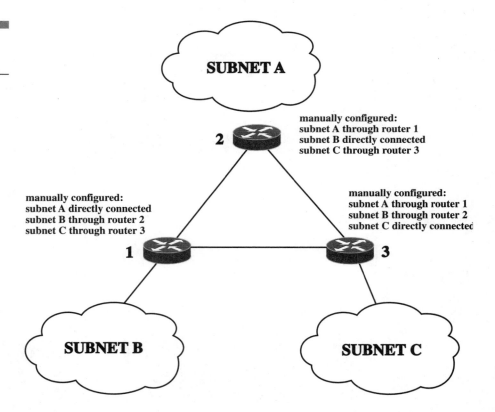

If you only have a couple of routers with a very few interfaces each in your campus network, it is not too much work to enter each static route into every router assuming the routes would not change. However, your network is likely to change over time when subnets are moved or added, or more routers deployed. After more than a couple of routers exist in the network, manually configuring static routes can become more than a full-time job.

The solution is to implement dynamic route propagation throughout your campus network as shown in Figure 10-2. This is where routing protocols come into play. Routing protocols allow routers to pass known subnets and their location to each router in the network.

This chapter covers one category of unicast routing protocols known as classful routing protocols. Both classful and classless routing protocols are covered early in the chapter.

Figure 10-2
Dynamic routing
protocols

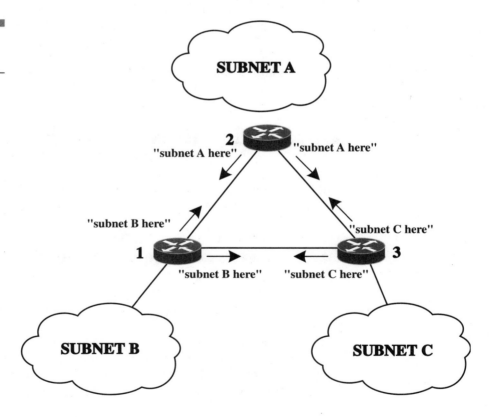

Objectives Covered in the Chapter

The following topics are covered in this chapter:

- Routing Protocol Categories
- *Routing Information Protocol* (RIP)
- *Interior Gateway Routing Protocol* (IGRP)

In this chapter, we explore the different types of routing protocols. Interior, exterior, classful, and classless routing protocol categories are discussed.

The *Routing Information Protocol* (RIP) is covered in detail. Information about its historical value, operation, simplicity, and limitations is discussed.

Next, Cisco's IGRP is covered. The IGRP is Cisco's answer to RIP's limitations. The details of the operation and configuration of this protocol are covered.

The chapter also includes a case study that shows a practical example of implementing RIP and IGRP in your campus network.

This information gives you a framework from which to increase your knowledge of unicast routing protocols. The next chapter covers classless routing protocols and their configuration in a campus network.

Categories of Routing Protocols

Several categories of routing protocols exist. Knowledge of these categories will help you grasp the material in this chapter which covers classful interior routing protocols.

Interior versus Exterior Routing Protocols

The two main categories of routing protocols are interior and exterior routing. These categories are derived from the span of control of administration for the network.

Interior routing protocols, as illustrated in Figure 10-3, are designed for routing within a campus network where one group controls the policies and administration. The policies throughout this type of network are consistent and provide for communication within the network. These campus net-

Figure 10-3
Interior routing
protocol

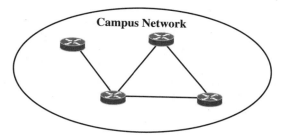

Figure 10-4
Exterior routing
protocol

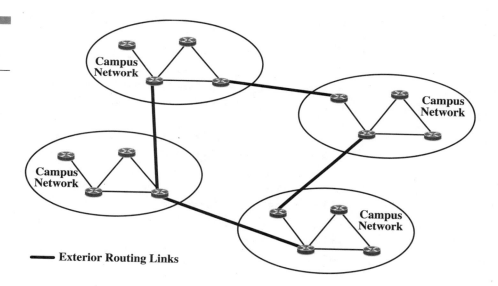

works where one group controls the internal policies of the networks are called autonomous systems.

Exterior routing protocols, as illustrated in Figure 10-4, are designed to handle routing between large networks that are controlled by different groups which tend to have individual and sometimes conflicting networking policies. The group responsible for routing between the large campus networks doesn't want to concern itself with the individual routing policies and configurations of these autonomous networks. Therefore, the routing protocols used to connect autonomous campus networks are designed to achieve routing between the networks without having to monitor the internal structures of the networks.

As you can see, we are mainly concerned with interior routing protocols in this book because we assume that you or your group will be building and maintaining campus networks.

Before we move on to the specifics of interior routing protocols, let's break interior routing protocols down further into two categories—classless and classful.

Classless versus Classful Routing Protocols

In the previous section, we explain the difference between interior and exterior routing protocols. To further explain interior routing protocols, let's explore classless and classful routing protocols.

Recall from an earlier chapter the notion of classes of IP addresses. Class A addresses have 8 bit network fields, Class B addresses have 16 bit network fields and Class C addresses have 24 bit network fields. Each class has a specified number of bits in the network field that defines how many network addresses can exist in each class. Classful routing protocols use this class distinction to derive the subnet masks for a particular address. Because of this distinction, classful routing protocols are very simple, but they are also somewhat limited in their flexibility.

Examples of classful routing protocols include RIP and Cisco's proprietary IGRP.

Classless routing protocols propagate the subnet mask as well as the subnet to determine the number of hosts in the subnet. There is no notion of Class A, Class B, and Class C addresses with classless routing protocols.

Examples of classless routing protocols include RIPv2, Cisco's proprietary EIGRP, and OSPF.

In this chapter we cover the theory, operation and configuration of two classful interior routing protocols—RIP and IGRP.

RIP

Background

RIP is a distance vector routing protocol. Distance vector protocols were derived from the work of two individuals, Bellman and Ford, who devised the Bellman-Ford algorithm. This algorithm is used to define the protocol and its operation. The basic assumption of the Bellman-Ford algorithm is that networks will converge as long as the topology is stable.

Distance vector protocols advertise the directly connected interfaces' subnets to neighboring routers and additional routes learned from other routers. Each route is advertised with a parameter that signifies the distance of the router to the destination route.

RIP is specified in RFC 1058 and is derived from the *Xerox Networking Services* (XNS) protocol suite developed in the late 1970s. RIP is the first interior routing protocol to be used in networks. It was initially developed and distributed with Unix as the "routed" demon process. Since that time, RIP implementations have been developed on a number of specialized routing hardware platforms, such a Cisco routers and multilayer switches.

Overview

Since RIP is a distance vector routing protocol, it constructs a routing table that lists the routes that are directly connected to the router or are learned from RIP advertisements sent over the network. These advertisements are carried by RIP updates sent by RIP-enabled routers periodically. The RIP updates are only sent to neighboring routers.

When the routers receive RIP updates, they use an algorithm to decide how the routing table should be updated, if at all.

RIP Packet Format

RIP updates are sent over UDP port 520. The UDP/IP encapsulation is shown in Figure 10-5.

RIP transmits two types of messages, Requests and Responses. Requests ask neighboring routers for routing information and Responses transmit the responding router's route table. The packet format for a RIP message is shown in Figure 10-6.

The command field contains either a 0x1 for a RIP request or a 0x2 for a RIP response.

The version field contains the RIP version number. This field is set to one for RIPv1.

The Address Family Identifier field is set to two to signify that the routes are for IP.

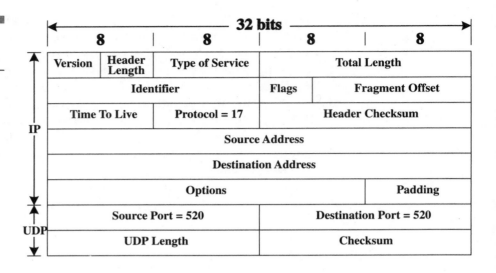

Figure 10-5
RIP UDP/IP
encapsulation

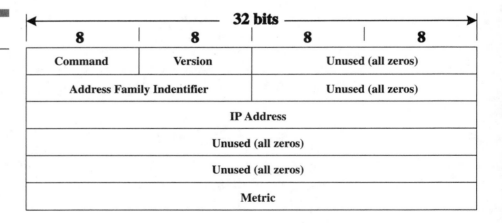

Figure 10-6
RIP packet format

The IP Address field contains the address of the route destination. This can be any valid IP address that represents a network, subnet, or host.

The Metric Field   A RIP update (RIP response) can list as many as 25 routes. If more than 25 routes are to be transmitted to a neighboring router, more that one route update packet must be sent.

Operation

Route Information Updates When a RIP-enabled router becomes operational, it broadcasts a RIP Request Message on each RIP-enabled interface. Neighboring routers respond to the RIP Request Message with a RIP Response Message that includes that router's routing table. If the responding router has more than 25 routes, the limit of a RIP Response packet, more than one RIP Response will be sent to transmit the router's entire routing table.

Once operational, a RIP router sends a RIP response message every 30 seconds by default. The network administrator can configure the frequency of the RIP responses. The message includes the following information:

■ Destination address of a host or network
■ IP address of the router sending the update
■ The number of hops to the destination (metric)

NOTE: *It is useful to note that an interface can be active or passive. An active RIP interface listens to and sends RIP updates. A passive RIP interface only **listens** to RIP updates.*

RIP updates are transmitted over UDP port 520. When an update is received the router takes one of the following actions:

■ If the routing update includes a new destination network, the new route is added to the routing table.
■ If the router receives a route with a smaller metric than a route that is already listed in the routing table, the metric and next hop information are updated in the routing protocol.
■ If the router receives an existing route with a different metric, the metric information is updated in the routing table.

This only illustrates how routes are added and modified. Other algorithms have been devised that allow RIP to handle the case of a route being removed from a routing table if a link or a router goes down. Also with this simple operation, routing loops can be created. Routing loops can send traffic in a circle through the network until the packet's TTL field decrements to zero at which time the packet is removed. This can create a large number of unnecessary packets in the network.

Split Horizon, Poison Reverse, and Triggered Updates Split horizon reduces the occurrence of routing loops between two routers. Simply stated, split horizon does not allow a router to propagate a route over the same port that supplied the route. Routing loops of three routers or more can still occur.

When used with poison reverse, split horizon causes the router to send a route to the same interface that supplied the route with a metric of 16. A metric of 16 specifies that the route is unreachable. A limitation of RIP is that the maximum number of hops allowed in the network is 15.

You may wonder why a router would send a route with a metric of 16 to specify that the route is unreachable. The router specifies reachable *and* unreachable routes to its neighbors. This further reduces the occurrence of routing loops and helps to increase the convergence time of route information throughout the network.

Poison reverse is an option that can be enabled or disabled by the network administrator. The disadvantage of poison reverse is the increased size of the routing table because of the combined storage of reachable and unreachable routes.

With poison reverse, routing loops can still occur between three or more routers. Using triggered updates reduces the network route convergence time in this case. The operation is quite simple. When a router receives an update that in turn causes it to update the metric of a route, a RIP update is automatically sent to all neighboring routes, rather than waiting for the next update time. This helps reduce convergence time in the case of routing loops of more than two routers.

Route States The four route states are as follows:

- Up
- Garbage Collection
- Hold-down
- Down

Figure 10-7 illustrates the state machine diagram for RIP route states.

A route is in the Up state if it is reachable with a finite metric (value of 0-15). The route remains in the Up state for six times the update interval, an interval that is configurable by the network administrator. Because the default update time is 30 seconds, the route remains in the Up state for 3 minutes by default. The route timer is reset each time a new update for the route is received. If the route timer ever expires, the route enters the Garbage Collection state.

Figure 10-7
RIP route state
diagram

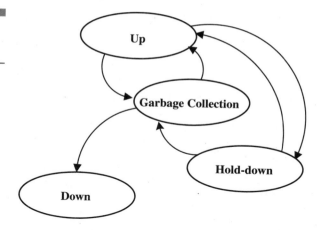

A route enters the Garbage Collection state from the Up state if the route timer expires. A route can remain in the Garbage Collection state for a maximum of four times the value of the update interval—2 minutes by default. If no route update containing this route is received during the garbage collection interval, the route is moved to the Down state. If an update is received that includes this route, the route is updated and moved to the Up state.

A route enters the Hold-down state if the router receives a RIP update for the route with a metric of 16. The route can remain in the Hold-down state for a maximum of four times the value of the update timer—2 minutes by default. The hold-down timer tracks this length of time. If the router does not receive a route update within the hold-down time, it is moved to the Garbage Collection state. If the router receives a route with a metric less than infinity, the route is moved to the Up state. The Hold-down state is a Cisco enhancement to RIP operation and is not defined by RFC 1058.

A route is moved to the Down state when the garbage collection timer expires. The route is instantly deleted.

RIP Limitations

The following list describes some of the limitations of RIP:

- RIP is limited to 15 router hops in the network.
- Subnetting is not possible.
- RIP is bandwidth intensive.

- RIP is difficult to troubleshoot.
- RIP has weak security.
- RIP sees two routes of the same hop count but different bandwidth capacities as equal.
- RIP offers no load balancing between routes.

The metric field is only 4 bits wide. Therefore, there can only be 16 values for the metric information, which limits the number of router hops to 15. A value of 16 represents infinity.

RIP has no concept of subnetting. A subnet mask can be used, but all interfaces on all routers must have the same subnet mask for all subnets. There is no allowance for *Variable Length Subnet Masks* (VLSM) in RIP. This leads to an inefficient use of IP address space.

RIP sends route updates to all neighboring routers every 30 seconds by default. This can be an inefficient use of bandwidth throughout the campus network.

RIP is a distance vector routing protocol that sends periodic updates to all neighboring routers. Therefore, all routers can have an inaccurate view of network route information if network topology has changed. This is a very difficult situation to diagnose and troubleshoot.

RIP has no built-in restrictions on receiving updates from neighbors. Therefore, routes can be spoofed by any device that is capable of creating RIP packets.

Because hop count is the only parameter for determining the route metric, a one-hop route with Gigabit Ethernet links is seen as equal to a one-hop route with 10BaseT links. One of RIP's fundamental assumptions is that all links in the network are the same.

If there are two routes to a destination, RIP picks one. There is no mechanism for load-balancing traffic over both links to provide increased bandwidth and fault tolerance.

RIP Configuration

Enabling IP routing using RIP is a three-step process:

1. Enable IP Routing
2. Enable RIP
3. Specify networks for which to perform routing

Enabling IP routing is done using the following Cisco IOS command:

```
Router(config)# ip routing
```

Next, to enable RIP, the following command is used:

```
Router(config)# router rip
```

Lastly, to specify the network addresses that RIP will actively participate with other routers on the network, you must use the following command:

```
Router(config-router)# network network-address
```

An example of a fully functional routing configuration for a router that routes for the 101.1.1.0 network would look as follows:

```
Router> enable
Router# configure terminal
Router(config)# ip routing
Router(config)# router rip
Router(config-router)# network 101.1.0.0
Router(config-router)# end
```

Notice that the network address was entered as a Class B address. If you're unsure of the network address class, you can enter the full address and the router will change it appropriately. The resulting configuration file would appear as follows:

```
Router# show running-config
. . .
ip routing
!
router rip
   network 101.1.0.0
. . .
```

A useful, but optional, configuration option allows you to prevent RIP from sending routing updates on a particular interface.

```
Router(config-router)# passive-interface interface-name
```

An example of disabling routing updates on the Ethernet 0 interface would appear as follows:

```
Router> enable
Router# configure terminal
Router(config)# router rip
```

```
Router(config-router)# passive-interface Ethernet 0
Router(config-router)# end
```

The resulting configuration file using show interface would appear as follows:

```
Router# show running-config
. . .
ip routing
!
router rip
    network 101.1.0.0
    passive-interface Ethernet 0
. . .
```

Once configured, you should confirm the routes that each router knows and has received. You may do this with the following Cisco IOS command:

```
Router# show ip route
```

This will break down the routing table into routes that it knows locally and those it has learned from other routers.

Configuring RIP is straightforward; however, other routing protocols are as simple to configure, but have features that would make them more desirable.

IGRP

Background

Cisco designed IGRP to address some of the limitations of RIP, such as the limit of 15 router hops through the network and the limit of only using the hop count for the metric calculation. In general, IGRP is similar to RIP—it is a classful interior distance vector routing protocol, but when you closely examine the the protocol, you can see that they are quite different.

IGRP is a Cisco proprietary routing protocol. Therefore, IGRP can only be used between Cisco equipment. Other companies have been able to reverse engineer IGRP operation and implement their own versions of IGRP (like Ipsilon, now owned by Nokia), but IGRP remains a closed protocol. RIP however, is interoperable between vendors.

IGRP can be deployed in networks that have up to 255 hops, as opposed to RIP's limit of 15 hops. Also, IGRP can use parameters other than hop count to determine link metrics. IGRP can factor information such as delay, bandwidth, reliability, *Maximum Transmission Unit* (MTU) and load into the metric calculation. This gives IGRP the ability to route within networks with different types of links which are common in today's campus networks. Network administrators can set the weightings of each of these parameters for determining the route metric.

IGRP supports multipath routing. It can route one stream of traffic over multiple existing paths to a destination. If the paths are equal in metric, the paths will be utilized equally. If one path is four times more desirable than another path (signified by the more desirable path having one-fourth the metric value), it will have four times the load of the less desirable path. One stream is routed over multiple paths only if all the metric values are within a certain range.

IGRP Packet Format

IGRP messages are encapsulated directly in IP with a protocol number of 0x9.

The IGRP protocol uses both an IGRP Request and IGRP Update packet for its operation. The general packet format for an IGRP message is shown in Figure 10-8.

The four-bit version field contains the version number of IGRP. The version number for IGRP is 1.

The four-bit opcode field is used to signify an update or request message.

The eight-bit edition field contains the version number of the route update. This number is incremented when a change occurs in the routing table. The idea is to let the receiving router know if it should process the route updates. If the edition field doesn't change, then the router knows that it already has the information in the update message and will ignore

Figure 10-8
IGRP packet format

32 bits				
8	**8**		**8**	**8**
Version	Opcode	Edition	Autonomous System Number	
Number of Interior Routes			Number of System Routes	
Number of Exterior Routes			Checksum	
Route Entries...				

the packet. This field is typically unused because dropped packets can make this field invalid. The data in the field is maintained, but the receiving router ignores the field.

The 16-bit autonomous system field contains the autonomous system number.

The 16-bit N interior field contains the number of route entries that are in the autonomous system.

The 16-bit system field contains the number of system route entries.

The 16-bit exterior field contains the number of route entries that are outside the autonomous system.

The 16-bit checksum field is a checksum computed on the IGRP header and route entries. The checksum field is assumed to be 0 when computing the checksum. This is necessary because the checksum field is part of the IGRP header.

Figure 10-9 shows the format of the route entry. These route entries are appended to the IGRP Update message header.

Each route entry is 14 bytes long. The fields are as follows:

- The network number is three bytes long. There is no need to transmit four bytes of the address because the network number is known. This information is given in the configuration of IGRP if the route is an interior route. Therefore, only the last three bytes are needed for an interior route. If the route is a system or exterior route, only the first three bytes of the network number are needed because the last byte is always zero.

- The delay and bandwidth values are three bytes each.

- The least MTU of the route is given in a two-byte field.

- The reliability, load, and hop count values are each placed in a one-byte field.

Figure 10-9
IGRP route entry

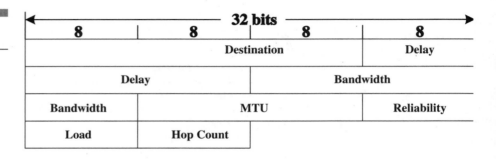

IGRP Operation

Routing Updates   Routers running IGRP that are all administered and controlled by the same group of administrators are given an Autonomous System Number. The Autonomous System Number of a router receiving a routing update must match the Autonomous System Number of the routing update. If the Autonomous System Numbers do not match, the update is ignored. This helps ensure that received routing updates are valid.

When an IGRP-enabled router first becomes operational, it sends an IGRP request message to its neighboring routers. This allows the router to learn routes without having to wait for the next scheduled update from its neighboring routers.

IGRP routers transmit periodic updates by default every 90 seconds and is configurable by the network administrator. These IGRP updates contain routes from the transmitting router's routing table.

Hold Down   To increase route stability in the network, IGRP implements a principle called hold down. The principle is very simple. When a router receives a route update that shows a route to be down, the router waits a period of time, equal to the length of time for the network to converge, before updating its routing table. This helps to reduce the number of times routes are changed from up to down as the network learns the actual state of all its routes.

These frequent changes from up to down can happen when a router fails and another router sees that routes are down and begins to propagate the downed routes to its neighbors. Its neighbors will see this update, but may receive other updates from different routers that signify that the route is still up. The route table will be changed many times for no reason until the network converges. This extends the network convergence time. The hold down period helps to reduce the chance of this happening.

Split Horizon   The split horizon feature is used in IGRP to reduce the chances of a routing loop forming between two routers. IGRP routers do not send routing information in the direction from which it came.

Consider the following simple network of two routers with directly attached LANs as illustrated in Figure 10-10.

If Router 1 sends a routing update to Router 2 about its directly connected network without split horizon, Router 2 then sends an update back

Figure 10-10
Potential routing loop
with two routers

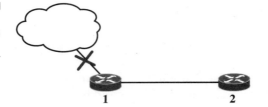

to Router 1 about Router 1's directly connected network with an increased metric. If Router 1's directly connected network goes down, it will see the route from Router 2 that incorrectly states that the network is up. Router 1 will then send forward traffic to Router 2 for its own directly connected network. Router 2 then forwards the packet back. This process will continue until Router 2 learns that Router 1's directly connected network is down.

With split horizon, Router 2 would never send an update about Router 1's directly connected network back to Router 1.

Poison Reverse Updates Split horizon prevents routing loops between two routers, but cannot guarantee that routing loops will not occur with more than two routers. Poison Reverse Updates help reduce the incidence of larger routing loops.

We can derive from the previous discussion about split horizon that one of the symptoms of a routing loop is an increasing metric value for a route. With IGRP, a Poison Reverse Update will be sent to the router that sent the original route update if the metric increases by a factor of 1.1 or more.

IGRP Metrics IGRP metric values are derived from bandwidth and delay information by default. A network administrator can configure Cisco routers to define the metrics by load and reliability as well. IGRP tracks the smallest *Maximum Transmission Unit* (MTU) of each path, but the MTU is not used in the calculation of the route metric.

Bandwidth is expressed in kilobits. For example, a bandwidth value of 100,000 would represent a 100Mbps path. The bandwidth value is set by default by the interface type, but the network administrator can also set this value. IGRP divides 10^7 by the bandwidth value to find the value transmitted in the update packet. For example, a bandwidth value of 100,000 (to represent 100Mbps) would be represented by $10^7/100,000 = 100$.

Delay is a value defined by the network administrator. It is not gathered dynamically from the network. The value, represented in microseconds, is divided by 10 before being placed in the delay field for a route update. A value of 0xFFFFFF represents an unreachable route. Therefore, the maximum delay that IGRP can account for is 167 seconds.

The formula for deriving the route metric is as follows:

$$\text{metric} = \left[k1 \times BW + \frac{k2 \times BW}{265 - \text{LOAD}} + k3 \times \text{DLY} \right] \times \left[\frac{k5}{\text{RELIABILITY} + k4} \right]$$

The variables k1, k2, k3, k4, and k5 are configurable by the network administrator. By default, k1 = k3 = 1 and k2 = k4 = k5 = 0 which means only bandwidth and delay are used to calculate the IGRP route metric by default. The following equation is the default metric formula:

$$\text{metric} = BW^{\min} + \text{DLY}$$

All the previous bandwidth values are the minimum value for the path. In addition, all the previous delay values are the sum of the delays for the path.

IGRP Multipath Routing   IGRP supports routing over multiple paths for one route. It can support up to six parallel equal cost (equal metric) routes in later releases of IOS and up to four parallel equal-cost routes in earlier releases.

IGRP can route over multiple unequal cost paths too, as long as the following conditions are met:

- The neighboring next hop router must be closer to the destination. This prevents mutlipath routing to be set up over inefficient routes.
- The metric advertised by the neighbor must be less than the variance of the local metric. The variance is found by multiplying the configurable variance factor with the local metric.

Multipath routing allows routers to have fault tolerant routes set up in case a link fails. In the event of a link failure, a path is already set up and the network does not have to converge on a new route.

IGRP Configuration

Enabling IP routing using IGRP is a three-step process:

1. Enable IP Routing
2. Enable IGRP
3. Specify networks for which to perform routing

Enabling IP routing is done using the following Cisco IOS command:

```
Router(config)# ip routing
```

Next, to enable IGRP, the following command is used:

```
Router(config)# router igrp 80
```

Lastly, to specify the network addresses where IGRP will actively participate with other routers on the network, you must use the following command:

```
Router(config-router)# network network-address
```

An example of a fully functional routing configuration for a router that routes for the 101.1.1.0 network would look as follows:

```
Router> enable
Router# configure terminal
Router(config)# ip routing
Router(config)# router igrp 80
Router(config-router)# network 101.1.0.0
Router(config-router)# end
```

Notice that the network address was entered as a Class B address. If you're unsure of the network address class, you can enter the full address and the router will change it appropriately. The resulting configuration file would look as follows:

```
Router# show running-config
. . .
ip routing
!
router igrp
   network 101.1.0.0
. . .
```

A useful, but optional, configuration option allows you to prevent IGRP from sending routing updates on a particular interface.

```
Router(config-router)# passive-interface interface-name
```

An example of disabling routing updates on the Ethernet 0 interface would look as follows:

```
Router> enable
Router# configure terminal
Router(config)# router igrp
Router(config-router)# passive-interface Ethernet 0
Router(config-router)# end
```

The resulting configuration file using show interface would appear as follows:

```
Router# show running-config
. . .
ip routing
!
router igrp
   network 101.1.0.0
   passive-interface Ethernet 0
. . .
```

Once configured, you should confirm the routes that each router knows and has received. You may do this with the following Cisco IOS command:

```
Router# show ip route
```

This will break down the routing table into routes that it knows locally and those it has learned from other routers.

Configuring IGRP is straightforward; however, other routing protocols are as simple to configure, but have features that would make them more desirable. More routing protocols are covered in the next chapter.

Chapter Summary

This chapter covers the following topics:

- Routing Protocol Categories
- *Routing Information Protocol* (RIP)
- *Interior Gateway Routing Protocol* (IGRP)

In this chapter, we discuss the differences between interior and exterior routing protocols. We are only concerned with interior routing protocols because this book is focused on building campus networks. Exterior routing protocols address routing between campus networks where the routing information of the campus networks is to remain under the control of the individual campus network administrators.

We also cover the differences between link state and distance vector routing protocols. An example of link state routing protocols is OSPF. Examples of distance vector routing protocols include RIP, IGRP, and EIGRP.

The concept of classful versus classless routing is covered. Classful routing has no concept of a subnet, therefore no subnet mask is passed with routing updates. Classless routing protocols, on the other hand, transmit the subnet mask along with the route. Classless routing protocols have the ability to summarize contiguous routes into one route to reduce the size of routing tables. Examples of classful routing protocols are RIP and IGRP. Examples of classless routing protocols are EIGRP, RIPv2, and OSPF.

This chapter explores classful routing protocols. Here we cover RIP and IGRP. RIP is a simple routing protocol that was the first IP routing protocol devised. It has a number of limitations because of its simple nature, but it works very well within its limits. Cisco developed a routing protocol called

IGRP to address some of the limitations of RIP. IGRP handles multiple path routing, metrics that are based on more than just hop count, and a hop count up to 255. RIP, on the other hand, can only route over one path at a time for a particular route. RIP's metric value is only based on hop count, and RIP can only handle 15 hops.

The next chapter explores link state routing protocols. This will round out your understanding of unicast routing to help you build more elaborate, reliable and efficient campus networks.

Frequently Asked Questions (FAQ)

Question: Are there other tools to help troubleshoot routing problems?

Answer: Yes, the most predominate is the Cisco IOS command `traceroute`. Traceroute takes an IP address as an argument and will attempt to determine the hop-by-hop route taken by the IP packet. Examining the routing table only shows you the next hop to a destination. Using traceroute allows you to see all hops from source to destination.

Case Study

In this case study, we continue to work with *Cubby Products International's* (CPI's) campus network. Recall that in Chapter 6 we had you enable the devices to allow communication between VLANs. In Chapter 6, we told you how to configure and use IGRP. Now that you are more familiar with the routing protocols, we want to examine this more closely.

Objective

Your objective is to first implement RIP as the routing protocol and then implement IGRP as the routing protocol for CPI's network.

The following are the devices for reference:

Switch Name	IP Address
IT-1-dist-5505	100.1.1.11
RD-1-dist-5505	100.1.1.16
Mfg-1-dist-5505	100.1.1.21
SR-1-dist-5505	100.1.1.26
Admin-1-dist-5505	100.1.1.31

Approach

The approach is straightforward. Knowing which protocol you need to implement, your tasks are to get it configured properly and verify operation. First, we'll implement RIP and then move to IGRP.

Configuring RIP in 5505s   The following lists the commands to set up routing in the 5505s. Note that the 5505s are the only devices that perform routing.

Enabling routing is the same for each of the Catalyst 5505s.

```
IT-1-dist-5505(config)# ip routing
IT-1-dist-5505(config)# router rip
IT-1-dist-5505(config-router)# network 100.0.0.0
```

With routing enabled, your Catalyst 5505 will now perform interVLAN routing. Repeat the commands for each Catalyst 5505.

Verifying RIP Operation   To verify that routing is operational, you can verify the information each device has in its routing table. When enabled on the first device as shown earlier, using the `show ip route` command will result in output as follows:

```
IT-1-dist-5505# show ip route
Codes: C - connected, S - static, I - IGRP, R - RIP, M - mobile, B
       - BGP
         D - EIGRP, EX - EIGRP external, O - OSPF, IA - OSPF inter area
         N1 - OSPF NSSA external type 1, N2 - OSPF NSSA external type 2
         E1 - OSPF external type 1, E2 - OSPF external type 2, E - EGP
         i - IS-IS, L1 - IS-IS level-1, L2 - IS-IS level-2
* - candidate default
         U - per-user static route, o - ODR
P - periodic downloaded static route
         T - traffic engineered route

Gateway of last resort is not set

      100.1.0.0/16 is contains 2 subnets
C        100.1.6.0/24 is directly connected, Vlan5
C        100.1.1.0/24 is directly connected, Vlan0
```

As more devices are added, the routing table will grow, and will look similar to the following:

```
IT-1-dist-5505# show ip route
Codes: C - connected, S - static, I - IGRP, R - RIP, M - mobile, B
       - BGP
         D - EIGRP, EX - EIGRP external, O - OSPF, IA - OSPF inter area
         N1 - OSPF NSSA external type 1, N2 - OSPF NSSA external type 2
         E1 - OSPF external type 1, E2 - OSPF external type 2, E - EGP
         i - IS-IS, L1 - IS-IS level-1, L2 - IS-IS level-2
* - candidate default
         U - per-user static route, o - ODR
P - periodic downloaded static route
         T - traffic engineered route

Gateway of last resort is not set

      100.1.0.0/16 is contains 6 subnets
C        100.1.6.0/24 is directly connected, Vlan5
C        100.1.1.0/24 is directly connected, Vlan0
R        100.1.2.0/24 via 100.1.1.16, Vlan1
R        100.1.3.0/24 via 100.1.1.21, Vlan2
R        100.1.4.0/24 via 100.1.1.26, Vlan3
R         100.1.5.0/24 via 100.1.1.31, Vlan4
```

Note that the routes from the other routers show up with an R to the left. This signifies that they were learned from RIP updates. Furthermore, the IP address of the router from which the route was heard is given.

Configuring IGRP in 5505s   The following lists the commands to set up routing in the 5505s. Note that the 5505s are the only devices that perform routing.

Enabling routing is the same for each of the Catalyst 5505s.

```
IT-1-dist-5505(config)# ip routing
IT-1-dist-5505(config)# router igrp 80
IT-1-dist-5505(config-router)# network 100.0.0.0
```

With routing enabled, your Catalyst 5505 will now perform interVLAN routing. Repeat the commands for each Catalyst 5505.

Verifying IGRP Operation   To verify that routing is operational, you can verify the information each device has in its routing table. When enabled on the first device as shown earlier, using the show ip route command will result in output as follows:

```
IT-1-dist-5505# show ip route
Codes: C - connected, S - static, I - IGRP, R - RIP, M - mobile, B
       - BGP
       D - EIGRP, EX - EIGRP external, O - OSPF, IA - OSPF inter area
       N1 - OSPF NSSA external type 1, N2 - OSPF NSSA external type 2
       E1 - OSPF external type 1, E2 - OSPF external type 2, E - EGP
       i - IS-IS, L1 - IS-IS level-1, L2 - IS-IS level-2
* - candidate default
       U - per-user static route, o - ODR
P - periodic downloaded static route
       T - traffic engineered route

Gateway of last resort is not set

     100.1.0.0/16 is contains 2 subnets
C       100.1.6.0/24 is directly connected, Vlan5
C       100.1.1.0/24 is directly connected, Vlan0
```

As more devices are added, the routing table will grow, and will look similar to the following:

```
IT-1-dist-5505# show ip route
Codes: C - connected, S - static, I - IGRP, R - RIP, M - mobile, B
       - BGP
       D - EIGRP, EX - EIGRP external, O - OSPF, IA - OSPF inter area
       N1 - OSPF NSSA external type 1, N2 - OSPF NSSA external type 2
       E1 - OSPF external type 1, E2 - OSPF external type 2, E - EGP
```

```
        i - IS-IS, L1 - IS-IS level-1, L2 - IS-IS level-2
* - candidate default
        U - per-user static route, o - ODR
P - periodic downloaded static route
        T - traffic engineered route

Gateway of last resort is not set

        100.1.0.0/16 is contains 6 subnets
C          100.1.6.0/24 is directly connected, Vlan5
C          100.1.1.0/24 is directly connected, Vlan0
I          100.1.2.0/24 via 100.1.1.16, Vlan1
I          100.1.3.0/24 via 100.1.1.21, Vlan2
I          100.1.4.0/24 via 100.1.1.26, Vlan3
I          100.1.5.0/24 via 100.1.1.31, Vlan4
```

Note that the routes from the other routers show up with an I to the left. This signifies that they were learned from IGRP updates. Furthermore, the IP address of the router from which the route was heard is given.

Case Study Summary

The objective of this case study was to implement routing using two different protocols: RIP and IGRP. As discussed in this chapter, both operate in a similar fashion. To achieve the objective, we used the appropriate commands for each protocol to enable and configure the protocol. Next, we verified routing operation using the show ip route command.

While RIP and IGRP are very capable routing protocols, in Chapter 11 we examine some protocols that are more full-featured. Again, IP routing is not covered on the BCMSN exam.

▬▬ ▬▬ Questions

1. Interior routing protocols are designed for routing
   - **a.** between the CAN and Internet Service Provider
   - **b.** within the CAN
   - **c.** in the WAN
   - **d.** Ethernet

2. Exterior routing protocols are designed for routing
   - **a.** between the CAN and Internet Service Provider
   - **b.** within the CAN
   - **c.** in the WAN
   - **d.** Ethernet

3. Classful routing protocols include:
   - **a.** RIP
   - **b.** IGRP
   - **c.** EIGRP
   - **d.** Both a and b

4. Classless routing protocols include:
   - **a.** RIPv2
   - **b.** OSPF
   - **c.** EIGRP
   - **d.** All of the above

5. RIP is a _____ _____ routing protocol.
   - **a.** link state
   - **b.** distance vector
   - **c.** static processing
   - **d.** exterior gateway

6. RIP uses UDP port ____ to advertise routing updates.
   - **a.** 1058
   - **b.** 1970
   - **c.** 520
   - **d.** 1023

7. RIP can send a maximum of _____ IP routes in an update packet.
   - **a.** 25
   - **b.** 30
   - **c.** 64
   - **d.** 512

8. RIP response messages are sent every ____ seconds by default.

    a. 5
    b. 10
    c. 30
    d. 120

9. Passive interfaces:

    a. Do not participate in route processing
    b. Receive updates but do not send updates
    c. Send updates but do not receive updates
    d. Are non-aggressive

10. The maximum number of hops that can exist in a RIP network is ____.

    a. 7
    b. 15
    c. 31
    d. 42

11. The maximum number of hops that can exist in an IGRP network is ____.

    a. 15
    b. 63
    c. 127
    d. 255

12. IGRP

    a. is Cisco proprietary
    b. supports load balancing over multiple paths
    c. has IP protocol number of 0x9
    d. all the above

13. IGRP default update interval is ___ seconds.

    a. 5
    b. 30
    c. 90
    d. 120

14. The IGRP metric is calculated using _____ and _____.

    a. hop count, AS number
    b. Bellman-Ford, hop count
    c. IP address, link speed
    d. bandwidth, delay

15. Routing hold down refers to:

   a. Delaying routing table changes after an update is received

   b. Delaying route update notifications when a link goes down

   c. Delaying route update notifications when a router goes down

   d. Clamping the router to an equipment rack

16. Split horizon states that:

   a. A router ignores duplicate route information from more than one interface.

   b. A router does not send routing information on the interface that it was received.

   c. A router splits up traffic between multiple interfaces if a duplicate route exists.

   d. A router uses hold down to suppress duplicate routes.

17. Poison reverse states that:

   a. A router sends a duplicate routing packet on an interface before any other router.

   b. A router sends an invalid update packet to all interfaces.

   c. A router sends an update packet with routes received on an interface set to infinity.

   d. A router sends an update packet with routes received on an interface set to zero.

18. The latest Cisco IOS release supports ___ IGRP multipath routes.

   a. 2

   b. 4

   c. 6

   d. 8

19. RIP stands for _____ _____ _____ _____.

   a. Rest In Peace

   b. Routing Information Protocol

   c. Routing Interface Protocol

   d. Reliable Information Protocol

20. IGRP stands for _____ _____ _____
_____.

    a. Internet Group Routing Protocol
    b. Internet Geographic Routing Protocol
    c. Interior Gateway Routing Protocol
    d. Interior Group Routing Protocol

Answers

1. Interior routing protocols are designed for routing

   b. within the CAN

   Which is usually administered by a single entity

2. Exterior routing protocols are designed for routing

   a. between the CAN and Internet Service Provider

   Which involves connection between two different administrative entities.

3. Classful routing protocols include:

   d. Both a and b

   Subnet/netmask information is not included in routing updates.

4. Classless routing protocols include:

   d. All of the above

   All include netmask information in the routing updates.

5. RIP is a _____ _____ routing protocol.

   b. distance vector

6. RIP uses UDP port ____ to advertise routing updates.

   c. 520

7. RIP can send a maximum of ____ IP routes in an update packet.

   a. 25

8. RIP response messages are sent every ____ seconds by default.

   c. 30

9. Passive interfaces:

   b. Receive updates but do not send updates

   Passive means do not send routing updates on that interface, but it will still listen to updates/routing information.

10. The maximum number of hops that can exist in a RIP network is ____.

    b. 15

11. The maximum number of hops that can exist in an IGRP network is ____.

    d. 255

12. IGRP

    d.   all the above

IGRP was developed by Cisco and supports load balancing. It also uses IP for transport, but does not use TCP or UDP. It has it's own IP protocol value of 0x9.

13. IGRP default update interval is ___ seconds.

    c.   90

14. The IGRP metric is calculated using _____ and

_____.

    d.   bandwidth, delay

The IGRP metric is based on bandwidth and delay by default. Reliability, load and MTU can be configured manually.

15. Routing hold down refers to:

    a.   Delaying routing table changes after an update is received

16. Split horizon states that:

    b.   A router does not send routing information on the interface that it was received.

Split horizon is used as a route loop avoidance mechanism.

17. Poison reverse states that:

    c.   A router sends an update packet with routes received on an interface set to infinity.

Poison reverse is a mechanism to help reduce convergence time of the routing tables, but does increase memory resources.

18. The latest Cisco IOS release supports ___ IGRP multipath routes.

    c.   6

19. RIP stands for _____ _____ _____

_____.

    b.   Routing Information Protocol

20. IGRP stands for _____ _____ _____

_____.

    c.   Interior Gateway Routing Protocol

Classless Interior Routing Protocols

The previous chapters in this book cover the material in the Building Cisco MultiLayer Switched Networks course to prepare you for the certification exam. To give you a more thorough understanding of the material, we have included this chapter to provide an overview of unicast routing protocols. This chapter is outside the scope of the course, but the information is necessary for you to successfully build a routed IP campus network.

Recall the notion of communicating routes between routers from Chapter 6. The network must propagate the location of all subnets within the network so routers will know how to forward packets to their destination. One way of propagating routes through the network is by manually configuring static routes on every router throughout the network as shown in Figure 11-1.

If you have only a couple of routers with a very few interfaces each in your campus network, it is not too much work to enter each static route into every router assuming the routes would not change. However, your network

Figure 11-1

Static routes in a campus network

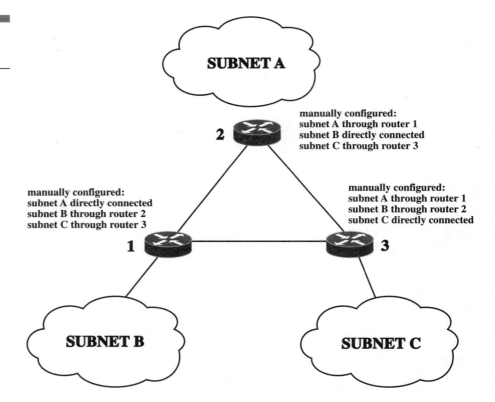

SUBNET A

2

manually configured:
subnet A through router 1
subnet B directly connected
subnet C through router 3

manually configured:
subnet A directly connected
subnet B through router 2
subnet C through router 3

manually configured:
subnet A through router 1
subnet B through router 2
subnet C directly connected

1   3

SUBNET B

SUBNET C

is likely to change over time when subnets are moved or added, or more routers deployed. Once more than a couple of routers exist in the network, manually configuring static routes can become more than a full-time job.

The solution is to implement dynamic route propagation through your campus network as shown in Figure 11-2. This is where routing protocols come into play. Routing protocols allow routers to pass known subnets and their location to each router in the network.

This chapter covers one category of unicast routing protocols known as classless routing protocols. Both classful and classless routing protocols will be covered early in the chapter.

Figure 11-2
Dynamic routing
protocols

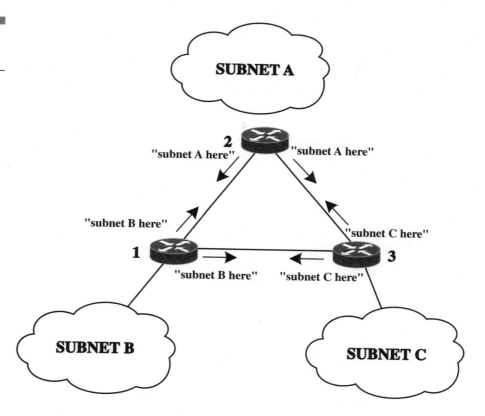

Objectives Covered in the Chapter

The following topics are covered in this chapter:

- Routing Protocol Categories
- *Routing Information Protocol Version 2* (RIPv2)
- *Enhanced Interior Gateway Routing Protocol* (EIGRP)
- *Open Shortest Path First* (OSPF)

Categories of Routing Protocols

Several categories of routing protocols exist. Knowledge of these categories will help you grasp the material in this chapter, which covers classful interior routing protocols.

Interior versus Exterior Routing Protocols

The two main categories of routing protocols are interior and exterior. These categories are derived from the span of control of administration for the network.

Interior routing protocols, as illustrated in Figure 11-3, are designed for routing within a campus network where one group controls the policies and administration. The network-wide policies are consistent and provide communication throughout the network. These campus networks where one group controls the internal policies of the networks are called autonomous systems.

Figure 11-3
Interior routing
protocol

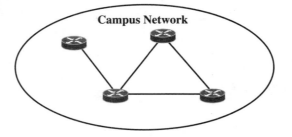

Figure 11-4
Exterior routing
protocol

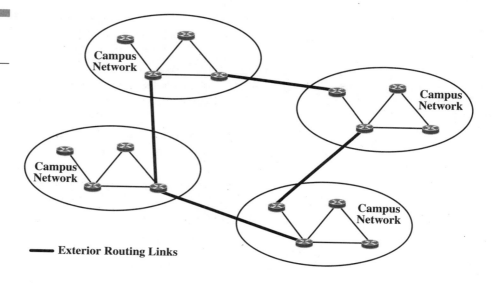

—— Exterior Routing Links

Exterior routing protocols, as illustrated in Figure 11-4, are designed to handle routing between large networks that are controlled by different groups which tend to have individual and sometimes conflicting networking policies. The group responsible for routing between the large campus networks doesn't want to concern itself with the individual routing policies and configurations of these autonomous networks. Therefore, the routing protocols used to connect autonomous campus networks are designed to achieve routing between the networks without having to monitor the internal structures of the networks.

As you can see, we are mainly concerned with interior routing protocols in this book because we assume that you or your group will be building and maintaining campus networks.

Before we move on to the specifics of interior routing protocols, let's break interior routing protocols down further into two categories—classless and classful.

Classless versus Classful Routing Protocols

In the previous section, we explain the difference between interior and exterior routing protocols. To further explain interior routing protocols, let's explore classless and classful routing protocols.

Recall from an earlier chapter the notion of classes of IP addresses. Class A addresses have 8 bit network fields, class B addresses have 16 bit network fields and class C addresses have 24 bit network fields. Each class has a specified number of bits in the network field that defines how many network addresses can exist in each class. Classful routing protocols use this class distinction to derive the subnet masks for a particular address. Because of this distinction, classful routing protocols are very simple, but they are also somewhat limited in their flexibility.

Examples of classful routing protocols includeRIP and Cisco's proprietary IGRP.

Classless routing protocols propagate the subnet mask as well as the subnet to determine the number hosts in the subnet. There is no notion of Class A, Class B, and Class C addresses with classless routing protocols.

Examples of classless routing protocols include RIPv2, Cisco's proprietary EIGRP, and OSPF.

In this chapter we cover the theory, operation and configuration of three classless interior routing protocols—RIPv2, EIGRP, and OSPF.

RIPv2

Overview

RIPv2 is fully specified in RFC 1723. It is supported in IOS versions 11.1 and later. RIPv2 is basically RIPv1 with a few improvements. See the previous chapter for a discussion on RIPv1. The features of RIPv2 are as follows:

- Subnet masks are sent with each route entry in the routing updates, enabling the use of VLSM.
- The next hop address is sent with each route entry in the routing updates.
- The routing updates are authenticated.
- Route updates are sent to a multicast group.

Because the subnet masks are sent with each route entry in the routing updates, RIPv2 supports VLSMs. This feature allows LANs to have different subnet masks. This is an effective way to conserve IP address space by tailoring the subnet mask to have just enough node addresses. Without a VLSM, all subnet masks must be the same, which can lead to a wasted address space.

Another benefit of transmitting the subnet mask with each route entry is the classless nature of RIPv2. RIPv2 isn't restricted to the classful designations of IP address space and therefore is much more flexible in the method by which IP addresses can be used.

Because RIPv2 is a distance vector routing protocol, it constructs a routing table that lists the routes that are directly connected to the router or are learned from RIP advertisements sent over the network. Unlike RIPv1, RIPv2 route advertisements are periodically sent by RIP-enabled routers to a well-known multicast address.

When the routers receive RIP updates, they use an algorithm to decide how the routing table should be updated— if at all.

Now that you have an overview of RIPv2, let's move on to a more detailed discussion about how RIPv2 works.

RIPv2 Packet Format

RIPv2 messages are encapsulated in UDP messages over IP. Figure 11-5 shows the encapsulation of RIPv2 messages.

RIPv2 updates are sent to the reserved multicast address of 224.0.0.9, an address that represents all RIPv2 routers. The reason for sending the updates to a multicast address instead of a broadcast address is so other

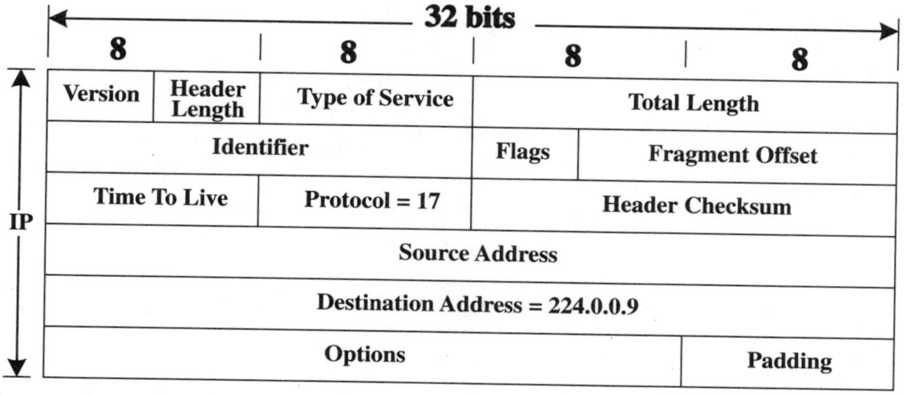

Figure 11-5
RIPv2 message encapsulation

32 bits			
8	8	8	8
Version / Header Length	Type of Service	Total Length	
Identifier		Flags	Fragment Offset
Time To Live	Protocol = 17	Header Checksum	
Source Address			
Destination Address = 224.0.0.9			
Options			Padding

IP

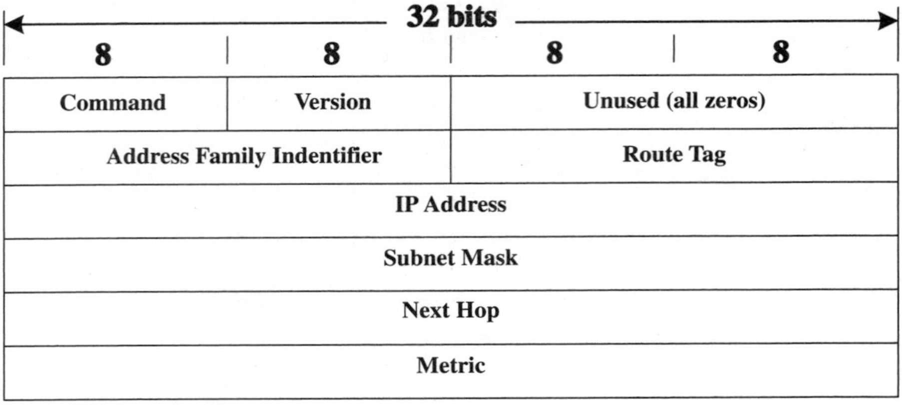

Figure 11-6
RIPv2 packet format

◄──── **32 bits** ────►			
8	**8**	**8**	**8**
Command	Version	Unused (all zeros)	
Address Family Indentifier		Route Tag	
IP Address			
Subnet Mask			
Next Hop			
Metric			

hosts on the local LAN do not have to process the packets. Only hosts that belong to the "all RIPv2 routers" multicast address must process the packets.

Figure 11-6 shows the packet format for the RIPv2 packet.

Notice that the structure of the message is very similar to the RIPv1 message. Remember that the RIPv1 message has an unused field for each route entry. These fields, that are explained in more detail later, are used for the subnet mask and next hop address. Each RIPv2 message can have up to 25 route entries. If more than 25 routes are to be transmitted to a neighboring router, more than one route update packet must be sent.

The command field contains either a 0x1 for a RIP request or a 0x2 for a RIP response.

The version field contains the RIP version number. This field is set to 0x2 for RIPv1.

The Address Family Identifier field is set to 0x02 to signify that the routes are for IP. If the message is a request for a routers complete route table, the field is set to 0x00.

The Route Tag field is for determining whether the routes are external or routes that have been redistributed into RIPv2. Route redistribution is the process of advertising the routes from one routing protocol into another. RIPv2 doesn't use the Route Tag field. The use of this field is outside the scope of this book.

The IP Address field contains the address of the route destination. This can be any valid IP address that represents a network, subnet, or host.

The Subnet Mask field is a 32-bit field that determines the length of the network and subnet fields in the IP route.

The Metric field represents a hop count between 1 and 16.

RIPv2 Operation

Route Information Updates   When a RIPv2-enabled router becomes operational, it sends a RIPv2 Request Message. Routers respond to the RIPv2 Request Message with a RIPv2 Response Message that includes that router's routing table. If the responding router has more than 25 routes, the limit of a RIPv2 Response packet, more than one RIPv2 Response will be sent to transmit the router's entire routing table.

Once operational, a RIPv2 router sends a RIP Response Message every 30 seconds by default. The network administrator can configure the frequency of the RIPv2 responses.

NOTE: *It is useful to note that an interface can be active or passive. An active RIPv2 interface listens to and sends RIPv2 updates. A passive RIPv2 interface only **listens** to RIPv2 updates.*

When an update is received, the router takes one of the following actions:

- If the routing update includes a new destination network, the new route is added to the routing table.

- If the router receives a route with a metric smaller than a route that is already listed in the routing table, the metric and next hop information are updated in the routing protocol.

- If the router receives an existing route with a different metric, the metric information is updated in the routing table.

This only shows how routes are added and modified. Other algorithms have been devised that allow RIPv2 to handle the case of route removal from a routing table if a link or router goes down. Also with this simple operation, routing loops can be created, causing traffic to be sent in a circle throughout the network. When the *time-to-live* (TTL) field is decremented to zero, the packet is removed from the network. This can create many unnecessary packets in the network.

Split Horizon, Poison Reverse, and Triggered Updates   Split horizon is used to reduce the occurrence of routing loops between two routers. Simply stated, Split Horizon does not allow a router to propagate a route over the same port that supplied the route. However, routing loops of three routers or more can still occur.

When used with Poison Reverse, split horizon causes the router to send a route to the same interface that supplied the route with a metric of 16. A metric of 16 specifies that the route is unreachable. In RIPv2, the maximum number of hops allowed in the network is 15. As with RIPv1, this is a limitation of RIPv2.

You may wonder why a router would send a route with a metric of 16 to specify that the route is unreachable. The router specifies reachable *and* unreachable routes to its neighbors. This further reduces the occurrence of routing loops and helps increase the convergence time of route information throughout the network.

Poison Reverse is an option that can be enabled or disabled by the network administrator. The disadvantage of Poison Reverse is the increased size of the routing table because of the combined storage of unreachable and reachable routes.

With Poison Reverse, routing loops can still occur between three or more routers. However, the network route convergence time is reduced with the use of triggered updates. This operation is quite simple. When a router receives an update that causes it to in turn update the metric of a route, a RIP update is automatically sent to all neighboring routes and does not wait for the next update time. This helps reduce convergence time in the event of routing loops involving more than two routers.

Route States   The four route states are as follows:

- Up
- Garbage Collection
- Hold-down
- Down

Figure 11-7

RIP route state
diagram

32 bits			
8	**8**	**8**	**8**
Command	Version	Unused (all zeros)	
0xFFFF		Authentication Type	
Password (bytes 0–3)			
Password (bytes 4–7)			
Password (bytes 8–11)			
Password (bytes 12–15)			
Address Family Indentifier		Route Tag	
IP Address			
Subnet Mask			
Next Hop			
Metric			

Figure 11-7 illustrates the state machine diagram for RIP route states.

A route is in the Up state if it is reachable with a finite metric (value of 0–15). The route remains in the Up state for six times the update interval, an interval that is configurable by the network administrator. Because the default update time is 30 seconds, the route remains in the Up state for 3 minutes by default. The route timer is reset each time a new update for the route is received. If the route timer expires, the route enters the Garbage Collection state.

A route enters the Garbage collection state from the Up state if the route timer expires. A route can remain in the Garbage Collection state for a maximum of four times the value of the update interval—2 minutes by default. If no route update containing this route is received during the garbage collection interval, the route is moved to the Down state. If an update is received that includes this route, the route is updated and moved to the Up state.

A route enters the Hold-Down state if the router receives a RIP update for the route with a metric of 16. The route can remain in the Hold-Down state for a maximum of four times the value of the update timer—2 minutes by default. The hold-down timer tracks this period of time. If the router does not receive a route update within the hold-down time, it is moved to the Garbage Collection state. If the router receives a route with a metric less than infinity, the route is moved to the Up state.

A route is moved to the Down state when the garbage collection timer expires and the route is instantly deleted.

Interoperability with RIPv1

RIPv1 has an interesting feature that works well with RIPv2. RIPv1 routers will ignore an update packet if the update is declared as version 1 and the unused fields are non-zero. However, if the version field is set to 2 to specify RIPv2, a RIPv1 router will still process the packet and ignore the unused fields. Therefore, RIPv2 is backward compatible with RIPv1.

To cope with RIPv1 and RIPv2 interoperability, RFC 1723 specifies four compatibility settings for transmitting RIPv2 updates. These settings are as follows:

- *RIP-1*   Only RIPv1 messages are transmitted.
- *RIP-1 Compatibility*   RIPv2 messages are broadcast instead of multicast.
- *RIP-2*   Normal RIPv2 update mode
- *None*   No updates are sent

RFC 1723 also defines interoperability parameters for receiving RIP updates. The settings are as follows:

- RIP-1 only
- RIP-2 only
- Both RIP-1 and RIP-2
- None

Classless Routing Protocols

What is the real benefit of classless routing protocols? One of the benefits is that they allow routers to distinguish an "all-zeros" subnet from a network address. For example, the address 128.109.0.0 is seen as a network address in RIPv1. In RIPv2, the address can be further specified. In another example, 128.109.0.0/16 represents an address of 128.109.0.0 with a 16-bit subnet mask or 255.255.0.0. This IP address/subnet bits convention is used in all classless routing protocols. Therefore, 128.109.0.0/16 is a network address and is invalid to use as a subnet address. The route designation of 128.109.0.0/24 represents a valid subnet. Now these addresses that were once invalid can be used.

Another benefit of classless routing protocols is the ability to use VLSMs in your network. Each routing update has route entries that specify the address and the subnet mask. This allows a network designer to make full use of his allotted IP address space. Also, routers are able to create "supernets" which are best match summarizations of multiple contiguous routes.

Route Update Authentication

To ensure that RIPv2 updates are valid, a password is included in the RIP update to let the receiving router know that the update can be trusted. This is done by modifying the first route entry in a route update message. This reduces the maximum number of routes in one update message to 24.

The message format for RIPv2 with authentication is shown in Figure 11-8.

Setting the Address Family Identifier field to all ones designates the presence of authentication.

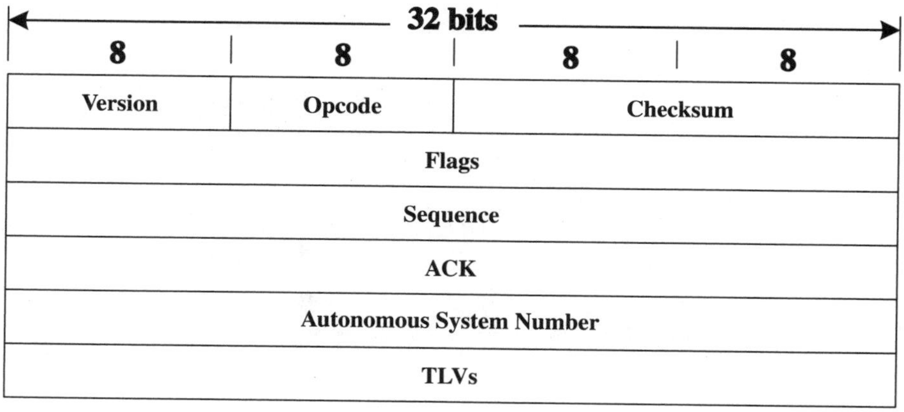

Figure 11-8
RIPv2 with
authentication
message format

The Authentication Type field is set to 0x0002 for simple password authentication.

The Password field contains an alphanumeric password of up to 16 characters. This password is left justified in the field and if the password is less than 16 characters, the remaining space in the password field is set to zeros.

This method of transmitting the password can be a little risky because the password is transmitted in simple ASCII format that is readable by a sniffer. Cisco extended the authentication method to include an MD5 style password encryption that does not transmit the passwords in plain ASCII format. RFC 1723 only specifies simple password authentication and Cisco designates this new type by setting the Authentication Type field to 0x0003. Since this type is not specified in the RFC, this method of authentication will not interoperate with other vendors' equipment.

EIGRP

Overview

EIGRP is a completely different protocol than IGRP. RIPv2 is basically RIPv1 with a few enhancements, but this is not the case with EIGRP and IGRP. Despite their differences, however, some things are the same. For instance, both EIGRP and IGRP are distance vector and interior routing protocols. Their similarities end there. For the purposes of this discussion, we'll treat EIGRP like a completely different protocol.

Distance vector protocols typically use the Bellman-Ford algorithm for route computation. There's no need to go into the details of the rules of the Bellman-Ford algorithm, because the algorithm is straightforward and easy to implement. The Bellman-Ford algorithm doesn't require many computing resources on the router to do the job. The disadvantage of the Bellman-Ford algorithm is that the algorithm is susceptible to routing loops. Mechanisms such as Split Horizon, Poison Reverse, and hold-down timers are added to the Bellman-Ford algorithm to improve the routing loop functions.

Link-state routing protocols use the Dijkstra routing algorithm. This algorithm is complex and requires a significant amount of computing resources on the router to implement. The good news is that routing loops are not a problem with this algorithm. Routing information converges much faster with the Dijkstra routing algorithm than with Bellman-Ford.

In contrast, EIGRP uses a diffusing computation to maintain the routing information across the network while eliminating routing loops. Having said this, EIGRP remains a distance vector routing protocol that has the following characteristics:

- Non-periodic
- Partial
- Bounded

First, non-periodic means that routing information is only transmitted when necessary. Thus, there are no scheduled routing updates. Second, partial indicates that the router doesn't transmit all the routing information. The only information that is transmitted to neighboring routers is information pertaining to a change. Finally, bounded means that the routing updates are only sent to the affected routers.

Because of these characteristics, EIGRP behaves like a link-state routing protocol, similar to OSPF. Therefore, this protocol is very efficient for low bandwidth links, such as with WAN. In fact, the bandwidth utilized on a link by EIGRP can be specified in terms of the percentage utilization of the link.

EIGRP is a classless protocol much like RIPv2. Subnet mask information is transmitted with each route entry change. This gives EIGRP the capability for VLSM and route summarization.

The composite metric information is similar to IGRP in that the metric can be defined from a number of parameters.

EIGRP also takes into consideration authentication by using MD5 encryption mechanism much in the same way that Cisco does with RIPv2.

EIGRP Packet Format

Figure 11-9 shows the EIGRP packet header.

The 8-bit Version field contains the version of the EIGRP implementation. Note that there is only one version of EIGRP even though there have been several improvements to EIGRP since EIGRP was made available in IOS 9.21. It is recommended that latest version of IOS software is used to guarantee the maximum amount of stability.

Figure 11-9
EIGRP packet header

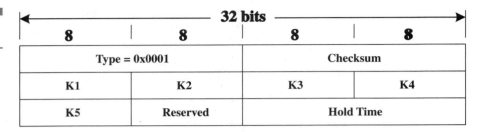

32 bits			
8	8	8	8
Type = 0x0001		Checksum	
K1	K2	K3	K4
K5	Reserved	Hold Time	

Table 11-1

EIGRP opcode field
values

Opcode Value	Description
1	Update
3	Query
4	Reply
5	Hello
6	IPX SAP

The 8-bit Opcode field specifies the EIGRP message type. Table 11-1 lists the possible values and their descriptions. The IPX SAP opcode is for routing IPX.

The 16-bit Checksum field is a checksum that is calculated for the entire EIGRP message.

The 32-bit Flags field is used for specifying special characteristics about the EIGRP message. Only two valid values exist. If the field is set to 0x00000001, the EIGRP message contains route entries that are the first in a new neighbor relationship. If the field is set to 0x00000002, the Cisco proprietary Reliable Multicasting algorithm is being used. Reliable Multicasting is not discussed in this book.

The 32-bit ACK field is a sequence number last seen by the device sending the message.

The 32-bit Autonomous System Number is the identification number of the EIGRP routing domain.

The "payload" of the EIGRP message carries *Type/Length/Value* (TLV) triplets. Multiple TLVs can be carried in one EIGRP message. There are many types of TLVs, but in this book we discuss only six of them. Each TLV format begins with a 16-bit Type field followed by a 16-bit Length field. Table 11-2 lists the six TLV Types that are discussed in this book.

Table 11-2

TLV type values

TLV Type Value	Description
0x0001	EIGRP Parameters
0x0003	Sequence
0x0004	Software Version
0x0005	Next Multicast Sequence
0x0102	IP Internal Routes
0x0103	IP External Routes

Figure 11-10
EIGRP parameters
TLV format

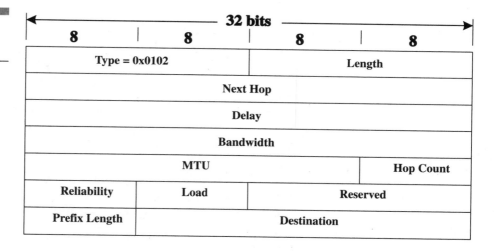

Figure 11-10 shows the format for an EIGRP Parameters TLV.

Note that this TLV is used to transmit the metric parameters k1 through k5. These parameters are similar to the IGRP metric parameters and are discussed later in this chapter. The Hold Time parameter is also sent in this TLV.

The Sequence, Software Version, and Next Multicast Sequence are used by Cisco's proprietary Reliable Multicast and are not covered in this book.

Because we focus on interior routing in this book, we will not cover the operation of the IP External Routes TLV. The format for the IP Internal Routes TLV is shown in Figure 11-11.

The Next Hop field (32 bits) is the next-hop IP address.

Figure 11-11
IP Internal routes
TLV format

Protocol Dependent Modules		
IPX	IP	Appletalk
Diffusing Update Algorithm (DUAL)		
Neighbor Discovery/Recovery		
Reliable Transport Protocol		

The 32-bit Delay field is sum of the configured delays of each link in the path. The sum has units of 10 microseconds. A delay of 0xFFFFFFFF specifies an unreachable route.

The 32-bit Bandwidth field is $256*BW^{IGRP(min)}$ or $256*10,000,000$ divided by the lowest bandwidth (in bps) of all the links in the path.

The 24-bit MTU field is the smallest MTU of all the links in the route path.

The 8-bit Hop Count field is the number of hops to the destination. A directly connected network will have a hop count of 0x00.

The 8-bit Reliability field is a 5-minute exponentially weighted-average that describes the reliability of a link. A value of 0xFF is a perfectly reliable link.

The 8-bit Load field is a 5-minute exponentially weighted-average that describes the load of a link. A value of 0x01 is a minimally loaded link.

The Reserved field is always set to 0x0000.

The 8-bit Prefix Length field specifies the number of network and subnet bits of the address mask.

The Destination field contains the Destination address of the route. The mask determines the length of this field. If the Prefix length of a route is 16, then the Destination field will be two bytes long. The TLV will be padded with zeros to make sure that the TLV ends on a 32-bit boundary. For example, a route of 128.109.240.0/24 will have a value of 24 in the Prefix Length field and 128.109.240 in the Destination field.

EIGRP Operation

Metric Calculation As with IGRP, EIGRP is primarily based on bandwidth and delay. This formula is as follows:

$$\text{metric} = \left[k1 \times BW + \frac{k2 \times BW}{256 - LOAD} + k3 \times DLY \right] \times \left[\frac{k5}{RELIABILITY + k4} \right]$$

The only difference is that this metric is scaled by a factor of 256 to increase the number of possible metrics to better distinguish routes.

EIGRP Components

EIGRP has four components:

- Protocol dependent modules
- *Reliable Transport Protocol* (RTP)
- Neighbor Discovery/Recovery
- *Diffusing Update Algorithm* (DUAL)

Figure 11-12 shows the relationship between the components.

Protocol Dependent Modules

EIGRP has separate modules to handle routing for IP, IPX, and AppleTalk. We only cover IP routing in this book.

Note that EIGRP will automatically distribute (share) routes with IGRP if both routing protocols are in the same Autonomous System.

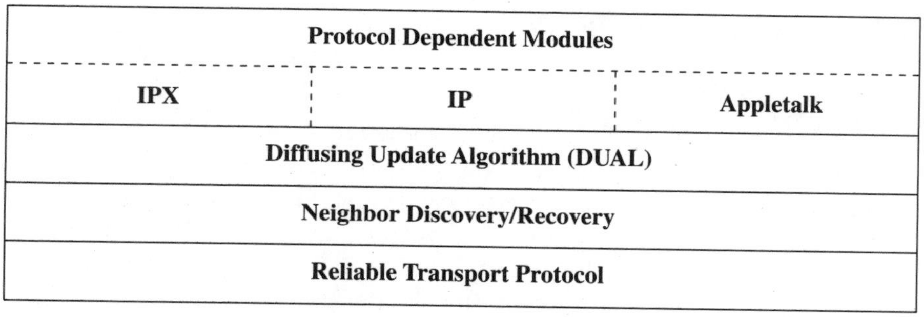

Figure 11-12
EIGRP components

Protocol Dependent Modules		
IPX	IP	Appletalk
Diffusing Update Algorithm (DUAL)		
Neighbor Discovery/Recovery		
Reliable Transport Protocol		

Reliable Transport Protocol (RTP)

EIGRP has a reliable mechanism for transmitting EIGRP messages. This mechanism is a proprietary algorithm called Reliable Multicast. The multicast group address of 224.0.0.10 is used for the destination address of most EIGRP packets that are acknowledged by the receivers. An acknowledgement message is then sent back to the unicast address of the sender of the original EIGRP message.

Two sequence numbers are included in an EIGRP message sent with Reliable Multicast. The sending router generates one sequence number and the other sequence number is the last one seen by the sending router. This guarantees the ability to sequence the packets if they arrive out of order.

EIGRP acknowledgements do not use Reliable Multicast and do not include any sequence numbers.

As we discussed in the EIGRP packet format section, the several EIGRP packet types are as follows:

- Hellos
- Acknowledgements
- Updates
- Queries
- Replies
- Requests

EIGRP Hellos are used in the EIGRP Neighbor Discovery/Recovery process covered in the next section.

EIGRP Acknowledgements are EIGRP Hello packets with no data. These packets are addressed to the unicast address of the router that sent the original data.

EIGRP Updates carry routing information and are only sent when there is a need to send them. Updates are sent when requested by another router or when there is a change in the topology of the network. If the Update is directed to one router, a unicast address is used for the destination address of the packet. If the Update is directed to many routers, a multicast address is used. In either case, the receiver should acknowledge the Updates. Therefore, a reliable transport mechanism is necessary.

EIGRP Queries and Replies are used by the DUAL algorithm and use a reliable transmission mechanism.

EIGRP Requests have not been used in recent EIGRP implementations and are not discussed further.

Reliable Transmission requires that an acknowledgement is received from the destination. If an acknowledgement is not received after 16 retransmissions, the neighbor is considered down.

The waiting time before sending the first unicast retransmission is called the Multicast Flow Time. The time between subsequent unicast retransmissions is called *Retransmission Timeout* (RTO). These timers are calculated for each neighbor from the *Smooth Round-Trip Time* (SRTT). The SRTT is the average time in milliseconds between sending the Hello multicast and receiving a unicast acknowledgement. The algorithm for determining these times is not published by Cisco and remains proprietary.

Neighbor Discovery/Recovery

EIGRP routers maintain knowledge of their neighbors by multicasting Hello packets every 5 seconds. This Hello period applies to high-speed links such as Ethernet. The Hello multicast period is extended to 60 seconds for links of rates of 1.544 Mbps or less (low speed links traditionally used for WAN connections) to keep from wasting bandwidth. Hellos are not acknowledged.

The Hello packet includes a hold time value to let neighbors know the maximum amount of time to wait for another Hello packet before declaring the neighbor to be dead. This time is three times the Hello period by default. This relatively short amount of time to detect that a neighbor is down is one of the elements of EIGRP's operation that leads to shorter convergence times. Compare this 15-second default hold down time to RIP's 180 seconds or IGRP's 270 seconds.

Each EIGRP router maintains a neighbor table that keeps up with the following:

- Neighbors IP address
- Local interface that connects the neighbor
- Hold time advertised by the neighbor
- SRTT
- RTO
- Number of times the router has retransmitted a Hello

- Sequence number of the last Hello
- Amount of time that the neighbor has been registered

This process of discovering neighbors begins when the router becomes operational. The virtual link that connects two routers is called an adjacency. Adjacencies are used so that routers can exchange routing information.

Diffusing Update Algorithm (DUAL)

Initially proposed by Dijkstra in 1980, the *Diffusing Update Algorithm* (DUAL) was not developed until the early 1990s by J. J. Garcia-Luna-Aceves. The algorithm makes the following assumptions:

- A node detects the existence or nonexistence of a neighbor in a finite length of time.
- All messages transmitted over a link are received in order and error-free in a finite length of time.
- All messages are processed in a finite amount of time in the order that they arrive.

EIGRP's Neighbor Discovery and Reliable Multicast meet the following assumptions: Routers use their adjacencies to exchange routing information. When a router receives an Update message for one of its neighbors, it calculates a distance value based on the metric of the route and the cost of the link used to connect the neighbor.

Here are a few definitions for use in understanding the DUAL algorithm. The *Feasible Distance* (FD) is the path to a destination with the lowest distance value. A *Feasibility Condition* (FC) is met if a neighbor's advertised distance for a route is lower than the router's FD for that route. A Feasible Successor is a neighbor that advertises a distance value that meets the FC for a particular route.

The FC, FD, and Feasible Successor are used to avoid routing loops. If the route forwards packets to the Feasible Successor for a particular destination, the packet will go downstream and not be seen again by the router.

Each router maintains a Topological Table that includes the routes' FD, a list of Feasible Successors, each Feasible Successor's distance value, the local distance value to the destination, and the interface that connects to the Feasible Successor. The local distance value to the destination is calculated by factoring the advertised distance value and the cost of the interface that connects to the Feasible Successor.

The Topological Table is processed to find the path with the lowest local distance value for each route. This path is placed in the routing table. The neighbor that advertises this route becomes the Successor or the next hop router for the route. If more than one neighbor has an equally lowest local distance value and can be named a Successor for a particular route, the router enters all the routes in the routing table and load balances among the routes to the destination.

If a change occurs in the network and a Feasible Successor has a lower distance than the Successor, the Feasible Successor becomes the Successor. The following section describes the DUAL state machine.

DUAL State Machine

When an *Input Event* (IE) occurs, the router will reevaluate the list of Feasible Successors to determine if there should be a new Successor. The following list describes examples of valid IEs:

- The cost changes for a directly connected link
- A directly connected link's interface goes down
- An EIGRP Update message is received
- An EIGRP Query message is received
- An EIGRP Reply message is received

When an IE is detected, the router does a Local Computation to determine the distance to the destination for all Feasible Successors. The following outcomes can occur:

- If a Feasible Successor has a lower distance value than the Successor, the Feasible Successor becomes the new Successor for that route.
- If the distance value is less than the FD, the FD is updated.
- If the new distance value is different, an update will be sent to neighboring routers.

The route is in a Passive State when the Local Computation is in process. If a Feasible Successor is found for a route, an Update is sent to all neighbors and no state change occurs. If no Feasible Successor can be found, the route changes state to the Active State and the router will start a Diffusing Computation. While a router is in the Active State, the router cannot perform the following:

■ Change the Successor for the route

■ Change the distance value the router is advertising for the route

■ Change the route's Feasible Distance

■ Start another Diffusing Computation for the route

The Diffusion Computation begins by sending EIGRP Queries to all neighboring routers. When the neighboring router receives the EIGRP Query message, it performs a Local Computation and the following can occur:

■ If the neighboring router has a Feasible Successor for the route, an EIGRP Reply message is sent back to the router that originated the EIGRP Query. This Reply message includes the neighbor's locally calculated distance value for the route.

■ If the neighboring router does not have a Feasible Successor for the route, this router will put the route in Active State and begin a Diffusing Computation.

The router that began the Diffusing Computation keeps up with the neighbors that respond to its Query messages. If a neighbor doesn't respond before an Active Timer expires, which is set for 3 minutes by default, the route moves to a *Stuck-In-Active* (SIA) state. The neighbor that did not reply will be removed from the neighbor table and it will be assumed that the neighbor responded with a distance value of an infinite metric.

After all the neighbors respond, the Diffusing Computation is complete. This means that all routers that began Diffusing Computations of their own are also complete. The originating router set FD to infinity so that any neighbors that reply will meet the FC and become a Feasible Successor.

Table 11-3 lists all the possible Input Events for the DUAL State Machine.

Table 11-3

DUAL state machine input events

Input Event	Description
IE1	Any input event for which FC is satisfied or the destination is unreachable
IE2	Query received from the successor; FC not satisfied
IE3	Input event other than a query from the successor; FC not satisfied
IE4	Input event other than last reply or a query from the successor
IE5	Input event other than last reply, a query from the successor, or an increase in distance to destination
IE6	Input event other than last reply
IE7	Input event other than last reply or increase in distance to destination
IE8	Increase in distance to destination
IE9	Last reply received; FC not met with current FD
IE10	Query received from the successor
IE11	Last reply received; FC met with current FD
IE12	Last reply received; set FD to infinity

Figure 11-13 shows the DUAL State Machine. Refer to the Table 11-13 for a description of each of the IEs. The Query Origin Flag "O" is used to indicate the current state of the route. The Reply Status Flag value is represented by an "r."

Configuring EIGRP

Enabling IP routing using EIGRP is a three-step process:

1. Enable IP Routing
2. Enable EIGRP
3. Specify networks for which to perform routing

Figure 11-13
DUAL state machine
diagram

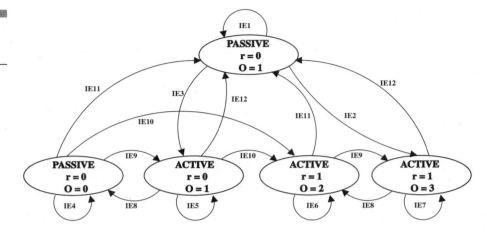

Enabling IP routing is done using the following Cisco IOS command:

```
Router(config)# ip routing
```

Next, to enable EIGRP, the following command is used:

```
Router(config)# router eigrp [AS-number]
```

The AS number is an *Autonomous System number*. The AS number should be a unique number within the campus area network. EIGRP will only exchange routes with routers in the same Autonomous System. Lastly, to specify the network addresses that EIGRP will actively participate with other routers on the network, you must use the following command:

```
Router(config-router)# network network-address
```

An example of a fully functional routing configuration for a router that routes for the 101.1.1.0 network would appear as follows:

```
Router> enable
Router# configure terminal
Router(config)# ip routing
Router(config)# router eigrp 10
Router(config-router)# network 101.1.1.0
Router(config-router)# end
```

Notice that the network address was entered as a classless address. The resulting configuration file would appear as follows:

```
Router# show running-config
. . .
ip routing
!
router eigrp 10
    network 101.1.1.0
. . .
```

A useful, but optional, configuration option allows you to prevent EIRGP from sending routing updates on a particular interface.

```
Router(config-router)# passive-interface interface-name
```

An example of disabling routing updates on the Ethernet 0 interface would appear as follows:

```
Router> enable
Router# configure terminal
Router(config)# router eigrp 10
Router(config-router)# passive-interface Ethernet 0
Router(config-router)# end
```

The resulting configuration file using show interface would appear as follows:

```
Router# show running-config
. . .
ip routing
!
router eigrp 10
    network 101.1.0.0
    passive-interface Ethernet 0
. . .
```

Once configured, you should confirm the routes that each router knows and has received. You may do this with the following Cisco IOS command.

```
Router# show ip route
```

This will break down the routing table into routes that it knows locally and those it has learned from other routers.

OSPF

OSPF protocol was developed in the late 1980s and is fully specified in RFC 2178. This RFC defines Version 2 of OSPF. OSPF is a link state, interior, classless routing protocol. OSPF was designed to address the shortcomings of RIP and has become the interior routing protocol that is recommended by the *Internet Engineering Task Force* (IETF). The OSPF specification is available to the public. Thus, the "open" nomenclature.

OSPF has several key advantages that are listed:

- Fast convergence
- Efficient use of bandwidth
- Support for *Variable Length Subnet Mask* (VLSM)
- Good scalability
- Good path selection metric

Convergence in OSPF is very good because updates occur at the same time as network changes. With RIP and IGRP, updates occur periodically and this will delay the propagation of new routing information.

OSPF creates minimal impact on the network by sending routing information only when it is needed via a multicast group address. No periodic routing table advertisements exist as with a distance vector routing protocol. Also, since the routing updates are sent to a multicast address, only those devices that are members of the multicast group must process the update packets. Some other routing protocols, such as RIP, broadcast their updates, which causes all devices on the network to parse the packet.

Because subnet information is transmitted in the routing information, OSPF allows VLSMs. This results in an efficient use of network address space.

OSPF derives a cost metric instead of a hop count. With RIP, the metric is the hop count and the number of router hops in the network is limited to 15. With OSPF, the number of router hops can be very large. Also, OSPF routing architectures can be segmented off into areas to reduce the size of the routing tables within an area. Areas can be interconnected to create a very large network.

Because OSPF factors in the bandwidth of a link, a path with more hops and greater bandwidth can appear more advantageous than a path with fewer hops and less bandwidth. RIP, on the other hand, only looks at the hop count and will choose a path with lower bandwidth if it has a lower hop count.

Operation

OSPF is a link state routing protocol and therefore keeps up with the topology of the network by receiving neighbor updates when there is a change in the state of a link. In contrast, RIP receives periodic (timer-based) updates from neighbors. The routing information from RIP is passed from router to router throughout the network. OSPF directly updates the network with changes in network topology. Unlike RIP's "second-hand" route communication, OSPF directly communicates routing information. The direct method of communication in OSPF tends to be more accurate and therefore reduces the convergence time of the network routing information.

The OSPF specification determines the following: router communication with neighbors (Adjacency), the Link-State Database, router path choice, and the maintenance of routing information. These topics are described in the following sections.

Adjacency

Adjacency is a relationship in which OSPF routers exchange routing information. The first step to establishing adjacency is by forming a neighbor relationship using the Hello protocol.

The Hello protocol is a simple transaction whereby routers periodically send a Hello packet to each other to communicate that they are still operational. It's analogous to saying "Hello" to your friend. No information is exchanged other than an acknowledgement of their presence. The OSPF Hello packet contains the following information:

- The router ID of the source
- Hello interval
- Dead interval
- Routing IDs of neighboring routers on the same link
- Area ID
- Router priority
- Designated router and backup designated router for this network
- Authentication type and password
- Stub area flag

The router ID is a unique 32-bit identifier for the router sending the OSPF Hello. Cisco routers typically use the highest IP address of all the interfaces on the router as the router ID.

The hello interval is the time between the transmission of Hello packets. By default, the hello interval is set to 10 seconds.

The dead timer is the amount of time the receiving router should wait before determining that the neighbor is down. By default, this value is four times the Hello interval.

The router IDs of other routers on the same link will be listed in the Hello packet.

The Area ID communicates the area where the transmitting router is found.

The router priority helps in determining the designated router on the link. We cover the designated router's responsibilities and the way in which it is chosen later.

The authentication type and password is placed in the Hello packets if authentication is being used. The use of authentication is optional in OSPF. If authentication is used, the type of authentication used is optional.

The Hello packet declares if the area identified in the packet is a stub area. The use of stub areas allows for the reduction of routing tables within the area.

To become neighbors the following must match from all the routers on the link: the Hello Interval, Dead Interval, Area ID, Authentication type, Password (if authentication is used), and stub area flag.

Each router must maintain a neighbor table to monitor each of its neighbors. This table keeps information in the last Hello packet received about the state of the neighbor relationship.

The three neighbor states in OSPF are as follows:

- Down State
- Init State
- Two-way State

The router begins in the Down state, signifying that the router's neighbor table is empty. The router then begins sending Hello packets to find neighbors.

The router moves to the Init State when it receives a Hello packet from a neighbor. The next Hello packet sent from this receiving router will have the IP address of the neighbor from which it received the Hello packet.

The router enters the Two-way State when it receives a Hello packet that has its own IP address in it.

When two routers enter the Two-way neighbor State, they may now become Adjacent. These routers may not exchange routing information until they are Adjacent. When two routers decide to become adjacent, they begin exchanging link-state database descriptor, request, and update packets until all the information has been synchronized on the routers. When both routers have the same link-state information, they are considered to be fully adjacent.

When several OSPF routers are on a multi-access link, all the routers maintain a neighbor relationship with each other, but do not necessarily maintain Adjacency. One router is elected to be the *Designated Router* (DR) and another router is elected to be the *Backup Designated Router* (BDR). These routers are required to maintain Adjacencies with each of the routers on multiple access networks.

When an OSPF router first comes online, it sends a Hello packet to the multicast address 224.0.0.5. This address is a reserved address that includes all OSPF routers. The router assumes the role of a DR if it gets no response. The next router that comes online assumes the role of a BDR after seeing the DR. Any subsequent routers that come online will recognize the DR and BDR on the network. The DR and BDR will not change unless an election occurs, regardless of the IP address and priority of a router that comes online on the same link.

Figure 11-14 shows DR and BDR Adjacencies on a multi-access link.

A DR election occurs when routers do not see Hellos from the DR within the Dead Interval. When there are multiple routers on the link vying for DR and BDR, the router with the highest priority gets the job. The next highest priority gets the responsibilities of a BDR. In the case of a priority tie, the router with the largest Router ID wins.

Once the DR and BDR have been elected, all link state changes are sent to the DR. Updates are sent to 224.0.0.6, the multicast address for all DRs. The DR will then repeat the update to 224.0.0.5, all OSPF routers.

Once routers form a two-way state neighbor relationship, they begin to form an adjacency. The following states are part of the adjacency state machine:

- Two-Way State
- Exstart State
- Exchange State

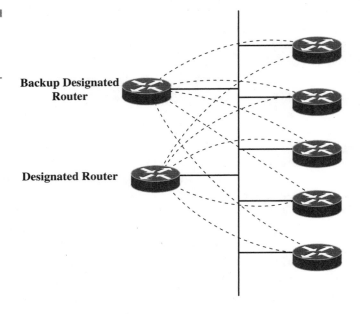

Figure 11-14
DR and BDR
adjacencies on a
multi-access link

**Backup Designated
Router**

Designated Router

- Loading State
- Full State

The Two-Way State means that the routers have successfully formed a neighbor relationship. The routers move to the Exstart State when they begin exchanging Hello packets.

From the Exstart State, the routers move to the Exchange state. In this state, one router becomes the master and begins the exchange process by sending a *Database Description Packet* (DBD or DDP) that contains a sequence number. The other router, the slave, will respond by sending a DBD within its link state database. This DBD has the same sequence number, thus forming an acknowledgement. The master then sends a DBD with its link state database information. If the link state database is large, this exchange could take several packets. There can never be more than one unacknowledged DBD at a time.

When all DBDs are acknowledged, the routers move to the Loading State. In this state, the router requests link state information with *Link State Request* (LSR) packets. The other router responds with link state information in *Link State Update* (LSU) packets. Link state information elements are called *Link State Advertisements* (LSAs).

When all the LSAs have been received from both routers, the routers move to the Full State. In the Full State, routers have synchronized their link state information and have formed an adjacency.

Selecting a Path

OSPF routers use the Dijkstra routing algorithm to determine the shortest path to a destination. The SPF algorithm determines all possible paths to a destination and calculates the cost of each path. The paths are sorted in the link state database by cost. The path with the lowest cost is considered the "shortest" path. To determine the "shortest" path, more factors than the number of hops are considered. This "shortest" path is placed in the IP routing table and is used to make forwarding decisions.

Maintaining the Link State Database

When there is a change in the state of any link in the network topology, the routers that are directly connected to this link will form an LSA to describe the change. LSAs will also be sent to neighbors when the LSRefresh Timer has expired. This ensures that the link state information in each OSPF router link-state database remains fresh.

Configuring OSPF

Enabling IP routing using OSPF is a three-step process:

1. Enable IP Routing
2. Enable OSPF
3. Specify networks for which to perform routing

   Enabling IP routing is done using the following Cisco IOS command:

   ```
   Router(config)# ip routing
   ```

   Next, to enable OSPF, the following command is used:

   ```
   Router(config)# router ospf [process-id]
   ```

The process ID specifies an instance of the OSPF routing engine. You may run multiple instances of a routing protocol on the router; however, that topic is far beyond the scope of this book. Lastly, to specify the network addresses that OSPF will actively participate with other routers on the network, you must use the following command:

```
Router(config-router)# network network-address area area-id
```

The area-id must be the same for all routers in a network that want to exchange routing information. An example of a fully functional routing configuration for a router that routes for the 101.1.1.0 network would look as follows:

```
Router> enable
Router# configure terminal
Router(config)# ip routing
Router(config)# router ospf 101
Router(config-router)# network 101.1.1.0 area 0
Router(config-router)# end
```

Notice that the network address was entered as a classless address. The resulting configuration file would appear as follows:

```
Router# show running-config
. . .
ip routing
!
router ospf 101
   network 101.1.1.0 area 0
. . .
```

A useful, but optional, configuration option allows you to prevent OSPF from sending routing updates on a particular interface.

```
Router(config-router)# passive-interface interface-name
```

An example of disabling routing updates on the Ethernet 0 interface would appear as follows:

```
Router> enable
Router# configure terminal
Router(config)# router ospf 101
Router(config-router)# passive-interface Ethernet 0
Router(config-router)# end
```

The resulting configuration file using show interface would appear as follows:

```
Router# show running-config
. . .
ip routing
!
router ospf 101
   network 101.1.0.0 area 0
   passive-interface Ethernet 0
. . .
```

Once configured, you should confirm the routes that each router knows and has received. You may do this with the following Cisco IOS command:

```
Router# show ip route
```

This will break down the routing table into routes that it knows locally and those it has learned from other routers.

OSPF offers three commands to aid in troubleshooting.

- show ip ospf neighbors
- show ip ospf database
- show ip ospf interface

These three commands enable you to view the router states, and examine the database information as described earlier. For example output of these commands, refer to the case study at the end of this chapter.

Chapter Summary

This chapter describes three classless interior routing protocols that are used in a campus network where there is one administration domain. The classless routing protocols allow VLSM because subnet mask information is transmitted with route information.

The routing protocols covered in this chapter are as follows:

- *Routing Information Protocol Version 2* (RIPv2)
- *Enhanced Interior Gateway Routing Protocol* (EIGRP)
- *Open Shortest Path First* (OSPF)

RIPv2, a distance vector interior classless routing protocol, is an enhancement of RIPv1. Subnet information is transmitted with route information to implement VLSM. RIPv2 includes an authentication option to validate the routing updates from the network and thus, has more security than RIPv1. The routing updates are sent to a multicast address to reduce the amount of processing time in non-RIPv2 devices.

RIPv2 is simply RIPv1 with a few enhancements. The operation of RIPv2 is basically the same as RIPv1. The hop count limitations exist with both RIPv1 and RIPv2.

EIGRP is much more than IGRP with a few enhancements. It is a completely different protocol that allows VLSM and fast convergence. It used the *Diffusion Update Algorithm* (DUAL) as the routing algorithm. Technically, EIGRP is a distance vector routing protocol, but it has many of the characteristics of a link state routing protocol. It is often referred to as a hybrid routing protocol—a combination of distance vector and link state routing protocols. EIGRP has fast convergence times and the benefits of a classless routing protocol. Updates are only sent when necessary, not periodically as with RIP and IGRP.

EIGRP is a proprietary routing protocol designed by Cisco for Cisco routers. This routing protocol will not interoperate with products from vendors other than Cisco.

OSPF is a link state classless interior routing protocol. It is an open standard, thus the "open" in its name. Currently, it is the interior routing protocol recommended by the IETF. Updates are sent only when the router first comes online and when there is a change in the network topology. OSPF typically takes more computing resources on the router, but the bandwidth resulting from the distribution of routing information is minimal.

OSPF supports VLSM and has relatively quick convergence times because any changes in the network are immediately sent to neighboring routers to propagate throughout the network.

This chapter concludes the supplemental information on routing protocols. This material is not on the BCMSN exam, but is necessary in fully understanding the design and implementation of campus networks.

Frequently Asked Questions (FAQ)

Question: Which routing protocol is best?

Answer: This is the subject of many debates. There is no right answer; however, you will find a majority of large CANs and MANs running OSPF or IS-IS. IS-IS is another interior gateway protocol that stresses hierarchy, like OSPF.

Case Study

As we continue to work with *Cubby Products International* (CPI) campus network, recall that in Chapter 6 we had you enable the devices to allow communication between VLANs. In Chapter 6 we told you how to configure and use IGRP. Now that you are more familiar with the routing protocols, we want to examine this more closely.

Objective

Your objective is to first implement OSPF as the routing protocol and then implement EIGRP as the routing protocol for CPI's network.

The following are the devices for reference:

Switch Name	IP Address
IT-1-dist-5505	100.1.1.11
RD-1-dist-5505	100.1.1.16
Mfg-1-dist-5505	100.1.1.21
SR-1-dist-5505	100.1.1.26
Admin-1-dist-5505	100.1.1.31

Approach

The approach is straightforward. Knowing which protocol you need to implement, your tasks are to get it configured properly and verify operation. First, we'll implement OSPF and then move to EIGRP.

Configuring OSPF in 5505s   The following lists the commands to set up routing in the 5505s. Note that the 5505s are the only devices that perform routing.

Enabling routing is the same for each of the Catalyst 5505s.

```
IT-1-dist-5505(config)# ip routing
IT-1-dist-5505(config)# router ospf 101
IT-1-dist-5505(config-router)# network 100.0.0.0 area 0
```

With routing enabled, your Catalyst 5505 will now perform interVLAN routing. Repeat the commands for each Catalyst 5505.

Verifying OSPF Operation   To verify that routing is operational, you can verify the information that each device has in its routing table. When enabled on the first device as previously shown, using the show ip route command will result in output as follows:

```
IT-1-dist-5505# show ip route
Codes: C - connected, S - static, I - IGRP, R - RIP, M - mobile, B
       - BGP
       D - EIGRP, EX - EIGRP external, O - OSPF, IA - OSPF inter area
       N1 - OSPF NSSA external type 1, N2 - OSPF NSSA external type 2
       E1 - OSPF external type 1, E2 - OSPF external type 2, E - EGP
       i - IS-IS, L1 - IS-IS level-1, L2 - IS-IS level-2
* - candidate default
       U - per-user static route, o - ODR
P - periodic downloaded static route
       T - traffic engineered route

Gateway of last resort is not set

     100.1.0.0/16 is contains 2 subnets
C       100.1.6.0/24 is directly connected, Vlan5
C       100.1.1.0/24 is directly connected, Vlan0
```

As more devices are added, the routing table will grow, and will look similar to the following:

```
IT-1-dist-5505# show ip route
Codes: C - connected, S - static, I - IGRP, R - RIP, M - mobile, B
       - BGP
       D - EIGRP, EX - EIGRP external, O - OSPF, IA - OSPF inter area
       N1 - OSPF NSSA external type 1, N2 - OSPF NSSA external type 2
       E1 - OSPF external type 1, E2 - OSPF external type 2, E - EGP
       i - IS-IS, L1 - IS-IS level-1, L2 - IS-IS level-2
* - candidate default
       U - per-user static route, o - ODR
P - periodic downloaded static route
       T - traffic engineered route

Gateway of last resort is not set

     100.1.0.0/16 is contains 6 subnets
C       100.1.6.0/24 is directly connected, Vlan5
```

```
C        100.1.1.0/24 is directly connected, Vlan0
O        100.1.2.0/24 via 100.1.1.16, Vlan1
O        100.1.3.0/24 via 100.1.1.21, Vlan2
O        100.1.4.0/24 via 100.1.1.26, Vlan3
O        100.1.5.0/24 via 100.1.1.31, Vlan4
```

Note that the routes from the other routers show up with an O to the left. This signifies that they were learned from OSPF updates. Furthermore, the IP address of the router from which the route was heard is given.

Furthermore, we can verify the state of OSPF on the other routers:

```
IT-1-dist-5505# show ip ospf neighbors
Neighbor ID   Pri    State       Dead Time   Address       Interface
100.1.6.254   1    2WAY/DROTHER  00:00:36    100.1.1.11    Vlan0
100.1.2.254   1    2WAY/DROTHER  00:00:36    100.1.1.16    Vlan0
100.1.3.254   1    2WAY/DROTHER  00:00:32    100.1.1.21    Vlan0
100.1.4.254   1    FULL/BDR      00:00:35    100.1.1.26    Vlan0
100.1.5.254   1    FULL/DR       00:00:35    100.1.1.31    Vlan0
```

In addition to the list of neighbors, the status shows us which router is the DR and which is the BDR.

In addition, we can view the OSPF route database:

```
IT-1-dist-5505# show ip ospf database
OSPF Router with ID (100.1.6.254) (Process ID 100)
                Router Link States (Area 0)
Link ID       ADV Router     Age    Seq#           Checksum Link cnt
100.1.1.11    100.1.1.11     1353   0x80001A0A 0xE1F8        8
100.1.1.16    100.1.1.16     1461   0x80000141 0x229F        1
100.1.1.21    100.1.1.21     549    0x8000021C 0x91F0        15
100.1.1.26    100.1.1.26     789    0x80001101 0xD013        1
100.1.1.31    100.1.1.31     1868   0x80000526 0xAE17        1
```

Here you see the links, and how long the link has been active. Because routing protocols are very dynamic, it is very important to understand how they function. The OSPF database and neighbor status are critical in understanding OSPF.

Lastly, you can view the OSPF status on a per-interface basis.

```
IT-1-dist-5505# show ip ospf interface Vlan0
Vlan0 is up, line protocol is up
  Internet Address 100.1.1.11/24, Area 0
  Process ID 100, Router ID 100.1.6.254, Network Type BROADCAST,
  Cost: 1
  Transmit Delay is 1 sec, State DROTHER, Priority 1
  Designated Router (ID) 100.1.5.254, Interface address 100.1.1.11
  Backup Designated router (ID) 100.1.4.254, Interface address
  100.1.1.11
```

```
      Timer intervals configured, Hello 10, Dead 40, Wait 40,
      Retransmit 5
        Hello due in 00:00:04
      Index 1/1, flood queue length 0
      Next 0x0(0)/0x0(0)
      Last flood scan length is 0, maximum is 16
      Last flood scan time is 0 msec, maximum is 4 msec
      Neighbor Count is 4, Adjacent neighbor count is 4
        Adjacent with neighbor 100.1.4.254  (Backup Designated Router)
        Adjacent with neighbor 100.1.5.254  (Designated Router)
        Adjacent with neighbor 100.1.3.254  (Designated Router)
        Adjacent with neighbor 100.1.2.254  (Designated Router)
  Suppress hello for 0 neighbor(s)
```

Here you are able to view exactly how OSPF is interacting with this interface. This includes all timers and neighbors adjacent to this interface.

Configuring EIGRP in 5505s   The commands to set up routing in the 5505s are listed. Note that the 5505s are the only devices that perform routing.

Enabling routing is the same for each of the Catalyst 5505s.

```
IT-1-dist-5505(config)# ip routing
IT-1-dist-5505(config)# router eigrp 10
IT-1-dist-5505(config-router)# network 100.0.0.0
```

With routing enabled, your Catalyst 5505 will now perform interVLAN routing. Repeat the commands for each Catalyst 5505.

Verifying EIGRP Operation   To verify that routing is operational, you can verify the information that each device has in its routing table. When enabled on the first device as previously shown, using the show ip route command will result in output as follows:

```
IT-1-dist-5505# show ip route
Codes: C - connected, S - static, I - IGRP, R - RIP, M - mobile, B
       - BGP
       D - EIGRP, EX - EIGRP external, O - OSPF, IA - OSPF inter area
       N1 - OSPF NSSA external type 1, N2 - OSPF NSSA external type 2
       E1 - OSPF external type 1, E2 - OSPF external type 2, E - EGP
       i - IS-IS, L1 - IS-IS level-1, L2 - IS-IS level-2
* - candidate default
       U - per-user static route, o - ODR
P - periodic downloaded static route
       T - traffic engineered route
```

```
Gateway of last resort is not set

        100.1.0.0/16 is contains 2 subnets
C       100.1.6.0/24 is directly connected, Vlan5
C       100.1.1.0/24 is directly connected, Vlan0
```

As more devices are added, the routing table will grow and will look similar to the following:

```
IT-1-dist-5505# show ip route
Codes: C - connected, S - static, I - IGRP, R - RIP, M - mobile, B
       - BGP
       D - EIGRP, EX - EIGRP external, O - OSPF, IA - OSPF inter area
       N1 - OSPF NSSA external type 1, N2 - OSPF NSSA external type 2
       E1 - OSPF external type 1, E2 - OSPF external type 2, E - EGP
       i - IS-IS, L1 - IS-IS level-1, L2 - IS-IS level-2
* - candidate default
       U - per-user static route, o - ODR
P - periodic downloaded static route
       T - traffic engineered route

Gateway of last resort is not set

        100.1.0.0/16 is contains 6 subnets
C       100.1.6.0/24 is directly connected, Vlan5
C       100.1.1.0/24 is directly connected, Vlan0
D       100.1.2.0/24 via 100.1.1.16, Vlan1
D       100.1.3.0/24 via 100.1.1.21, Vlan2
D       100.1.4.0/24 via 100.1.1.26, Vlan3
D       100.1.5.0/24 via 100.1.1.31, Vlan4
```

Note that the routes from the other routers show up with a D to the left. This indicates that they were learned from EIGRP updates. Furthermore, it indicates the IP address of the router from which the route was given.

Case Study Summary

The objective of this case study was to implement routing using two different protocols: OSPF and EIGRP. To achieve the objective, we used the appropriate commands for each protocol to enable and configure the protocol. Next, we verified routing operation using the show ip route command. In addition, we used some additional commands to augment our understanding of OSPF.

As a reminder, IP routing is not covered on the BCMSN exam.

Questions

1. Interior routing protocols are designed for routing
   a. between the CAN and Internet Service Provider
   b. within the CAN
   c. in the WAN
   d. Ethernet

2. Exterior routing protocols are designed for routing
   a. between the CAN and the Internet Service Provider
   b. within the CAN
   c. in the WAN
   d. Ethernet

3. Classful routing protocols include:
   a. RIP
   b. IGRP
   c. EIGRP
   d. Both a and b

4. Classless routing protocols include:
   a. RIPv2
   b. OSPF
   c. EIGRP
   d. All of the above

5. RIPv2 is a _____ _____ routing protocol.
   a. link state
   b. distance vector
   c. static processing
   d. exterior gateway

6. RIPv2 uses _____ to advertise routing updates.
   a. UDP
   b. multicast
   c. TCP
   d. RTP

7. RIPv2 can send a maximum of _____ IP routes in an update packet.

   a. 25
   b. 30
   c. 64
   d. 512

8. RIPv2 response messages are sent every _____ seconds by default.

   a. 5
   b. 10
   c. 30
   d. 120

9. Passive interfaces:

   a. Do not participate in route processing.
   b. Receive updates but do not send updates.
   c. Send updates but do not receive updates
   d. Are non-aggressive

10. The maximum number of hops that can exist in a RIPv2 network is _____.

    a. 7
    b. 15
    c. 31
    d. 42

11. The maximum number of hops that can exist in an EIGRP network is _____.

    a. 15
    b. 63
    c. 127
    d. 255

12. EIGRP

    a. is Cisco proprietary
    b. supports load balancing over multiple paths
    c. uses MD5 for authentication
    d. all the above

13. EIGRP default update interval is _____ seconds.

    a. 5
    b. 15
    c. 30
    d. 90

14. The default EIGRP metric is calculated using _____ and _____.

    a. hop count, AS number

    b. Bellman-Ford, hop count

    c. IP address, link speed

    d. bandwidth, delay

15. OSPF stands for:

    a. Open Standard Protocol Family

    b. Open Shortest Path First

    c. Open Shortest Protocol Family

    d. Original Stable Protocol Family

16. OSPF is a _____ _____ protocol.

    a. link state

    b. delayed update

    c. reverse path

    d. Bellman-Ford

17. Instead of a hop count, OSPF uses a _____ _____.

    a. path count

    b. metric count

    c. cost metric

    d. router count

18. The OSPF Hello packet aids in the establishment of _____.

    a. friendship

    b. routes

    c. links

    d. adjacencies

19. OSPF neighbors must have:

    a. Identical Area IDs

    b. Identical Hello and Dead intervals

    c. Identical passwords

    d. All the above

20. The Designated Router is the router with the largest _____ _____.

    a. Hello Timer

    b. Router ID

    c. Area ID

    d. Router Priority

Answers

1. Interior routing protocols are designed for routing

   b. within the CAN

   Which is usually administered by a single entity.

2. Exterior routing protocols are designed for routing

   a. between the CAN and Internet Service Provider

   Which involves connection between two different administrative entities.

3. Classful routing protocols include:

   d. Both a and b

   Subnet/netmask information is not included in routing updates.

4. Classless routing protocols include:

   d. All of the above

   All include netmask information in the routing updates.

5. RIPv2 is a _____ _____ routing protocol.

   b. distance vector

6. RIPv2 uses _____ to advertise routing updates.

   b. multicast

7. RIPv2 can send a maximum of _____ IP routes in an update packet.

   a. 25

8. RIPv2 response messages are sent every ____ seconds by default.

   c. 30

9. Passive interfaces:

   b. Receive updates but do not send updates

   Passive means do not send routing updates on that interface, but it will still listen to updates/routing information.

10. The maximum number of hops that can exist in a RIPv2 network is ____.

    b. 15

11. The maximum number of hops that can exist in an EIGRP network is ____.

    d. 255

12. EIGRP

    d. all the above

    IGRP was developed by Cisco and supports load balancing. It also uses a MD5 checksum for authentication of neighboring routers.

13. EIGRP default update interval is ___ seconds.

    b. 15

14. The default EIGRP metric is calculated using _____ and _____.

    d. bandwidth, delay

    The EIGRP metric is based on bandwidth and delay by default. Reliability, load and MTU can be configured manually.

15. OSPF stands for:

    b. Open Shortest Path First

16. OSPF is a _____ _____ protocol.

    a. link state

    Routing updates are triggered by link state changes.

17. Instead of a hop count, OSPF uses a _____ _____.

    c. cost metric

    This gives far more flexibility in route administration and aids the routing protocol in making better routing decisions when multiple paths exist.

18. The OSPF Hello packet aids in the establishment of _____.

    d. adjacencies

19. OSPF neighbors must have:

    d. All the above

    All the parameters of the Hello packet must match with the receiving router to become established as a neighbor.

20. The Designated Router is the router with the largest

    b. Router ID

    Cisco routers typically use the highest IP address of all the interfaces on the router as the router ID.

APPENDIX A

Glossary

Many of the following terms are taken, with permission, from *Thomas' Concise Networking & Telecom Dictionary*.

10Base2 10-Mbps, baseband Ethernet deployed in 185-meter segments. The IEEE 802.3 substandard for ThinWire and coaxial

10Base-2A A 10-Mbit/s baseband network using thin Ethernet coaxial cable

10Base5 The original IEEE 802.3 cabling standard for Ethernet that uses coaxial cables (type RG-8). The name derives from the fact that the maximum data transfer speed is 10 Mbps, it uses baseband transmission, and the maximum length of cables is 500 meters (1,640 feet) long and a maximum of 100 MAUs. The maximum end-to-end propagation delay for a coaxial segment is 2165 ns (nanoseconds). Maximum attenuation for the segment shall not exceed 8.5 dB (17 dB/km) for each 500m segment. 10Base5 is also known as thick Ethernet, ThickWire, or ThickNet.

10Base-5A A 10-Mbit/s baseband network using thick Ethernet coaxial cable

10BaseF 10 Mbps, baseband, over fiber optic cabling. The IEEE 802.3 substandard for fiber optic Ethernet that refers to the 10BaseFB, 10BaseFL, and 10BaseFP standards for Ethernet over fiber optic cabling

10Base-FB Part of the IEEE 10Base-F specification providing a synchronous signaling backbone that enables additional segments and repeaters to be connected to the network

10Base-FL IEEE 10Base-Fiber specification designed to replace the *Fiber-Optic Inter-Repeater Link* (FOIRL) standard providing Ethernet over fiber optic cabling. Interoperability is provided between the old and new standards. 10BaseFL is a part of the IEEE 10BaseF specification and, although able to interoperate with FOIRL, it is designed to replace the FOIRL specification. 10BaseFL segments can be up to 3,280 feet (1,000 meters) long if used with FOIRL, and up to 1.24 miles (2,000 meters) if 10BaseFL is used exclusively in the deployment.

10Base-FP   Part of the IEEE 10Base-F specification that enables the organization of a number of end nodes into a star topology without the use of repeaters. *See* 10Base-FB, 10Base-FL, and 10Base-FP.

10Base-FT   The IEEE specification for baseband Ethernet over fiber optic cabling. *See* 10Base-FB, 10Base-FL, and 10Base-FP.

10Base-Fx   An Ethernet technology with a transmission rate of 10 Mbps carried over multimode fiber optic cable

10Base-T   An IEEE 802.3 physical layer specification enabling telephone UTP cable to be used for 10-Mbps Ethernet over two pairs of *unshielded twisted pair* wiring (UTP). One of several adaptations of the Ethernet (IEEE 802.3) standard for *Local Area Networks* (LANs). The purpose of the 10Base-T standard is to provide a simple, inexpensive, and flexible means of attaching devices to the ubiquitous twisted-pair cable. 10Base-T is a multisegment 10-Mbps baseband network operating as a single collision domain.

100Base-F   A standard for fiber optic cabling used with Fast Ethernet, often used to mean Fast Ethernet with fiber optic cabling

100Base-FX   This system is designed to enable fiber optic segments of up to 412 meters in length. The 100Base-FX specification requires one pair of *multimode fiber* (MMF) cable per link. The typical fiber optic cable used for a fiber link segment is a graded index MMF cable with a 62.5 micron core and 125 micron cladding. The wavelength specified is 1,350 nanometers with an 11-dB loss budget per link.

100Base-T   An IEEE 802.3 physical layer specification for 100-Mbps Ethernet over different grades of *unshielded twisted-pair* wiring (UTP). Fast Ethernet offers a natural migration from traditional 10-Mbps Ethernet because it uses the same CSMA/CD access mechanism. Officially, the 100BASE-T standard is IEEE 802.3u.

100Base-TX   An IEEE 802.3 specification for Fast Ethernet over two pairs of Category 5 *unshielded twisted-pair* (UTP) or Type 1 shielded twisted-pair (STP) wire. The first pair of wires is used to receive data; the second pair is used to transmit data. The maximum distance for a segment is 100 meters. Two 100-meter transmission segments can be connected together through a single Class I or Class II repeater, thereby providing up to 200 meters between DTE devices.

100Base-VG   A joint AT&T and Hewlett-Packard proposal for a 100Mbps, four-pair, category 3 Ethernet. It is being standardized by the IEEE 802.12 working group.

100Base-X   A Grand Junction Networks' proposal for 100-Mbps Ethernet using two pairs of category 5 wire and CSMA/CD. It is being standardized by the IEEE 802.13 working group.

100VG-AnyLAN   A new 100-Mbps LAN technology originally developed by Hewlett-Packard and currently refined and described in the IEEE 802.12 standard. 100VG-AnyLAN departs from traditional Ethernet in that it uses a centrally controlled demand priority access protocol instead of CSMA/CD. It builds on the positive aspects of both Token Ring and Ethernet to run at 100 Mbits/s with resilience and a high realization of potential. Generally considered better technically than the alternative Fast Ethernet, 100VG-AnyLAN has been less than successful in the marketplace.

1000Base-Lx   An Ethernet technology with a transmission rate of 1,000 Mbps carried over a single-mode fiber optic cable

1000Base-Sx   An Ethernet technology with a transmission rate of 1,000 Mbps carried over a multimode fiber optic cable

802.1d   An IEEE standard for Spanning Tree

802.1Q   The IEEE encapsulation standard, which calls for adding four bytes to a packet to tag it for virtual LAN purposes. *See* VLANs and tagging.

802.x   The set of IEEE standards for the definition of LAN protocols

access layer   The outside layer of a hierarchical campus network topology. This layer is responsible for providing hosts access to the network.

active router   The router in a *Hot Standby Router Protocol* (HSRP) virtual router group that is responsible for all the routing responsibilities of the virtual router.

adapter   (a) Short for expansion board. (b) The circuitry required to support a particular device. For example, video adapters enable the computer to support graphics monitors, and network adapters enable a computer to attach to a network. Adapters can be built into the main circuitry of a computer or they can be separate add-ons that come in the form of expansion boards. *See* MAC address.

adapter address   Twelve hexadecimal digits that identify a LAN adapter

adapter card   A hardware card that provides the interface between the computer (DTE) and the physical network circuit. *See* NIC.

address   A designation referencing a particular location. This could refer to memory, the adapter card identification, the data structure location in storage, and other such points referenced.

address class   The original Internet IP routing scheme was developed in the 1970s, and sites and hosts were assigned IP addresses from one of the following three classes: Class A, Class B, and Class C. The address classes differ in both their size and number of networks/hosts allowed within each. Class A addresses are the largest, but there are just a few of them. Class B's are medium in size. Class C's are the smallest, but they are numerous. Classes D and E are also defined, but not used in normal operations. The official description of IP addresses is found in RFC 1166, "Internet Numbers." To receive an assigned network number, contact your Internet Service Provider. *See* IP addressing and RFC 1166.

address mask   A bit combination used to describe which portion of an address refers to the network or subnet and which part refers to the host. Sometimes referred to simply as the mask. Each class of IP address has a default mask. *See* subnet mask, address class, and IP addressing.

Address Resolution Protocol (ARP)   The TCP/IP protocol used to dynamically bind a high-level IP address to low-level physical (MAC) hardware addresses. ARP works across single physical networks and is limited to networks that support hardware broadcasts. *See* RARP and Inverse ARP.

address space   Addresses used to uniquely identify network-accessible units, sessions, adjacent link stations, and links in a node for each network in which the node participates. This is the set of all legal addresses in memory for a given application. The address space represents the amount of memory available to a program. Interestingly, the address space can be larger than physical memory through a technique called virtual memory.

addressing   In data communication, the way in which a station identifies the station to which it is supposed to send data. *See* address class and IP addressing.

adjacency   A relationship formed between neighboring OSPF routers for the purpose of exchanging link state information. *See* OSPF, ABR, and DR.

adjacent   In an internetwork, devices, nodes, or domains that are directly connected by a physical connection. *See* adjacencies.

Advanced Research Projects Agency (ARPA)   The U.S. government entity focused upon what would become known as the Internet.

Advanced Research Projects Agency Network (ARPANET)   A large *Wide Area Network* (WAN) created by the U.S. Defense Advanced Research Project Agency and the precursor to the Internet, established in 1969

algorithm   A clearly-defined mathematical formula used to solve a problem or run an operation

alignment error   In IEEE 802.3 networks, an error usually caused by frame damage due to collisions that occur when the total number of bits of a received frame is not divisible by eight

alphanumeric   Describes the combined set of all letters in the alphabet and the numbers 0 through 9

American National Standards Institute (ANSI)   A voluntary organization that creates standards in programming languages, electrical specifications, communications protocols, and many other issues affecting the computer industry

American Standard Code for Information Interchange   *See* ASCII.

ANSI   *See* American National Standards Institute.

AppleTalk   An ancient (though still active) communication media created by Apple Computer. *See also* Token Ring.

application   A program or group of programs designed for end users. Software can be divided into two general classes: systems software and applications software

application layer   The highest layer of the OSI Reference Model. This layer is responsible for connecting the network to applications. Some examples of application-layer protocols are the *File Transfer Protocol* (FTP) and Telnet.

architecture   A design that can refer to either hardware or software.

ARP   *See* Address Resolution Protocol.

ARP table   A list of known IP and MAC address pairs maintained by a host or router

ARPA   *See* Advanced Research Projects Agency.

ARPANET   *See* Advanced Research Projects Agency Network.

AS   *See* autonomous system.

Asynchronous Transfer Mode (ATM)   A switching technology that organizes data into 53-byte cells and transmits them over a physical medium. Each cell is processed asynchronously relative to other related cells and is queued before being multiplexed over the transmission path.

ATM   *See* Asynchronous Transfer Mode.

attachment unit interface (AUI)   The portion of the Ethernet standard that specifies how a cable is to be connected to an Ethernet card. AUI specifies a coaxial cable connected to a transceiver that plugs into a 15-pin socket on the *network interface card* (NIC).

authentication   A process of establishing identity. *See* authorization.

Authentication, Authorization, and Accounting (AAA)   A security method that enables you to implement three unique aspects of security (authentication, authorization, and accounting) into a cohesive whole. AAA uses protocols such as RADIUS, TACACS+, and Kerberos to administer and control its security functions.

authorization   The process of granting or denying a user access to a network resource. To gain authorization, authentication must first be verified. *See* authentication.

autonomous system (AS)   An internetwork that is part of the Internet and has a single routing policy. Each AS is assigned an AS number.

backbone   In a multisegment LAN configuration, a centrally located LAN segment to which other LAN segments are connected by means of bridges or routers

BackboneFast   A Cisco proprietary update to the Spanning Tree protocol that enables a bridge to more quickly find an alternate path to a root bridge in the event of a link failure

backoff   A retransmission delay randomly determined and enforced by contentious MAC protocols after a network node with data to transmit determines that the physical medium is already in use, typically through the detection of a collision

backplane   (a) A circuit board containing sockets into which other circuit boards can be plugged in. In PCs, the backplane is the circuit board that contains sockets for expansion cards. Backplanes can be classified as active or passive. Active backplanes contain a logical circuitry that performs computing functions in addition to the sockets. Passive backplanes contain almost no computing circuitry. (b) The physical connection between an interface processor or card and the data buses and power distribution buses inside a chassis.

bandwidth (BW)   The transmission capacity of a communications medium. It is the amount of data that can be transmitted in a fixed amount of time. Bandwidth is usually expressed in bits per second or bytes per second for digital devices. For analog devices, bandwidth is expressed in cycles per second or *Hertz* (Hz). A subtle difference should be noted with the definition of bandwidth: the number of bits a communications line can transmit may not be the total bandwidth for data because some bits may be used for control signals. This leaves a lesser amount as real bandwidth for the user. For example, an OC3 SONET line in ATM, which is rated at 155 Mbits, really only has 149.76 of real data bits available to the user.

Bellman-Ford Routing Algorithm   *See* Distance-Vector Routing Algorithm.

BGP   *See* border gateway protocol.

binary numbers   A number system that has just two unique digits, 1 and 0. Computers are based on the binary numbering system. All mathematical operations that are possible in the decimal numbering system (addition, subtraction, multiplication, and division) are equally possible in the binary system. The decimal system is used in everyday life because it seems more natural (we have 10 fingers). For the computer, the binary system is more natural because of its electrical nature (charged versus uncharged).

bit   An abbreviation for binary digit which is digital representation of the smallest possible unit of information. It can be in one of two states: off or on, 0 or 1. The meaning of the bit, which can represent almost anything, is unimportant at this point. The thing to remember is that all computer data (a text file on disk, a program in memory, or a packet on a network) is ultimately a collection of bits.

bit rate   The number of bits of data transmitted over a communications line each second

bits/s   *See* bits per second.

bits per second (Bps)   A measurement of how fast data is moved from one place to another. A 28.8-K modem can move 28,800 bits per second. *See* bandwidth and bit.

BNC connector   British Naval Connector or Bayonet Nut Connector or Bayonet Neil Consulman. A bayonet-locking connector for slim coaxial cables which is a type of connector used with the 10Base2 Ethernet coaxial cables, such as the RG-58 A/U cable

Border Gateway Protocol (BGP)   A protocol for exchanging routing information between gateway routers in a network of autonomous systems. BGP is often the protocol used between gateway routers on the Internet

BPDU   *See* bridge protocol data unit.

Bps   *See* bits per second.

branch   In tree structures, a single section of the tree that ends with a leaf

bridge   (a) An interface connecting two similar or dissimilar LAN media types. (b) A device that connects two LANs. It performs its functions at the *data link control* (DLC) layer.

bridge forwarding   A process that uses entries in a filtering database to determine whether frames with a given MAC destination address can be forwarded to a given port or ports. Described in the IEEE 802.1 standard. *See* IEEE 802.1.

bridge protocol data unit (BPDU)   A Spanning Tree protocol hello packet that is sent out at regular intervals to exchange information among switches/bridges in the network. *See* spanning tree, PDU, and bridging.

bridging   A method of path selection (contrast routing). In a bridged network, no correspondence is required between addresses and paths. Put another way, addresses don't imply anything about where hosts are physically attached to the network. Any address can thus appear at any location. In contrast, routing requires a more thoughtful address assignment, corresponding to physical placement. Bridging relies heavily on broadcasting. Because a packet may contain no information other than the destination address, and that implies nothing about the path that should be used, the only option may be to send the packet everywhere. This is one of bridging's most severe limitations, because this is a very inefficient method of data delivery and can trigger broadcast storms. In networks with low-speed links, this can introduce crippling overhead. *See* translational and transparent bridging.

broadcast   The simultaneous transmission of data to more than one destination. A source sends one copy of a message to all the nodes on the network even if any node does not want to receive such messages. *See* anycast, unicast, multicast, and IP multicasting.

broadcast address   Generally, a MAC destination address of all ones. It is reserved for sending to all stations on an internetwork. Compare this with multicast addresses and unicast addresses.

broadcast domain   The part of a network that receives the same broadcasts

broadcast storm   A condition where a significant amount of available network bandwidth is used for broadcast traffic

broadcast transmission   *See* broadcast.

Building Cisco Multilayer Switching Networks (BCMSN)   (a) The title of this book. (b) One of the three exams necessary to acquire CCNP certification.

bus   (a) A network configuration in which nodes are interconnected through a bidirectional transmission medium. (b) A collection of wires through which data is transmitted from one part of a computer to another. This is a sort of highway that data travels on within a computer.

bus network   A network in which all nodes are connected to a single wire (the bus) that has two end points. Ethernet 10Base-2 and 10Base-5 networks, for example, are bus networks.

bus topology   One of the three principal topologies used in LANs. All devices are connected to a central cable, called the bus or backbone. Bus networks are relatively inexpensive and easy to install. Ethernet systems use a bus topology. *See* ring topology and star topology.

BW   *See* bandwidth.

byte   A set of eight bits that represents a single character. *See* bit.

cable   A physical transmission medium that consists of copper wire or optical fiber wrapped in a protective cover

cache   A high-speed storage buffer. It can be either a reserved section of main memory or an independent high-speed storage device. The two types of caching commonly used in personal computers are memory caching and disk caching.

CAM   *See* content-addressable memory.

campus   A networking environment in which users of voice, video, and data transmissions are spread out over a broad geographic area as in a university, hospital, or medical center. Several LANs may exist on a campus. They will be connected with bridges and/or routers communicating over telephone or fiber optic cable.

campus backbone   A link between buildings that contains the cabling and resources for a *Campus Area Network* (CAN)

CAN   Campus Area Network. *See* campus.

cards   Adapter cards or *network interface cards* (NICs) are circuit boards installed in a device's chassis slots to provide network communication capabilities to and from other devices.

carrier   In data communication, a continuous frequency capable of being modulated

carrier sense   A device (transceiver, interface board, or other entity) capable of detecting a constant frequency. The channel access method used by the Ethernet and ISO 8802-3 LANs

carrier-sense multiple access with collision detection (CSMA/CD) A protocol that utilizes equipment capable of detecting a carrier that permits multiple access to a common medium. This protocol also has the capability to detect a collision because this type of technology is broadcast-oriented. *See* Ethernet.

Category1 cabling The cabling is most commonly used for telephone communication systems. It is typically not suitable for transmitting data. It is one of five grades of *unshielded twisted-pair* (UTP) cabling, as described in the EIA/TIA-586 standard. Compare this with Category2 cabling, Category3 cabling, Category4 cabling, and Category5 cabling. *See* UTP.

Category2 cabling One of five grades of *unshielded twisted-pair* (UTP) cabling described in the EIA/TIA-586 standard. Category2 cabling is capable of transmitting data at speeds of up to four Mbps. Compare this with Category1 cabling, Category3 cabling, Category4 cabling, and Category5 cabling. *See* EIA/TIA-586 and UTP.

Category3 cabling One of five grades of *unshielded twisted-pair* (UTP) cabling described in the EIA/TIA-586 standard. Category3 cabling is used in 10BaseT or low-speed ATM networks capable of transmitting data at speeds of up to 10 Mbps. Compare this with Category1 cabling, Category2 cabling, Category4 cabling, and Category5 cabling. *See* UTP.

Category4 cabling One of five grades of UTP cabling described in the EIA/TIA-586 standard. Category4 cabling is used in Token Ring networks and is capable of transmitting data at speeds of up to 16 Mbps. Compare this with Category1 cabling, Category2 cabling, Category3 cabling, and Category5 cabling. *See* UTP.

Category5 cabling One of five grades of *unshielded twisted-pair* (UTP) cabling described in the EIA/TIA-586 standard. Category5 cabling is used for running *copper distributed-data interfaces* (CDDIs) and can transmit data at speeds of up to 100 Mbps. Compare this with Category1 cabling, Category2 cabling, Category3 cabling, and Category4 cabling. It is a type of UTP commonly used with *Asynchronous Transfer Mode* (ATM) interfaces for higher speed cell transmissions (more than 50 Mbps). *See* UTP.

CBT *See* core-based trees.

CCIE *See* Cisco Certified Internetworking Engineer.

CCNP *See* Cisco Certified Networking Professional.

CGMP *See* Cisco Group Management Protocol.

chassis A metal frame that serves as the structural support for electronic components. Every computer system requires at least one chassis to house the circuit boards and wiring.

checksum   A numeric value used to verify the integrity of a block of data. The value is computed using a checksum procedure. A crypto checksum incorporates secret information in the checksum procedure so that it can't be reproduced by third parties that don't know the secret information.

Cisco Certified Internetworking Engineer (CCIE)   A difficult, mind-numbing, hands-on network certification test conducted by Cisco Systems

Cisco Certified Networking Professional (CCNP)   The second-level certification available from Cisco Systems. It involves passing three exams, one being the BCMSN.

Cisco Group Management Protocol (CGMP)   A protocol developed by Cisco that provides a mechanism for routers to forward multicast group information to switches to limit unnecessary multicast traffic in the broadcast domain.

Cisco Visual Switch Manager (CVSM)   Cisco's Web-based switch management software

CiscoWorks for Switched Internetworks (CWSI)   A network management system application for managing Cisco network devices

class A IP address   A type of unicast IP address that segments the address space into many network addresses and few host addresses

class B IP address   A type of unicast IP address that segments the address space into a medium number of network and host addresses

class C IP address   A type of unicast IP address that segments the address space into many host addresses and few network addresses

class D IP address   This specifies multicast host groups in IPv4-based networks

Classful Routing Protocol   A routing protocol that does not transmit the subnet mask information with the routing entries. This class of routing protocol only recognizes the IP address class categorizations.

Classless Routing Protocol   A routing protocol that transmits subnet mask information with the route entries. This class of routing protocol is not dependent on IP address class categorization.

collapsed core   A core layer topology where the core layer is simply connections between distribution-layer switches

collision   An event where two or more devices simultaneously perform a broadcast on the same medium. This term is used in Ethernet networks and also in networks where broadcast technology is implemented. *See* collision domain.

collision detection   The process of detecting simultaneous transmissions (collisions) on a shared medium. Typically, each transmitting workstation that detects a collision will wait some period of time and try again. Collision detection is an essential part of the *Carrier-Sense Multiple Access with Collision Detection* (CSMA/CD) access method. Workstations detect collisions if, after sending data, they fail to receive an acknowledgment from the receiving station.

collision domain   In Ethernet, the network area where frames that have collided are propagated. Repeaters and hubs propagate collisions; LAN switches, bridges, and routers do not.

command line   The line on the display screen where a command is entered

command-line interface (CLI)   The text-based interface common to all IOS-based (Cisco) routers. This text-based interface is being copied as the command interface on network devices besides those sold by Cisco.

Common Spanning Tree (CST)   An IEEE specification that defines that there is one instance of Spanning Tree for all VLANs implemented throughout a layer-2 switch network

conductors   A piece of wire. For 10BaseT purposes, it is solid, copper wire, not stranded.

connection   In data communications, two types of connections exist: physical and logical. A physical connection consists of a tangible path between two or more points. A logical connection has the capability to communicate between two or more end points.

connectionless   A type of network protocol that enables a host to send a message without establishing a connection with the recipient. That is, the host simply puts the message onto the network with the destination address and hopes that it arrives. Examples of connectionless protocols include Ethernet, IPX, and UDP.

connection-oriented   A communications service where an initial connection between the end points (source and destination) has to be set up. Examples are ATM and Frame Relay. *See* virtual circuit.

console port   A port on a network device that provides administrative control. Typically, the port is an RS-232 serial port, but other connection types such as Ethernet can be used for the console port.

Content Addressable Memory (CAM)   A bridge table in a layer-2 switch

convergence   The result of a network finding its structure. For example, a Spanning Tree network must instruct the Spanning Tree to define paths through the network. The conclusion of this distributed calculation is known as convergence. Routing protocols also have the notion of convergence.

core-based trees (CBT)   A shared tree multicast routing protocol. This protocol is not implemented by Cisco.

core block   A group of core-layer switches. Except for the most complex networks, only one core block exists in a campus network.

core layer   The center of a hierarchical campus network topology. This layer is responsible for switching packets between switch blocks.

CPU   *See* central processing unit.

CRC   *See* cyclic redundancy check.

crossover cable   A twisted-pair Ethernet cable with pinouts as follows: pin 1-pin 3, pin 2-pin 6, pin 3-pin 1, pin 6-pin 2

CSMA/CA   *See* Carrier-Sense Multiple Access with Collision Avoidance.

CSMA/CD   *See* Carrier-Sense Multiple Access with Collision Detection.

CST   *See* Common Spanning Tree.

CVSM   *See* Cisco Visual Switch Manager.

CWSI   *See* CiscoWorks for Switched Internetworks.

cyclic redundancy check (CRC)   A common technique for detecting data transmission errors. A number of file transfer protocols, including Zmodem, use CRC in addition to checksum. It is a bit-errors detection technique that employs a mathematical algorithm, where, based on the transmitted bits, it calculates a value attached to the information bits in the same packet. The receiver, using the same algorithm, recalculates that value and compares it to the one received. If the two values do not agree, the transmitted packet is then considered to be in error.

DARPA   Obsolete term referring to the Internet. *See also* Internet and Defense Advanced Research Projects Agency.

data   (a) Distinct pieces of information usually formatted in a special way. All software is divided into two general categories: data and programs. Programs are collections of instructions for manipulating data. (b) A term often used to distinguish binary machine-readable information from textual human-readable information. (c) In database management systems, data files store the database information, whereas other files, such as index files and data dictionaries, store administrative information, known as metadata.

data communication   The transmission and reception of data

data compression   Storing data in a format that requires less space than usual. Compressing data is the same as packing data. Data compression is particularly useful in communications because it enables devices to transmit the same amount of data in fewer bits. A variety of data compression techniques exist, but only a few have been standardized. The CCITT has defined a standard data compression technique for transmitting faxes (Group 3 standard) and a compression standard for data communications through modems (CCITT V.42bis). In addition, file compression formats can be used, such as ARC and ZIP.

datagram   In IP networks, a packet of data in which a data message is randomly broken into parts that are correctly reassembled by the receiving machine. Each message part contains information about itself, including its destination and source.

data link control (DLC)   (a) A set of rules used by nodes at layer 2 within a network. The data link is governed by data link protocols such as Ethernet, FDDI, and Token Ring. (b) The physical means of connecting one location to another for the purpose of transmitting and receiving data. (c) In SNA, the second layer of the seven-layer architecture. In OSI, the second layer of the seven-layer architecture. (d) The second lowest layer in the OSI reference model. Every *network interface card* (NIC) has a DLC address or *DLC identifier* (DLCI) that uniquely identifies the node on the network. Some network protocols, such as Ethernet and Token Ring, use the DLC addresses exclusively. Other protocols, such as TCP/IP, use a logical address at the network layer to identify nodes. For networks that conform to the IEEE 802 standards (such as Ethernet), the DLC address is usually called the *Media Access Control* (MAC) address.

data link layer   Layer 2 of the OSI reference model. It synchronizes transmission and handles error corrections for a data link.

data network   An arrangement of data circuits and switching facilities for establishing connections between data terminal equipment

data packet   A packet used for the transmission of user data on a virtual circuit at the *data terminal equipment/data circuit-terminating equipment* (DTE/DCE) interface

data rate   *See* data transfer rate.

decimal   Numbers in base 10 (the numbers we use in everyday life). The numbers 9, 100,345,000, and _256 are all decimal numbers. Note that a decimal number is not necessarily a number with a decimal point in it. Numbers with decimal points (that is, numbers with a fractional part) are called fixed-point or floating-point numbers. In addition to the decimal format, computer data is often represented in binary, octal, and hexadecimal formats.

DECNet   An ancient (though still in use) communication media created by Digital Equipment Corporation. *See also* Token Ring.

default route   A routing table entry that is used to direct frames for which a next hop is not explicitly listed in the routing table

Defense Advanced Research Projects Agency (DARPA)   Formerly ARPA. The government agency that funded research and experimentation with the ARPANET. *See* ARPA.

delay   The time between the initiation of a transaction by a sender and the first response received by the sender. Also, it is the time required to move a packet from its source to destination over a given path.

Dense Mode Multicast Routing Protocol   A multicast routing protocol that assumes that bandwidth is plentiful and that multicast group members are not a minority of the entire population of hosts on a network. Typically, these routing protocols flood multicast traffic unless an explicit leave message is received.

designated bridge   The bridge that incurs the lowest path cost when forwarding a frame from a segment to the route bridge

designated router   An OSPF router that generates LSAs for a multi-access network and has other special responsibilities in running OSPF. Each multi-access OSPF network that has at least two attached routers has a designated router elected by the OSPF hello protocol. The designated router reduces the number of adjacencies required on a multi-access network, which in turn reduces the amount of routing protocol traffic and the size of the topological database.

destination   In a network, any point or location such as a node, station, or terminal to which data is sent

destination address (DA)   The part of a message that indicates for whom the message is intended. It is synonymous with the address on an envelope. IBM Token Ring network addresses are 48 bits in length.

device   (a) In networking, a generic term describing a modem, host, terminal, or other entity. (b) Any machine or component that attaches to a computer. Examples of devices include disk drives, printers, mice, and modems.

Distance-Vector Multicast Routing Protocol (DVMRP)   An internetwork gateway protocol, largely based on RIP, that implements a typical dense-mode IP multicast scheme. DVMRP uses IGMP to exchange routing datagrams with its neighbors. *See* IGMP.

Distance-Vector Routing Algorithm   A class of routing algorithms that iterate on the number of hops in a route to find a shortest-path Spanning Tree. Distance-Vector Routing Algorithms call for each router to send its entire routing table in each update, but only to its neighbors. These algorithms can be prone to routing loops but are computationally simpler than Link-State Routing Algorithms. Also called Bellman-Ford Routing Algorithms. *See* Link-State Routing Algorithm and SPF.

Distance-Vector Routing Protocol   A routing protocol that requires that each router to simply inform its neighbors of its routing table. For each network path, the receiving routers pick the neighbor advertising the lowest cost and then add this entry into its routing table for re-advertisement. Hello and RIP are common Distance-Vector Routing Protocols. Common enhancements to Distance-Vector Algorithms include Split Horizon, Poison Reverse, triggered updates, and holddown. See the discussion of Distance-Vector or Bellman-Ford Algorithms in RIP's protocol specification, RFC 1058.

distribution layer   The next layer out from the core layer in a hierarchical campus network topology. This layer is responsible for routing in the campus network.

distribution tree   The logical structure established by multicast routing protocols to determine how to forward multicast packets. A distribution tree may or may not be optimal.

DNS   *See* domain name service.

Domain Name Services (DNS)   A service and protocol that resolves a DNS name such as www.cisco.com to an IP address

dotted-decimal notation   The addressing scheme of the *Internet Protocol* (IP). It is the representation of a 32-bit address consisting of four 8-bit numbers written in base 10 with periods separating them.

down   When a computer system is not working or not available to users

dual core   A core layer topology with two core switches in the core layer. Each core layer switch is connected to all distribution layer switches. There is also a connection between the core layer switches. This topology provides a fully redundant, fault-tolerant core layer.

duplex   Pertaining to communication in which data can be sent and received at the same time

DVMRP   *See* Distance-Vector Multicast Routing Protocol.

dynamic route   A route that is obtained from a routing protocol as opposed to a static route, which is manually configured

Dynamic Trunking Protocol (DTP)   A Cisco proprietary protocol for negotiating the *Virtual Local Area Network* (VLAN) tagging method for the trunk links. *See also* ISL, 802.1Q.

dynamic VLAN   *Virtual Local Area Networks* (VLANS) grouped by host *Media Access Control* (MAC) addresses

EHSA   *See* enhanced high-system availability.

encapsulate   In the internetworking community, to surround one protocol with another protocol for the purpose of passing the foreign protocol through the native environment

end-to-end VLAN   A *Virtual Local Area Network* (VLAN) where hosts are geographically distant; the path between two hosts may cross several switches

end user   The individual who uses a product after it has been fully developed and implemented or marketed

Enhanced High-System Availability (EHSA)   An architecture developed by Cisco that includes a processor redundancy scheme that reduces switchover time by requiring that the redundant processor be running in standby mode

enterprise network   The computer network of (usually) a large commercial organization. It may include mail servers, Web servers, Web sites, and e-commerce facilities, as well as a client/server database system.

Ethernet   A popular LAN technology that has a bus topology and CSMA/CD operations

exponential backoff   A mechanism by which an Ethernet device will wait double the average random amount of wait time after each successive collision. Increasing the time between retransmissions causes an overloaded Ethernet network to regain stability.

Extended Internet Gateway Routing Protocol (EIGRP)   A proprietary dynamic routing protocol developed by Cisco to address the problems associated with routing in large, heterogeneous networks. *See* IGRP, OSPF, and RIP.

exterior routing   Routing that occurs between *autonomous systems* (ASs). It is of concern to service providers and other large or complex networks. The basic routable element is the AS, a collection of *Classless Interdomain Routing* (CIDR) prefixes identified by an AS number. Although there may be many different interior routing schemes, a single exterior routing system manages the global Internet, based primarily on the BGP-4 exterior routing protocol.

Fast Etherchannel (FEC)   A Cisco proprietary mechanism that bundles four Fast Ethernet ports together into one logical link. *See also* link aggregation.

Fast Ethernet   The 100-Mbps version of IEEE 802.3. Fast Ethernet offers a speed increase 10 times that of the 10BaseT Ethernet specification while preserving qualities such as frame format, *Media Access Control* (MAC) mechanisms, and the *Maximum Transmission Unit* (MTU). These similarities enable the use of existing 10BaseT applications and network management tools on Fast Ethernet networks. Based on an extension to the IEEE 802.3 specification. Compare with Ethernet. *See* 100BaseFX, 100BaseT, 100BaseT4, 100BaseTX, 100BaseX, and IEEE 802.3.

FDDI   *See* fiber distributed data interface.

FEC   *See* Fast Etherchannel.

Fiber Distributed Data Interface (FDDI)   A communication media that is characterized by a fault-tolerant logical ring topology that operates at a speed of 100 Mbps over fiber optic cable

fiber optic cable   A thin, flexible (usually glass or plastic) physical medium capable of conducting modulated light for data transmission. A fiber optic cable consists of a bundle of glass threads, each of which is capable of transmitting messages close to the speed of light. Compared with other physical transmission media, fiber is not susceptible to electromagnetic interference (but it is susceptible to changes from radiation), capable of higher data rates, and occupies far less physical volume for an equivalent transmission capacity.

File Transfer Protocol (FTP)   In TCP/IP, a common method of moving files between two Internet sites. FTP is a way to log in to another Internet site to retrieve and/or send files between different machines across a network.

filter   (a) A program that accepts a certain type of data as input, transforms it in some manner, and then outputs the transformed data in accordance with specified criteria. (b) A pattern through which data is passed. Only data that matches the pattern is allowed to pass through the filter. (c) In paint programs and image editors, an effect that can be applied to a bitmap. (d) Utilities that enable data to be imported and exported.

firewall   A set of related programs located at a network gateway server that protect the resources of a private network from users of other networks. The term also implies the security policy that is used with the programs. An enterprise with an intranet that allows its workers access to the Internet will install a firewall to prevent outsiders from accessing its own private data resources and for controlling the outside resources that its own users can access.

flow   A group of packets with a common IP source, destination, or IP and TCP port addresses

frame   A layer-2 (data link layer) PDU

frame-check sequence (FCS)   Extra characters added to a frame for error control purposes. It is used in HDLC, frame relay, and other data link layer protocols.

frame tagging   The act of marking a packet with special *Virtual Local Area Network* (VLAN) identifiers. A packet that must be forwarded to another switch via an interswitch link or must go through a router to another VLAN carries a unique *VLAN identifier* (VLAN ID) as it leaves its local switch. The VLAN ID enables the VLAN switches and routers to selectively forward the packet to ports with the same VLAN ID. It is the responsibility of the local switch (which receives the packet from the source station) to insert the VLAN ID in the packet header. Similarly, it is the responsibility of the destination switch (on whose port the destination end user is located) to remove the VLAN ID and forward the packet to the appropriate port.

full-duplex Ethernet   An Ethernet transmission mode that enables the host to send and receive frames at the same time

gateway   A network point that acts as an entrance to another network. On the Internet, in terms of routing, the network consists of gateway nodes and host nodes. The computers of network users and the computers that serve content (such as Web pages) are host nodes. The computers that control traffic within a company's network or at local *Internet service providers* (ISPs) are gateway nodes.

GBIC   *See* Gigabit Interface Converter.

GEC   *See* Giga Etherchannel.

giga (G)   (a) In decimal notation, 10 to the ninth power. For example, a gigavolt is 1,000,000,000 volts. (b) In computers that use the binary notation system, giga represents 2 to the 30th power, which is 1,073,741,824, a little more than one billion. A gigabyte therefore is about 1.073 billion bytes.

Giga Etherchannel (GEC)   A Cisco proprietary mechanism that can bundle up to four gigabit Ethernet ports together into one logical link. *See also* link aggregation.

Gigabit Ethernet   A high-speed version of Ethernet (a billion bits per second) under development by the IEEE

Gigabit Interface Converter (GBIC)   A Gigabit Ethernet hardware standard for allowing interchangable physical ports (a copper or fiber optic port)

grafting   The process of adding an interface or network to a multicast distribution tree

Group Destination Address (GDA)   In CGMP, a packet field that is six-bytes long and holds the destination multicast group address

half-duplex   A method of data transmission where data can be transmitted in both directions on a signal carrier, but not at the same time. For example, on a *Local Area Network* (LAN) using a technology that has half-duplex transmission, one workstation can send data on the line and then immediately receive data on the line from the same direction in which data was just transmitted.

hardware   The physical aspect of computers, telecommunications, and other information technology devices. The term arose as a way to distinguish the "box" and the electronic components of a computer from the programs put in it to make it perform. The programs came to be known as software.

hardware address   Also called a burned-in or MAC address. In Ethernet networks, the 48-bit address assigned to the Ethernet *network interface card* (NIC). In Token Ring, the 12-digit hex address assigned to the NIC. *See* MAC address.

header   (a) Control information that precedes user data in a frame or datagram that passes through networks. Specifically, this portion of a message contains control information. Usually found at the beginning of a frame. (b) In word processing, one or more lines of text that appear at the top of each page of a document. Once specified, the text is automatically inserted by the word processor.

hello packet   Multicast packet used by routers for neighbor discovery and recovery. Hello packets indicate that a client is still operating and network-ready. They are also used in *Asynchronous Transfer Mode* (ATM) networks with the *Private Network Node Interface* (PNNI) protocol to discover adjacent switches.

hello protocol   Protocol used by OSPF systems for establishing and maintaining neighbor relationships. The are not to be confused with the HELLO routing protocol.

hexadecimal   A base-16 number system containing 16 sequential numbers as base units (including 0) before adding a new position for the next number. (Note that we're using 16 here as a decimal number to explain a number that would be 10 in hexadecimal.) The hexadecimal numbers are 0 through 9 and use the letters A through F. To convert a value from hexadecimal to binary, you merely translate each hexadecimal digit into its four-bit binary equivalent. Hexadecimal numbers have either a 0x prefix or an h suffix.

hierarchical   Systems organized in the shape of a pyramid with each row of objects linked to objects directly beneath it. Hierarchical systems pervade everyday life. The army, for example, which has generals at the top of the pyramid and privates at the bottom, is a hierarchical system. Similarly, the system for classifying plants and animals according to species, family, genus, and so on is also hierarchical.

holddown   A state into which a route is placed so that routers will neither advertise the route nor accept advertisements about the route for a specific length of time (the holddown period). Holddown is used to flush bad information about a route from all routers in the network. A route is typically placed in holddown when a link in that route fails.

host   (a) Any computer on a network that is a repository for services available to other computers on the network. It is quite common to have one host machine provide several services such as Web and Usenet access. (b) A computer system that is accessed by a user working at a remote location. Typically, the term is used when two computer systems are connected by modems and telephone lines. The system that contains the data is called the host, while the computer at which the user sits is called the remote terminal. (c) A computer that is connected to a TCP/IP network, including the Internet. Each host has a unique IP address. *See* node and network.

Hot Standby Router Protocol (HSRP)   A protocol developed by Cisco Systems that provides high network availability and transparent network topology changes. HSRP creates a hot standby router group with a lead router that uses a virtual IP address that services all packets sent to the hot standby (virtual) address. The lead router's operation is monitored by other routers in the group, and if it fails, one of these standby routers inherits the lead position and the hot standby (virtual) group address.

HSRP   *See* Hot Standby Routing Protocol.

HTTP   *See* HyperText Transfer Protocol.

HyperText Transfer Protocol (HTTP)   The protocol that defines communication between Web clients (browsers) and Web servers.

IANA *See* Internet Assigned Numbers Authority.

ICMP *See* Internet Control Message Protocol.

IEEE *See* Institute of Electrical and Electronics Engineers.

IEEE 802.1 The IEEE standard for packet tagging for security within *Local Area Networks* (LANs). It is also used by some companies (such as Cisco Systems) to tag packets for *Virtual LANs* (VLANs).

IEEE 802.1Q The IEEE specification that defines a method for the tagging of packets with a *Virtual Local Area Network* (VLAN) identifier across trunk links

IEEE 802.1z The IEEE specification that defines the *Gigabit Interface Converter* (GBIC) interface

IEEE 802.2 The IEEE standard for the control of the lower part of the layer-2 logical link control of the seven-layer OSI reference model

IEEE 802.3 The IEEE broadband bus networking system that uses the *Carrier-Sense Multiple Access with Collision Detection* (CSMA/CD) protocol. Ethernet has become the commonly used name, although it is one trademarked version of 802.3.

IEEE 802.4 The IEEE physical layer standard specifying a *Local Area Network* (LAN) with a token-passing access method on a bus topology. It is sed with the *Manufacturing Automation Protocol* (MAP) LANs. Its typical transmission speed is 10 Mbps.

IESG *See* Internet Engineering Steering Group.

IETF *See* Internet Engineering Task Force.

IGMP *See* Internet Group Management Protocol.

IGRP *See* Interior Gateway Routing Protocol.

Institute of Electrical and Electronics Engineers (IEEE)
Pronounced "I triple E." Founded in 1884, the IEEE is an organization composed of engineers, scientists, and students. The IEEE is best known for developing standards for the computer and electronics industry. In particular, the IEEE 802 standards for Local Area Networks (LANs) are widely followed.

Integrated Services Digital Network (ISDN) A standard for digital transmission over ordinary telephone copper wire at speeds of up to 128 Kbps

Interior Gateway Routing Protocol (IGRP) A proprietary dynamic routing protocol developed by Cisco to address the problems associated with routing in large, heterogeneous networks. *See* Enhanced IGRP, IGP, OSPF, and RIP.

interior routing A type of routing that occurs within an autonomous system (AS). Most common routing protocols such as the *Routing Information Protocol* (RIP) and *Open Shortest Path First* (OSPF) are interior routing protocols. The basic routable element is the IP network or subnetwork, or the *Classless Interdomain Routing* (CIDR) prefix for newer protocols.

International Organization for Standardization (IOS) An organization of national standards-making bodies from various countries established to promote the development of standards to facilitate the international exchange of goods and services, and to develop cooperation in intellectual, scientific, technological, and economic activity. One such standard is *Open Systems Interconnection* (OSI).

International Standardization for Organization (ISO) A special agency of the United Nations charged with the development of communication standards for computers. Membership in the ISO consists of representatives from international standards organizations throughout the world. Note that ISO is not an acronym; instead, the name derives from the Greek word *iso*, which means equal.

Internet address A 32-bit address assigned to the host. It is a software address that on local networks is locally managed, but on the central Internet it is dictated to the user or entity desiring access to the Internet. The current Internet addressing scheme follows what is called IPV4. Over the past few years, work has been done to increase the Internet address space. This effort is called IPv6. *See* IP address.

Internet Assigned Number Authority (IANA) Many protocol specifications include numbers, keywords, and other parameters that must be uniquely assigned. Examples include version numbers, protocol numbers, port numbers, and MIB numbers. The IAB has delegated to the *Internet Assigned Numbers Authority* (IANA) the task of assigning such protocol parameters for the Internet. The IANA publishes tables of all currently assigned numbers and parameters in RFCs titled "Assigned Numbers" (RFC 1602). *See* IAB, ISOC, and NIC.

Internet Control Message Protocol (ICMP) An extension to the Internet Protocol (IP) defined by RFC 792 and specific to the TCP/IP protocol suite. It is an integral part of the IP. ICMP supports packets containing error, control, and informational messages. The ping command, for example, uses ICMP to test an Internet connection. ICMP messages, delivered in IP packets, are used for out-of-band messages related to network operations or misoperations. Of course, since ICMP uses IP, ICMP packet delivery is unreliable, so hosts can't count on receiving ICMP packets for any network problem.

Internet datagram   The unit of data exchanged between an Internet module and the higher level protocol together with the Internet header

Internet Engineering Steering Group (IESG)   The organization responsible for technical management of *Internet Engineering Task Force* (IETF) activities and the Internet standards process. As part of the *Internet Society* (ISOC), it administers the process according to the rules and procedures that have been ratified by the ISOC trustees. The IESG is directly responsible for the actions associated with entry into and movement along the Internet's "standards track," including final approval of specifications as Internet standards. The IESG can be contacted at `iesg@cnri.reston.va.us`. *See* IAB and IETF.

Internet Engineering Task Force (IETF)   The main standards organization of the Internet. A loosely self-organized group of network designers, operators, vendors, and researchers who make technical and other contributions to the engineering and evolution of the Internet and its technologies. It is the principle body engaged in the development of new Internet standard specifications.

Internet Gateway Routing Protocol (IGRP)   A proprietary routing protocol designed for Cisco routers

Internet group   Multicast routers use this protocol to learn the existence of the host group

Internet Group Management Protocol (IGMP)   A protocol documented in Appendix I of RFC 1112 that enables Internet hosts to participate in multicasting. RFC 1112 describes the basics of multicasting IP traffic, including the format of multicast IP addresses, multicast Ethernet encapsulation, and the concept of a host group, which is the set of hosts interested in traffic for a particular multicast address. Important multicast addresses are documented in the most recent Assigned Numbers RFC, currently RFC 1700. IGMP enables a router to determine which host groups have members on a given network segment. The exchange of multicast packets between routers is not addressed by IGMP.

Internet Protocol (IP)   A protocol used to route data from its source to its destination. It is a part of the TCP/IP protocol.

Internetwork Packet eXchange (IPX)   A communication protocol created by Novell that is characterized by a lack of real layer-3 routing functionality and heavy broadcast traffic generated by service announcement requests

Internetworking Operating System (IOS)   The operating system of most Cisco devices

IOS   *See* Internetworking Operating System.

IP   *See* Internet Protocol.

IP address   The 32-bit dotted-decimal address assigned to hosts as an identifier for a computer or device on a TCP/IP network that wants to participate in a local TCP/IP Internet or the central (connected) Internet. IP addresses are software addresses. It is an IP address consists of a network portion and a host portion. The partition makes routing efficient. Networks using the TCP/IP protocol route messages based on the IP address of the destination.

IP datagram   In TCP/IP networks, a basic unit of information passed across the Internet. An IP datagram is to the Internet as a hardware packet is to a physical network. It contains a source address and a destination address along with data.

IP multicast   A one-to-many transmission described in RFC 1112. The RFC describes IP multicasting as "the transmission of an IP datagram to a host group, a set of zero or more hosts identified by a single IP destination address. A multicast datagram is delivered to all members of its destination host group with the same best-efforts reliability as regular unicast IP datagrams. The membership of a host group is dynamic; that is, hosts may join and leave groups at any time. There is no restriction on the location or number of members in a host group. A host may be a member of more than one group at a time."

IPX   *See* Internetwork Packet eXchange.

ISDN   *See* Integrated Services Digital Network.

ISO   *See* International Organization for Standardization.

K   *See* kilo-.

KB   *See* kilobyte.

kbits   *See* kilobits.

Kbps   *See* kilobits per second.

kbyte   *See* kilobyte.

kilo- (K)   A unit of measure equaling 1,000 in the metric system. Often seen as an abbreviation for *kilobyte* (KB). *See* kilobyte.

kilobits (kbits)   One thousand bits. The measurement of kilobits per second (kbits/s) is used to designate a data transfer rate of 1,000 bits per second.

kilobits per second (Kbps)   A measure of data transfer speed

kilobyte (KB)   In the metric system, 1,000 bytes. However, KB can also represent 1,024 bytes when used to describe data storage because the binary value closest to 1,000 bytes is 1,024.

LAN   *See* Local Area Network.

LAN adapter   A circuit board installed in workstations that connects the workstation with the LAN media

laser diode   Also called an injection laser or diode laser. A semiconductor device that produces coherent radiation in the visible or *infrared* (IR) spectrum when current passes through it. Laser diodes are used in fiber optic systems, *compact disc* (CD) players, laser printers, remote control devices, and intrusion detection systems.

layer   In networking architectures, a collection of network processing functions that together comprise a set of rules and standards for successful data communication.

layer 1   The physical layer of the OSI Reference Model

layer 2   The data link layer of the OSI Reference Model

layer 3   The network layer of the OSI Reference Model

layer 4   The transport layer of the OSI Reference Model

layer 5   The session layer of the OSI Reference Model

layer 6   The presentation layer of the OSI Reference Model

layer 7   The application layer of the OSI Reference Model

leaf   Items at the top of a hierarchical tree structure

link aggregation   The process of creating a single logical link by utilizing multiple networking interfaces

Link Control Protocol (LPP)   A part of the *Point-to-Point Protocol* (PPP) negotiation scheme

Link State Routing Algorithm   A type of routing algorithm used in link state protocols, such as *Open Shortest Path First* (OSPF). The router running this protocol uses the Link State Routing Algorithm broadcast or multicast link (routing) information regarding the cost of reaching each of its neighbors in relation to all other devices in the internetwork.

Link State Routing Protocols   A routing protocol that requires each router to maintain at least a partial map of the links within a network. When a network link changes state (up to down, or vice versa), a notification, called a *link-state advertisement* (LSA), is flooded throughout the network. All the routers note the change and recompute their routes accordingly. This method is more reliable, easier to debug, and less bandwidth-intensive than a Distance-Vector Routing Protocol. It is also more complex and more processor- and memory-intensive. OSPF and IS-IS are examples of Link State Routing Protocols. *See Open Shortest Path First* (OSPF) and *Intermediate-System-to-Intermediate System* (IS-IS) for additional information.

LLC   *See* Logical Link Control.

Local Area Network (LAN)   A data communication network of interconnected workstations, PCs, terminals, servers, printers, and other peripherals operating at a high speed over short distances (usually within the same floor or building) and sharing the resources of a single processor or server within a relatively small geographic area. Various LAN standards have been developed.

Local VLAN   A *Virtual Local Area Network* (VLAN) where hosts are geographically close, all connected to the same switch or the same group of switches on a particular floor or a building.

Logical Link Control (LLC)   An implementation of the OSI layer-2 data link control. It was originally designed by IBM as a sublayer in the IBM Token Ring architecture and provides connectionless and connection-oriented data transfer.

MAC   *See* Media Access Control.

MAC address   Also known as an Ethernet address, hardware address, station address, burned-in address, or physical address. It uniquely identifies each node in a network. It is a set of six two-digit hexadecimal numbers burned into an Ethernet product by its manufacturer.

MAC frame   A frame used to carry information to maintain the ring protocol and to exchange management information

MAC protocol   The *data link control* (DLC) sublayer protocol that includes functions for recognizing adapter addresses, copying message units from the physical network, and message-unit format recognition, error detection, and routing within the processor

MAN   *See* Metropolitan Area Network.

MB   *See* megabyte.

Mbits   *See* megabits.

Mbits/s   *See* megabits per second.

Mbone   *See* Multicast Backbone on the Internet.

Mbps   *See* megabits per second.

Mbyte   *See* megabyte.

Mbytes/s   *See* megabytes per second.

media   (a) Physical carriers of electrons or photons. The medium may be hard, as in a type of cable, or soft, in the sense of microwaves, for example. (b) Objects on which data can be stored. These include hard disks, floppy disks, CD-ROMs, and tapes. (c) In computer networks, the cables linking workstations together. Many different types of transmission media exist, the most popular being twisted-pair wire (normal electrical wire), coaxial cable (the type of cable used for cable television), and fiber optic cable (cables made out of glass). (d) The form and technology used to communicate information. Multimedia presentations, for example, combine sound, pictures, and videos.

Media Access Control (MAC)   (a) The lowest of the two sublayers of the data link layer defined by the IEEE. The MAC sublayer handles access to shared media, such as whether token passing or contention will be used. (b) According to OSI nomenclature, a sublayer in the data link layer, which controls access to the physical medium of a network. It supports topology-dependent functions and uses services of the physical layer to provide services to the *logical link control* (LLC) sublayer. *See* data link layer, MAC address, and LLC

Media Access Unit (MAU)   An Ethernet transceiver.

Media Independent Interface (MII)   A standard 40-pin connector that requires users to attach a transceiver to provide the appropriate media interface

megabit (Mbits)   (a) When used to describe data storage, 1,048,576 (2 to the 20th power) bytes. (b) When used to describe data transfer rates, it refers to one million bits. Networks are often measured in megabits per second, abbreviated as Mbps.

megabits per second (Mbits/s)   The transmission speed or rate of one million bits per second

megabyte (MB)   One million (actually 1,048,576) bytes

megabytes per second (Mbytes/s)   The transmission speed or rate of one million bytes per second

Metropolitan Area Network (MAN)   A data network that extends to a 50-kilometer range, spanning an entire metropolitan area such as a city or town. Generally, MANs span a larger geographic area than LANs but a smaller area than WANs. They are essentially somewhere in between them. MANs operate at speeds from one Mbps up to the gigabit level; these high-speed connections are common characteristics.

MII   *See* Media Independent Interface.

MLS   *See* multilayer switching.

MLS-RP   *See* Multilayer Switching Route Processor.

MLS-SE   *See* Multilayer Switching Switch Engine.

MOSPF   *See* Multicast OSPF.

multicast   A method of transmitting messages from a host using a single transmission to a selected subset of all the hosts that can receive the messages. This is also a message that is sent out to multiple devices on the network by a host. A simple example of multicasting is sending an e-mail message to a mailing list. Teleconferencing and videoconferencing also use multicasting but require more robust protocols and networks. Standards are being developed to support multicasting over a TCP/IP network such as the Internet. These standards, IP multicast and Mbone, will enable users to easily join multicast groups. *See* anycast, unicast, broadcast, and IP.

Multicast Backbone on the Internet (Mbone)   An extension to the Internet to support IP multicasting, or the two-way transmission of data between multiple sites. The TCP/IP protocol used by the Internet divides messages into packets and sends each packet independently. Packets can travel different routes to their destination, which means that they can arrive in any order and with sizable delays between the first and last packets. In addition, each recipient of the data requires that separate packets be sent from the source to the destination.

multicast group   A group set up to receive messages from a source

multicast OSPF (MOSPF)   A series of extensions applied to the *Open Shortest Path First* (OSPF) intradomain routing protocol for all OSPFs to support IP multicast routing.

multicast routing   The process of sending information about how to forward multicast packets between routers on a network

multicast scooping   The process of restricting how far a multicast packet can be forwarded

multicast transmission   *See* multicast.

multilayer switching (MLS)   A mechanism developed by Cisco to implement cut-through routing. The route information is determined once and then passed to the forwarding device. From that point on, the forwarding device knows how to forward that particular flow.

multilayer switching (MLS) cache   The component of an MLS-SE that keeps up with known flows and their routes

Multilayer Switching Route Processor (MLS-RP)   The device in MLS that determines the route for a flow

Multilayer Switching Switch Engine (MLS-SE)   The device in MLS that forwards packets

multimode   The transmission of multiple modes of light

multimode fiber (MMF)   A type of fiber mostly used for short distances such as those found on a campus LAN. It can carry 100 Mbs/sec for typical campus distances, the actual maximum speed (given the right electronics) depending upon the actual distance. It is easier to connect to than a single-mode fiber, but its limit on speed times distance is lower.

network interface card (NIC)   A *network interface device* (NID) in the form of a circuit card that is installed in the expansion slot of a computer to provide network access. Examples of NICs are cards that interface a computer with an Ethernet *Local Area Network* (LAN) and cards that interface a computer with an *Fiber Distributed Data Interface* (FDDI) ring network.

network layer   Layer 3 of the seven-layer *Open Systems Interconnection* (OSI) stack. It is responsible for data transfers across the network. It functions independently of network media and topology. Seven network layers can be found in the *Open Systems Interconnection Reference Model* (OSI-RM), which is an abstract description of the digital communications between application processes running in distinct systems. The model employs a hierarchical structure. Each layer performs value-added services at the request of the adjacent higher layer and in turn requests more basic services from the adjacent lower layer.

Network Management System (NMS)   A software system, such as *CiscoWorks for Switched Internetworks* (CWSI) or *Cisco Visual Switch Manager* (CVSM), that enables a network administrator to configure and monitor networking hardware

Network Time Protocol (NTP)   A protocol for exchanging time information over a network. It is useful for keeping many devices in a close time synchronization.

NIC   *See* network interface card.

NMS   *See* network management system.

NTP   *See* Network Time Protocol.

Open Shortest Path First (OSPF)   A routing protocol developed for IP networks based on the shortest path first or link-state algorithm. OSPF uses the Djikstra or Shortest Path Algorithm to calculate the shortest path between routers in an internetwork.

Open System Interconnection (OSI)   Also known as the OSI Reference Model or OSI Model. In the 1980s, the *International Standards Organization* (ISO) began to develop the *Open Systems Interconnection* (OSI) networking suite. The result was an ISO standard for worldwide communications that defines a networking framework for implementing protocols in seven layers.

Open Systems Interconnection (OSI)   The only internationally accepted framework for communication between two systems made by different vendors. It is a seven-layer architecture developed by the ISO.

operating system   A software program that manages the basic operation of a computer system

OS   *See* operating system.

OSI Reference Model   A stacked seven-layer model that defines modular network functions. Each layer has a unique defined function. Interfaces are defined to determine how a layer communicates with the layer above and the layer below.

OSPF   *See* Open Shortest Path First.

Packet   A layer-3 (network layer) *protocol data unit* (PDU). It is a series of bits logically grouped together and found at the network layer of the OSI model. A packet contains data and control information, including the source and destination addresses formatted with a header, to ready it for transmission from one end station (host) to another. The terms datagram, frame, message, and segment are also used to describe logical information groupings at various layers of the OSI Reference Model and in various technology circles. *See* PDU.

packet Internet groper   Erroneous definition of the word ping, which has become something of an urban legend. *See* ping.

packets per second (PPS)   A measure of router processing speed

PAgP   *See* port aggregation protocol.

PC   *See* personal computer.

PDU   *See* protocol data unit.

personal computer (PC)   (a) A desktop computational device capable of millions of calculations per second. (b) A computer for your home that can be programmed in Basic and be utilized for home accounting. (c) A machine with the power of a super-computer that operates efficiently running Linux. (d) Any home appliance created after 1/1/2002.

Per VLAN Spanning Tree (PVST)   A Cisco proprietary solution for handling Spanning Tree over VLANs. PVST runs a separate instance of Spanning Tree for each *Virtual Local Area Network* (VLAN). PVST requires that *Cisco's Inter Switch Link* (ISL) run on trunk links between switches.

Per VLAN Spanning Tree with CST (PVST+)   A Cisco proprietary solution for handling Spanning Tree over *Virtual Local Area Network* (VLANs). PVST+ enables CST information to be passed to *Per VLAN Spanning Tree* (PVST) for interoperating with other vendors using Spanning Tree over VLAN implementations.

PHY   *See* physical layer.

physical layer (PHY)   Layer 1 of the OSI model, the lowest of the seven hierarchical layers. The physical layer performs services requested by the data link layer. The major functions and services performed by the physical layer are as follows: (a) to establish and terminate a connection to a communications medium; (b) to participate in the process whereby the communication resources are effectively shared among multiple users, such as contention resolution and flow control; and (c) to convert between the representation of digital data in user equipment and the corresponding signals transmitted over a communications channel.

PIM   *See* Protocol-Independent Multicast.

PIMDM   *See* Protocol-Independent Multicast Dense Mode.

PIMSM   *See* Protocol-Independent Multicast Sparse Mode.

ping   A TCP/IP utility based upon the *Internet Control Message Protocol* (ICMP). It takes its name from a sonar search; a short sound burst is sent out and an echo or "ping" is received. The ping utility works by sending an ICMP echo request packet to the specified address and waiting for a reply. Ping is implemented using the required ICMP Echo function, as documented in RFC 792.

Plain Old Telephone Service (POTS)   The telephone service running to your house

point-to-point   A type of network topology where each physical network has two hosts connected. An Ethernet with two hosts or a T1 is point-to-point.

Poison Reverse   A mechanism by which downed routes are transmitted by sending an infinite metric. This lets the receiving router know that this route is not existent. Poison Reverse, along with Split Horizon, eliminates routing loops between three contiguously connected routers.

Port Aggregation Protocol (PAgP)   A Cisco proprietary protocol designed to ease the configuration of the Fast Etherchannel links by placing ports into an automatic channel mode

PortFast   A Cisco proprietary update to the Spanning Tree protocol that enables a network administrator to exclude ports from participating in the Spanning Tree

presentation layer   The sixth layer of the OSI reference model. This layer is responsible for providing data encryption, data compression, and code conversion.

protocol data unit (PDU)   A general term used to refer to what is exchanged between peer-layer entities. Originally used in the OSI model to describe what passes across two adjoining layers, it contains header, data, and trailer information.

Protocol Independent Multicast (PIM)   *See* PIMDM or PIMSM.

Protocol-Independent Multicast Dense Mode (PIMDM)   A Dense Mode Multicast Routing Protocol. This protocol does not have a built-in routing protocol. Instead, it uses the unicast routing protocol routing tables to find the path back to the multicast source.

Protocol-Independent Multicast Sparse Mode (PIMSM)   A Sparse Mode Multicast Routing Protocol. This protocol does not have a built-in routing protocol. Instead, it uses the unicast routing protocol routing tables to find the path back to the multicast source.

Pruning   The process of removing an interface or network from a multicast distribution tree

PVST   *See* Per VLAN Spanning Tree.

PVST+   *See* Per VLAN Spanning Tree with CST.

QoS   *See* Quality of Service.

Quality of Service (QoS)   A measure of performance for a network device or system that reflects its transmission quality and service availability

queue   (a) To line up. (b) A group of jobs waiting to be executed. (c) In programming, a data structure in which elements are removed in the same order they were entered.

queuing theory   Scientific principles governing the formation or lack of formation of congestion on a network or at an interface

RAM   *See* random access memory.

random access memory (RAM)   A type of computer memory that can be accessed randomly; that is, any byte of memory can be accessed without touching the preceding bytes. RAM is the most common type of memory found in computers and other devices, such as printers. Two basic types of RAM exist: *dynamic RAM* (DRAM) and *static RAM* (SRAM).

rendezvous point   The center of a shared tree in *Protocol-Independent Multicast Sparse Mode* (PIMSM)

repeater   A network device that reconstructs and retimes signals received on one interface to its other interfaces. A repeater operates at layer 1 (physical layer) of the OSI reference model.

resource   Generally, any item that can be used, such as main storage, secondary storage, input/output devices, the processing unit, files, and control or processing programs, or anything else that can be used by a user either directly or indirectly

Resource Reservation Protocol (RSVP)   A protocol that enables channels or paths on the Internet to be reserved for the multicast transmission of video or other high-bandwidth messages.

Reverse Path Forwarding (RPF)   A method for determining how to forward multicast packets. Only packets received from an interface that is in the path back to the source are allowed to be forwarded. This interface is known as the RPF interface.

RFC 2236   IGMPv2 specification

RIP   *See* Routing Information Protocol.

RJ-45   Registered Jack-45; an eight-wire connector commonly used to connect computers onto *Local Area Networks* (LANs), especially Ethernets. RJ-45 connectors look similar to the RJ-11 connectors used for connecting telephone equipment, but they are somewhat wider. Four-pair wire is the standard. Pair 1 is Blue, Pair 2 Orange, Pair 3 Green, and Pair 4 Brown. Colors are always shown with the base color first, and then the stripe color.

root bridge switch   A bridge or switch responsible for exchanging topology information with designated bridges in a Spanning Tree implementation in order to notify all other bridges in the network when topology changes are required. This prevents loops and provides a measure of protection against link failures.

route   An ordered sequence between origin and destination stations that represents a path in a network between the stations

router   A special-purpose device that connects two or more networks at the network layer (layer 3) of the OSI model; it operates like a bridge but can choose routes through a network. Routers spend all their time looking at the destination addresses of the packets passing through them and deciding which route to send them on. Routers use headers and a routing table to determine where packets go. *See* network and packet switching.

Router Switch Module (RSM)   A hardware module that adds layer-3 support to layer-2 switching products

Routing Information Protocol (RIP)   An early BSD Unix dynamic routing protocol that has become an industry standard. It is often used because WIN NT and Unix systems can understand it. RIP is considered an outdated router protocol. *See* OSPF and EIGRP.

routing tables   In Internet routing, each entry in a routing table has at least two fields: the IP Address Prefix and Next Hop. The next hop is the IP address of another host or router that is directly reachable via an Ethernet, serial link, or some other physical connection.

routing update   A message sent from a router that indicates network reachability and associated cost information. Routing updates are typically sent at regular intervals and after a change in network topology. *See* flash update.

RPF   *See* Reverse Path Forwarding.

RSM   *See* Route Switch Module.

RSVP   *See* Resource Reservation Protocol.

session layer   The fifth layer of the OSI reference model. The session layer is responsible for how sessions are to be started, ended, and controlled.

set commands   A *command-line interface* (CLI) that consists of set, clear, and show commands to perform system management tasks

Shared Tree   A multicast distribution tree that is established to include every source and destination for a multicast group

Simple Network Management Protocol   A protocol defined over the *User Datagram Protocol* (UDP) that specifies how a network management system communicates with network devices

SNMP   *See* Simple Network Management Protocol.

source-based tree   A multicast distribution tree that is established for each source in a multicast group

SPAN   *See* switch port analyzer.

Spanning Tree Protocol (STP)   A protocol used to prevent forwarding loops in a switched or bridged network

Sparse Mode Multicast Routing Protocol   A multicast routing protocol that assumes that bandwidth is expensive and that multicast group members are a minority of the entire population of hosts on a network. Typically, these routing protocols require an explicit join before multicast traffic is forwarded to a particular network.

Split Horizon   A mechanism that prevents routing updates for a network from being sent back to the network they were received on. This mechanism eliminates the possibility of routing loops between two connected routers.

standby router   A router in a *Hot Standby Router Protocol* (HSRP) virtual router group that can become the active router if the current active router fails

static route   A route that is manually configured as opposed to being obtained from a routing protocol

static VLAN   *Virtual Local Area Networks* (VLANs) grouped by switch ports

STP   *See* Spanning Tree Protocol.

straight-through cable   A twisted-pair Ethernet cable with pinouts as follows: pin 1 - pin 1, pin 2 - pin 2, pin 3 - pin 3, pin 6 - pin 6

subnet   A group of IP addresses with a common prefix

subnet mask   A 32-bit value used to determine the length of the node field of an IP address

switch   A network device that forwards network frames from one interface to appropriate interfaces. A switch is the functional equivalent of a bridge. *See also* bridge.

switch block   A group of networks with a distribution layer and an access layer component. Typically, the switch block is a geographically centered concept.

Switched Port Analyzer (SPAN)   A software feature that enables a network administrator to monitor traffic that is traversing a switch. Traffic is forced out a specified port in addition to any other port that should receive the traffic.

Tag Control Information (TCI)   In IEEE 802.1Q, the field is made up of a three-bit user priority field, a one-bit canonical format indicator, and a 12-bit *Virtual Local Area Networks* (VLAN) identifier.

Tag Protocol Identifier (TPID)   In IEEE 802.1Q, the two-byte field that designates that a packet is 802.1Q-encoded

TCI   *See* Tag Control Information.

TCP   *See* Transmission Control Protocol.

Telnet   An application that utilizes TCP to communicate text between two peers

Time to Live (TTL)   A field in the IP header that is decremented each time the IP packet traverses a router. If a router receives an IP packet with the TTL field equal to zero, the packet is dropped. This provides a mechanism to eventually rid the network of packets if a routing loop occurs.

TLV   *See* type-length value.

Token Ring   (a) An ancient (though still active) communication media based on a logical ring topology. Created by *International Business Machines* (IBM). (b) The subject of many jokes within today's networking community. *See also* DECNet.

TPID   *See* Tag Protocol Identifier.

Transmission Control Protocol (TCP)   A transmission layer protocol with guaranteed transmissions

transport layer   The fourth layer of the OSI Reference Model. This layer is responsible for multiplexing between many transport layer addresses known as ports. Transport layer PDUs are known as messages. Examples of transport layer protocols are *Transfer Control Protocol* (TCP) and *User Datagram Protocol* (UDP).

triggered update   An update that is sent immediately when an event occurs instead of waiting for a default time interval to pass

TTL   *See* Time to Live.

Type-Length Value (TLV)   A parameter that is first specified by a type field, then a length field specifying the number of bytes in the data, and finally the value or data

UDP   *See* user datagram protocol.

Unicast   A transmission method with one source and one destination

Unicast Source Address (USA)   In the *Cisco Group Management Protocol* (CGMP), a six-byte packet field that contains the *Media Access Address* (MAC) address of a source host

Unshielded Twisted Pair (UTP)   A type of twisted pair cable without a foil shield to protect the cable from external noise to lower the cost of the cable. It is commonly called twisted-pair cable and used in twisted-pair Ethernet links.

UplinkFast   A Cisco proprietary update to the spanning tree protocol that enables a network administrator to specify which links are redundant links from the access layer switches into the distribution layer. In the event of a redundant link failure, an alternate link can be brought up almost immediately without waiting for Spanning Tree to converge.

USA   *See* unicast source address.

User Datagram Protocol (UDP)   A transmission layer protocol with no mechanism for retransmission

UTP   *See* unshielded twisted pair.

VID   *See* VLAN identifier.

Virtual LAN (VLAN)   A *Local Area Network* (LAN) that can span an entire campus network. A VLAN is defined by groups of ports or MAC addresses regardless of geography. A traditional LAN is limited by its geographical bounds.

Virtual Router   A group of routers in HSRP that are members of a pool of devices that can at any time become the active router.

Virtual Terminal (vty)   An interface to a network device that simulates a console port and is usually accessed by a Telnet application.

VLAN   *See* virtual LAN.

VLAN Identifier   In IEEE 802.1Q, the label designating the originating VLAN a packet was sourced on

VLAN Trunking Protocol (VTP)   A protocol for automatically adding and removing VLANs from a switch group defined in a VTP domain

VTP   *See* VLAN trunking protocol.

vty   *See* virtual terminal.

WAN   *See* Wide Area Network.

Wide Area Network (WAN)   A class of networking technology that interconnects *Campus Area Networks* (CANs) and *Metropolitan Area Networks* (MANs) and can have a global reach

APPENDIX B

Bibliography

Bertsekas, D. and Gallager, R., *Data Networks Second Edition*, 1992, Prentice Hall.

Caslow, B., *Cisco Certification: Bridges, Routers, and Switches for CCIEs*, 1998, Prentice Hall.

Doyle, J., *Routing TCP/IP, Volume I*, 1998, Macmillan Technical Publishing.

Giles, R., *Cisco CCIE Study Guide*, 1998, McGraw-Hill.

Global Knowledge, *Advanced Cisco Routing Configuration Study Guide*, 1999, McGraw-Hill.

Held, Gil and Kent Hundley, *Cisco Security Architectures*, 1999, McGraw-Hill

Lewis, C., *Cisco TCP/IP Routing Professional Reference Second Edition*, 1999, McGraw-Hill.

Parkhurst, William R., *Cisco Multicast Routing & Switching*, 1999, McGraw-Hill

Perlman, R., *Interconnections Second Edition: Bridges, Routers, Switches, and Internetworking Protocols*, 1999, Addison-Wesley Professional Computing Series.

Slattery, T. and Burton, B., *Advanced IP Routing in Cisco Networks*, 1999, McGraw-Hill.

Stallings, William, *Data and Computer Communications*, 1994, MacMillan

Thomas, Tom, *Thomas' Concise Networking & Telecom Dictionary*, 2000, McGraw-Hill

APPENDIX C

Webliography

802.1Q
http://www.manta.ieee.org/groups/802/1/pages/802.1Q.html

http://www.manta.ieee.org/groups/802/1/pages/802.1u.html

http://www.cisco.com/univercd/cc/td/doc/product/software/ios120/
120newft/120t/120t1/8021q.htm

Access Lists
http://www.cisco.com/cpress/cc/td/cpress/ccie/ndcs798/nd2016.htm

http://www.cisco.com/univercd/cc/td/doc/product/software/ios113ed/
113ed_cr/secur_c/scprt3/screflex.htm

http://www.cisco.com/univercd/cc/td/doc/product/software/ios113ed/
113t/113t_3/stdlog.htm

http://www.cisco.com/univercd/cc/td/doc/product/software/ios120/
120newft/120t/120t2/comment.htm

Access Policies
http://www.sans.org/newlook/resources/policies/policies.htm

http://www.cisco.com/univercd/cc/td/doc/product/software/ios120/
12cgcr/secur_c/scoverv.htm

Catalyst 1900
http://www.cisco.com/warp/public/cc/cisco/mkt/switch/cat/c1928/

Catalyst 2926
http://www.cisco.com/warp/public/cc/cisco/mkt/switch/cat/2900/prodlit/
c2926_ds.htm

Catalyst 2900
http://www.cisco.com/warp/public/cc/cisco/mkt/switch/cat/2900/

Catalyst 3500
http://www.cisco.com/warp/public/cc/cisco/mkt/switch/cat/3500xl/

Catalyst 4000
http://www.cisco.com/warp/public/cc/cisco/mkt/switch/cat/c4000/

Catalyst 5000
http://www.cisco.com/warp/public/cc/cisco/mkt/switch/cat/c5000/

Catalyst 6000

http://www.cisco.com/warp/public/cc/cisco/mkt/switch/cat/6000/

Catalyst 8500

http://www.cisco.com/warp/public/cc/cisco/mkt/switch/cat/8500/

CGMP

http://www.cisco.com/univercd/cc/td/doc/product/lan/28201900/1928v67x/
    eescg67x/03cgmp1.htm

http://www.cisco.com/warp/public/795/5.html

http://www.cisco.com/univercd/cc/td/doc/product/software/ios120/
    12cgcr/np1_c/1cprt1/1cmulti.htm

http://www.cisco.com/univercd/cc/td/doc/product/software/ios120/
    120newft/120t/120t5/ipmctmls.htm

http://www.cisco.com/univercd/cc/td/doc/product/software/ios120/
    12cgcr/np1_r/1rprt1/1rmulti.htm

Cisco IOS

http://www.cisco.com/warp/public/732/

http://www.cisco.com/warp/public/534/15.html

http://www.cisco.com/warp/public/732/ciscoios.html

http://www.cisco.com/warp/public/710/access1/IOStutorial.htm

Cisco Switching Products

http://www.cisco.com/warp/public/534/16.html

http://www.cisco.com/warp/public/779/largeent/learn/topologies/
    campus.html

http://www.cisco.com/warp/public/779/largeent/select_products/
    requirements.html

CiscoWorks/CiscoView

http://www.cisco.com/warp/public/641/11.html

http://www.cisco.com/warp/public/732/iosben.html

http://www.cisco.com/warp/public/732/index.html

http://www.cisco.com/warp/public/779/servpro/

Classless IP Routing

http://ds.internic.net/rfc/rfc1786.txt

http://www.cisco.com/univercd/cc/td/doc/product/software/ios112/
    112cg_cr/5cbook/5cip.htm

Designing Switched LAN Internetworks

http://www.cisco.com/cpress/cc/td/cpress/ccie/ndcs798/nd2012.htm

http://www.cisco.com/warp/public/cc/cisco/mkt/switch/cat/6000/tech/campn_wp.htm

http://www.cisco.com/warp/public/cc/cisco/mkt/switch/cat/3500xl/prodlit/lan_dg.htm

EIGRP

http://www.cisco.com/univercd/cc/td/doc/product/software/ios11/cbook/ciproute.htm

http://www.cisco.com/univercd/cc/td/doc/product/software/ios113ed/113ed_cr/np1_c/1cindep.htm

http://www.cisco.com/cpress/cc/td/doc/cisintwk/ics/cs004.htm

Ethernet

http://wwwhost.ots.utexas.edu/ethernet/enet-faqs/ethernet-faq

http://gatsby.lit.tas.edu.au/tibs/lans/step3/lssb.htm

http://www.cisco.com/cpress/cc/td/cpress/fund/ith2nd/it2407.htm

HSRP Configuration

http://www.cisco.com/cpress/cc/td/cpress/ccie/ndcs798/nd2022.htm

IGMP

http://www.ipmulticast.com/community/whitepapers/netinfra.html

http://www.nanog.org/mtg-9806/ppt/davemeyer/

http://www.winsock2.com/multicast/whitepapers/apis.htm

http://www.ietf.org/internet-drafts/draft-ietf-idmr-igmp-v3-02.txt

http://ds.internic.net/rfc/rfc1112.txt

http://ds.internic.net/rfc/rfc1700.txt

IGRP

http://www.cisco.com/cpress/cc/td/cpress/ccie/ndcs798/nd2017.htm

http://www.cisco.com/warp/public/459/2.html

http://cio.cisco.com/warp/public/103/index.shtml

InterVLAN routing

http://www.cisco.com/cpress/cc/td/cpress/fund/ith2nd/it2407.htm

IP Multicast
http://www.cisco.com/cpress/cc/td/cpress/ccie/ndcs798/nd2013.htm

http://www.winsock2.com/ipmulticast/community/whitepapers/
howipmcworks.html

http://www.cisco.com/univercd/cc/td/doc/product/software/ios120/
12cgcr/np1_c/1cprt1/1cmulti.htm

http://www.cisco.com/warp/public/cc/cisco/mkt/ios/mcastip/tech/
ipcas_dg.htm

http://www.ipmulticast.com/community/whitepapers/highprot.html

http://www.cisco.com/univercd/cc/td/doc/product/software/ios120/
120newft/120t/120t5/ipmctmls.htm

http://ganges.cs.tcd.ie/4ba2/multicast/

IP Multicast Routing
http://www.cisco.com/cpress/cc/td/cpress/ccie/ndcs798/nd2024.htm

http://www.cisco.com/univercd/cc/td/doc/product/software/ios102/
accscg/76713.htm

IP Routing
http://www.cisco.com/cpress/cc/td/cpress/ccie/ndcs798/nd2002.htm

http://www.cisco.com/cpress/cc/td/cpress/ccie/ndcs798/nd2003.htm

ISL
http://www.cisco.com/warp/public/cc/sol/mkt/ent/cmps/netsr_wp.htm

http://www.cisco.com/warp/public/793/lan_switching/2.html

http://www.cisco.com/warp/public/793/lan_switching/4.html

http://www.tu-chemnitz.de/~sger/isl/

Link Aggregation
http://www.nwfusion.com/newsletters/lans/1026lan1.html

http://www.manta.ieee.org/groups/802/3/trunk_study/tutorial/

http://www.cisco.com/warp/public/cc/cisco/mkt/switch/fec/tech/
fetec_wp.htm

Mbone Multicast Network Information
http://www.mbone.com/

Multilayer Switching
http://www.cisco.com/univercd/cc/td/doc/product/l3sw/
2948g-l3/rel_12_0/config/dom_over.htm

http://www.cisco.com/univercd/cc/td/doc/product/lan/cat5000/rel_4_1/
netflow/03cnfg.htm

Network Security

http://www.sans.org/

http://www.cisco.com/warp/public/779/largeent/learn/technologies/
network_security.html

http://www.securityfocus.com/

OSI Reference Model

http://www.rad.com/networks/1994/osi/osi.htm

OSPF

http://www.ietf.org/html.charters/ospf-charter.html

http://www.cisco.com/univercd/cc/td/doc/cisintwk/ito_doc/ospf.htm

http://www.cisco.com/cpress/cc/td/cpress/design/ospf/on0407.htm

http://www.cisco.com/univercd/cc/td/doc/cisintwk/ics/cs001.htm

http://www.cisco.com/warp/public/104/2.html

http://ds.internic.net/rfc/rfc1583.txt

RIP

http://www.cisco.com/cpress/cc/td/cpress/ccie/ndcs798/nd2014.htm

http://www.rad.com/networks/1995/rip/content.htm

RIPv2

http://ds.internic.net/rfc/rfc1058.txt

http://ds.internic.net/rfc/rfc1721.txt

http://ds.internic.net/rfc/rfc2453.txt

http://www.cisco.com/warp/public/784/packet/oct98/8.html

http://www.cisco.com/univercd/cc/td/doc/product/software/ios113ed/
113ed_cr/np1_c/1crip.htm

STP

http://www.cisco.com/warp/public/cc/sol/mkt/ent/ndsgn/spane_an.htm

http://www.cisco.com/univercd/cc/td/doc/product/software/ios120/
120newft/120t/120t1/stpenh.htm

TCP/IP

http://whatis.com/tcpip.htm

http://www.cisco.com/cpress/cc/td/cpress/fund/ith2nd/it2407.htm

Virtual LANs

http://www.cisco.com/warp/public/cc/cisco/mkt/ios/rel/prodlit/
627_pp.htm

http://www.cisco.com/warp/public/cc/cisco/mkt/enm/cwsiman/tech/
vlan_wp.htm

http://www.whatis.com/virtuall.htm

VLAN Trunking

http://www.cisco.com/warp/public/cc/cisco/mkt/switch/fec/prodlit/
faste_an.htm

http://www.cisco.com/univercd/cc/td/doc/product/lan/cat5000/rel_5_4/
config/e_trunk.htm

APPENDIX D

Ethernet Performance

This appendix explores how a shared Ethernet behaves. This book spends a lot of time discussing how to get the most out of the features of multilayer switching equipment to build a reliable, scalable, and feature-rich campus network. The details of how Ethernet behaves in a point-to-point topology versus a shared topology are often overlooked. This appendix will develop the mathematics behind how an Ethernet behaves in a shared topology to help you understand the true benefits of deploying switched Ethernet networks.

Before we get started, note that this material is not on the BCMSN exam. This material is included to help you be more informed when you design your networks.

The next section will describe the differences between switched and shared Ethernet networks.

Switched versus Shared Ethernet

Consider the Ethernet network in Figure D-1 configured in a point-to-point fashion with an Ethernet switch connecting the hosts.

Figure D-1
A point-to-point network with an Ethernet switch connecting the hosts

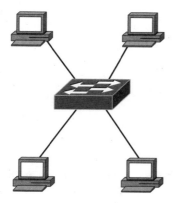

This network has all the hosts accessing the network with their own Ethernet port on a switch. Even though Ethernet is a multiple access medium, this network is a point-to-point dedicated link topology. If the links are configured to be full-duplex, all the bandwidth of the link is available to both hosts on the link. Therefore, the bandwidth afforded each host on a switched Ethernet link is N, where N is the bandwidth of the Ethernet link.

Now consider the Ethernet network configured in a shared fashion in Figure D-2. This is illustrated by showing the hosts connected by a bus cabling system.

This network has many hosts connected to one Ethernet. All the hosts must share the bandwidth of the Ethernet. If all the hosts use the Ethernet equally, it would appear that each host would get $1/N$ amount of bandwidth, where N is the total bandwidth of the Ethernet. The interesting detail in this situation is what happens to the available bandwidth of the Ethernet. Note that this network is in a half-duplex configuration.

The benefit of the shared Ethernet is a reduction in overall costs of the network. The per-port cost of an Ethernet repeater or hub is less than that of an Ethernet switch. Note, however, that the per-port cost of Ethernet switches are decreasing.

Now that switched Ethernet and shared Ethernet has been defined, let's look a little deeper into the performance of shared Ethernet.

Figure D-2
A shared Ethernet network with the hosts connected by a bus cabling system

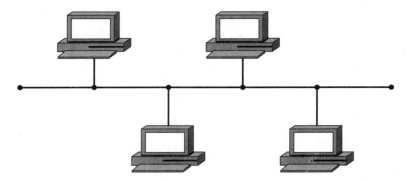

Shared Ethernet Performance

Before we get into the mathematics of shared Ethernet performance, we need to lay the foundation of Ethernet operations. The following discussion defines Ethernet operations.

Ethernet Operation

Ethernet is known as having *Carrier Sense Multiple Access with Collision Detect* (CSMA/CD) capabilities with exponential backoff. Here are a few examples to explain the meaning of CSMA/CD with exponential backoff.

Consider the shared Ethernet network in Figure D-3. Notice the bus topology of the network. If host A would like to send a packet to host B, host A listens to the bus and waits for all packets currently being transmitted on the bus to pass. Once the bus is quiet, host A begins sending an Ethernet frame onto the bus. All the hosts connected to the bus see the packet being sent from A. Host B sees the packet and recognizes the destination MAC address as its own address and then keeps the packet. The other hosts on the network ignore the packet destined to B. This property of waiting for the bus to be silent is called *Carrier Sense*. Since there are many devices using the Ethernet bus, it is a Multiple Access network.

Now consider a similar scenario where host A waits for the bus to be silent and begins to transmit a frame at the same time that host C begins

Figure D-3
A shared Ethernet
network

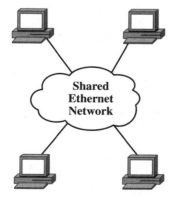

to send a frame onto the bus. This is called a *collision*. Since the transmitting hosts listen to the bus at the same time they are transmitting, they can detect a collision. After detecting a collision, the transmitting hosts stop sending their packets and wait for a random period of time before sending the packet again. This random period of time is based on an average wait time. The ability for an Ethernet host to know if another host begins transmitting at the same time is called *Collision Detection*.

If, after waiting a random period of time, a host experiences another collision, the host will stop transmitting the packet. This time the host will wait a random amount of time based on twice the average wait time after the last collision. Therefore, if succeeding collisions are experienced, the host waits exponentially longer to retransmit the packet. This is called *exponential backoff*.

Earlier network bus protocols used different methods to deal with collisions. One method is called 1-persistent CSMA where the stations retransmit immediately with a probability of 1. This arrangement can lead to instability of the bus due to constant collisions. Another method is called non-persistent CSMA where the collided stations wait a length of time drawn from a probability distribution. This fixes the instability problem but wastes the capacity of the bus since stations are spending a lot of time waiting to retransmit. A compromise of these methods is called p-persistent CSMA where the station transmits to an idle bus with probability p and waits a pre-specified amount of time with probability $(1 - p)$.

Ethernet uses a hybrid of these methods with a 1-persistent CSMA with binary exponential backoff. This specifies that a station will transmit to an idle bus with probability 1, and if a collision is detected, the station waits for an amount of time before retransmission. This time is doubled for each repeated collision. In other words, the probability of retransmission is cut in half for each collision, thus the term binary exponential backoff. This method gives good performance in a variety of load conditions since the station can utilize more of the bus in low loads and can remain stable in high loads.

Stochastics of Ethernet

The term *stochastics* is derived from a Greek term meaning "the art of aiming." Stochastics refers to the probabilities of behavior. The following is a mathematical development of the stochastics of Ethernet considering its rules of operation. Note that this mathematical development is not considered a complete characterization of the problem. Refer to the book by Bertsekas and Gallager for a more mathematically rigorous treatment of the problem.

First, the amount of time needed to start sending a packet without a collision is

$$A = kp(1 - p)^{k-1}$$

where k is the number of stations ready to transmit and p is the probability that a station begins to transmit in an open slot. This is simply the binomial probability that one station attempts to transmit and others do not. When $p = 1/k$, A is maximized. Therefore,

$$A = \left(1 - \frac{1}{k}\right)^{k-1}.$$

The maximum Ethernet utilization, or Ethernet efficiency, is the length of a transmission interval over the sum of the length of a transmission interval and the length of a collision interval. If the average frame takes P seconds to transmit, when k stations are ready to transmit, the system efficiency is

$$S = \frac{P}{P + \frac{2\tau}{A}}$$

where 2τ is the round trip time. Considering the maximum propagation time for Ethernet, the round trip time can be no more than 51.2μsec.

Since

$$P = \frac{F}{B}$$

where F is the frame length and B is the transmission rate, the above equation can be rewritten to solve for the system efficiency in terms of frame length.

$$S = \frac{1}{1 + \dfrac{2\tau B}{FA}}$$

where B is the transmission rate, 2τ is assumed to be 51.2μsec, and F is the frame size.

The curves in Figure D-4 derive from the above equations showing the system efficiency versus the number of stations for various frame sizes.

Note from the figure that the worst-case maximum efficiency is 30 percent of the transmission rate for 64B packets and 15 hosts. This is an enormous hit in throughput on a large access network. Therefore, understand that throwing a few hosts on a shared Ethernet to save money may have a more detrimental effect on the hosts' perceived performance of the network than simply dividing the transmission rate of the Ethernet by the number of hosts of the shared Ethernet.

Figure D-4
The system efficiency versus the number of stations for various frame sizes

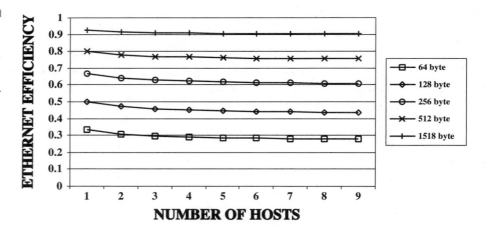

APPENDIX E

OSI Model

The OSI Model is used to describe how information from one application on one computer can move to an application on another computer. Developed by the *International Organization for Standardization* (ISO) in 1984, it is the primary architectural model for internetworking communications. The OSI Model has seven layers:

- Physical layer
- Data link layer
- Network layer
- Transport layer
- Session layer
- Presentation layer
- Application layer

We will now take a look at their purposes within the OSI Model and give an example of a technology that correlates to that particular layer.

Layer 1: The Physical Layer

The definition of the physical layer is that it is Layer 1 of the OSI Reference Model. The physical layer defines the electrical, mechanical, procedural, and functional specifications for activating, maintaining, and deactivating the physical link between end systems. It is comprised of three components. These components, in some instances, are the same in *Local Area Network* (LAN) and *Wide Area Network* (WAN) environments. They are cables or wires, connectors, and encoding.

Cables and Wires

The majority of the cable in place today falls into three types: *Unshielded Twisted Pair* (UTP), coaxial, and fiber optic. The majority of modern internal cable plant wiring is UTP. However, coaxial cable is still used today for specific LAN applications as well as for some high-speed WAN applications. Finally, the high-speed cable of choice is fiber. Fiber is used as the backbone for all high-speed LAN and WAN connections today.

Unshielded Twisted Pair (UTP)　UTP has many uses. It is used for voice communication, key card readers, alarm systems, and data communications. The first distinction in the type of UTP that can be used is the rating of the cable. UTP cable is rated for *either* or *plenum* use. If an area is a plenum or air return space, plenum rated cable must be used. Otherwise, standard cable is acceptable for use.

NOTE:　*Plenum-rated cable is approximately twice the cost of standard UTP cable.*

The next distinction, and probably most important, is the category designator. The category, often abbreviated as CAT, levels officially run from Category 1 to Category 5:

- *CAT 1*　Here cable performance is intended for basic communications and power-limited circuit cable. No performance criteria exist for cable at this level.

- *CAT 2*　Low performance UTP. Typical applications are voice and low-speed data. This is not specified in the *Electronic Industries Association/Telecommunications Industry Association* (EIA/TIA) 568A for data use.

- *CAT 3*　This is data cable that complies with the transmission requirements in the EIA/TIA 568A. It has a maximum transmission speed of 16Mbps. In current installations, this is the grade most often used for voice cabling.

- *CAT 4*   An infrequently used category. It has a maximum transmission speed of 20Mbps.
- *CAT 5*   The most commonly used UTP category. Its maximum transmission speed is 100Mbps.

Coaxial cable   The coaxial cable used in networks is a relative of the coax cable used in many households for cable TV reception. Just like UTP, there can be both PVC and plenum-rated varieties for each variation. Many variations of this cable exist, but only three are used for data communications. The impedance or resistance of the cable is the item that differentiates the specific cables. RG58, RG59, and RG62 have approximately the same diameter, but each cable has a different amount of impedance. Table E-1 summarizes the coax categories, as follows:

- *RG58*   Also called ThinNet. Rated for 10MHz transmissions over a distance of 185 meters.
- *RG8*   Also called ThickNet. Rated for 10MHz transmissions over a distance of 500 meters.
- *RG62*   Used for IBM controller cabling.
- *RG59*   Not used for data transmissions. Used primarily for video transmissions and household cable TV.

Fiber optic cable   Fiber optic cable is the cable of choice for high-speed, long-distance communications. Simply put, a light source such as a low-powered laser is used to generate the optical or light signals down this type of cable. These cables are constructed out of small, thin strands of glass that

Table E-1

Coaxial Cable
Variations

Type of Coaxial Cable	Impedance	Cable Diameter	Usage
RG8	50 Ohm	10mm	10Base5, Thick Ethernet
RG58	50 Ohm	5mm	10 Base2, Thin Ethernet
RG59	75 Ohm	6mm	Video
RG62	93 Ohm	6mm	IBM 3270, Arcnet

look like fibers. The distance limitation of fiber is often measured in kilometers. Fiber optic cable, like UTP and coax, is rated either for PVC or plenum use. Two different types of fiber optic cable exist:

- *Multimode Fiber (MMF)*   Multimode fiber enables light to travel over one of many possible paths. Light, for example, could bounce under various angles in the core of the multimode cable. Because of the larger diameter of the core, it is much easier to get the light within it, allowing for less expensive electronics and connectors. The maximum distance for MMF is two km.

- *Single Mode Fiber (SMF)*   This offers the light only one route to travel through. SMF has a much smaller core than MMF (eight micron for SMF versus 50 or 62.5 micron for MMF). The smaller core enables much longer distances than MMF. Telephone companies interconnect their network equipment with SMF. The typical distance is between five and 1,000 miles. Simply put, if you want more distance, use a stronger laser.

NOTE: *SMF equipment is much more expensive than the equipment for MMF.*

Physical Terminations and Connectors

Without connectors and terminations, cables would have to be "hard-wired" to the end device. This would make quick disconnects and reconnects impossible. Connectors usually vary depending on the media type.

UTP   Four basic modular jack styles are used in UTP. Figure E-1 shows the eight-position and eight-position keyed modular jacks. These jacks are commonly and incorrectly referred to as RJ45 and keyed RJ45 respectively.

The six-position modular jack is commonly referred to as RJ11. Using these terms can sometimes lead to confusion since the RJ designations actually refer to specific wiring configurations called *Universal Service Ordering Codes* (USOC).

Figure E-1
UTP jacks

8-position · 8-position keyed

6-position · 6-position modified

Figure E-2
EIA/TIA and USOC
jack pinouts

Pair ID	PIN #
T1	5
R1	4
T2	1
R2	6
T3	3
R3	2
T4	7
R4	8

T568A

Pair ID	PIN #
T1	5
R1	4
T2	2
R2	1
T3	3
R3	6
T4	7
R4	8

T568B

Pair ID	PIN #
T1	1
R1	2
T2	3
R2	6

10BASE-T
(802.3)

Pair ID	PIN #
T1	4
R1	3
T2	2
R2	5
T3	1
R4	6

USOC 1-, 2-
or 3-pair

Pair ID	PIN #
T1	5
R1	4
T2	3
R2	6
T3	2
R3	7
T4	1
R4	8

USOC 4-
pair

Pair ID	PIN #
T1	5
R1	4
T2	3
R2	6

Token-Ring
(802.5)

The designation RJ means "registered jack." Each of these three basic jack styles can be wired for different RJ configurations. For example, the six-position jack can be wired as an RJ11C (one-pair), RJ14C (two-pair), or RJ25C (three-pair) configuration. An eight-position jack can be wired for configurations such as RJ61C (four-pair) and RJ48C. The keyed eight-position jack can be wired for RJ45S, RJ46S, and RJ47S.

The fourth modular jack style is a modified version of the six-position jack (modified modular jack or MMJ). It was designed by *Digital Equipment Corporation*® (DEC) along with the *modified modular plug* (MMP) to eliminate the possibility of connecting DEC data equipment to voice lines and vice versa.

Cable Termination Practices for UTP   Two primary wiring standards exist. One set of standards is set by the EIA/TIA; the other is set by the USOC. The various pinouts are detailed in Figure E-2.

Two wiring schemes have been adopted by the EIA/TIA 568-A standard. They are nearly identical, except that pairs two and three are reversed.

T568A is the preferred scheme because it is compatible with one or two-pair USOC systems. Either configuration can be used for *Integrated Services Digital Network* (ISDN) and high-speed data applications.

USOC wiring is available for one-, two-, three-, or four-pair systems. Pair 1 occupies the center conductors; pair 2 occupies the next two contacts out, and so on. One advantage to this scheme is that a six-position plug configured with one or two pairs can be inserted into an eight-position jack and maintain pair continuity.

Ethernet uses either of the EIA/TIA standards in an eight-position jack. However, only two pairs are used. On the other hand, Token Ring wiring uses either an eight-position or six-position jack. The eight-position format is compatible with T568A, T568B, and USOC wiring schemes. The six-position format is compatible with one- or two-pair USOC wiring.

Coaxial connectors Coaxial cables use two different connectors. One type is used specifically for ThickNet. All other types of coax use the same type of connector.

All ThinNet and other coax cables, except RG8 (ThickNet), use the *Bayonet Neil-Concelman* (BNC) connector, shown in Figure E-3. The acronym BNC has also been purported to mean British Naval Connector and Bayonet Nut Connector, but those references are incorrect.

NOTE: *If the connector is not firmly connected to the cable, the connection will have intermittent connection issues. This is not acceptable for DS3 WAN circuits.*

ThickNet (RG8) uses an *Attachment Unit Interface* (AUI) connector to connect devices to the cable. The AUI connector itself is a standard male DB-15M with studs instead of mounting screws; the female is a DB-15F

Figure E-3
BNC connector for coaxial cable

Table E-2

AUI and RJ45
Pinouts

AUI Pin No.	Ethernet V2.0	IEEE 802.3	RJ45 (EIA/TIA568A) Pin #
1	Shield	Control in Shield	
2	Collision Presence +	Control in A	
3	Transmit +	Data out A	1
4	Reserved	Data in Shield	
5	Receive +	Data in A	3
6	Power Return	Voltage Common	
7	Reserved	Control out A	
8	Reserved	Control out Shield	
9	Collision Presence −	Control in B	
10	Transmit −	Data out B	2
11	Reserved	Data out Shield	
12	Receive −	Data in B	6
13	Power	Voltage	
14	Reserved	Voltage Shield	
15	Reserved	Control out B	
Connector Shield ──────────────────────── Protective Ground			

with a slide-clip that attempts to lock onto the studs. Table E-2 lists the pinouts for an AUI connector as well as an RJ45-pinned connector.

Fiber optic connectors Five popular types of fiber connectors exist. They can be used for both MMF and SMF. The most common types of connectors, ST, SC, and MIC, are pictured in Figure E-4. The less common connector types are ESCON and MT-RJ. The following is a brief description of each of the connectors:

- *ST* A commonly used connector in the earlier days of fiber installations.

- *SC* The most commonly used connector type today. Almost every connector on Cisco equipment uses an SC connector.

Figure E-4
Common types of
fiber connectors

A) ST Connector   B) SC Connector

C) MIC Connector

Figure E-5
Common encoding
methods

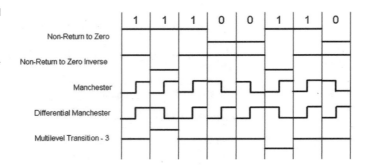

- *MIC/FSD*   The *Medium Interface Connector/Fiber Shroud Duplex* (MIC/FSD) connector is used for fiber-based Fiber Distributed Data Interfaces (FDDI) connections. It is polarized so that TX/RX are always correct.

- *ESCON*   This is used to connect to IBM equipment as well as channel interface processors.

- *MT-RJ*   A new fiber connector that is able to fit into a standard 110 patch panel. It almost doubles the port capacity of an SC module.

Physical Encoding Methods

An encoding method is the method that a device uses to put data on the media. Although the media and connectors for LANs and WANs are similar, the encoding variations for LANs and WANs are different.

LAN encoding   Four basic LAN encoding schemes exist. The first encoding scheme is the foundation for all the other encoding schemes. Thus, it is important that you understand the basic encoding scheme that everything is based on, the *Non-Return To Zero-Level* (NRZ-L). Figure E-5 shows how the various encoding methods reduce the binary numbers to electrical or optical signals.

The common encoding methods are as follows:

- *Non-Return to Zero-Level (NRZ-L)*   This is the basic type of encoding upon which all others are based. A *one* is positive voltage; a *zero* is no voltage. The problem with this is that timing information cannot be retrieved from a string of zeros. Thus, other encoding methods have been developed to overcome this problem.
- *Non-Return to Zero Inverted (NRZI)*   Used in 100Base-Fx fiber networks, NRZI uses a change in signal to represent a one.
- *Manchester*   Used in Ethernet, this encoding is based on the signal transition in the middle of the bit. An upward transition is a one. A downward transition represents a zero.
- *Differential Manchester*   Used in Token Ring networks, this always has a transition in the middle. However, the encoding is based on the transition at the bit boundaries. A transition indicates a zero. No transition indicates a one.
- *MLT-3*   Used in Fast Ethernet Networks. Instead of two voltage levels (voltage and no voltage), MLT-3 uses three layers: positive voltage, no voltage, and negative voltage. Changing the voltage represents a one. For instance, a series of ones would be represented as $0,1,0,-1,0,1,0,-1$.

WAN connectors   Remember that the same types of media are used in WANs as LANs. However, the connectors used in WANs differ depending upon their use. Too many WAN connectors exist for us to cover every type, but the most common WAN connectors terminate T1 and E1 lines. Table E-3 displays the pinouts of T1 and E1 Lines.

NOTE: *The use of the terms tip and ring are typically not used today. Their usage is historical in perspective when testing was done with a tone tester. This test would allow a different tone to be present depending on which tip or ring was tested.*

WAN encoding   Before the topic of WAN encoding can be addressed, the concept of the digital hierarchy must be familiar to the reader. The digital hierarchy is a classification of circuit speeds. In North America, it is called the North American Digital Hierarchy. In Europe and the majority of the

Table E-3

The Pinouts of T1 and E1 Lines

Eight Position Jack Pinouts	T1/EI
1	Receive (tip)
2	Receive (ring)
3	Not used
4	Transmit (tip)
5	Transmit (ring)
6	Not used
7	Not used
8	Not used

Table E-4

Various Circuit Names and Speeds

Optical Circuit	Speed
OC-1	51.8Mbps
OC-3	155.5Mbps
OC-12	622.1Mbps
OC-48	2488.3Mbps

world, it is called the CCITT Digital Hierarchy. Both begin at the DS0 level with a single 64Kbps circuit. Then differences appear in the two systems.

In the North American Digital Hierarchy, this DS0 circuit is multiplied 24 times into a DS1 circuit with a speed of 1.544Mbps. This DS1 is then multiplied 28 times into a DS3 circuit with a speed of over 44Mbps.

The CCITT Digital Hierarchy combines 30 DS0s into an E1 circuit with a speed of 2.048Mbps. Next, 16 E1 circuits are combined to form an E3 circuit with a speed of over 34Mbps.

The WAN media type used depends on the circuit speed. T1 and E1 circuits generally use UTP. DS3 and E3 circuits use coax. However, all speeds above DS3/E3 require the use of fiber optic cables. The terms *North American Synchronous Optical Network* (SONET) and *International Synchronous Digital Network* (SDH) identify the circuits in this range. Table E-4 denotes the various circuit names and speeds.

The variations in WAN encoding first occur at the DS1 level. When a DS1 line is ordered, it is necessary to specify the framing and line coding. These settings must match the Channel Service Unit/Data Service Unit (CSU/DSU) and the other end of the circuit.

NOTE: *One of the most difficult issues to troubleshoot is the incorrect encoding of a circuit. More that once, I have seen a service provider finally determine that the cause of a line fault is improper encoding at one end of the circuit.*

The two frame types available for DS1s are *D4/Super Frame* (SF) and *Extended Super Frame* (ESF). The two frame types for E1s are CRC4 and no CRC4.

The available line codings for DS1s are *Alternate Mark Inversion* (AMI) and *Bipolar Eight-Zero Substitution* (B8ZS). The only available line codings for E1s are AMI and *High-Density Bipolar 3* (HDB3).

Conclusion

The physical layer may be seen as the most trivial or least important of the seven layers. After all, no fancy things like routing or switching happen at this layer. No addresses are used at the physical layer. However, many of the issues faced in the networking world are solved at the physical layer. A UTP cable might run too close to a fluorescent light or an OC-3 fiber patch cord might get accidentally crushed. When troubleshooting network problems, one of the most effective methods is to follow the OSI Model and troubleshoot by layers. Thus, you would start at the physical layer and move up once you have determined each layer is operating correctly.

Layer 2: The Data Link Layer

Layer 2 of the OSI Reference Model is the data link layer. Figure E-6 shows the placement of the network layer in the OSI Reference Model.

Figure E-6
The data link layer in
the OSI Reference
Model

7	Application Layer
6	Presentation Layer
5	Session Layer
4	Transport Layer
3	Network Layer
2	**Data Link Layer**
1	Physical Layer

The data link layer is responsible for describing the specifications for topology and communication between local systems. Many examples of data link layer technology exist:

- Ethernet
- Fast Ethernet
- Token Ring
- Frame Relay
- HDLC
- Point-to-Point Protocol (PPP)
- Serial Line Interface Protocol (SLIP)

All of these services describe how conversations take place between two devices on the same media. Remember that the data link layer implementation used is independent of the physical layer. For example, Ethernet can use UTP or coaxial cable. It does not matter which physical layer media it uses; the rules that govern the technology are the same. This is the beauty of the OSI Model: any layer can be replaced without concerns about the lower or upper layers.

Communication at the data link layer is between two hosts on the same network. Those two hosts can be a desktop computer communicating with a local file server or a local host sending data to a router that is destined for a remote host (see Figure E-7).

Figure E-7
An example of data link layer conversations

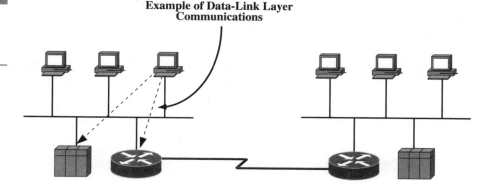

Example of Data-Link Layer Communications

Figure E-8
Ethernet frame format

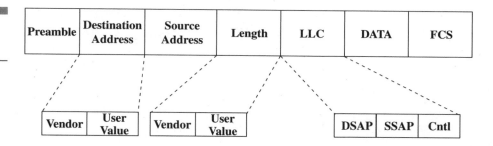

Data Link Layer Example

The following section focuses on Ethernet, one of the most commonly used data link layer standards. If we look at the frame format of an Ethernet frame, we can get a better understanding of each component's purpose. In Figure E-8, we see a standard IEEE 802.3 Ethernet frame format. If we look at each component, we can easily see its purpose.

Preamble The preamble is an alternating pattern of ones and zeros. It tells the other stations on the media that a frame is coming. The IEEE 802.3 preamble ends with two consecutive ones, which serves to synchronize the frame reception of all stations on the LAN.

Data link layer addressing (Destination and source address) The capability to distinguish one host from another is critical when multiple hosts have access to the same media. Compare that to point-to-point connections in which the capability to distinguish the end point is irrelevant because there is only one other node on the network that can hear the data.

The address used by end hosts to identify each other is called the *Media Access Control* (MAC) address. It is often referred to as the physical address, burned-in address, or hardware address. The MAC address of each Ethernet *Network Interface Card* (NIC) is by definition unique. It is a 48-bit address built into the NIC that uniquely identifies the station. It is generally represented in one of three formats:

- 00-60-94-EB-41-9F
- 00:60:94:EB:41:9F
- 0060.94EB.419F

If we look closely at the MAC address, we will see that it can be broken down into two distinct components: the vendor's address and a unique host identifier. The first three octets (24 bits) identify the vendor. Using the example listed above, we can look up 00-60-94 at `http://standards.ieee.org/regauth/oui/oui.txt`.

We can see that this NIC was manufactured by IBM. This can be useful when attempting to locate a device on the network that is malfunctioning.

Length   The Length field indicates the number of bytes contained in the Data field. Although all of the other fields are of a predetermined length (the Destination and Source addresses are six bytes) the Data field can be up to 1,500 bytes. If the data in the frame is insufficient to fill the frame to a minimum 64-byte size, the frame is padded to ensure at least a 64-byte frame.

Logical Link Control (LLC)   The IEEE 802.2 *Logical Link Control* (LLC) header is used to specify which upper layer protocol is contained in the data. Without the capability to distinguish which upper layer protocol a packet belongs to, it is impossible to carry multiple network layer protocols over a data link layer implementation. For example, because Novell's 802.3 RAW frame format does not have a method to distinguish between network layer protocols, it could only carry a single network layer protocol. This is one of the reasons why Novell's 802.3 frame format is generally not employed.

Another example of a data link layer technology not using a type field is SLIP. Even though it enjoyed some success in the late '80s and early '90s as a dialup protocol, its incapability to distinguish between different network layer protocols has allowed PPP to become the standard dialup protocol.

The following fields all play a part in LLC identification:

■ *DSAP*   The *Destination Service Access Point* (DSAP) is a one-byte field that acts like a pointer in the receiving station. It tells the receiving NIC which buffer to put this information in. This function is critical when users are running multiple network layer protocols.

■ *SSAP*   The *Source Service Access Point* (SSAP) is identical to the DSAP, except that it indicates the source of the sending application.

■ *Control*   This one-byte field is used to indicate the type of LLC frame of this data frame. Three different types of LLC frames exist:

- *LLC1*   An unacknowledged connectionless service. It uses unsequenced information to set up communication between two network stations. This type of LLC is generally used with Novell's *Internetwork Packet Exchange* (IPX), TCP/IP, and Vines IP.

- *LLC2*   A connection-oriented service between two network stations. This type of service is generally used in SNA and NetBIOS sessions.

- *LLC3*   A connectionless but acknowledged-oriented service between two different stations. This type of service can be used by SDLC.

Data   The Data field in an IEEE 802.3 frame can be between 43 and 1,497 bytes. However, depending upon the type of frame being used, this size can vary. For example, an Ethernet II frame can hold between 46 and 1,497 bytes of data, while a frame using Novell's RAW 802.3 frame format can hold between 46 and 1,500 bytes of data.

Frame Check Sequence (FCS)   The last four bytes of a IEEE 802.3 frame are used to verify that the frame is not corrupt. By using a complex polynomial, the NIC can detect errors in the frame. If errors are detected, then the frame is discarded and it never reaches the memory buffers.

Now that we understand the frame format of an IEEE 802.3 frame, we need to discuss how those frames get on the wire.

Carrier Sense Media Access with Collision Detection (CSMA/CD)
Ethernet is one of the most common network topologies. The basic rule behind Ethernet communication is called *Carrier Sense Multiple Access*

with Collision Detection (CSMA/CD). If we break down each phrase, we can interpret its meaning:

■ *Carrier Sense* All Ethernet stations are required to listen to the network to see if any other devices are sending data. This serves two purposes: one, it keeps the station from sending data when someone else is sending data and, two, it enables the station to be ready when another station wants to send it data.

■ *Multiple Access* This means more than two stations can be connected to the same network at the same time and that all stations can transmit data whenever the network is free. In order for data to be transmitted, the station must wait until the Ethernet channel is idle. Once the channel is idle, the station can transmit a frame, but it must listen to see if there is a collision.

■ *Collision Detection* If there is a collision, then both stations must immediately back off and use a backoff algorithm to randomly determine how long they should wait before trying to transmit again. It is important that a random number be generated for this timer, because if some standard number were used, then both stations would wait the same length of time and then attempt to transmit again, thus causing another collision.

NOTE: *A collision is the simultaneous transmitting of a frame by two different stations. A station can detect a collision within the first 64 bytes of the transmission.*

Conclusion

Many different types of data link layer technologies exist, and Ethernet is one of those technologies. Although a data link layer technology can theoretically use any physical layer implementation, generally the actual implementation of a data link layer technology goes hand in hand with the physical layer implementation. For example, PPP is generally used over dialup networks or WAN networks, while Ethernet and Token Ring are used in LAN environments. This means that you probably won't see very many implementations of PPP using CAT 5 cable for its wiring infrastructure. Likewise, you probably won't see Token Ring being deployed from a corporate office to a telecommuter's home using the Telco's wiring infrastructure.

Layer 3: Network Layer

Layer 3 of the OSI Reference Model is the network layer. Figure E-9 shows the placement of the network layer in the OSI Reference Model.

This layer is responsible for providing routing for the network. Routing, in a generic sense, is simply finding a path to a destination. In the context of the network layer, routing means finding a path to a destination that is a member of a different Layer 2 network than the source. Physical networks can be connected together with bridges to form larger Layer 2 networks. Unfortunately, Layer 2 networks cannot scale to an infinite size. As these networks grow, more bandwidth is used to transmit broadcast packets that flood the entire Layer 2 network. These broadcast packets are used to find the destination host.

Figure E-9
The network layer
and the OSI
reference model

7	Application Layer
6	Presentation Layer
5	Session Layer
4	Transport Layer
3	**Network Layer**
2	Data Link Layer
1	Physical Layer

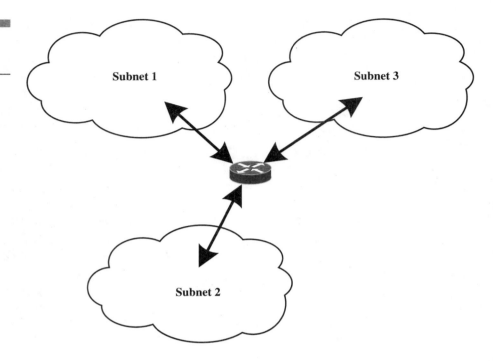

Routing enables Layer 2 networks to be broken into smaller segments, enabling the network to grow to support more hosts. Figure E-10 shows the concept of routing.

The data link control layer passes packets up to the network layer. These packets have headers to define the source and destination addresses and other network layer parameters of the data in the packet. The network layer only uses the data in the network layer packet header for information to perform its functions. This maintains the modularity of the network layer. Therefore, there is no dependency on the information from the data link control layer headers and the transport layer headers.

Network layer communication is not guaranteed. This means that there is no mechanism to determine if the destination node received the network layer packets. Guaranteed delivery is maintained at other layers in the OSI Reference Model. The most obvious reason for not implementing guaranteed delivery at the network layer is because this layer has no concept of end-to-end delivery. It would be more appropriate for upper layer protocols that implement more connection-oriented services to make sure that the data reaches its destination. The network layer routes data on a packet-by-packet basis.

Only one network layer process exists for each network node. Several data link control layer processes may be found below the network layer, depending on the number of physical interfaces in the node, and several transport layer processes may be found above the network layer, depending on the number of connection-oriented streams terminating at the node. Several network layer protocols may be running on a node, but each of these protocols corresponds to a separate logical internetwork and they do not intercommunicate.

A special node called a *gateway* connects logical networks formed by network layer addressing schemes. Gateways have a special sublayer in the upper portion of the network layer called the *Internet sublayer*. This sublayer handles the intercommunication between subnets. When a packet arrives from one subnet that is destined for another, the packet will be passed from the network layer to the Internet sublayer. The Internet sublayer in turn determines the destination subnet and forwards the packet back down to the lower portion of the network layer to the destination subnet. This is the basic idea behind routing. Figure E-11 illustrates the concept of a network node.

Each network layer process at each node is a peer process. These peer processes work together to implement distributed algorithms. These distributed algorithms are the routing algorithms corresponding to various routing protocols. These protocols provide a means to automatically discover and transmit routing information between gateways.

The Internet Protocol (IP)

The most familiar protocol that operates at the network layer is the *Internet Protocol* (IP). IP is by far the most widely deployed network layer protocol due to the success of the Internet. This protocol is the foundation of the

Figure E-11
Network node model

	Internet Sublayer
3	Network Layer
2	Data Link Layer
1	Physical Layer

Internet in terms of addressing and packet routing. The Internet employs multiple protocols in the other OSI Reference Model layers, but it only uses IP in the network layer.

Another example of a network protocol is Novell's *Internet Packet Exchange* (IPX). Novell has since refined NetWare to use IP as the native network layer protocol instead of IPX.

IP Node Operation

If an IP host wants to communicate with another IP host, the transmitting IP source must determine if the destination IP address is in the same subnet or not. If the destination is in the same subnet, the host must send an *Address Resolution Protocol* (ARP) request packet to obtain the MAC address of the destination, assuming the destination MAC address isn't already in its ARP table. If the destination is not in the same subnet as the source, the source must send the packet to the MAC address of the gateway for that subnet. Most IP hosts have one IP address to send their packets to if they are destined for any subnet other than their own. This is called the *default gateway* or *default router address*. The user configures the default gateway address.

Once the default gateway (router) gets the packet and sees that the packet is destined for its own MAC address and at the same time destined for another IP host, the router knows that it must forward the packet to another interface to move the packet closer to its destination.

The mechanism for determining if the destination IP host is in the same subnet is as follows. The subnet mask is bitwise ANDed with both the source IP address and the destination IP address. The logic table for the AND operation is shown in Table E-5.

The result of these two functions is exclusively ORed (XORed). If this final result is not zero, then the destination IP address is in another subnet. The logic table for the XOR operation is shown in Table E-6.

Table E-5

Logic table for
AND operations

	1	0
1	1	0
0	0	0

Table E-6

Logic table for OR operations

	1	0
1	0	1
0	1	0

Here is an example of determining if the destination address is in the same subnet as the host:

Source IP address:

$(100.1.43.1)_{\text{dotted-decimal}}$ $(01100100.00000001.00101011.00000001)_{\text{binary}}$

Subnet mask:

$(255.255.255.0)_{\text{dotted-decimal}}$ $(11111111.11111111.11111111.00000000)_{\text{binary}}$

Destination IP address:

$(100.1.44.2)_{\text{dotted-decimal}}$ $(01100100.00000001.00101100.00000010)_{\text{binary}}$

Source IP address ANDed with subnet mask:

01100100.00000001.00101011.00000001
11111111.11111111.11111111.00000000
01100100.00000001.00101011.00000000

Destination IP address ANDed with subnet mask:

01100100.00000001.00101100.00000010
11111111.11111111.11111111.00000000
01100100.00000001.00101100.00000000

The two results XORed:

01100100.00000001.00101011.00000000
01100100.00000001.00101100.00000000
00000000.00000000.00000111.00000000

The result of the XOR function is not zero. Therefore, the destination IP address is in another subnet than the source and the packet must be sent to the default gateway to be routed to the destination subnet.

When the router gets a packet to be forwarded to another subnet, the router must manipulate the MAC and IP header fields to ensure that the packet is forwarded toward its destination.

Three things must happen when the router forwards the packet at the network layer:

■ The interface to forward the packet to must be determined.

■ The destination MAC address must be updated with the MAC address of the next-hop router or destination host.

■ The *Time to Live* (TTL) field must be decremented in the IP header.

The interface that the packet is forwarded out of is determined by looking through the route table that the router maintains. This route table associates a route to a destination with a physical interface.

The destination MAC address must be updated with the MAC address of the destination IP host if the host is directly connected to the router. If the destination host is not directly connected to one of the ports of the router, the router must forward the packet to the next router to move the packet toward the destination IP host. In either case, if the router doesn't know the MAC address of the next hop toward the destination, it must ARP for the MAC address.

The TTL field is then decremented. This field provides a mechanism for the packet to be removed from the network if it gets caught in a loop. Without such a mechanism, the packet may be forwarded for as long as the routing loop is active. The packet is removed by a router if its TTL field is zero.

Internetwork Packet Exchange (IPX) Operation

Another example of a Layer 3 protocol is the IPX protocol. The IPX protocol was developed by Novell NetWare. Novell NetWare is a *Network Operating System* (NOS) that provides network file and print services. IPX is quickly being replaced by IP since NetWare now provides native IP support, but there remains a large installed base of IPX networks in campus networks.

Unlike IP, IPX has no concept of multiple subnets per the Layer 2 network. Instead, IPX has only one address per physical network called a *net-*

work number. The full network layer address for a network device is made of two parts: the 32-bit network number and the node's 48-bit MAC address.

Some argue that the combination of Layer 2 and Layer 3 addresses to form a Layer 3 address undermines the modularity of the OSI Reference Model. This is due to the fact that IPX (Layer 3) network numbers depend on the Layer 2 addressing scheme. This argument is purely academic since the MAC address scheme is so prevalent. The real limitation to IPX is its inability to logically subnet hosts on the same physical network.

Layer 4: Transport Layer

Layer 4 of the OSI Reference Model is the transport layer. Figure E-12 shows the placement of the network layer in the OSI Reference Model.

The transport layer is responsible for data transfer issues such as reliability of the connection, establishing error detections, recovery, and flow control. In addition, this layer is responsible for delivering packets from the network layer to the upper layers of the OSI Model.

If we think of the network layer as responsible for delivering packets from one host to another, the transport layer is responsible for identifying

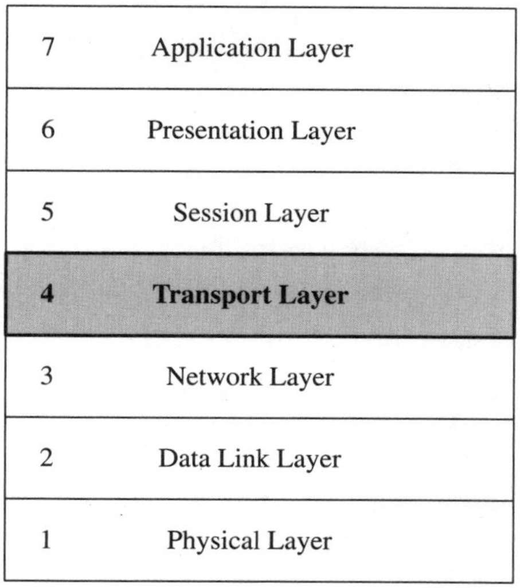

Figure E-12
The transport layer
and the OSI
reference model

7	Application Layer
6	Presentation Layer
5	Session Layer
4	**Transport Layer**
3	Network Layer
2	Data Link Layer
1	Physical Layer

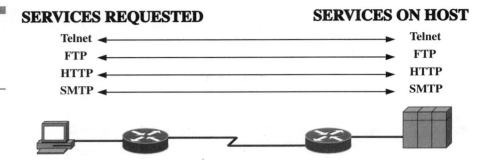

the conversations between two hosts. For example, Figure E-13 shows an example of how the transport layer keeps the conversations between the different applications separate.

Two different variants of transport layer protocols are used. The first provides a reliable, connection-oriented service, while the second method is a best-effort delivery. The difference between these two protocols dictates the paradigm in which they operate. When using TCP/IP, the two different protocols are TCP and UDP. Inside an IP packet is a protocol number that enables the host to identify whether the packet contains a TCP message or a UDP message. The TCP protocol value is 6 and for UDP it is 17. Many other (~130) protocols types exist, but these two are commonly used to transport user messages from one host to another.

Transport Layer Protocol Examples

In this section, we'll examine some examples of transport layer protocols.

Transmission Control Protocol (TCP)   The TCP described in RFC 793 provides applications with a reliable connection-oriented service. Three basic instruments are used to make TCP a connection-oriented service:

- Sequence numbers
- Acknowledgments
- Windowing

In order for data to be handed down to the network layer, the data must be broken down into messages. These messages are then given a sequence number by TCP before being handed off to the network layer. The purpose of the sequence number is so that in case the packets arrive out of order the remote host can reassemble the data using the sequence numbers. This only guarantees that the data is reassembled correctly.

In addition to sequence numbers, acknowledgements are used by the remote host to tell the local host that the data was received, guaranteeing the delivery of data. If, for whatever reason, a packet gets dropped along the way, the remote host can see that it is missing a message and request it again, as shown in Figure E-14.

Although windowing enables TCP to regulate the flow of packets between two hosts, this minimizes the chances of packets being dropped because the buffers are full in the remote host.

In order for a TCP connection to be established, a three-step handshake is exchanged between the local host and the remote host. This three-way handshake starts with the local host initiating a conversation by sending a *Synchronize Sequence Numbers* (SYN) packet to the remote host, as shown in Figure E-15.

The remote host acknowledges the SYN and sends an SYN acknowledgement back to the local host. The local host responds by sending an acknowledgement and then starts sending data. The purpose of this handshake is to synchronize the sequence numbers that identify the proper order used to reconstruct the messages throughout the conversation.

User Datagram Protocol (UDP) The UDP, as described in RFC 768, provides applications with a connectionless best-effort delivery service. Because there is no time wasted setting up a connection, applications that

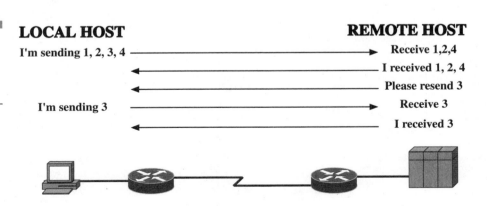

Figure E-14
Using
acknowledgements
for guaranteed
delivery

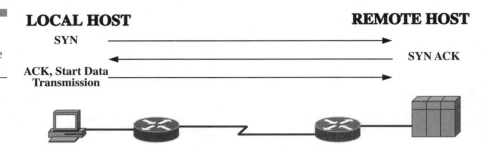

utilize UDP are very fast. Applications that send short bursts of data can take advantage of UDP's speed, but if the messages get delivered out of order or a message gets dropped, then the entire message fails.

Well-Known Ports   We've seen how we can guarantee the delivery of a packet through the use of TCP and how we can improve throughput by using a connectionless delivery service, but how are discrete conversations between two hosts handled? Both TCP and UDP utilize a mechanism called a port (also known as a socket). By utilizing a source port and a destination port, two hosts can distinguish between multiple conversations.

In order to provide services to unknown callers, a host will use a well-known port number. Well-known port numbers are assigned by the *Internet Assigned Numbers Authority* (IANA). By adhering to the well-known port numbers published by the IANA, we can make sure that various services do not utilize the same port. Both TCP and UDP use port numbers and when a service can utilize both TCP and UDP, the port number is identical. Table E-7 shows us a sampling of the well-known port numbers.

Until recently, the assigned port range was from 0 to 255. However, the range has been expanded from 0 to 1,023.

Conclusion

The transport layer protocol helps end devices distinguish between simultaneous conversations between the same two hosts. The protocol that is used, connection-oriented or connectionless, is dependent upon the needs of the upper layer application. Some applications want the speed of UDP and will implement their own form of reliability-checking in an effort to speed up the transmission of the data. Although this obviously adds a lot of over-

Table E-7

Well-known port
numbers

Port Number	Service
20	FTP (Data)
21	FTP (Control)
23	Telnet
25	SMTP
42	Host Name Server
53	Domain Name Service
80	HTTP

Figure E-16
The session layer and
the OSI reference
model

7	Application Layer
6	Presentation Layer
5	**Session Layer**
4	Transport Layer
3	Network Layer
2	Data Link Layer
1	Physical Layer

head to the programmer's job, it can be worth it, depending upon the applications requirements.

Layer 5: Session Layer

Layer 5 of the OSI Reference Model is the session layer. Figure E-16 shows the placement of the session layer in the OSI Reference Model.

The session layer is responsible for providing such functions as directory service and access rights. The session layer has a defined role in the OSI Reference Model, but its functions are not as critical as the lower layers to all networks. For example, a network without the physical layer, the data link layer, network layer, or the transport layer would be lacking basic functionality that would make the network useful. Until recently, the session layer has been ignored or at least not seen as absolutely necessary in data networks. Session layer functionality has been seen as a host responsibility, not a network function. As networks become larger and more secure, functions such as directory services and access rights become more necessary.

Access rights functionality deals with a user's access to various network resources such as computer access and authentication, file access, and printer access. Devices providing the service such as file and print servers have typically implemented access rights. There has been a shift in responsibility for these functions in recent years. Authentication can now be distributed using authentication services such as Kerberos. File and print service access control is moving to network directory services such as Novell's *Network Directory Service* (NDS) or Microsoft's *Active Directory Services* (ADS). These services control what resources a host may access.

Directory services are services that find resources on the network. Typically, a user would have to have prior knowledge of a service to gain access to the service. Some services have the capability of broadcasting their presence, but that methodology does not scale well in a large network with many hosts and many services. True directory services act as a redirection point for hosts to be given addressing information to find a particular resource. Novell's NDS or Microsoft's ADS can act as directory services as well as define a user's access rights, as mentioned above.

The session layer has no hard and fast rules for interfacing with the presentation layer since the presentation layer is optional in many cases. The session layer services are typically accessed via TCP or UDP port numbers, therefore defining the interface to the transport layer.

Layer 6: Presentation Layer

Layer 6 of the OSI Reference Model is the presentation layer. Figure E-17 shows the placement of the network layer in the OSI Reference Model.

The presentation layer is responsible for providing data encryption, data compression, and code conversion. The functions in this layer have

Figure E-17
The presentation
layer and the OSI
reference model

7	Application Layer
6	**Presentation Layer**
5	Session Layer
4	Transport Layer
3	Network Layer
2	Data Link Layer
1	Physical Layer

not been considered a function of the network and have been handled by various applications. In recent years, data encryption, compression, and code conversion have moved into the mainstream of the network protocol functionality.

Data encryption is moving to the forefront of networking since networks are carrying more sensitive data. Encryption can be handled in a number of ways. The easiest and most secure method for encrypting data is to encrypt all the data on a particular link. This requires a device on both ends of a path to encrypt and decrypt the payload of each packet that passes over the link. This requires that sensitive data always pass over a path installed with an encryption device. This does not scale well for a large network. The more scalable method for encryption is for the applications at both ends of a session to set up a means for encrypting the data. This method of encryption requires that a device have more processing power to handle the application and the data encryption in real time.

Data compression conserves bandwidth over a link. Like data encryption, data compression can be done on both ends of a path through a network. This requires an external device to compress the network data. This method does not scale well in large networks where there can be many paths through a network. A more scalable method for data compression is to allow the application at both ends of a session to compress the data. The tradeoff in this method is more processing power is required on the host to support the application and real-time compression/decompression.

Code conversion involves converting a set of data or a data stream from one format to another. Data formats can be for character sets, video formats, graphics formats, and presentation formats. Examples of character set formats are ASCII and EBCDIC, video formats are MPEG and MJPEG, graphics formats are GIF, TIFF, JPEG, and bitmap, and presentation formats are HTML, XML, and SHTML.

No hard and fast rules define the interface between the presentation layer and the session layer since the session layer may be optional for a particular network. The presentation layer communicates to the application layer by addressing the application with an appropriate transport layer (session) address such as a TCP port number.

Layer 7: Application Layer

The final layer, Layer 7, of the OSI Model is the application layer. This section will define the application layer and examine in moderate detail what takes place at Layer 7.

The application layer consists of an application that requires the use of a network to perform its task. Communication between applications takes place at Layer 7. As with the previous layers, Layer 7 exchanges messages with Layer 7 only. Restated, an application communicates with only a peer application. Figure E-18 depicts this layer-to-layer communication.

Figure E-18
Layer 7 application communication

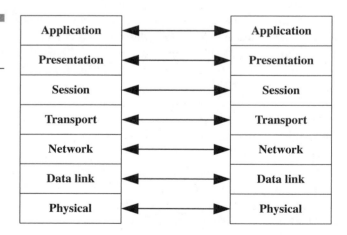

An example application could be something as simple as a *chat* program. The application connects to its peer application and sends characters that are entered on the keyboard. It also displays characters received from the peer application. The applications communicating at Layer 7 use the lower layers and the services they provide to send and receive application-specific information.

Furthermore, it is common for applications to further define the contents of the data that is being exchanged. Even with the simple chat program, a protocol is defined: "Each message received from a peer application contains a single character." This creates a challenge for troubleshooting network-related problems.

Although only a handful of protocols are used at the lower layers, the protocols are usually well specified. As you can see, anyone can define a new protocol for his or her specific application. This makes it difficult for vendors that develop network analyzers to provide the capability of troubleshooting application, or Layer 7, problems.

As you can see, this layer can be any application that requires network communication. The application communicates with its peer application at Layer 7, and an application may arbitrarily define a protocol that specifies application-to-application communication.

Conclusion

It is important to remember that the OSI Model is only for reference. Not all protocols and technologies have a direct correlation to one of the seven layers. Frequently, a protocol may straddle different layers, such as ARP, which is used when a computer knows the IP address it needs to communicate with (network layer) but it doesn't know its MAC address (data link layer). ARP enables a computer to map an IP address to a MAC address. So is ARP a data link layer-protocol or a network-layer protocol? Technically, it straddles both layers, so it doesn't really fit the OSI Model, but without it IP communication on a LAN couldn't happen.

INDEX

Symbols

A

S

W-Z

ABOUT THE CD-ROM

FastTrakExpress™

FastTrak Express provides interactive certification exams to help you prepare for certification. With the enclosed CD, you can test your knowledge of the topics covered in this book with over 200 multiple choice questions.

To Install FastTrak Express:

1. Insert the CD-ROM in your CD-ROM drive.
2. FastTrak Express Setup will launch automatically. Follow the instructions to complete the Setup.
3. When the Setup is finished, you may immediately begin using FastTrak Express.

FastTrak Express offers two testing options: the Adaptive exam and the Standard exam.

The Adaptive Exam

FastTrack Express (FTE) is fully adaptive.

Adaptive testing is a time-saving option used to identify the candidates' strengths and weaknesses. The FTE Adaptive exam style does not simulate all of the exam environments that are found on certification exams but it does cover the most popular styles.

The FTE Adaptive exam selects questions based on the previous topic and will increase or decrease the level of question difficulty depending upon a correct or incorrect answer. The number of correct answers to questions required to pass an FTE exam varies with the specific certification exam. The number of questions in each adaptive exam will vary between 25 and 40 questions. Depending on the type of adaptive exam taken, a passing grade will be given when 17 to 33 questions are answered correctly.

Once an adaptive exam question has been answered you cannot go back to a previous question. You have a time limit in which to complete the adaptive exam. This time varies between certification exams ranging between 25 and 40 minutes maximum per certification exam. If you have not passed before the maximum time limit has been reached, your exam automatically ends.

To take the Adaptive Exam:

1. Click the Adaptive Exam button from the Main window. The Adaptive Exam window will appear.
2. Click the circle or square to the left of the correct answer.

NOTE: *There may be more than one correct answer. The text in the bottom left corner of the window instructs you to Choose the Best Answer (if there is only one answer) or Mark All Correct Answers (if there is more than one correct answer.)*

3. Click the Next button to continue.
4. To quit the test at any time, click the Finish button. After about 30 minutes, the exam exits to review mode.

After you have completed the Adaptive exam, FastTrak Express displays your score and the passing score required for the test.

- ■ Click Details to display a chapter-by-chapter review of your exam results.
- ■ Click on Report to get a full analysis of your score.

To review the Adaptive exam   After you have taken an Adaptive exam, you can review the questions, your answers, and the correct answers. You may only review your questions immediately after an Adaptive exam. To review your questions:

1. Click the Correct Answer button.
2. To see your answer, click the Your Answer button.

The Standard Exam

After you have learned about your subject using the Adaptive sessions, you can take a Standard exam. This mode simulates the environment that might be found on an actual certification exam.

You cannot choose subcategories for a Standard exam. You have a time limit (this time varies from subject to subject, although it is usually 75 minutes) to complete the Standard exam. When this time limit has been reached, your exam automatically ends.

To take the Standard exam:

1. Click the Standard Exam button from the Main window. The Standard Exam window will appear.
2. Click the circle or square to the left of the correct answer.

NOTE: *There may be more than one correct answer. The text in the bottom left corner of the window instructs you to Choose the Best Answer (if there is only one answer) or Mark All Correct Answers (if there is more than one correct answer).*

3. If you are unsure of the answer and wish to mark the question so you can return to it later, check the Mark box in the upper left hand corner.
4. To review which questions you have marked, which you have answered, and which you have not answered, click the Review button.
5. Click the Next button to continue.
6. To quit the test at any time, click the Finish button. After about 75 minutes, the exam exits to review mode.

After you have completed the Standard exam, FastTrak Express displays your score and the passing score required for the test.

- Click Details to display a chapter-by-chapter review of your exam results.
- Click on Report to get a full analysis of your score.

To review a Standard Exam   After you have taken a Standard exam, you can review the questions, your answers, and the correct answers.

You may only review your questions immediately after a Standard exam.

To review your questions:

1. Click the Correct Answer button.
2. To see your answer, click the Your Answer button.

Changing Exams   FastTrakExpress provides several practice exams to test your knowledge. To change exams:

1. Select the exam for the test you want to run from the Select Exam window.

If you experience technical difficulties please call (888) 992-3131. Outside the U.S. call (281) 992-3131. Or, you may e-mail brucem@bfq.com. For more information, visit the BeachFrontQuizzer site at www.bfq.com.

SOFTWARE AND INFORMATION LICENSE

The software and information on this diskette (collectively referred to as the "Product") are the property of The McGraw-Hill Companies, Inc. ("McGraw-Hill") and are protected by both United States copyright law and international copyright treaty provision. You must treat this Product just like a book, except that you may copy it into a computer to be used and you may make archival copies of the Products for the sole purpose of backing up our software and protecting your investment from loss.

By saying "just like a book," McGraw-Hill means, for example, that the Product may be used by any number of people and may be freely moved from one computer location to another, so long as there is no possibility of the Product (or any part of the Product) being used at one location or on one computer while it is being used at another. Just as a book cannot be read by two different people in two different places at the same time, neither can the Product be used by two different people in two different places at the same time (unless, of course, McGraw-Hill's rights are being violated).

McGraw-Hill reserves the right to alter or modify the contents of the Product at any time.

This agreement is effective until terminated. The Agreement will terminate automatically without notice if you fail to comply with any provisions of this Agreement. In the event of termination by reason of your breach, you will destroy or erase all copies of the Product installed on any computer system or made for backup purposes and shall expunge the Product from your data storage facilities.

LIMITED WARRANTY

McGraw-Hill warrants the physical diskette(s) enclosed herein to be free of defects in materials and workmanship for a period of sixty days from the purchase date. If McGraw-Hill receives written notification within the warranty period of defects in materials or workmanship, and such notification is determined by McGraw-Hill to be correct, McGraw-Hill will replace the defective diskette(s). Send request to:

Customer Service
McGraw-Hill
Gahanna Industrial Park
860 Taylor Station Road
Blacklick, OH 43004-9615

The entire and exclusive liability and remedy for breach of this Limited Warranty shall be limited to replacement of defective diskette(s) and shall not include or extend any claim for or right to cover any other damages, including but not limited to, loss of profit, data, or use of the software, or special, incidental, or consequential damages or other similar claims, even if McGraw-Hill has been specifically advised as to the possibility of such damages. In no event will McGraw-Hill's liability for any damages to you or any other person ever exceed the lower of suggested list price or actual price paid for the license to use the Product, regardless of any form of the claim.

THE McGRAW-HILL COMPANIES, INC. SPECIFICALLY DISCLAIMS ALL OTHER WARRANTIES, EXPRESS OR IMPLIED, INCLUDING BUT NOT LIMITED TO, ANY IMPLIED WARRANTY OF MERCHANTABILITY OR FITNESS FOR A PARTICULAR PURPOSE. Specifically, McGraw-Hill makes no representation or warranty that the Product is fit for any particular purpose and any implied warranty of merchantability is limited to the sixty day duration of the Limited Warranty covering the physical diskette(s) only (and not the software or information) and is otherwise expressly and specifically disclaimed.

This Limited Warranty gives you specific legal rights; you may have others which may vary from state to state. Some states do not allow the exclusion of incidental or consequential damages, or the limitation on how long an implied warranty lasts, so some of the above may not apply to you.

This Agreement constitutes the entire agreement between the parties relating to use of the Product. The terms of any purchase order shall have no effect on the terms of this Agreement. Failure of McGraw-Hill to insist at any time on strict compliance with this Agreement shall not constitute a waiver of any rights under this Agreement. This Agreement shall be construed and governed in accordance with the laws of New York. If any provision of this Agreement is held to be contrary to law, that provision will be enforced to the maximum extent permissible and the remaining provisions will remain in force and effect.